W9-BWB-401

PSYCHOSOCIAL DEVELOPMENT
DURING ADOLESCENCE

Psychosocial Development During Adolescence

Edited by

GERALD R. ADAMS

RAYMOND MONTEMAYOR

THOMAS P. GULLOTTA

ADVANCES IN ADOLESCENT DEVELOPMENT

An Annual Book Series   Volume 8

SAGE PUBLICATIONS
International Educational and Professional Publisher
Thousand Oaks   London   New Delhi

For information address:

SAGE Publications, Inc.
2455 Teller Road
Thousand Oaks, California 91320
E-mail: order@sagepub.com

SAGE Publications Ltd.
6 Bonhill Street
London EC2A 4PU
United Kingdom

SAGE Publications India Pvt. Ltd.
M-32 Market
Greater Kailash I
New Delhi 110 048 India

Printed in the United States of America

Library of Congress: 90-657291

ISSN 1050-8589
ISBN 0-7619-0532-4 (cl.)
ISBN 0-7619-0533-2 (pbk.)

This book is printed on acid-free paper.

96 97 98 99 10 9 8 7 6 5 4 3 2 1

Sage Production Editor: Sherrise Purdum

Contents

Preface

Advances in Adolescent Development is a serial publication designed to address an integrative understanding of existing knowledge or the introduction of new developments in theory and research. The series is managed by three associate editors. Each volume is assigned to a given associate editor for development and preparation. The senior series editor coordinates the totality of the series, whereas individual editors determine the direction, nature, and essence of a given volume. This volume focuses on advances in psychosocial development during adolescence. Given an expanding interest in developmental contextualism by scholars investigating adolescence, the editor of this volume selected John Hill's statements in 1973 as a starting point for the formulation of this text. In 1993, two decades after Hill's initial government report, we selected authors with excellent research histories focusing on the content of each chapter and asked them to review progress over this time period. Broad, general guidelines were offered for the nature of the volume, leaving ample room for individual creativity. Contributors from the United States and Canada were chosen to write the chapters within this volume. I am thankful for their diligence, their openness to constructive feedback, and their standards of excellence in preparing each chapter.

Again, I am thankful for the energy, creativity, and involvement of my fellow associate editors. The mixture between us in our different training and intellectual foci allows us to continue to build a multidisciplinary perspective in the series. In that adolescence, as a field, is owned by no single discipline but shared by many, **Advances in Adolescent Development** should continue to assume a multidisciplinary orientation. Due to the cooperative nature of the editorial team, we have been able to maintain a continuing commitment to this goal throughout the series.

From the original conception of this series and right through the preparation of this volume, C. Deborah Laughton, of Sage Publications,

Inc., has provided continuous encouragement and support. As an editor and businesswoman, she excels. But more important, she builds and maintains both a friendship with the editors and a mutually shared commitment to the advancement of research on adolescent development. We are likewise thankful to her many assistants, production editors, and colleagues at Sage.

This volume speaks to our cumulative knowledge on psychosocial development during adolescence. It tells us much about the role of gender, race and ethnicity, and socioeconomic features of individual differences and adolescent development. It provides a marker for an assessment of where we have, or have not, come in our understanding of adolescence from the perspective of developmental contextualism. This volume celebrates our advances and enlightens us on our shortcomings. We hope it demonstrates that we have traveled far but must travel much farther to have a truly complete understanding from a contextualist framework.

I thank the authors for their analyses and examinations of many important features to the study of psychosocial development during adolescence. Editors and authors alike hope you, the reader, will find this text useful in your own research, teaching, and practice.

—GERALD R. ADAMS
Senior Series Editor

Acknowledgments

The editorial review process, of necessity, must rely on the dedicated service of external reviewers. A review process ensures that our profession will strive toward reachable editorial standards of excellence. In the preparation of this volume, assistance was provided by the following scholars: Brent Miller, Steve Jorgensen, J. Richard Udry, Lorah Dorn, Sally L. Archer, Alan Waterman, Jean S. Phinney, Larry Steinberg, Grayson N. Holmbeck, Ronald M. Sabatelli, Ellen Greenberger, and Linda Bakken.

A portion of this text was prepared while I was on sabbatical leave with support from the University of Guelph. I am thankful to the Division of Family Resources, West Virginia University, for providing me with office space and library privileges. Likewise, I thank Carol Markstrom for assistance in coordinating this opportunity.

—GERALD R. ADAMS
Senior Series Editor

1. Psychosocial Development During Adolescence: The Legacy of John Hill

Gerald R. Adams
Raymond Montemayor
Thomas P. Gullotta

Many individuals have had a substantive effect on our understanding of adolescent development and behavior. John Hill was such a person. In 1973, Hill prepared a position statement for the Office of Child Development, U. S. Department of Health, Education and Welfare, titled *Some Perspectives on Adolescence in American Society*. This document and a later extension (Hill, 1983) provide (among other things) an important historical benchmark for judging the progress of certain aspects of the field of adolescent development over the past two decades. Hill's statement covers an array of issues, all of which remain important to the contemporary study of adolescent behavior. In this volume, we focus on Hill's concerns about (a) psychosocial variables as central to the study of normal development in adolescence; (b) the role of bio-psychosocial factors (e.g., puberty, cognition, self-definition) in understanding adolescent behavior and development; and (c) the contextual influences of gender, race-ethnicity, and social class.

The influence of many theorists is seen in Hill's treatise as he recognized detachment-autonomy, intimacy, sexuality, achievement, and identity as the central psychosocial themes of adolescent development and the biological, cognitive, and social dimensions underpinning individual development. Hill's selection of these psychosocial constructs was an early indication of the growing interest in the study of dimensions of individuality and connectedness that are focal to many contemporary scholars' research and theoretical interests. Likewise, Hill proposed the need for a bio-psychosocial perspective in the study of adolescent development. Arguments for this perspective foretold of the developmental contextualism that now dominates the field (for examples, see Ford & Lerner, 1992; Hayes,

Hayes, Reese, & Sarbin, 1993). In particular, Hill indicated that (a) issues of social class, ethnicity-race, and gender are important contextual factors in which individual development is embedded; (b) biological factors of genital maturation, pubertal timing and physical growth, and changes in physical development interact with relationship roles that influence individual development; and (c) a comprehensive understanding of psychosocial development must include motivational, behavioral, and cognitive components.

We are suggesting that Hill's (1973) original commissioned paper was not only a signpost of emerging work from the 1970s but also a visionary (if not determining) document of what was to unfold in the years to come. Therefore, we shall provide for readers a summary of John Hill's statements on psychosocial development and the mediating influences of contextual factors—as he conceived it in the early 1970s. We recognize that by the 1980s, Hill (1983) narrowed his focus primarily to biological and cognitive development (self-cognition, mostly) and broadened his contextual theme to include gender roles, families, peers, and school. Furthermore, he expanded his interest to health behavior through his interest in cognitive and pubertal development. Recognizing the expanding complexity of Hill's evolving treatise and knowing we cannot adequately address all of his ideas in this volume, we have chosen to focus on the evolution of research on psychosocial development during adolescence. We conclude this introductory chapter with a summary of Hill's (1973) conceptual model for the study of individual development and a brief rationale for the use of a historical perspective in the preparation of this volume.

A series of solicited chapters have been prepared to either describe historical progression or to assess prominent advances since 1973 in the research and accumulating knowledge of adolescent psychosocial development. Such perspectives provide a portrait of the unfolding and evolving landscape of each theme and provide the backdrop for understanding recent advances. Each contributor has been asked (where appropriate to his or her goals) to (a) use a historical perspective in identifying the most common definitions and operationalizations of a given psychosocial construct; (b) delineate the major theoretical or conceptual frameworks and focal research hypotheses tested during the past 20 years; (c) summarize the documented individual differences and developmental trends, patterns, and trajectories from early, through middle, to late adolescence; and (d) exam-

ine the role of gender, ethnicity-race, and social class in understanding adolescent psychosocial development. The authors have, to
varying degrees, addressed some or all of these dimensions in the
chapters in this volume. In that Hill argued that biological and
cognitive change are central aspects of adolescent development,
chapters have also been included that examine pubertal effects (a) on
psychosocial development and (b) on cognitive development (including self-cognition and social-cognition) and psychosocial functioning. All contributors have been asked to use a blend of historical
description, analytic explanation, and critique in preparing their
chapters. Each author (or group of authors) has been encouraged to
end the chapter with a statement on new or emerging directions for
research. The concluding chapter integrates the many themes and
trends in this volume.

PSYCHOSOCIAL CONSTRUCTS:
EARLY DEFINITIONS AND DISTINCTIONS

Drawing on the writings of Sigmund and Anna Freud, Peter Blos,
Elizabeth Douvan, Joseph Adelson, Harry S. Sullivan, David
McClelland, J. S. Coleman, and Erik Erikson (among others), Hill
identified six central psychosocial variables to the study of adolescence. He recognized that this list of variables was far from exhaustive but was representative of current theoretical perspectives that
included both a *personality* and a *situational* dimension.

Detachment referred to aspects of object relations that involve
emotional independence from parents. At the time of writing the
commissioned paper, Hill maintained that only a psychoanalytic
perspective was driving empirical inquiry. Hill (1973) offered the
following summary of this perspective:

> The important developmental task of adolescence according to this
> view is the reorganization of (sexual) object ties such that attachments
> to parents come to be replaced by attachments to peers. The *sturm und
> drang* of adolescents—for themselves and for others—is seen as the
> result of this reorganization. The "rebelliousness is normal" point of
> view about adolescence has its major theoretical roots in psychoana-
> lytic theory: rebelliousness is seen as the natural behavioral manifes-
> tation of working through the change in object ties. (p. 32)

Hill argued, however, that the available evidence examining stormy family relations with teenagers due to parenting styles tended to confound detachment and autonomy. Therefore, he indicated a need to differentiate between detachment and autonomy and argued that the association between the two variables needed to be carefully investigated.

For Hill (1973), *autonomy* denoted "instrumental independence-striving" (p. 35), which refers to "independence in decision-making and to feelings of confidence in personal goals and standards of behavior" (p. 37). In regard to developmental issues, it is suggested that an intrapsychic model would view increased autonomy as being based on an increasing sense of detachment, whereas an interpersonal model would propose that situational demands for autonomous behavior, acted out in the form of individual decision making and supported by others (family or peers), would either instigate or maintain the process of detachment. Neither model was viewed by Hill as having the greater substantive support.

Up to the 1970s, studies of autonomy were primarily undertaken by sociologists studying parental practices using survey-questionnaire methodology and rarely by educational or child psychologists studying autonomy through the use of behavior ratings by teachers. Neither forms of investigation were viewed as being directed toward conceptual issues involving the construct of autonomy as a possible set of related overt behaviors, a phenomenon of consciousness and as such, a self-cognition, or the conceptualization of either a separate or congruent pathway in development between detachment and autonomy. Because of such shortcomings, Hill proposed that further analysis and refinement of the concept would provide important new research directions. To make his point, he referred to the following quotation from Douvan and Adelson (1966):

There are autonomies and autonomies. The American adolescent asks for and is freely given an unusual degree of behavioral freedom—the right to come and go, to share in setting rules, and so on. But it is far more problematic whether he asks for or achieves a high degree of emotional autonomy [detachment], and it is even more doubtful that he manages much in the way of value autonomy. Indeed, the ease with which the adolescent acquires behavioral freedom may tend to interfere with the achievement of emotional and ideological freedom. (p. 352)[1]

Sexuality, as yet another psychosocial construct of importance to adolescence, is presented by different disciplines through varying perspectives. In traditional psychoanalytic views, childhood sexuality is recognized, and the process of development in sexuality is seen as a gradual and continuous one, with a new phase occurring due to puberty and the formation of a new sexual motive away from parents to peers. Yet others have viewed sexuality as a discontinuous developmental process. Hill referred to a quotation from Simon and Gagnon (1969) in a reference to the view that sexuality (in the form of sexual activity) is discontinuous. To repeat a portion of this longer quotation:

> Even for persons with prior sexual experience, the newly acquired definition of their social status as adolescents qualitatively alters the meaning of both current and prior sexual activity; they must now integrate such meanings in more complex ways, ways that are related to both spheres of social life and senses of self. (p. 741)

In that notions of sexuality are inferred in the process of learning sex roles (the term *gender identity* is preferred by Hill to that of sex roles) during childhood, Hill argued that knowledge of the association between gender identity and sexual behavior is a preferred direction for the study of childhood and adolescent sexual relations.

Intimacy is fundamentally connected with sexuality. To demonstrate this connection, Hill referred to Sullivan's (1953) notion that one task of adolescence is the development of intimate relationships with opposite-sex peers. This process begins through a need for interpersonal intimacy with a close friend or chum and, with genital maturity, expands to opposite-sex relationships that satisfy the lust dynamism. Thus, satisfaction of the lust dynamism through sexual activity and the need for intimacy are two separate but potentially intertwined need systems. Hill suggested that the integration of the two systems is one of the primary tasks of adolescence.

Hill (1973) maintained that

> intimacy has been little studied outside the Sullivanian framework. . . . We know little about its relation to earlier parental attachment and to adolescent detachment . . . [however,] it would appear that the differential socialization of boys and girls in childhood means that girls are more competent in this area. (pp. 46-47)

He goes on to imply that our knowledge of the childhood and adolescent genesis of intimacy is greatly limited.

It is suggested by Hill that of all the psychosocial constructs selected for inclusion, the most was known about *achievement motivation and behavior*. Hill (1973) defined the achievement situation as one that requires the individual to make a personal evaluation in the form of adequacy—"a standard of excellence is applied to performance and relative proficiency is established" (p. 49). His discussion focused primarily on studies dealing with subjects high versus low in need for achievement (e.g., Atkinson & Feather, 1969; McClelland, Atkinson, Clark, & Lowell, 1953). Hill draws distinctions between such things as abilities and skills, motivation for performance, dispositions to respond to achievement situations, and situational factors that determine the intensity of effort. He argued that we should make distinctions between achievement motivation and achievement behavior that may be affected by other motives too. This discussion highlights the concern for recognizing situational, contextual, and interactional factors in the study of psychosocial development during adolescence.

Last, it is argued through an Eriksonian perspective that the *identity crisis and its resolution* is the major developmental task of adolescence. Furthermore, this resolution functions as an integrating force regarding issues of the concept of self, body image changes, sexuality, and intimacy, among other psychosocial features. Hill turns to Erikson's discussion of the role of the peer group as a major social mechanism for resolving the identity crisis. He stated, "with his peers, the adolescent can 'try on' new roles behaviorally and test their fit to his image of himself by observing the reactions of others" (Hill, 1973, p. 60).

In a summary statement on the concept of identity as an integrating variable, Hill (1973) wrote,

> One of the appealing features of the concept of identity as Erikson has proposed it is that it appears to integrate much of what is known about adolescence. The identity crisis is triggered by the primary changes and by the reaction of others to them. The cognition of self and others is now potentially far more powerful, thus permitting more complex analysis of options and permitting the self to be measured against ideals in a way not possible before. Detachment from parents and questioning of old identifications must be a part of the

process. Autonomy, intimacy, and achievement appear to be implicated, with different valences in our society today for males and
females. (p. 64)

However, Hill questioned whether the process of identity formation is clearly and sufficiently detailed in the research and writing of
the time to permit adequate empirical tests of hypotheses from an
Eriksonian viewpoint. In particular, he wondered if the motivational,
behavioral, and cognitive components of the Eriksonian formulation
were adequately conceptualized and measured.

In Hill's (1973) paper, one finds both specific and general definitions of the six psychosocial variables. In each case, he was searching
for behavioral, motivational, and cognitive components; dispositions and situational factors; and interrelationships, associations,
and parallels between the six psychosocial constructs. In general, he
viewed most definitions as underdeveloped, the research literature
fragmented, narrow, or incomplete, and the need for conceptual
models that broadened the interplay between individual psychological variables and contextual factors that minimally include gender,
ethnicity-race, and social class. In his later elaboration, Hill (1983)
restates that in adolescence research, insufficient attention is given
to careful conceptual definitions of variables, selection of measures
that are coordinated with these definitions, the use of both interview-
questionnaire and observational methodologies, and the application
of multitrait, multimethod strategies that are fundamental to a developmental contextualist perspective.

AN EARLY
THEORETICAL PERSPECTIVE

Hill provided us with a valuable critique of the then contemporary
lay perspectives to the study of adolescent development and outlined an heuristic framework for considering adolescence. He maintained that three widely held perspectives dominated general conceptions of adolescence. One perspective perceived adolescence as a
period of total discontinuity from other stages of the life cycle.
Another perspective viewed adolescents as a broadly homogeneous
and undifferentiated group. The third perspective primarily viewed
adolescent behavior and development from an endogenously pro-

grammed intrapsychic perspective. Each of these perspectives was recognized as useful but greatly limited. To borrow Hill's (1973) words regarding limitations and distortions,

> As a result the continuities which bind adolescence to childhood and adulthood are likely to be ignored. . . . The diversity of the settings in which children become adolescents and adolescents adults is de-emphasized and, consequently, the varieties of adolescent experiences are disregarded . . . [and] little public knowledge [is available] about the ways in which the social environment interacts with the person in the determination of adolescent behavior. (p. 2)

To address the limitations, Hill provided a recipe for necessary attributes of an adequate theory. He proposed the following attributes:

> First, it should be a conceptual framework which applies to the life cycle as a whole since only a consistent conceptual framework applied to each period will reveal the extent and the nature of continuities and discontinuities in development. Second, the theory should provide concepts useful in describing variations in environments as well as variations in persons. Only then can the universal be disentangled from the particular. Third, the theory should be based upon thoroughgoing interactionist kinds of assumptions about development rather than a strictly "inner" or "outer" bias. By this is meant that developmental change is also likely to be a matter of genetically-programmed and environmental events acting together in some way. Fourth, behavior at any given point in space and time should be considered a function of personal and situational variables. Using some shorthand labels, one might say that the attributes of the desired theory are that it be: life-span, contextual, interactionist, and life-space. (p. 12)

In that Hill's framework is concerned with the associations between the organism (person) and environment (situation) throughout the life course, he recognized it as an ecological theory of human development.

Four classes of variables and their interrelations were used by Hill to conceptualize the phenomenon of adolescence. The four classes included (a) dimension of change, (b) roles, (c) psychosocial characteristics, and (d) demographics. Under dimensions of change, Hill was particularly interested in (a) biological events that resulted in changes in the body as a social stimulus, physical capacities, motor skills, and sexual motivations; (b) cognitive changes in information processing; and (c) the reconstitution and redefinition of adolescence by norms applied throughout society regarding the beginning, duration, and end of adolescence. Based on these three dimensions of change, Hill pursued the nature of the interrelations with roles (son or daughter, peer, pupil, community member, worker), demographics (gender, social class, ethnicity-race), and psychosocial functioning (detachment-autonomy, intimacy, sexuality, achievement, and identity).

The interrelation between person variables of biological and psychosocial characteristics and situational features, such as social setting and roles within the larger embedded context of social class, ethnicity-race, or gender for understanding adolescent development (change), foretold of the general contemporary movement from an organicism to a contextualism zeitgeist for the study of individual development. Indeed, we believe that Hill was a leading advocate of his day for a developmental contextualist view of adolescence.

CONCLUSION

In the chapters to follow, authors provide differing forms of analysis on the degree to which the classes of variables suggested by Hill have been useful to the conceptualization, investigation, and understanding of adolescent psychosocial development. We have requested that authors use (where appropriate) a historical perspective to examine changes in the study of adolescence so as to provide insight on the evolving and changing nature of the research enterprise.

Many reasons exist for the value of adopting a historical perspective. Indeed, several prior historical treatises can be found that offer important insight on adolescent development (e.g., L'Abata, 1971; Petersen, 1988). Nonetheless, in this volume, we have focused on two such reasons for using a historical perspective. First of all, a study of history can provide the scientist with a sense of perspective on the field of investigation. It allows one to recognize multiple viewpoints and approaches; in turn, it affords vigilance against the potential egocentric view of one's own work. A historical perspective may even suggest that currently espoused ideas are actually modern reflections of similar notions from the past. Second, we suggest that a historical perspective provides a way to deal with the vastness and complexity found within a given scientific discipline. For example, a historical perspective offers the possibility of seeing how various ideas, methodologies, and theories are related.

Today's view of adolescent development is the outgrowth of yesterday's study of adolescence. Hence, a historical perspective in the study of this field permits us to understand to some degree the problems of definitions of what we study, how it is studied, and (selectively determined by the historian) who studies it.

In 1983, Hill concluded his paper on a proposed research agenda with statements of hope for the potential to make important advancements in the study of the transition from childhood to adolescence. He concluded,

> During the past decade [1970s], there have been dramatic increases in the number of scholars attracted to the study of adolescence. . . . As research on adolescence has begun to move into the mainstream, its quality has increased. New investigators are young, talented, and committed. . . . [S]tudents of adolescence . . . can look to 1984 and beyond with hope. There is little reason for Orwellian Dread in this domain. (p. 17)

This volume in the **Advances in Adolescent Development** series focuses on the recognizable advances in the study of psychosocial development throughout the decades since the 1970s. The goal is to describe the unfolding research agendas in the study of psychosocial development of adolescence as it is understood from the developmental contextualist perspective outlined here. To this end, we are thankful to the authors of each chapter for preparing a historical or analytic (or both) review that is constructed using the organization summarized in this introductory chapter.

NOTE

1. In that detachment and autonomy are interrelated psychosocial constructs, both are addressed in a single chapter.

REFERENCES

Atkinson, J. W., & Feather, N. (1969). *A theory of achievement motivation*. New York: John Wiley.

Douvan, E. A., & Adelson, J. (1966). *The adolescent experience*. New York: John Wiley.

Ford, D. H., & Lerner, R. M. (1992). *Developmental systems theory: An integrative approach*. Newbury Park, CA: Sage.

Hayes, S., Hayes, L. J., Reese, H. W., & Sarbin, T. R. (1993). *Varieties of scientific contextualism*. Reno, NV: Context Press.

Hill, J. P. (1973). *Some perspectives on adolescence in American society*. An unpublished position paper prepared for the Office of Child Development, United States Department of Health, Education, and Welfare.

Hill, J. P. (1983). Early adolescence: A research agenda. *Journal of Early Adolescence, 3*(1-2), 1-21.

L'Abata, L. (1971). The status of adolescent psychology. *Developmental Psychology, 4*, 201-205.

McClelland, D. C., Atkinson, J., Clark, R., & Lowell, E. (1953). *The achievement motive*. New York: Appleton-Century-Crofts.

Petersen, A. C. (1988). Adolescent development. *Annual Review of Psychology, 39*, 583-607.

Simon, W., & Gagnon, J. H. (1969). On psychosexual development. In D. A. Goslin (Ed.), *Handbook of socialization theory and research* (pp. 733-752). Chicago: Rand McNally.

Sullivan, H. S. (1953). *The interpersonal theory of psychiatry*. New York: Norton.

2. Autonomy in Adolescence: A Contextualized Perspective

Susan B. Silverberg
Dawn M. Gondoli

Of the six domains of psychosocial development identified by John Hill in his 1973 paper, the one that Hill himself studied and reported on most carefully is *autonomy*. Indeed, as recently as 1986, Hill and Holmbeck wrote a chapter titled "Attachment and Autonomy During Adolescence." In it, they covered theoretical streams of influence; key sociohistorical considerations in the study of autonomy; and selected empirical work on familial, biological, and cognitive influences on the development of autonomy and the maintenance of close relationships. Thus, as we developed our account of the notable conceptual and empirical scholarship in this area for the present chapter, we often turned to Hill and Holmbeck's chapter as a rich source of guidance, and we strongly encourage others to read that work as well (see also Hill & Steinberg, 1976). The literature on topics related directly and indirectly to autonomy has grown since 1986. It is this more recent literature that we will emphasize in the present chapter.

OVERVIEW

When one scans the recent research efforts on autonomy and closely related constructs, there emerge some clear advances. Many of these advances in scholarship were suggested or at least anticipated in Hill's insightful conceptual work (Hill, 1973, 1983; Hill &

AUTHORS' NOTE: We would like to express our gratitude to Marie Davila-Woolsey, Mary Lynn McGee, and James Sudakow for their help in conducting numerous literature searches for this chapter. In addition, we extend special thanks to S. Shirley Feldman, Ellen Greenberger, Rebecca Turner, Laurence Steinberg, and Grayson Holmbeck; our conversations with these scholars were very valuable as we conceptualized and revised our work.

12

Steinberg, 1976). For example, researchers since the mid-1980s have devoted greater attention to age differences in autonomy-related domains from late childhood through early adulthood (e.g., Brown, Clasen, & Eicher, 1986; Greenberger, 1984; Smollar & Youniss, 1989; Steinberg & Silverberg, 1986; White, Speisman, & Costos, 1983). Also, investigators have begun to ground their research in theory or systematic conceptual frameworks (e.g., Frank, Pirsch, & Wright, 1990; Hauser, Powers, & Noam, 1991; Kobak, Cole, Ferenz-Gillies, Fleming, & Gamble, 1993; Smetana, 1988b; Steinberg & Silverberg, 1986). In addition, researchers have made further attempts to make critical yet sometimes subtle distinctions among various aspects of autonomy (e.g., Hoffman, 1984; Moore, 1987); autonomy continues, however, to be a fuzzy and elusive concept. Contemporary investigators have also begun to examine systematically (a) the interrelationships between aspects of autonomy (e.g., Frank, Avery, & Laman, 1988; Steinberg & Silverberg, 1986), (b) the place of emotional distance from parents in the process of healthy development (Frank & Jackson-Walker, in press; Fuhrman & Holmbeck, 1995; Lamborn & Steinberg, 1993; Ryan & Lynch, 1989), and (c) the influence of familial and nonfamilial roles and contexts on the development of self-reliance and responsible independence (e.g., Allen, Hauser, Bell, & O'Connor, 1994; Eccles et al., 1991; Fuhrman & Holmbeck, 1995; Lamborn & Steinberg, 1993; Steinberg, Fegley, & Dornbusch, 1993; Tremper & Kelly, 1987). In brief, the recent literature on autonomy at adolescence is quite engaging as controversies persist and new directions for study are launched.

In keeping with our focus on the recent literature, we have organized this chapter around a number of key themes that have driven much of the scholarship on autonomy in the last decade. To set the stage, we begin with a brief discussion of the enduring interest in the study of adolescent autonomy. Next, we turn our attention to the continuing debate over the adaptive value of emotional distance or detachment from parents at adolescence. This is followed by a discussion of parent-adolescent relationships and the challenge of encouraging individuality and self-reliance on the one hand, and maintaining emotional connection and guidance on the other; in this section, we also review research on the value of opportunities for decision making in the context of the family. Fourth, we consider the arenas of school and work as contexts that have the potential to enhance adolescents' self-reliance and responsible independence. Last, we consider the restricted legal rights of adolescents to be self-governing individuals and the empirical literature that may call such restrictions into question. Within this thematic approach, we will touch on issues of definition, measurement, sex differences, and developmental trends, as appropriate.

AUTONOMY AS AN ENDURING FOCUS OF STUDY

It is not surprising that autonomy continues to figure prominently in the work of U.S. social and behavioral scientists. There are at least two interrelated reasons for the enduring interest in autonomy and its development at adolescence. First, the United States has been described as a culture that emphasizes, and is even preoccupied by, issues of self-reliance and independence (see Bellah, Madsen, Sullivan, Swidler, & Tipton, 1985). Within this U.S. context, much of socialization may be seen as preparation for being independent in the world. Second, although autonomy is probably more realistically considered a psychosocial concern across the life span (Baltes & Silverberg, 1994), issues of autonomy and of preparation for leaving home are of particular concern in the "launching" phase of adolescence.

Viewing autonomy as independence and self-reliance, free of emotional attachments and social commitments, however, has come under criticism by a number of contemporary scholars (e.g., Bellah et al., 1985; Cooper, 1994; Gilligan, 1988; Greenberger, 1984; Jordan, Kaplan, Miller, Stiver, & Surrey, 1991; Josselson, 1988; Sampson, 1985; Spence, 1985). Gilligan (1988) expressed this concern:

Psychologists in characterizing adolescence as a "second individuation" (Blos, 1967) and in celebrating an identity that is "self-wrought" (Erikson, 1962), have encouraged a way of thinking in which the interdependence of human life and the reliance of people on one another becomes either problematic or tacit." (p. xii)[1]

As described by Bellah et al. (1985),

Clearly, the meaning of one's life for most Americans is to become one's own person, almost to give birth to oneself. Much of this process . . . is negative. It involves breaking free from family, community, and inherited ideas. Our culture does not give us much guidance as to how to fill the contours of this autonomous, self-responsible self. (pp. 82-83)

Bellah and his colleagues seem to be referring primarily to European Americans; the goal of a primarily autonomous self could not be as easily said of Asian Americans, for example. Nonetheless, many current researchers interested in the period of adolescence have taken these concerns quite seriously and have, in turn, accorded greater significance to relational ties, support, and social commitment in their studies of autonomy at this period of the life span. Evidence for this revised approach can be found in recent empirical work in which investigators have conceptualized healthy ego development, identity formation, and self-esteem as growing from familial climates that promote a sense of connection as well as individuation (e.g., Allen et al., 1994; Grotevant & Cooper, 1986; Hauser et al., 1991; Turner, Irwin, Tschann, & Millstein, 1994; also see Knudson-Martin, 1994).

Further evidence for a shift in scholarship is notable in Greenberger's (1984) multifaceted conceptualization of psychosocial maturity. According to Greenberger's model, psychosocial maturity entails the complementary development of autonomy on the one hand, and social responsibility on the other. Greenberger argues that "self-reliance is perhaps the most basic disposition that underlies the capacity for autonomy". Self-reliance, in her model, entails the absence of excessive dependence on others, a sense of control or agency over one's life, and an action orientation or sense of initiative. Social commitment, an underlying feature of social responsibility, entails "feelings of 'community' with others; willingness to modify or relinquish personal goals in the interest of social goals; readiness to form alliances with others to promote social goals; and investment in long-term social goals". Thus, Greenberger's model of psychosocial maturity at adolescence is one in which a sense of responsibility toward others is placed on equal par with a sense of independence or autonomy.

Greenberger and her colleagues have operationalized this model of psychosocial maturity in a self-report instrument (Greenberger, Josselson, Knerr, & Knerr, 1974) that is often used in research on adolescent development (see section on adolescent work to follow, for example). Several studies using this instrument have indicated that both autonomy and social responsibility show signs of development across the adolescent years, with an especially clear progression for the indexes of autonomy (for a review, see Greenberger, 1984). Studies of adolescents' values, however, suggest that U.S. teens tend to place somewhat greater importance on developing and expressing self-reliance than social responsibility or commitment (this discrepancy is less consistent among adolescent girls than boys because girls appear to be more likely to value both autonomy and social commitment).

In summary, contemporary U.S. researchers continue to focus on issues of separation and independence in their studies of adolescents, and adolescents themselves continue to hold self-reliance as a key developmental task as they progress toward young adulthood. None-theless, a prevailing movement in the recent scholarship on adoles-cent development is to understand autonomy-related growth in the context of relational support and enduring bonds (see Grotevant & Cooper, 1986; Steinberg, 1990) and in parallel with growth in a sense of responsibility toward one's family (Pipp, Shaver, Jennings, Lamborn, & Fischer, 1985; White et al., 1983; Youniss & Smollar, 1985) and one's community (Becker, 1976; Greenberger, 1984).

THE "DETACHMENT" DEBATE

One of the most prominent and lively debates in the recent litera-ture on autonomy at adolescence turns on the question of whether emotional distance from parents serves an adaptive function. In 1973, Hill noted that "unfortunately, very little is known about the issue of detachment outside the theory and evidence psychoanalysis pro-vides" (p. 32). Although we do have more theorizing and empirical data today, historically speaking, the psychoanalytic writings of Anna Freud (1958) probably advanced the strongest and most straight-forward assertion that emotional distance from parents plays a criti-cal role in healthy development at adolescence. From Freud's ortho-dox psychoanalytic viewpoint, it is detachment from parental ties (initially manifested in adolescent rebelliousness against parents) that makes possible emotional adjustment, healthy independence, and later attachment to extrafamilial objects.

In light of research findings that have accumulated over the past several decades on nonclinical samples of adolescents, it is no longer possible to enter into the debate over the adaptive value of emotional distance if one assumes that emotional distance entails a state of detachment from parents as described by Anna Freud (see Steinberg, 1990). Although adolescents and their parents engage in bickering, especially at the apex of pubertal development (Hill & Holmbeck, 1987; Montemayor, 1983; Paikoff & Brooks-Gunn, 1991; Steinberg, 1989) and adolescents seek out greater amounts of privacy (Larson & Richards, 1994), the vast majority of adolescents report that they feel rather close to and respect their parents (Frank et al., 1990; Kenny, 1987; Larson & Richards, 1994; Rutter, Graham, Chadwick, & Yule, 1976). Also, most young people continue to be influenced by their parents during adolescence. For example, when it comes to long-term questions concerning educational or occupational plans or questions of values, adolescents generally seem to follow parental advice even over peer advice (Brittain, 1963; Brown, 1990; Young & Ferguson, 1979).

Researchers have noted, however, that adolescence is a time of transformations in parent-child emotional relations. For example, Larson and Richards (1994) have shown that compared to preadolescents, middle adolescents' feelings of closeness to their parents appear somewhat more conditional or situation-specific, perhaps due to adolescents' greater cognitive complexity. Other researchers have found that in early to middle adolescence, most youngsters begin to disengage somewhat from idealized conceptualizations of their parents as all-knowing and all-powerful, recognizing parental fallibility (Kaul, 1995; Smollar & Youniss, 1989; Steinberg & Silverberg, 1986). Studies also suggest that youngsters begin to experience a differentiation of some aspects of self from parents, extending further the process of individuation that is often noted among toddlers (Kaul, 1995; Steinberg & Silverberg, 1986; see also Josselson, 1988). For most teens, these affective and conceptual changes, sometimes referred to as features of *emotional autonomy*, neither demand nor signify radical detachment from parents. Indeed, studies that address age differences in emotional autonomy from preadolescence to middle adolescence reveal rather modest increases in deidealization of parents, in feelings of individuation, and in lessened dependence on parents (Kaul, 1995; Steinberg & Silverberg, 1986; see also Frank et al., 1990). New appraisals of self and parent do begin to surface as part of the process of individuation, but there is no evidence to suggest that even most middle adolescents are consumed or preoccupied with thoughts of parental fallibility and feelings of the self as separate.

The gradual emergence of these new appraisals of self and parent is consistent to some extent with Blos's (1967) neoanalytic theory of adolescent individuation (see also Douvan & Adelson, 1966; Josselson, 1980). In contrast to Freud, Blos focused less on the severance of emotional ties between adolescent and parent and more on the process by which youngsters relinquish childish dependencies on, and conceptualizations of, their parents. Blos would, perhaps, be surprised that the extent to which most adolescents experience these new thoughts and feelings is fairly modest. In any case, he would argue that it is through this process of gaining emotional autonomy that adolescents come to rely on their own internal resources and take responsibility for their actions—that is, come to be mature, competent young people.

It is this proposal that is exactly the point of contemporary debate. Although there is empirical evidence to support a developmental component to emotional autonomy defined and operationalized from Blos's perspective (Kaul, 1995; Lamborn & Steinberg, 1993; Steinberg & Silverberg, 1986), there are of course individual differences in the level of emotional autonomy experienced by same-age adolescents. The issue of debate thus becomes whether stronger feelings of emotional autonomy are especially adaptive. Are youngsters who experience strong feelings of emotional autonomy vis-à-vis their parents more competent and well-adjusted than their peers?

Initial Research Using
the Emotional Autonomy Scale

Researchers interested in this issue have generally used the Emotional Autonomy Scale (EAS) in their investigations (Steinberg & Silverberg, 1986). This 20-item scale, which has aroused a good deal of debate itself, is composed of four subscales that are intended to reflect the features of emotional autonomy as outlined by Blos: (a) deidealization of parents (e.g., Even when my parents and I disagree, my parents are always right; reverse scored), (b) relinquishing of childish dependencies on parents (e.g., When I've done something wrong, I depend on my parents to straighten things out for me), (c) individuation (e.g., My parents know everything there is to know about me), and (d) perceiving parents as people (e.g., I might be surprised to see how my parents act at a party).

Steinberg and Silverberg's (1986) initial research using the EAS indicated that early adolescents with relatively high emotional autonomy scores tended to be more susceptible to peer pressure, at least in hypothetical situations. That is, the early adolescents who were most emotionally autonomous from their parents appeared to be least able to remain autonomous in the face of pressure from their friends to engage in antisocial behavior. This initial finding, based on cross-sectional data, seemed to suggest that emotional autonomy from parents, at least relatively strong feelings of emotional autonomy, leaves young adolescents in a rather vulnerable position and not one that most adults would consider promising of competence and adjustment (Ryan & Lynch, 1989). Lamborn and Steinberg's (1993) alternative, more optimistic and neoanalytic interpretation of these findings was this:

> Young people move through a transitional period in the progression to true self-reliance. Initially, young adolescents gain a sense of emotional autonomy from parents that leaves them susceptible to peer pressure. . . . The development of emotional autonomy in early adolescence is an important stepping stone in the process [toward true self-reliance and responsible decision making]. (p. 484)

Although this positive, transitional interpretation is plausible, in the absence of long-term longitudinal data and in light of additional research findings outlined here, it is open to debate. Notably, a number of researchers have reported findings that suggest that high EAS scores are uncorrelated with measures of global self-esteem and self-perceptions of competence (Ryan & Lynch, 1989) but are correlated with greater substance use and fighting among adolescents (Turner, Irwin, & Millstein, 1991) as well as with greater feelings of insecurity with parents and lower feelings of lovability (Ryan & Lynch, 1989). It is interesting, however, that when researchers who study late adolescents use only the deidealization subscale of the EAS, high scores tend to be associated with some positive outcomes, such as healthier identity development—less identity foreclosure and more identity achievement (Frank et al., 1990).

In short, the overall pattern of findings based on the studies cited thus far suggests that in late adolescence, a more realistic, somewhat deidealized view of parents may play a critical role in the process of identity formation, albeit with some uneasiness (Josselson, 1988), but that high scores on emotional autonomy as a whole are associated with a variety of behaviors and dispositions among adolescents that are not indicative of responsible independence. Although as a group, youngsters seem to experience some emotional distancing from their parents during the adolescent years, as ego development, human evolution, and family systems theorists would also expect (Allison & Sabatelli, 1988; Hess & Handel, 1967; Josselson, 1988; Steinberg, 1989), those young people who experience the greatest emotional autonomy—defined in Blos's terms and operationalized by the EAS—may be experiencing feelings of detachment. On the one hand, these feelings of detachment, especially during early and middle adolescence, may lay the foundation for problem behavior as well as for difficulty with emotional regulation (Kobak et al., 1993); alternatively, feelings of detachment, problem behavior, and difficulties with emotional regulation may all reflect a common internal or contextual source or both.

Emotional Autonomy in Context

The debate over the adaptive value of emotional autonomy as measured by the EAS has recently entered a second phase. In this most current scholarship, researchers have proposed that the meaning of emotional autonomy and, more specifically, its link to competence, adjustment, and interpersonal functioning can be understood only if considered in context—that the significance of adolescent emotional autonomy may differ depending on the quality of the parent-adolescent relationship (Lamborn & Steinberg, 1993) and the level of stress in the family environment (Fuhrman & Holmbeck, 1995). Researchers have differed considerably, however, with regard to the contextual conditions under which they predict emotional autonomy might be adaptive and thus positively associated with indexes of competence and adjustment.

On the one hand, Lamborn and Steinberg (1993) have taken the position that a negative profile of adjustment and competence would hold true for emotionally autonomous adolescents who also perceive their parents as relatively unsupportive and unavailable; these authors have proposed, however, that emotionally autonomous adolescents who perceive high levels of parental support and availability should score quite favorably on measures of competence and adjustment—indeed, even more favorably than adolescents who report high levels of parental support and availability but low levels of emotional autonomy as assessed by the EAS. In sharp contrast to Lamborn and Steinberg's predictions, Fuhrman and Holmbeck (1995) proposed that it is only under conditions of family stress—low maternal warmth, low family cohesion, parent-adolescent conflict, or nonintact family structures—that feelings of emotional autonomy can be adaptive and beneficial to adolescents. Emotional autonomy, or emotional distancing under these conditions, the authors reasoned, should serve a protective function and facilitate development (see Rutter, 1990). Under less stressful and more supportive conditions, high emotional autonomy would be maladaptive, with adolescents distancing themselves from the benefits of a supportive relationship with their parents.[2,3]

The findings that have emerged from the empirical investigations of these two research teams appear very much at odds on certain points but do share some critical commonalities. As Lamborn and Steinberg (1993) anticipated, their findings suggested that adolescents at greatest risk for internalizing and externalizing problems, as well as for low levels of both academic competence and psychosocial development, were those who reported strong feelings of emotional autonomy and who described their relationship with their parents as lacking in support. These findings appeared to confirm the argument that "emotional autonomy from parents when it is accompanied by a weakened parent-adolescent relationship may bode poorly for adolescent psychological development and adjustment" (Lamborn & Steinberg, 1993, p. 495). In contrast, Fuhrman and Holmbeck (1995) found that high emotional autonomy seemed to be associated with positive adjustment in less supportive family environments. This pattern was especially strong when maternal warmth was used as the index of family environment. Specifically, Fuhrman and Holmbeck found that among those dyads where mothers reported relatively low levels of warmth toward their adolescent, higher adolescent EAS scores were associated with fewer externalizing behavior problems, higher total competence scores, and higher school grades. These authors draw a tentative analogy to the deactivation of attachment behaviors seen in certain infant-parent dyads (Cassidy & Kobak, 1988) and argue that distancing oneself emotionally from parents— indeed, detaching oneself from parents—may be a strategy that can remove the adolescent psychologically from a stressful situation. Nonetheless, Fuhrman and Holmbeck suggest the following:

Even though adolescents may be advantaged in the short run if they emotionally distance themselves from stressful environments, such avoidance strategies may prove deleterious in the long run . . . particularly with respect to the quality and maintenance of future relationships. (p 806)

They go on to state,

Adolescents may also distance themselves from less optimal family environments in order to preserve their sense of self (Ryan, 1991); such distancing may be adaptive but is not likely to be facilitative of gains in self-governance (Hill & Holmbeck, 1986; Ryan, 1991). Simply put, just because a relationship strategy is adaptive does not necessarily mean that the strategy is optimal. (p. 806)

So, it appears that Lamborn and Steinberg (1993) and Fuhrman and Holmbeck (in press) do reach some consensus, at least in their final interpretations. Both research teams discuss negative outcomes of having an unsupportive family environment combined with a sense of emotional distance from parents. Whereas Lamborn and Steinberg's data implied that these negative outcomes manifest themselves during adolescence, Fuhrman and Holmbeck predict negative outcomes in the long term (and perhaps some in the short run as well).

Do feelings of emotional autonomy as measured by the EAS when combined with perceptions of parental support predict optimal adolescent adjustment and competence as Lamborn and Steinberg (1993) hypothesized? Their findings seem to suggest that "emotional autonomy in the context of a supportive adolescent-parent relationship may carry some developmental advantages as well as some deleterious consequences" (p. 483). On the positive side, the adolescents in this group—compared to their high support-low emotional autonomy peers—were generally superior with respect to academic competence and had higher (boys) or equivalent (girls) scores in the domain of psychosocial development (self-reliance, self-esteem, and work orientation). On the negative side, however, the adolescents in this group reported relatively greater negative affect (depression, anxiety) and were more likely to display problem behavior—not of the most serious sort, but including drug and alcohol use, school misconduct, and conformity to peer pressure to engage in minor antisocial behaviors. Overall, Lamborn and Steinberg's findings suggest that these are youngsters who are cognitively astute, as reflected not only in school but also in their more realistic views of their parents (Holmbeck, Paikoff, & Brooks-Gunn, in press); at the same time, these youngsters seem to be susceptible to peer influence and engage in behavior that may keep them in good stead with their peer group (Brown, 1990), a pattern that is of concern to many adults. Fuhrman and Holmbeck's study similarly indicated that adolescents who experience a supportive-warm parent-adolescent relationship but who report high levels of emotional autonomy tend to engage in relatively high amounts of problem behavior. Their study did not find any of the developmental advantages noted in Lamborn and Steinberg's work.[4]

A number of issues need to be taken into account in an attempt to make sense of the findings from these two studies. One issue is whether we view the "problem behavior" seen in the adolescents who score high on both emotional autonomy and parental support as part of a normative transition (Lamborn & Steinberg, 1993) or as something of greater concern (Fuhrman & Holmbeck, 1995). Another issue to consider is the circumstances under which emotional disengagement from a stressful family environment might be beneficial. For both issues, age (or, more broadly, developmental level) may be a critical variable to take into account.

One way to decide whether a given behavior reflects a normative transition or a problem would be to consider the age of the adolescent. This is especially important because many so-called problem behaviors of adolescence (e.g., drinking) are no longer considered deviant once the adolescent reaches majority just a few years down the road. For many older adolescents, experimentation with alcohol may be a part of a package of age-appropriate steps in the psychosocial transition to adulthood (Jessor, 1982) and may serve social integration functions (Silbereisen & Noack, 1988). On the other hand, the early onset of alcohol use, especially if it serves as a means of coping, is generally indicative of a larger pattern of problem behavior and is predictive of difficulties in the years to follow (Newcomb & Bentler, 1989)—perhaps because the young person has undermined his or her opportunity to develop alternative means of reducing distress. In short, the consequences of emotional autonomy or disengagement may take on different meanings for younger and older adolescents.[5]

Age may also be a critical variable with regard to the issue of the possible positive functions of emotional disengagement. Older ado-

24 PSYCHOSOCIAL DEVELOPMENT DURING ADOLESCENCE

lescents may be more capable than younger adolescents of a proactive response to relationship problems with parents. The greater cognitive and emotional maturity of most older adolescents may enable them to establish an identity and relationships that are indeed separate from parents but that are prosocial or beneficial for their development. In contrast, younger adolescents may react to relationship problems with parents by quickly gravitating toward peers who may be experiencing similar problems and who may provide a supportive context for delinquency (see Fuligni & Eccles, 1993).

Another issue and potential source of within-group differences not discussed by either Lamborn and Steinberg or Fuhrman and Holmbeck is the EAS itself. As the work of Frank and her colleagues (1990) has suggested, the multidimensional nature of this measure must not be overlooked. It is possible, for example, that certain subscales of the measure (e.g., deidealization) reflect emotional or cognitive maturity such that high scores would predict positive outcomes, at least among older adolescents. In contrast, other subscales (e.g., individuation), particularly in early adolescence, may reflect a reactive detachment from parents such that high scores would generally predict negative outcomes. It is important to note, however, that individuals could receive the same high *total* EAS score for different reasons; for example, one high score could be due largely to the endorsement of deidealization items, whereas another could be due largely to the endorsement of individuation (detachment) items. To the extent that different subscales of the EAS reflect more positive or negative aspects of autonomy, the meaning of high total EAS scores may not be equivalent for all individuals.

Last, we must bear in mind the subtle yet important distinctions between emotional autonomy as measured by the EAS and other aspects of psychological separation and individuation that are associated more consistently with personal adjustment and academic competence. Studies on adolescent development grounded in object relations and family systems theories—that have relied on scales other than the EAS—have indicated, for example, that adolescents and young adults who seem most well-adjusted are those who maintain appropriate boundaries relative to their parents, who are willing to express needs or values that may differ from those of their parents but without fear of threatening the parent-adolescent relationship, and who are free of excessive guilt in relation to their parents (see Cooper, Grotevant, & Condon, 1983; Frank et al., 1988; Hoffman, 1984; Moore, 1987; Sabatelli & Mazor, 1985).

Future Directions

Clearly, there are some unresolved questions with regard to emotional autonomy and its place in healthy development among adolescents. A valuable addition to the empirical literature would be long-term longitudinal studies that (a) focus on the distinctive subparts of emotional autonomy (e.g., distinguishing parental deidealization from other components); (b) consider possible curvilinear relations between emotional autonomy and adjustment; (c) look not only at the consequences but also at the precursors of high emotional autonomy scores, especially among early adolescents; and (d) discern potential differential implications of high emotional autonomy experienced continually from early through late adolescence versus high emotional autonomy experienced initially in late adolescence.

In addition, to understand emotional autonomy as well as its place in the development of adolescents and young adults, investigators need to extend their methods beyond researcher-driven questionnaire, and include in-depth interviews with young people (Cooper, 1994; Fontana & Frey, 1994). Interviews, if effectively conducted, may help researchers make sense of individual differences in the consequences of, and the meanings attached to, emotional autonomy among young people at different ages, from various cultural backgrounds, for males and females, and under different family circumstances. A qualitative approach will bring richness as well to recent survey data that suggest, for example, that among Indian immigrant families in the United States, adolescents who score higher on a measure of individual and family acculturation also report higher levels of emotional autonomy vis-à-vis their parents, as assessed by the EAS (Kaul, 1995). Propositions that emerge from the self-in-relation model of women's development (Surrey, 1991) and from the ecocultural model of family relations (Cooper, 1994; Weisner, Gallimore, & Jordan, 1988) are constructive starting points for future research. In short, researchers may profit most by adopting a long-range, contextual, and qualitative perspective in their future research on emotional autonomy.

STRIKING A BALANCE IN
THE PARENT-ADOLESCENT RELATIONSHIP

As the research on emotional autonomy would suggest, one of the most challenging aspects of the parent-child relationship at adolescence involves the process of establishing, maintaining, and renegotiating a healthy and age-appropriate balance of youngsters' individuality and self-reliance on the one hand, and a sense of connection and parental guidance on the other. This pervasive challenge is evidenced in the voices of parents who want to monitor their adolescent's behavior but at the same time grant decision-making privileges and promote feelings of self-reliance, and it is reflected in the desire of many parents to maintain a close relationship with their youngster but at the same time not to stifle their youngster's developing sense of self (Larson & Richards, 1994). Many contemporary researchers, whose work derives from fairly disparate theoretical roots, also recognize this challenge as a critical—even a defining—aspect of the parent-child relationship at adolescence (e.g., Allison & Sabatelli, 1988; Cooper et al., 1983; Eccles et al., 1991; Humphrey, 1989; Maccoby & Martin, 1983; Quintana & Lapsley, 1990; Ruebush, 1994). Although researchers have used a variety of constructs in their theoretical and empirical work in this area, they seem to maintain considerable agreement regarding the importance of striking an effective balance for youngsters' healthy development as they move through adolescence toward young adulthood.

Patterns of Parent-Adolescent Interaction:
Individuality and Connectedness

A theme that permeates the recent conceptual models of family interaction and adolescent development is the importance of acknowledging and fostering the adolescent's developing sense of individuality but in a context of parent-adolescent emotional connectedness and support (e.g., Allen et al., 1994; Cooper & Cooper, 1992; Grotevant & Cooper, 1986; Hauser et al., 1984; Hauser et al., 1991; Powers, Hauser, Schwartz, Noam, & Jacobson, 1983). Indeed, several research teams share the general guiding hypothesis that parent-adolescent interactions that encourage differentiation and an autonomous sense of self, but that also send a message of acceptance and connection, should facilitate a variety of positive outcomes in the adolescent, including healthy identity formation, perspective-taking skills, ego development, and self-esteem. For example, Hauser and Powers and their colleagues have attempted to specify the role that family interactions play in facilitating (enabling) or inhibiting (constraining) adolescent ego development (Hauser et al., 1984; Hauser et al., 1991; Powers et al., 1983). Their work is generally based on the premise that to stimulate youngsters' ego development, parent-child interactions must combine cognitive enabling behavior (communication of different viewpoints, challenging of views, focusing, problem solving) with affective support (acceptance, empathy, encouragement of discussion). Inhibiting interactions, according to these researchers, include those in which parents actively resist their child's differentiation (through devaluing, distortion, and avoidance), especially in the context of affective conflict.

Hauser's and Powers's empirical work provides support for these hypotheses. For example, in a structured interactional study of 14-year-old to 15-year-old adolescents and their parents, Powers et al. (1983) found that adolescent ego development was most advanced when families exhibited a high amount of noncompetitive sharing of perspectives or challenging behavior within a context of high affective support. Somewhat less advanced youngsters experienced sharing of perspectives in their family interactions as well; however, this was combined with high amounts of avoidance (perhaps indicating that family members felt uneasy about openly dealing with differences of opinion). Families whose youngsters were least advanced in ego development were most likely to exhibit high amounts of task rejection and distortion within a context of affective conflict. In short, in these latter families, opportunities for the sharing of alternative viewpoints and noncompetitive challenging or differentiation were denied.

Although the pattern of findings in Powers et al.'s (1983) work seems rather compelling, there remains a question of whether adolescent males and females benefit from a similar combination of overt affective support and encouragement of individuality. In fact, both additional analyses of the Hauser-Powers cross-sectional data set (Powers, Beardslee, Jacobson, & Noam, 1987) and analyses of a 4-year longitudinal follow-up (Leaper et al., 1989) point to possible differences in family interactions that appear to facilitate healthy ego development in adolescent males and females. Unfortunately, these two reports yielded conflicting results regarding the relative beneficial effects of the encouragement of individuality and overt affective support for the two sexes. Thus, future research that focuses on potential differences in facilitative family interaction for males and females—and that is grounded in theory (e.g., self-in-relation theory discussed in Jordan et al., 1991)—is clearly warranted (see, however, Allen et al., 1994).

Aside from this unresolved issue, recent longitudinal data begin to reveal the full import of Hauser and Powers's earlier cross-sectional results (Hauser et al., 1991; Hauser, Powers, Noam, & Bowlds, 1987). More specifically, by assessing the stage of adolescent ego development annually over 4 years (beginning at age 14), Hauser and his colleagues were able to map ego development *trajectories*—early arrested, consistent, precociously advanced, and progressive—and the antecedent family interactional patterns that appear to contribute to these various developmental paths. Analyses revealed that adolescents who subsequently showed trajectories of progressive ego development had parents who engaged in a good deal of cognitive and affective enabling. Parents in these families seemed to permit, encourage, and accept the expression of multiple perspectives or points of view, including the point of view of their adolescent.

In a separate program of research, Grotevant and Cooper (1986) have outlined a model of adolescent development that highlights the facilitative role of individuation in family dyadic relationships (Cooper, 1994; Cooper et al., 1983). According to this model, an individuated relationship is one that displays a balance between individuality and emotional connectedness. "Individuality involves processes that reflect the distinctiveness of 'self' whereas 'connectedness' involves processes that link the self to others" (Cooper, 1994). Using this model as a conceptual framework, Grotevant and Cooper developed a four-part system for coding family communication patterns. In their system, individuality is reflected in expressions of *separateness* (expressions of differentness of self from others) and *self-assertion* (expressions of one's own point of view), whereas connectedness is reflected in *mutuality* (being sensitive to and respectful of others' ideas) and *permeability* (expressing openness and responsiveness to others' views).

The results from Grotevant and Cooper's observational study of high school seniors and their families provide support for the view that an effective combination of cohesion and separation in family relationships is associated with adolescent identity exploration and perspective-taking skills (Cooper et al., 1983; Grotevant & Cooper, 1985). In general, "adolescents rated highest in both identity exploration and role-taking skill were found to have participated with at least one parent in an individuated relationship . . . examining their differences but within the context of connectedness" (Grotevant & Cooper, 1986, p. 92). The specific pattern of results, however, was complicated enough to underscore the importance of examining individuation at the level of particular dyads within the family (including the marital dyad) and of considering differences in communication patterns that are predictive of competence in males and females during adolescence.

It should be noted that the families who participated in the studies described above were European Americans. In her more recent work using self-report and focus group techniques, Cooper (1994) has begun to identify differing patterns of connectedness and individuality in parent-adolescent dyads across various ethnic groups living in the United States. Among her findings, she notes that "overall, Chinese, Filipino, Mexican, and Vietnamese descent adolescents saw themselves, their parents, and grandparents as placing greater value than European American adolescents on norms of support and the use of family for advice". A question to be tested empirically is whether different mixtures of individuality and connectedness in the mother-adolescent and father-adolescent relationship are beneficial to adolescents from various ethnic and cultural backgrounds.

In summary, it appears that adolescents (at least European American adolescents) thrive in families where the emotional climate is generally one of acceptance and support but where, at the same time, differentiation is encouraged and the expression of one's own point of view is permitted. Josselson (1988) captured this view of adolescence and the family well by using Mahler's concept of *rapprochement*, initially used to describe development during toddlerhood (Mahler, Pine, & Bergman, 1975). As Josselson (1988) states,

> Rapprochement is about preserving bonds of relationship in the presence of increasing autonomy. . . . The adolescent, as much as the toddler, brings [his or her] new ideas and [his or her] new ways of being home, to be recognized in the context of ongoing connection, to bring the relationship up to date. (pp. 94-95)

Decision Making and the Family

Fuligni and Eccles (1993) capture the adolescent's view in this challenge of parenting when they noted that "most early adolescents do not wish to withdraw completely from their relationships with their parents. Instead, they want greater control over their lives and their personal decision making" (p. 623). Stated alternatively, what adolescents seem to desire is greater self-governance or independence. In the context of research on family relations at adolescence, several investigators have, in fact, conceptualized autonomy as adolescents' participation in decision making regarding matters that concern both the self (e.g., what clothes to wear, when to go to sleep) and the family as a whole (e.g., whether to attend a family function).

A number of studies in this body of literature confirm that as youngsters progress through adolescence, they desire greater say in such day-to-day matters (Eccles et al., 1993; Smetana, 1988a, 1988b). This desire seems to be facilitated or provoked by a host of converging factors that fit well into Hill's (1973) model of adolescent development. First, as youngsters experience the physical changes of puberty, they see themselves as more deserving of the privilege of decision making, which may have been largely the domain of their parents in prior years (Paikoff & Brooks-Gunn, 1990). Second, more advanced cognitive abilities, including the capacity to engage in more adultlike reasoning and abstract thought, lead not only to improved abilities to make decisions but also to increased questioning of the legitimacy of parental control and parental rules over certain issues (Laursen & Collins, 1988; Smetana, 1988b). Third, increased amounts of time spent with peers, common to the period of adolescence, afford youngsters more opportunities to experience symmetry with respect to interpersonal power and authority in their relationships. These experiences outside the home may prompt adolescents to expect something similar in the context of family life (Eccles et al., 1993; Hill & Holmbeck, 1987). Last, cultural beliefs common to many Americans carry the notion that adolescence is a time of practice for adult roles, including responsible decision making (Bellah et al., 1985); adolescents are as, if not more, likely than their parents to embrace this idea (Collins, 1990).

Although youngsters tend to desire greater participation or freedom with respect to decision making as they move into and through adolescence, their desires do not always mesh well with those of their parents (Collins, 1990; Eccles et al., 1993; Feldman & Quatman, 1988; Holmbeck & O'Donnell, 1991); this mismatch is a major contributor to the challenge of parenting. Smetana's (1988a, 1988b, 1989) influential program of research has shown, for example, that whereas parents (especially mothers) tend to view a wide range of issues and topics as matters legitimately subject to at least some parental say throughout adolescence, young people over the course of adolescence perceive more and more matters as personal and as rightly and solely under their own decision-making jurisdiction. Smetana has found that this discrepancy in beliefs regarding legitimate authority, especially as it manifests itself in early and middle adolescence, appears to be associated with parent-adolescent conflict. This finding coincides well with Collins's (1990) work that suggests that families are especially vulnerable to conflict in early to middle adolescence— a time when parents' expectancies and ideal timetables for adolescent behavior, including decision-making participation, are most likely to be violated or challenged.

It is interesting that research indicates that conflicts over the balance of autonomy and control that do emerge present a stressful challenge to parents and their own sense of self and well-being (Silverberg, in press; Silverberg & Steinberg, 1987; Small, Eastman, & Cornelius, 1988; Steinberg & Steinberg, 1994); this is especially true for mothers and for parents who do not have strong psychological investments in extrafamilial roles. Nonetheless, conflict over issues of autonomy and control in an otherwise supportive environment may initiate a process of negotiation, leading eventually to concessions on the part of both parent and child and to a realignment of parental expectations for adolescent autonomous behavior (Collins, 1990; Cooper, 1988). Although not true in all families, many parents do "recognize their children's heightened skills and developmental needs and begin to relax their earlier restrictions and provide more opportunities for independence and involvement in decision making" (Fuligni & Eccles, 1993, p. 623)—that is, strike a new balance in the relationship with their adolescent.

In short, when there is a mismatch between adolescents' desire for decision-making autonomy and parents' willingness to grant such autonomy, the most common scenario is that adolescents desire greater autonomy than they are granted. Research reveals, however, that there are instances in which the tables are turned, and parents expect rather competent and autonomous decision making across a range of issues on the part of their young adolescent, or even preadolescent, due to factors such as the social stimulus value of early pubertal maturation (Holmbeck et al., in press), family unemployment (Flanagan, 1990), or a recent shift in the household from a two-parent to a single-parent family structure (Wallerstein & Blakeslee, 1990). In addition, recent research has suggested that certain handicapping conditions and chronic illnesses may influence the strength and timing of adolescents' desire for independence in the areas of decision making and supervision as well as parents' expectations and willingness to grant autonomy in these areas. Considerable variation in findings across studies involving adolescents with special needs highlights the importance of taking into account the specific health problems of adolescents and the differential effects these may have on the parent-adolescent relationship with regard to autonomy (see Holmbeck, Faier-Routman, Willis, & McLone, 1994; Murtaugh & Zetlin, 1988). Last, research comparing youngsters from nations and ethnic backgrounds that seem to vary with respect to the value placed on individualism reveals the significance of cultural attitudes in youngsters' and parents' expectations for independent decision making on the part of the adolescents (Cooper, 1994; Feldman & Quatman, 1988; Feldman & Rosenthal, 1991; Poole, Cooney, & Cheong, 1986).[6]

Benefits of Decision-Making Involvement

Although the research literature on parenting practices and adolescent behavior indicates that parents should be involved in their youngster's daily life, monitor their youngster's whereabouts and activities to a certain degree, and maintain reasonable guidelines for behavior throughout adolescence (Fuligni & Eccles, 1993; Patterson & Stouthamer-Loeber, 1984; Silverberg & Small, 1995; Steinberg, 1986), studies also suggest that a variety of favorable outcomes are associated with granting decision-making opportunities to teens. For example, Holmbeck and O'Donnell (1991) found that adolescents who were involved in decision making in their families displayed increases in self-concept over time; in contrast, those adolescents whose parents were unwilling to grant them opportunities for autonomous decision making experienced decreases in self-concept over time.

Opportunities for decision making in the family also appear to have implications for young adolescents' relationships with peers and parents. For example, in a 1-year longitudinal study that followed youngsters from sixth grade to seventh grade, Fuligni and Eccles (1993) found that those youngsters who perceived few opportunities to be involved in decision making, and no increase in these opportunities over time, showed an increased tendency to seek out advice from their peers as opposed to their parents about personal and future issues. Those teens who perceived not only limited opportunities for decision-making involvement but also increases in parental strictness were those most likely to be extreme in their peer orientation, endorsing items such as "It's okay to let your schoolwork slip or get a low grade to be popular with your friends" and "It's okay to break some of your parents' rules to keep your friends." Although the issue of direction of influence could not be fully addressed in their study, Fuligni and Eccles proposed that adolescents who are not granted decision-making opportunities and who perceive parental domination may be especially attracted to the peer group and even be willing to forego important responsibilities to maintain a connection to the peer group—a context in which these adolescents may perceive greater chances for "mutual and egalitarian interactions" (p. 628) and validation of their opinions and ideas. In short, for these youngsters, the peer group may provide a better "stage-environment" or need-context fit than might their families (Eccles et al., 1993).

Last, analyses of a nationally representative, longitudinal data set indicated that those adolescents (aged 11-16) who were involved in family decision making—adolescents who had some input into family rules, who made decisions regarding many of their own daily activities (e.g., buying clothes, regulating television watching), and whose parents talked over important decisions with them—were those who, 6 years later (aged 18-22), showed the greatest parent-adolescent attitude similarity across a wide variety of basic values on topics such as sex roles, marriage and divorce, and welfare (Brody, Moore, & Glei, 1994). This similarity may be due to a combination of factors. According to Brody and colleagues, decision-making involvement "enhances an adolescent's willing acceptance of, rather than forced compliance with, parental attitudes and values" (pp. 369-370). Moreover,

Involvement in the mutual give and take that characterizes the decision-making process provides the adolescent with an opportunity to learn about the parents' point of view. . . . Encouraging adolescents' participation in decision making also *acknowledges their developing individuality and autonomy.* [Italics added] It communicates to adolescents that *their points of view are legitimate,* [Italics added] and that they deserve to be treated more like adults than like children. (p. 373)

Thus, the research on decision-making involvement brings us back to the theme of individuality and connectedness. It offers further evidence that parent-adolescent interactions that Hauser and his colleagues would describe as enabling and that Cooper and Grotevant would describe as individuated provide a supportive base from which adolescents can develop positive feelings about themselves and their parents as well as the foundations for responsible, independent action.

Future Directions

Although we have a growing body of literature that confirms the beneficial effects of fostering a sense of individuality and decision-making opportunities in the context of ongoing, supportive parent-adolescent relationships, almost all of the empirical work has involved samples of middle-class European American families (see Cooper, 1994, for a notable exception). Future research in the area of renegotiating patterns of individuality and connectedness at adolescence must not only be broader with respect to the composition of study samples, it must also recognize the likely diversity of goals, meanings, and opportunities held by young people and parents from different backgrounds. Second, although existing research samples have included both male and female adolescents, there is some inconsistency regarding the pattern of mother-adolescent and father-adolescent relations that best fits the needs of boys and girls. Because we know from Larson and Richards's (1994) recent time-sampling study of emotions that some adolescent girls are dissatisfied with the ways that their fathers express closeness or connectedness—through teasing and joking—researchers should make efforts to examine boys' and girls' emotional reactions to mothers' and fathers' attempts at encouraging individuality. Not only may parents use different approaches when interacting with sons and daughters, but sons and daughters may attach different meanings to similar interaction patterns (see Gjerde, 1986).

Last, it is somewhat surprising to realize that we know very little about the determinants of an individuated parent-adolescent relationship. Belsky's (1984) model of the determinants of parenting would be a useful starting point for future research in this area. Belsky's model recognizes the delicate interplay of three factors: parents' personal resources (e.g., mental health, flexibility), child characteristics (e.g., temperament), and social sources of support and stress (e.g., marital relations, employment, and social network). Other theoretical models may also be useful in future research endeavors in this domain. For example, a symbolic interactionism framework (LaRossa & Reitzes, 1993) would call for the study of both intrapersonal processes (e.g., parents' cognitions, attributions, and expectations about adolescence and adolescents' behavior) and sociocultural influences (e.g., ethnicity, immigration history, socioeconomic opportunities and constraints).

AUTONOMY AND THE CONTEXTS
OF SCHOOL AND WORK

As a social phenomenon (e.g., resistance to peer pressure, reasonable independence in the family, development of responsible autonomy in the workplace), autonomy is influenced by the opportunities and boundaries of social organizations and contexts. Indeed, in recognizing the shortcomings of the extant scholarship in 1973, Hill stated, "Obviously, these sets of [psychosocial] variables [e.g., autonomy] are only analytically separable from the roles the adolescent plays" (p. 30), and that,

> To the extent that "inner" perspectives predominate, then, the impact of social institutions, roles, and organizations upon behavior and development are given short shrift in both policy-making and scientific investigation. . . . Very little is known in much beyond anecdotal ways about the impact of various social organizations, particularly schools and work settings, upon development and behavior in the adolescent period. (p. 11)

School

Of the main contexts of adolescent development, Hill (1983) believed that school was the one most neglected by researchers. At that time, he called for increased attention to the school setting, stating, "I view the conceptualization and measurement of schools as environments for development as our most pressing need" (p. 15). Part of the urgency in examining the school context stemmed from the emerging consensus that the United States's secondary schools were failing to meet the developmental needs of most adolescents, especially in regard to autonomy. If as a nation, we depended on our secondary schools to help socialize adolescents toward responsible independence, Hill (1973) believed we were in trouble. As he noted then,

> Friedenberg (1963) has been especially forceful in arguing that the typical high school fosters acquiescence rather than autonomy. The preoccupation with matters of control—often over the most petty matters—is extreme. (It must be noted, however, that the information we have on this point is largely unsystematic and informal, even if uniform.) It is unlikely that the high schools socialize for autonomy for any but a few students. Indeed it is widely held that they punish autonomy and positively reinforce a childlike passivity and obeisance to external authority. (p. 40)

Since the late 1970s, researchers have devoted more attention to describing the features of U.S. junior and senior high schools and to relating these features to the psychosocial development of adolescents (for a review, see Entwisle, 1990). Of most relevance to Hill's comments and to the present chapter, Eccles and colleagues have focused on the fit between the needs and capacities of early adolescents and the opportunities available to them within the typical junior high school. These authors contend that some of the negative school-related outcomes that often accompany the junior high transition, such as decreased intrinsic motivation and loss of interest in school, may be in part the result of a poor fit between early adolescents and the junior high school environment. More specifically, Eccles and colleagues contend that although early adolescents prefer increasing autonomy in regard to classroom decision making and self-management, junior high school classrooms, as compared to elementary school classrooms, actually reflect decreased opportunities for youngsters to participate in decisions about classroom activities (Midgley & Feldlaufer, 1987) and increased teacher control and discipline (Midgley, Feldlaufer, & Eccles, 1988). According to these authors, the lack of fit is one feature of the typical junior high school environment that may lead to motivational deficits, such as diminished intrinsic interest in academics. In contrast, an environment in which early adolescents are allowed to exercise autonomy in developmentally appropriate ways may be more likely to foster interest in, and involvement with, schoolwork.

To test their model of developmental mismatch at early adolescence, Eccles and colleagues conducted a longitudinal study that followed adolescents as they moved from sixth grade in an elementary school to seventh grade in a junior high school. As part of the data collection, students were asked to rate the degree to which they were allowed to have input into decisions regarding classroom structure and class work (e.g., seating arrangements, homework, class rules, and the sequence of class activities). The students were also asked whether they should have input into decisions about structure and class work. As the researchers expected, students reported that there was less opportunity for participation in decision making at the seventh-grade than at the sixth-grade level. Also as predicted, adolescents reported an increase in the desire for classroom autonomy from the sixth to the seventh grade. Thus, the discrepancy between students' desired and perceived involvement in decision making increased as these students made the transition from elementary school to junior high school.

In addition to desiring greater classroom autonomy as a function of increasing grade level, Eccles et al. (1993) reported that adolescents desired greater autonomy as a function of increasing physical maturation. Among junior high school students, for example, the more physically mature girls expressed a greater desire for involvement in classroom decisions than did the less mature girls. When the perceptions of the more and less physically mature girls were compared, however, it was the less mature girls who actually perceived greater opportunity for classroom decision making. Even more compelling, the early maturing girls felt that their decision-making input decreased over the school year, whereas the late maturing girls in the same classrooms felt that their decision-making input increased.

Why was the discrepancy between desired and perceived classroom autonomy larger for early maturing girls as compared to their on-time and late maturing peers? Furthermore, why did the early maturing girls perceive less opportunity for autonomy as the school year progressed? Eccles et al. (1993) suggested that the differences between early maturing and late maturing girls could reflect differences in the ways that these youngsters perceived the classroom environment, differences in the ways that more or less mature adolescents were treated by teachers, or some combination of both factors. For example, as part of the changing self-definitions that accompany the physical changes of puberty (Paikoff & Brooks-Gunn, 1990), early maturing girls may come to see themselves as more adultlike and thus deserving of more "say" in their day-to-day activities. Moreover, we do have some evidence to suggest that in the months following menarche, early adolescent girls perceive parents as less accepting and more controlling (Hill & Holmbeck, 1987); perhaps postmenarcheal girls develop similar perceptions of their teachers—something that would be especially apparent in early maturing girls at the start of seventh grade. It is possible, as well, that teachers may be concerned about being able to control the more adult-looking, early maturing girls and so may restrict these students more, rather than encouraging self-direction. Teachers may also worry about early maturing girls becoming more interested in peer relationships, especially interactions with boys, and so may exert more control over early maturing girls as a means of keeping them focused on academics. Unfortunately, this exertion of control may have the effect of undermining early maturing girls' intrinsic motivation and interest in school. Although these possibilities are intriguing, more research, including observational studies of teacher-student interaction, is needed to evaluate them.

It may also be worthwhile to broaden the scope of the inquiry to boys. In their review of their research program, Eccles et al. (1993) did not mention whether boys' maturation had an effect on desired and perceived classroom autonomy. Like early maturing girls, early maturing boys may desire greater classroom autonomy. Contrary to their female peers, however, early maturing boys may actually be granted more autonomy in the classroom because their more adult male appearance may be especially consistent with teachers' expectations for leadership and independence. There is some suggestion, for example, that adults may have higher expectations for early maturing boys in regard to responsibility and independence (Livson & Peskin, 1980). Thus, on the one hand, teachers may grant early maturing boys more classroom autonomy as part of greater expectations for mature behavior. On the other hand, early maturing boys have been characterized as acting out more than their late maturing or on-time-maturing peers, both in school and in nonschool contexts (Duncan, Ritter, Dornbusch, Gross, & Carlsmith, 1985). Given these findings, one would expect that teachers would be more concerned about controlling the behavior of early maturing boys. Clearly, more research is needed to investigate the potential interactive effects of adolescent gender and maturational status on teacher perception and behavior.

To summarize to this point, Eccles and colleagues have empirical support for their notion that there is often a mismatch between early adolescents' desires for classroom autonomy and the opportunities for classroom autonomy available to them. What about the second part of their theory? Does the discrepancy between perceived and desired classroom autonomy actually lead to decreases in intrinsic interest in schoolwork? Preliminary data reported by MacIver and Reuman (1988) suggest that it does. These authors charted changes in intrinsic interest in math among students making the transition from sixth grade to seventh grade. For a portion of the sample, a mismatch occurred between desired and perceived opportunities for autonomy in math classrooms such that desires for classroom autonomy increased, whereas perceived opportunities for autonomy decreased across the transition to seventh grade. Those students who experienced this type of mismatch were found to have the most consistent and substantial declines in intrinsic interest in math when compared to students who did not experience a mismatch or students who perceived more opportunities for classroom autonomy than they desired. Thus, exposure to what Eccles et al. (1993) have called a *developmentally regressive* environment was associated with the predicted declines in intrinsic interest in schoolwork.

Future Directions

The research by Eccles and her colleagues has made important inroads into questions regarding students' perceptions of autonomy in the context of school and the relationships between these perceptions and student motivation and interest. Nevertheless, more observational research of student-teacher interaction is needed to clarify the connections between youngsters' maturational status and opportunities for classroom autonomy. In addition, more attention needs to be directed toward understanding the forces that constrain opportunities for reasonable autonomy in junior high school. The typical

U.S. junior high school is characterized by large class size, departmentalized teaching, normative grading, and tracking (Carnegie Council on Adolescent Development, 1989). Junior high school teachers—like other adults in contemporary U.S. society—also appear to hold negative attitudes and stereotypes about early adolescents, including the view that young teens are more moody, unpredictable, and unreachable than younger children (Buchanan et al., 1990; Carnegie Council on Adolescent Development, 1989). The institutional characteristics of the junior high, combined with negative attitudes about young adolescents, may undermine a teacher's sense of efficacy and motivation, leading to an emphasis on control of students rather than on promotion of reasonable autonomy (Carnegie Council on Adolescent Development, 1989; Eccles et al., 1993). The Carnegie Council on Adolescent Development (1989) has recommended a number of changes in the junior high environment that may facilitate the promotion of autonomy, including the creation of smaller learning communities within the school (e.g., work groups and teams), the elimination of tracking, and special training and empowerment of teachers who work with early adolescents. Program evaluation research is needed to determine whether these kinds of changes help teachers develop and maintain a high level of efficacy and motivation and whether this, in turn, promotes a sense of "shared community" (Eccles et al., 1993, p. 95) for both teachers and students and greater involvement on the part of youngsters in their day-to-day education.

Of course, the classroom is a hierarchical setting in which adolescents and their adult teachers do not have equal power and authority. Perhaps researchers should thus look beyond the classroom to school-based extracurricular activities that may afford adolescents opportunities for self-direction and decision making. As nonclassroom activities are explored by researchers, however, several important issues should be considered. First, researchers should remember that not all students have the opportunity to participate in extracurricular activities, especially in large schools in which there is greater competition for relatively few positions on sports teams and other performance-oriented activities and in large families where the adolescent's help at home or afterschool earnings are needed. Second, researchers would do well to consider that many school-based activities and clubs are organized and controlled by adults rather than by students. Last, researchers should keep in mind that even student-run clubs and activities may actually encourage conformity to peers rather than self-direction and independent decision making—that is, autonomy.

Workplace

Much of what we know about the features and effects of adolescent employment is based on research conducted by Greenberger, Steinberg, and colleagues (e.g., Greenberger & Steinberg, 1981, 1986; Steinberg, Greenberger, Garduque, Ruggiero, & Vaux, 1982). In their research, these authors have investigated the effects of working on adolescent psychosocial competence, including psychological well-being, family and peer relationships, school involvement, problem behavior, attitudes about work, and, most relevant to the present chapter, autonomy-related variables, such as self-reliance and decision-making freedom within the family. Findings from this research program suggest that the effects of work on adolescent development are variable. The effects of work seem to depend on what outcome variables are considered, on whether employment status or hours of work are considered, and, in some cases, on the gender of the adolescent worker.

A short-term longitudinal study that followed first-time workers for 1 year (Steinberg et al., 1982) indicated that for girls, hours worked were positively associated with scores on a measure of self-reliance, which included items pertaining to initiative and absence of excessive dependence on others (Greenberger et al., 1974). In contrast, number of hours worked was associated with lower self-reliance scores among boys, especially for those boys who worked a substantial number of hours per week. The effect of work on adolescents' autonomy within the family also varied according to gender. For girls, being employed had a negative effect on scores on a multifaceted measure of parent-adolescent closeness; that is, over the 12-month period, girls who worked reported decreased emotional closeness to parents and were less likely to turn to parents to discuss problems. In contrast, for boys, being employed was associated with increased emotional closeness to parents and a greater frequency of turning to parents to discuss problems. Examination of parent-adolescent closeness as a function of hours worked (rather than work status per se) revealed a richer pattern of findings. For both boys and girls, working a limited number of hours was associated with increased closeness; for girls who spent a great deal of time in the workplace, perceived closeness to parents decreased sharply, whereas for boys, parent-adolescent closeness was positively associated with hours spent at work. In general, the pattern of findings in this study suggested that involvement in work was associated with greater autonomy for girls (as manifested in higher self-reliance scores and lower parent-adolescent closeness scores), especially if they worked long hours, whereas among boys, work involvement was associated with lower self-reliance scores and higher parent-adolescent closeness scores. In interpreting these findings, Steinberg et al. (1982) suggested that girls may gain in self-reliance through work because employment is less expected for girls. According to the authors,

> For girls, entering the labor force at an early age represents, in some respects, a departure from the expectations placed on them by significant others. In contrast, for boys, taking on a job is more consistent with social expectations and with socialization for adulthood. Thus, working may be viewed as an act of independence for girls but an act of conformity for boys. (p. 394)

Follow-up studies to the Steinberg et al. (1982) study have produced somewhat inconsistent findings. A cross-sectional study with a larger, more heterogeneous sample (Steinberg & Dornbusch, 1991), for example, indicated that employment was not associated with self-reliance, either for boys or girls. Consistent with the findings from the Steinberg et al. (1982) research, longer work hours were associated with greater autonomy from parents; however, this occurred for both boys and girls. More specifically, youngsters who worked more hours each week spent less time in family activities, were monitored less closely by their parents, and perceived higher levels of decision-making freedom in regard to day-to-day issues (e.g., curfew, money management, leisure activities).

A mixture of consistent and contradictory results were again found in a more recent longitudinal follow-up (Steinberg et al., 1993). Consistent with findings from the previous studies, involvement in work was associated with higher levels of adolescent decision-making autonomy in the family. More specifically, nonworkers who began extensive involvement in the labor force (at more than 20 hours per week) reported greater decision-making autonomy than their peers who remained nonemployed during the study's 1-year interval. In contrast to Steinberg and Dornbusch's (1991) findings, working long hours was associated with self-reliance for both boys and girls, such that extensive work hours were associated with *lower* self-reliance scores. Even more intriguing, an interaction indicated that the negative effect of employment status (employed versus nonemployed) on self-reliance was especially true among girls—a finding that was directly opposite to that reported by Steinberg et al. (1982). It is interesting that results of analyses focused on potential selection effects indicated that autonomy can also be considered an independent variable that predicts future behavior. For example, the results indicated that nonworkers who joined the labor force as the study progressed were granted more decision-making freedom by parents and experienced lower levels of parental monitoring *before* employment than did nonworkers who remained unemployed. Thus, although involvement in work appeared to increase youngsters' autonomy in the family, being granted more autonomy by parents also appeared to facilitate the movement into the labor force.

Future Directions

The research to date has yielded inconsistent findings about the effect of working on adolescent self-reliance and autonomy vis-à-vis parents. The inconsistencies do not appear to be the result of poorly designed studies; the extant research appears to be well designed, with large, heterogeneous samples and cross-sectional and longitudinal data collection. Perhaps a more consistent relationship between workplace involvement and self-reliance would be obtained if the measures of self-reliance were expanded to include specific behavioral indicators of self-reliance (see Feldman & Wood, 1994) as well as a subjective sense of autonomy. For example, a stronger relationship might emerge between work involvement and behaviors such as taking care of possessions, taking responsibility for one's own schedule and time management, and other details of life, such as getting one's own meals and obtaining needed items.

The existing research might also be expanded by determining whether the effect of employment on adolescent self-reliance and responsible independence is moderated by youngsters' perceptions of the costs and benefits of their jobs. Mortimer, Finch, Shanahan, and Ryu (1992), for example, reported that for ninth-graders, employment was positively associated with various indexes of mental health and behavioral adjustment if the adolescents believed that their jobs offered skill training that would be useful in the future and especially for girls, if the jobs were perceived as not interfering with school-work. Based on the Mortimer et al. finding, future research may find that employment fosters self-reliance and other indicators of auton-omy for those adolescents who believe that their current jobs provide important training for their future occupations and are complemen-tary to their school performance. If this moderator effect holds, then those youngsters who may be most likely to benefit from working during adolescence may be those who participate in apprenticeship programs—training for occupations they intend to pursue as adults—as is the case for large numbers of teens in European countries (Hamilton, 1987; Smith & Rojewski, 1993).

DECISION-MAKING COMPETENCE AND ADOLESCENT LEGAL RIGHTS: AUTONOMY AS SELF-GOVERNANCE

When autonomy is defined as *self-governance*, questions regarding the legal rights and status of adolescents naturally surface. As the U.S. system stands today, adolescents' legal rights to self-governance are restricted in many ways. The paradox, noted by Hill and Holmbeck (1986), is that

> We continue to associate adolescence with independence-striving, yet the emergence of adolescence—conceptually by Hall (1904) and operationally through policies regarding work, education, and jus-tice, for example (Bakan, 1972; Hill & Monks, 1977)—is historically yoked to a monumental preoccupation with protectiveness. (p. 147)

In fact, it is not until they reach adulthood or legal majority that individuals are granted certain constitutional rights. These rights hold the adult individual as a full and autonomous member of the commu-nity (Melton, 1983)—someone who is permitted to consent or refuse medical treatment and mental health interventions for themselves, to elect to terminate a pregnancy through abortion without parental notification, and so on.[7] The explicit justification that is offered for restricting the legal rights of adolescents most often rests on the argument or assumption that adolescents are not competent in decision making. In fact, in 1979, Chief Justice Burger of the U. S. Supreme Court maintained that "most children, even in adolescence, simply are not able to make sound judgments concerning many decisions, including their need for medical care or treatment. Parents can and must make those judgments" (quoted in Melton, 1983, p. 100).

Decision-Making Competence: Adolescents and Adults

Several authors have questioned the fundamental assumption that adolescents are in fact less competent decision makers than adults and thus have questioned public policies that restrict adolescents' rights and that make adolescents dependent on others to make critical decisions for them (Lewis, 1987; Melton, 1983; Quadrel, Fischhoff, & Davis, 1993; Tremper & Kelly, 1987). In a brief review of the psychological research literature through 1983, Melton concluded that "for most purposes, adolescents cannot be distinguished from adults on the ground of competence in decision making alone" (p. 100). He referred, for example, to Weithorn and Campbell's (1982) study in which young people 9, 14, 18, and 21 years old were presented with a series of hypothetical dilemmas about medical and psychological treatment in a laboratory situation. (See the following discussion of caveats to laboratory-based research.) The responses of the 14-year-olds did not differ from those of the 18-year-olds and 21-year-olds on a range of tests designed to measure decision-making competencies, including reasonable decision-making process and understanding of the facts. Other studies have also suggested that adolescents tend to use the same basic cognitive processes in decision making as do adults, such as identifying and weighing out alternatives and their consequences (see Fischhoff, 1992; Grisso & Vierling, 1978; Tremper & Kelly, 1987). In fact, in a recent study, a group of approximately 160 adolescents, aged 12 to 18 years, and their parents listed consequences that might follow from either taking or not taking the opportunity to engage in a risky behavior, such as a ride from friends who have been drinking (Beyth-Marom, Austin, Fischhoff, Palmgren, & Quadrel, 1993). The findings indicated that the adolescents and parents listed very similar consequences and with similar frequency.

There are some studies on decision making, however, that suggest that young adolescents—seventh and eighth graders, in particular—

are less likely than both older adolescents and adults to consider future consequences, to use information about options, to recommend consultation with specialists, and to recognize spontaneously the possible vested interests of advice givers (Gardner, Sherer, & Tester, 1989; Lewis, 1981). These deficiencies appear to be critical ones. Furthermore, research by Lewis (1981) and Weithorn and Campbell (1982) suggests that young adolescents may place more significance than appropriate on potential consequences that concern short-term issues of appearance when arriving at major decisions, at least in hypothetical situations. Youngsters in the age group from 12 to 15 could thus be viewed as in transition with respect to certain cognitive abilities essential to prudent decision making—for instance, the ability to recognize the value of objective sources of information (Lewis, 1987; Melton, 1983; see also Lewis, 1980). Moreover, there may be situational or topical variations in the quality of early adolescents' decision making. On certain topics—or with respect to certain treatment outcomes—their decision making may be less adult.

A small-scale study by Lewis (1980) on pregnancy decision-making plans of minors (17 and younger) and adults raises the possibility that adolescents often may possess decision-making competencies but may reach their decisions largely due to their social situations. In this study, conducted at the time of the pregnancy test, minors and adults did not differ with respect to knowledge of the legality and confidentiality of abortion, nor did they differ with respect to the significant others (boyfriend, peers, parents) with whom they had consulted or expected to consult about the pregnancy, nor did they differ with respect to the expectation of receiving conflicting advice from different sources.

Moreover, when presented with hypothetical situations (e.g., "Imagine someone your own age is asking your advice about what to do about her pregnancy"), minors and adults were equally likely to consider the child-raising abilities of the potential mother. Minors were, however, less likely than adults to mention child-rearing abilities when asked to give reasons for their own pregnancy decisions. In addition, they were more likely than adults to mention the effect of the decision on their family and on their parents, in particular. In many cases, the minors seemed externally compelled to accept a decision due to family influence, whereas other factors were outweighed or disregarded; they seemed to feel that they had only one realistic alternative. According to Lewis (1987),

One striking difference between minors and adults may be the influence of their social situation on pregnancy decision making. Even if minors and adults do not differ in their competence (latent ability) to imagine consequences of the pregnancy decision, they may differ in the social circumstances that permit them to apply their abilities to their own decisions. (p. 86)

One shortcoming of Lewis's 1980 study, with respect to its potential implications for granting legal rights to adolescents, is the fact that the subsample of minors was considered as an undifferentiated group, perhaps due to the study's small sample size. As a result, there was no opportunity to discover potential differences between younger and older adolescents in terms of their approach to decision making. Lewis's (1981) laboratory research suggests that there may indeed be important age differences in decision-making process during the adolescent years, including increases in the likelihood of thinking through future consequences and of using objective sources of information.

Peer-Parent Influence

It is interesting that it was parental influence and not peer influence that seemed to drive many of the minors' decisions in Lewis's (1980) pregnancy study. This pattern is consistent with the developmental literature on vulnerability to social (peer) influence—another reason that could be offered to restrict adolescents' rights as autonomous decision makers. Although it is widely assumed that adolescents tend to follow peer dictates, the existing research would suggest that on major decisions, most adolescents do not, at least once they reach middle adolescence (age 16 or 17 years) when major decisions are more likely to present themselves (Lewis, 1987). Self-report studies indicate that conformity to peer influence seems to peak during early adolescence (about eighth grade) and tends to decline thereafter (Berndt, 1979; Brown, 1990; Steinberg & Silverberg, 1986). Moreover, like Lewis's study, Rosen's (1980) research also indicates that most adolescents tend to involve their parents in major decisions even when they are not obligated to do so by law. In his study of pregnant women under age 18 living in Michigan (where legal, low-cost outpatient abortion was available to minors without the requirement of parental consent or notification), 57% of the adolescents involved their parents in the decision regarding pregnancy continuation or termination. In fact, most of the adolescents in the study reported that influence of mothers was greater than that of girlfriends or of male partners (the exception was among the sample's European American adolescents who planned to keep their children and to remain single). Although some research suggests that only a minority of women under age 18 notify their parents of their plans for abortion, it appears that younger minors (i.e., age 15 years and younger) are those most likely to involve parents in an abortion decision (Clary, 1982; Torres, Forrest, & Eisman, 1980).

Risk-Taking Behavior

It is very likely that the risk-taking behavior of some adolescents, such as reckless driving, unprotected sex, and decisions to drink, so often discussed in the media, has also influenced the reasoning of policymakers to restrict the legal rights of teens as a whole. If adolescents cannot make so-called rational choices in these areas, the argument may be, how can they be trusted to make competent decisions with respect to medical or psychological treatments for themselves? First, it may be important to point out that it is unlikely that individuals—adolescents or adults—always use a rational process in arriving at their decisions, whether those decisions concern drinking or financial investments (Quadrel et al., 1993; Steinberg, 1993). Second, as described above, research suggests that once most teens reach middle adolescence (age 16), they seem to apply similar decision-making processes as do adults when asked to consider issues such as medical and psychological interventions. Last, the risk-taking behaviors commonly associated with adolescence seem to entail choices that are most likely to be subject to peer influence, such as perceptions of how one will be judged for not taking a drink at a party (see Beyth-Marom et al., 1993).

Even with these points in mind, the relatively high rate of risk-taking behavior on the part of many adolescents clearly presents a special challenge to policymakers. Choice of policy seems to depend in part on political values, such as the degree of importance one places on individual autonomy and protection, as well as on beliefs regarding adolescents' general abilities to regulate and manage certain personal decisions (Quadrel et al., 1993). An empirical basis for understanding adolescent risk behavior can help policymakers decide whether it is valid to use such behavior as a justification for restricting the general legal rights of teenagers.

One widely cited explanation for adolescent risk-taking behavior is that adolescents ignore, or greatly underestimate, the likelihood that harmful outcomes would affect them—that adolescents view themselves as invulnerable to potential negative consequences and as a result, focus only on the benefits of risk behaviors (Quadrel et al., 1993). The notion that adolescents are especially susceptible to feelings of invulnerability or are especially likely to hold an optimistic bias has been discussed in the theoretical work of Elkind (1967) under the rubric of adolescent egocentrism and in particular, the personal fable. Quadrel et al. (1993) note that, "if it could be demonstrated [empirically] that adolescents were uniquely afflicted by such an exaggerated sense of personal invulnerability, then a stronger case could be made for restricting their freedom" (p. 111).

It is interesting that there is little empirical evidence to support the suggestion that perceived invulnerability (or at least an optimistic bias) is especially high during adolescence (for a review, see Quadrel et al., 1993). In a recent study, for example, Quadrel and her colleagues compared adults and teens (aged 11-18 years) on perceived vulnerability across a wide range of events (e.g., unplanned pregnancy, auto accident injury, alcohol dependency, sickness from air pollution). In general, the authors found that adults and teens seem to use similar, somewhat biased psychological processes in estimating their vulnerability. The most common pattern in the findings for both adults and adolescents was to see no difference between one's own level of risk and that of others; when differences were perceived, both adults and adolescents were likely to see themselves as facing somewhat less risk or vulnerability than others. In short, adolescents did not seem to hold especially exaggerated beliefs of their own invulnerability. Unfortunately, the age range of the adolescents in this study was wide, and the researchers did not analyze whether response patterns differed systematically as a function of adolescent age.

Caveats for Decision-Making and Risk-Taking Research

There are some important caveats to consider with respect to the external validity and generalizability of studies on perceived risk and decision making (Quadrel et al., 1993). In most research in this area, investigators rely on paper-and-pencil tests, present hypothetical situations, and administer their questionnaires in schoollike or laboratory settings. Participants are thus isolated from social pressures that are likely to accompany actual decision making. Not all researchers agree, however, on whether such research conditions enhance or diminish decision-making performance or whether the conditions affect adolescents and adults in similar ways. Quadrel et al. also raise the question of whether "similar performance deficits have similar consequences for adults and adolescents" (p. 114). This is a critical question when one considers possible policy implications for limiting adolescents' rights and advocating protective measures.

Summary

The evidence available to date suggests that adolescents—at least once they reach age 16—have acquired a host of critical decision-making skills that are comparable to those of adults. Prior to age 16, most teens display a good number of deficiencies in their decision-making skills, although this may vary with topic or situation; for example, early adolescents are less likely to consider future consequences and to recommend consultation with specialists when arriving at major decisions. Second, field research, which tends to focus on females, further suggests that adolescents often involve their parents, especially their mothers, in their decisions; and, in arriving at certain major decisions, mothers' influence seems to be more salient than that of peers. Because part of responsible decision making entails a sense of when it is appropriate to turn to others—including parents, peers, and nonfamilial adults—for input (Baltes & Silverberg, 1994; Ryan & Lynch, 1989), this is a notable finding. Third, laboratory-based research conducted to date suggests that teens (at least when considered as a group with no age differentiation) do not have a greater sense of invulnerability than do adults. Before policymakers could justify granting certain legal rights to adolescents at an earlier age than is now the case, however, further research is in order.

Future Directions

If policymakers decide to take research into account in their own decision making regarding the legal rights of adolescents, several changes are warranted. First, studies that inform policymakers need to move beyond the simple comparison of adults and adolescents and incorporate a systematic focus on developmental differences and progress during the adolescent years. Second, policymakers should request additional field research—in particular, field research with samples of boys making major decisions because it is possible that boys and girls employ different decision-making strategies and are influenced by different external sources. Third, even if policymakers accept the existing research findings that suggest that middle and late adolescents have the cognitive capacities to make major decisions, they must consider how adolescents manage emotionally in comparison to adults when they are faced with the burden of making real-life major decisions. If significant and meaningful differences were found at the emotional level, then perhaps the argument for restricting the decision-making rights of adolescents could be justified. According to Tremper and Kelly (1987), who are generally in favor of granting autonomy rights at an earlier age,

> The difficulty lies in formulating policies that appropriately balance minors' need for autonomy with opposing interests. Policies fostering minors' autonomy will be most preferable if they facilitate healthy identity development, concern matters with which youths are familiar, present little risk of aggravating parent-child conflict, minimize state intervention into family affairs, and rely upon measures other than absolute rules. (p. 126)

A final recommendation for future research would be to make comparisons of the health and well-being of adolescents who reside in different states throughout the United States, which vary with respect to legal rights afforded to teens.

CONCLUDING REMARKS

It is clear that researchers interested in the study of autonomy at adolescence can turn their investigations in myriad directions, ranging from the emotions associated with individuation in the parent-adolescent relationship, to opportunities for self-direction in the classroom, to the legal ramifications of adolescents' decision-making capabilities. Throughout this chapter, we have highlighted specific avenues for future research in these areas as well as in others. Rather than concluding with a summary of those suggestions, we offer four concepts central to a life span orientation on human development (Baltes, 1987) that can serve as an organizing framework for future research endeavors on autonomy. These concepts are (a) lifelong development, (b) multidimensionality-multidirectionality, (c) historical embeddedness, and (d) contextualism.

First, with respect to lifelong development, we must recognize that the changing demands, challenges, and opportunities that individuals face throughout their lives—whether they are primarily biological, interpersonal, or economic—will necessarily bring the issue of autonomy to the fore in the years following adolescence. What may be valuable to know is whether the skills and dispositions individuals hold during adolescence are good predictors of how they manage the autonomy challenges they face later in life. Second, we must bear in mind the multidimensional character of autonomy and devote more systematic attention toward tracing the interacting trajectories of each of these components. Third, we must recognize that the vast majority of the extant scholarship on autonomy at adolescence is based on samples of healthy youngsters who were adolescents in the 1980s, who were in school (i.e., had not dropped out), and who were growing up in middle-class, European American, two-parent families. A life span orientation to the study of human development reminds us that our expectations and norms regarding autonomy—whether defined in terms of emotions, behaviors, or relationship quality—are inextricably linked to historical period and social context. To the extent that our empirical findings are based on a selective group of adolescents, then, we have only a limited perspective on the salient and adaptive aspects of autonomy. Researchers must reach beyond easily accessible populations and contexts in their future efforts and study adolescents who, for example, face economic deprivation, poorly funded school systems, and dangerous communities. Our notion of autonomy at adolescence can only be complete when we step into the worlds of all adolescents and view their lives through a contextual and historical lens.

NOTES

1. Gilligan may have underestimated to some extent Erikson's notion that commitment to the past and integration of relations with others are key aspects of identity

2. To test their proposal, Lamborn and Steinberg studied a large, ethnically and socioeconomically diverse sample of high school students 14 to 18 years old (*N* = 2,416). Data were collected via a battery of self-report questionnaires. Fuhrman and Holmbeck's sample (*N* = 96) was socioeconomically diverse and composed of European American and African American adolescents aged 10 to 18 years. Data were collected via questionnaires completed by the adolescents and by mothers and teachers on certain variables.

3. Lamborn and Steinberg (1993) used only three of the four EAS subscales as their index of emotional autonomy. They chose not to include the "perceiving parents as people" subscale because previous research indicated that this aspect of emotional autonomy is slow to develop over the adolescent years (e.g., Steinberg & Silverberg, 1986). Note as well that there were other methodological differences between the Lamborn and Steinberg (1993) and Fuhrman and Holmbeck (1995) studies.

4. It is interesting that both studies indicated that adolescents who experience a supportive-warm parent-adolescent relationship and low levels of emotional autonomy as measured by the EAS are those who engage in the fewest problem behaviors.

5. In separate analyses involving age, however, Fuhrman and Holmbeck found few age interaction effects.

6. Cooper (1994) proposes that we should challenge the view of cultural groups as homogeneous, however. She states, "ecocultural analyses of activity settings can help us 'unpackage' global characterizations of diverse groups as 'communal' or 'individualistic' " and recognize heterogeneity within groups.

7. Generally speaking, in the United States, the age of majority is 18 years. Younger teens may become legally emancipated or act autonomously under certain circumstances (see Tremper & Kelly, 1987; Willemsen & Sanger, 1991). In addition, states are permitted to vary with respect to the issue of parental notification and abortion.

REFERENCES

Allen, J., Hauser, S., Bell, K., & O'Connor, T. (1994). Longitudinal assessment of autonomy and relatedness in adolescent-family interactions as predictors of adolescent ego development and self-esteem. *Child Development, 65,* 179-194.

Allison, M., & Sabatelli, R. (1988). Differentiation and individuation as mediators of identity and intimacy in adolescence. *Journal of Adolescent Research, 3,* 1-16.

Bakan, D. (1972). Adolescence in America: From idea to social fact. In J. Kagan & R. Coles (Eds.), *Twelve to sixteen: Early adolescence* (pp. 73-89). New York: Norton.

Baltes, M., & Silverberg, S. (1994). The dynamics between dependency and autonomy: Illustrations across the life span. In D. Featherman, R. Lerner, & M. Perlmutter (Eds.), *Life-span development and behavior* (pp. 41-90). Hillsdale, NJ: Lawrence Erlbaum.

Baltes, P. (1987). Theoretical propositions of life-span development psychology: On the dynamics between growth and decline. *Developmental Psychology, 23,* 611-626.

Becker, T. (1976). Self and social responsibility: A comparative view of American and Israeli youth. *American Journal of Psychoanalysis, 36,* 155-162.

Bellah, R., Madsen, R., Sullivan, W., Swidler, A., & Tipton, S. (1985). *Habits of the heart: Individualism and commitment in American life*. Berkeley: University of California Press.

Belsky, J. (1984). The determinants of parenting: A process model. *Child Development, 55*, 83-96.

Berndt, T. (1979). Developmental changes in conformity to peers and parents. *Developmental Psychology, 15*, 608-615.

Beyth-Marom, R., Austin, L., Fischhoff, B., Palmgren, C., & Quadrel, M. (1993). Perceived consequences of risky behaviors: Adolescents and adults. *Developmental Psychology, 29*, 549-563.

Blos, P. (1967). The second individuation process. *Psychoanalytic Study of the Child, 22*, 162-186.

Brittain, C. (1963). Adolescent choices and parent/peer cross-pressures. *American Sociological Review, 28*, 385-391.

Brody, G., Moore, K., & Glei, D. (1994). Family processes during adolescence as predictors of parent-young adult attitude similarity: A six-year longitudinal analysis. *Family Relations, 43*, 369-373.

Brown, B. B. (1990). Peer groups and peer culture. In S. Feldman & G. Elliott (Eds.), *At the threshold: The developing adolescent* (pp. 171-196). Cambridge, MA: Harvard University Press.

Brown, B. B., Clasen, D., & Eicher, S. (1986). Perceptions of peer pressure, peer conformity, and self-reported behavior among adolescents. *Developmental Psychology, 22*, 521-530.

Buchanan, C., Eccles, J., Flanagan, C., Midgley, C., Feldlaufer, M., & Harold, R. (1990). Parents' and teachers' beliefs about adolescents: Effects of sex and experience. *Journal of Youth and Adolescence, 19*, 363-394.

Carnegie Council on Adolescent Development. (1989). *Turning points: Preparing American youth for the 21st century*. New York: Carnegie.

Cassidy, J., & Kobak, R. (1988). Avoidance and its relation to other defense processes. In J. Belsky & T. Nezworski (Eds.), *Clinical implications of attachment* (pp. 300-323). Hillsdale, NJ: Lawrence Erlbaum.

Clary, F. (1982). Minor women obtaining abortions: A study of parental notification in a metropolitan area. *American Journal of Public Health, 72*, 283-285.

Collins, W. A. (1990). Parent-child relationships in the transition to adolescence: Continuity and change in interaction, affect, and cognition. In R. Montemayor, G. R. Adams, & T. P. Gullotta (Eds.), *From childhood to adolescence: A transitional period?* (pp. 85-106). Newbury Park, CA: Sage.

Cooper, C. (1988). Commentary: The role of conflict in adolescent-parent relationships. In M. Gunnar & W. A. Collins (Eds.), *Development during the transition to adolescence: Minnesota symposium on child development* (Vol. 21, pp. 181-187). Hillsdale, NJ: Lawrence Erlbaum.

Cooper, C. (1994). Cultural perspectives on continuity and change in adolescents' relationships. In R. Montemayor, G. R. Adams, & T. P. Gullotta (Eds.), *Personal relationships during adolescence* (pp. 78-100). Thousand Oaks, CA: Sage.

Cooper, C., & Cooper, R. (1992). Links between adolescents' relationships with their parents and peers: Models, evidence, and mechanisms. In R. Parke & G. Ladd (Eds.), *Family-peer relationships: Models of linkages* (pp. 135-158). Hillsdale, NJ: Lawrence Erlbaum.

Cooper, C., Grotevant, H., & Condon, S. (1983). Individuality and connectedness in the family as a context for adolescent identity formation and role-taking skill. In H. Grotevant & C. Cooper (Eds.), *Adolescent development in the family: New directions of child development* (pp. 43-59). San Francisco: Jossey-Bass.

Douvan, E., & Adelson, J. (1966). *The adolescent experience.* New York: John Wiley.

Duncan, P., Ritter, P., Dornbusch, S., Gross, R., & Carlsmith, J. M. (1985). The effects of pubertal timing on body image, school behavior, and deviance. *Journal of Youth and Adolescence, 14,* 227-235.

Eccles, J., Buchanan, C., Flanagan, C., Fuligni, A., Midgley, C., & Yee, D. (1991). Control versus autonomy during adolescence. *Journal of Social Issues, 47,* 53-68.

Eccles, J., Midgley, C., Wigfled, A., Buchanan, C., Reuman, D., Flanagan, C., & MacIver, D. (1993). Development during adolescence: The impact of stage-environment fit on young adolescents' experiences in schools and families. *American Psychologist, 48,* 90-101.

Elkind, D. (1967). Egocentrism in adolescence. *Child Development, 38,* 1025-1034.

Entwisle, D. (1990). Schools and the adolescent. In S. Feldman & G. Elliott (Eds.), *At the threshold: The developing adolescent* (pp. 197-224). Cambridge, MA: Harvard University Press.

Erikson, E. (1962). *Young man Luther.* New York: Norton.

Feldman, S., & Quatman, T. (1988). Factors influencing age expectations for adolescent autonomy: A study of early adolescents and parents. *Journal of Early Adolescence, 8,* 325-343.

Feldman, S., & Rosenthal, D. (1991). Age expectations for behavioral autonomy in Hong Kong, Australian, and American youth: The influence of family variables and adolescents' values. *International Journal of Psychology, 26,* 1-23.

Feldman, S., & Wood, D. (1994). Parents' expectations for preadolescent sons' behavioral autonomy: A longitudinal study of correlates and outcomes. *Journal of Research on Adolescence, 4,* 45-70.

Fischhoff, B. (1992). Risk taking: A developmental perspective. In J. Yates (Ed.), *Risk-taking behavior* (pp. 133-162). New York: John Wiley.

Flanagan, C. (1990). Changes in family work status: Effects on parent-adolescent decision making. *Child Development, 61,* 163-177.

Fontana, A., & Frey, J. (1994). Interviewing: The art of science. In N. Denzin & Y. Lincoln (Eds.), *Handbook of qualitative research* (pp. 361-376). Thousand Oaks, CA: Sage.

Frank, S., Avery, C., & Laman, M. (1988). Young adults' perceptions of their relationships with their parents: Individual differences in connectedness, competence, and emotional autonomy. *Developmental Psychology, 24,* 729-737.

Frank, S., & Jackson-Walker, S. (in press). Family experiences as moderators of the relationship between eating symptoms and personality disturbance. *Journal of Youth and Adolescence.*

Frank, S., Pirsch, L., & Wright, V. (1990). Late adolescents' perceptions of their relationships with their parents: Relationships among deidealization, autonomy, relatedness, and insecurity and implications for adolescent adjustment and ego identity status. *Journal of Youth and Adolescence, 19,* 571-588.

Freud, A. (1958). Adolescence. *Psychoanalytic Study of the Child, 13,* 255-278.

Friedenberg, E. (1963). *Coming of age in America: Growth and acquiescence.* New York: Knopf-Vintage.

Fuhrman, T., & Holmbeck, G. (1995). A contextual-moderator analysis of emotional autonomy and adjustment in adolescence. *Child Development*.

Fuligni, A., & Eccles, J. (1993). Perceived parent-child relationships and early adolescents' orientation toward peers. *Developmental Psychology, 29,* 622-632.

Gardner, W., Sherer, D., & Tester, T. (1989). Asserting scientific authority: Cognitive development and adolescent legal rights. *American Psychologist, 44,* 895-902.

Gilligan, C. (1988). Adolescent development reconsidered. In C. Gilligan, J. Ward, & J. Taylor (Eds.), *Mapping the moral domain* (pp. vii-xxxix). Cambridge, MA: Harvard University Press.

Gjerde, P. (1986). The interpersonal structure of family interaction settings: Parent-adolescent relations in dyads and triads. *Developmental Psychology, 22,* 297-304.

Greenberger, E. (1984). Defining psychosocial maturity in adolescence (revised manuscript). In P. Karoly & J. Steffen (Eds.), *Adolescent behavior disorders: Foundations and contemporary concerns* (pp. 54-81). Lexington, MA: Heath.

Greenberger, E., Josselson, R., Knerr, C., & Knerr, B. (1974). The measurement and structure of psychosocial maturity. *Journal of Youth and Adolescence, 4,* 127-143.

Greenberger, E., & Steinberg, L. (1981). The workplace as a context for the socialization of youth. *Journal of Youth and Adolescence, 10,* 185-210.

Greenberger, E., & Steinberg, L. (1986). *When teenagers work: The psychological and social costs of adolescents' employment.* New York: Basic Books.

Grisso, T., & Vierling, L. (1978). Minors' consent to treatment: A developmental perspective. *Professional Psychology, 9,* 412-417.

Grotevant, H., & Cooper, C. (1985). Patterns of interaction in family relationships and the development of identity exploration in adolescence. *Child Development, 56,* 415-428.

Grotevant, H., & Cooper, C. (1986). Individuation in family relationships: A perspective on individual differences in the development of identity and role-taking skill in adolescence. *Human Development, 29,* 82-100.

Hall, G. S. (1904). *Adolescence.* Englewood Cliffs, NJ: Prentice Hall.

Hamilton, S. (1987). Apprenticeship as a transition to adulthood in West Germany. *American Journal of Education, 95,* 314-345.

Hauser, S., Powers, S., & Noam, G. (1991). *Adolescents and their families: Paths of ego development.* New York: Free Press.

Hauser, S., Powers, S., Noam, G., & Bowlds, M. (1987). Family interiors of adolescent ego development trajectories. *Family Perspective, 21,* 263-282.

Hauser, S., Powers, S., Noam, G., Jacobson, A., Weiss, B., & Follansbee, D. (1984). Familial contexts of adolescent ego development. *Child Development, 55,* 195-213.

Hess, R., & Handel, G. (1967). The family as a psychosocial organization. In G. Handel (Ed.), *The psychosocial interior of the family* (pp. 10-24). Chicago: Aldine.

Hill, J. P. (1973). *Some perspectives on adolescence in American society.* A report prepared for the Office of Child Development, U.S. Department of Health, Education, and Welfare, Washington, DC.

Hill, J., & Holmbeck, G. (1986). Attachment and autonomy during adolescence. In G. Whitehurst (Ed.), *Annals of child development* (Vol. 3, pp. 145-189). Greenwich, CT: JAI.

Hill, J., & Holmbeck, G. (1987). Familial adaptation to biological change during adolescence. In R. Lerner & T. Foch (Eds.), *Biological-psychosocial interactions in early adolescence* (pp. 207-223). Hillsdale, NJ: Lawrence Erlbaum.

Hill, J., & Monks, F. (1977). Some perspectives of adolescence in modern societies. In J. Hill & F. Monks (Eds.), *Adolescence and youth in prospect*. Atlantic Highlands, NJ: Humanities Press.

Hill, J., & Steinberg, L. (1976). *The development of autonomy during adolescence*. Paper presented at the Symposium on Research on Youth Problems Today, Fundacion Faustino Orbegoza Eizaguirre, Madrid, Spain.

Hill, J. P. (1983). Early adolescence: A research agenda. *Journal of Early Adolescence, 3*, 1-21.

Hoffman, J. (1984). Psychological separation of late adolescents from their parents. *Journal of Counseling Psychology, 31*, 170-178.

Holmbeck, G., Faier-Routman, J., Willis, K., & McLone, D. (1994). *Autonomy and psychosocial adjustment in adolescents with and without spina bifida*. Unpublished manuscript.

Holmbeck, G., & O'Donnell, K. (1991). Discrepancies between perceptions of decision-making and behavioral autonomy. In R. Paikoff (Ed.), *Shared views of the family during adolescence: New directions for child development* (pp. 51-69). San Francisco: Jossey-Bass.

Holmbeck, G., Paikoff, R., & Brooks-Gunn, J. (in press). Parenting adolescents. In M. Bornstein (Ed.), *Handbook of parenting*. Hillsdale, NJ: Lawrence Erlbaum.

Humphrey, L. (1989). Observed family interactions among subtypes of eating disorders using structural analysis of social behavior. *Journal of Consulting and Clinical Psychology, 57*, 206-214.

Jessor, R. (1982). Problem behavior and developmental transition in adolescence. *Journal of School Health, 52*, 295-300.

Jordan, J., Kaplan, A., Miller, J., Stiver, I., & Surrey, J. (1991). *Women's growth in connection: Writings from the Stone Center*. New York: Guilford.

Josselson, R. (1980). Ego development in adolescence. In J. Adelson (Ed.), *Handbook of adolescent psychology*. New York: John Wiley.

Josselson, R. (1988). The embedded self: I and thou revisited. In D. Lapsley & F. Power (Eds.), *Self, ego, and identity: Integrative approaches* (pp. 91-106). New York: Springer-Verlag.

Kaul, S. (1995). *Emotional autonomy and acculturation among Indian-American adolescents*. Manuscript submitted for publication.

Kenny, M. (1987). The extent and function of parental attachment among first-year college students. *Journal of Youth and Adolescence, 16*, 17-29.

Knudson-Martin, C. (1994). The female voice: Applications of Bowen's family systems theory. *Journal of Marital and Family Therapy, 20*, 35-46.

Kobak, R., Cole, H., Ferenz-Gillies, R., Fleming, W., & Gamble, W. (1993). Attachment and emotion regulation during mother-teen problem-solving: A control theory analysis. *Child Development, 64*, 231-245.

Lamborn, S., & Steinberg, L. (1993). Emotional autonomy redux: Revisting Ryan and Lynch. *Child Development, 64*, 483-499.

LaRossa, R., & Reitzes, D. (1993). Symbolic interactionism and family studies. In P. Boss, W. Doherty, R. LaRossa, W. Schumm, & S. Steinmetz (Eds.), *Sourcebook of family theories and methods: A contextual approach* (pp. 135-163). New York: Plenum.

Larson, R., & Richards, M. (1994). *Divergent realities: The emotional lives of mothers, fathers, and adolescents.* New York: Basic Books.

Laursen, B., & Collins, W. A. (1988). Conceptual changes during adolescence and effects upon parent-child relationships. *Journal of Adolescent Research, 3,* 119-140.

Leaper, C., Hauser, S., Kremen, A., Powers, S., Jacobson, A., Noam, G., Weiss-Perry, B., & Follansbee, D. (1989). Adolescent-parent interactions in relation to adolescents' gender and ego development pathway: A longitudinal study. *Journal of Early Adolescence, 9,* 335-361.

Lewis, C. (1980). A comparison of minors' and adults' pregnancy decisions. *American Journal of Orthopsychiatry, 50,* 446-453.

Lewis, C. (1981). How adolescents approach decisions: Changes over grades seven through twelve and policy implications. *Child Development, 52,* 538-544.

Lewis, C. (1987). Minors' competence to consent to abortion. *American Psychologist, 42,* 84-88.

Livson, N., & Peskin, H. (1980). Perspectives on adolescence from longitudinal research. In J. Adelson (Ed.), *Handbook of adolescent psychology* (pp. 47-98). New York: John Wiley.

Maccoby, E., & Martin, J. (1983). Socialization in the context of the family: Parent-child interaction. In E. M. Hetherington (Ed.), *Handbook of child psychology: Vol. 4. Socialization, personality, and social development* (pp. 1-101). New York: John Wiley.

MacIver, D., & Reuman, D. (1988, April). *Decision-making in the classroom and early adolescents' valuing of mathematics.* Paper presented at the annual meeting of the American Educational Research Association, New Orleans, LA.

Mahler, M., Pine, F., & Bergman, A. (1975). *The psychological birth of the human infant.* New York: Basic Books.

Melton, G. (1983). Toward "personhood" for adolescents: Autonomy and privacy as values in public policy. *American Psychologist, 38,* 99-103.

Midgley, C., & Feldlaufer, H. (1987). Students' and teachers' decision-making fit before and after the transition to junior high school. *Journal of Early Adolescence, 7,* 225-241.

Midgley, C., Feldlaufer, H., & Eccles, J. (1988). The transition to junior high school: Beliefs of pre- and post-transition teachers. *Journal of Youth and Adolescence, 17,* 543-562.

Montemayor, R. (1983). Parents and adolescents in conflict: All of the families some of the time and some families most of the time. *Journal of Early Adolescence, 3,* 83-103.

Moore, D. (1987). Parent-adolescent separation: The construction of adulthood by late adolescents. *Developmental Psychology, 23,* 298-307.

Mortimer, J., Finch, M., Shanahan, M., & Ryu, S. (1992). Work experience, mental health, and behavioral adjustment in adolescence. *Journal of Research on Adolescence, 2,* 25-57.

Murtaugh, M., & Zetlin, A. (1988). Achievement of autonomy by nonhandicapped and mildly learning handicapped adolescents. *Journal of Youth and Adolescence, 17,* 445-460.

Newcomb, M., & Bentler, P. (1989). Substance use and abuse among children and teenagers. *American Psychologist, 44,* 242-248.

Paikoff, R., & Brooks-Gunn, J. (1990). Physiological processes: What role do they play during the transition to adolescence? In R. Montemayor, G. R. Adams, & T. P. Gullotta (Eds.), *From childhood to adolescence: A transitional period?* (pp. 63-81). Newbury Park, CA: Sage.

Paikoff, R., & Brooks-Gunn, J. (1991). Do parent-child relationships change during puberty? *Psychological Bulletin, 110,* 47-66.

Patterson, G., & Stouthamer-Loeber, M. (1984). The correlation of family management practices and delinquency. *Child Development, 55,* 1299-1307.

Pipp, S., Shaver, P., Jennings, S., Lamborn, S., & Fischer, K. (1985). Adolescents' theories about the development of the relationships with parents. *Journal of Personality and Social Psychology, 48,* 991-1001.

Poole, M., Cooney, G., & Cheong, A. (1986). Adolescent perceptions of family cohesiveness, autonomy and independence in Australia and Singapore. *Journal of Comparative Family Studies, 17,* 311-332.

Powers, S., Beardslee, W., Jacobson, A., & Noam, G. (1987, April). *Family influences on the development of adolescent coping processes.* Paper presented at the biennial meeting of the Society for Research in Child Development, Baltimore.

Powers, S., Hauser, S., Schwartz, J., Noam, G., & Jacobson, A. (1983). Adolescent ego development and family interaction: A structural-developmental perspective. In H. Grotevant & C. Cooper (Eds.), *Adolescent development in the family: New directions of child development* (pp. 5-24). San Francisco, CA: Jossey-Bass.

Quadrel, M., Fischhoff, B., & Davis, W. (1993). Adolescent (in)vulnerability. *American Psychologist, 48,* 102-116.

Quintana, S., & Lapsley, D. (1990). Rapprochement in late adolescent separation-individuation: A structural equations approach. *Journal of Adolescence, 13,* 371-385.

Rosen, R. (1980). Adolescent pregnancy decision-making: Are parents important? *Adolescence, 57,* 43-54.

Ruebush, K. (1994). The mother-daughter relationship and psychological separation in adolescence. *Journal of Research on Adolescence, 4,* 439-451.

Rutter, M. (1990). Psychosocial resilience and protective mechanisms. In J. Rolf, A. Masten, D. Cicchetti, K. Nuechterlein, & S. Weintraub (Eds.), *Risk and protective factors in the development of psychopathology* (pp. 181-214). New York: Cambridge University Press.

Rutter, M., Graham, M., Chadwick, O., & Yule, W. (1976). Adolescent turmoil: Fact or fiction? *Journal of Child Psychology and Psychiatry, 17,* 35-56.

Ryan, R. (1991). The nature of the self in autonomy and relatedness. In J. Strauss & G. Goethals (Eds.), *The self: Interdisciplinary approaches* (pp. 208-238). New York: Springer-Verlag.

Ryan, R., & Lynch, J. (1989). Emotional autonomy versus detachment: Revisiting the vicissitudes of adolescence and young adulthood. *Child Development, 60,* 340-356.

Sabatelli, R., & Mazor, A. (1985). Differentiation, individuation, and identity formation: The integration of family systems and individual development perspectives. *Adolescence, 20,* 619-633.

Sampson, E. (1985). The decentralization of identity: Toward a revised concept of personal and social order. *American Psychologist, 40,* 1203-1211.

Silbereisen, R., & Noack, P. (1988). On the constructive role of problem behavior in adolescence. In N. Bolger, A. Caspi, G. Downey, & M. Moorehouse (Eds.), *Persons in context: Developmental processes* (pp. 152-180). Cambridge, UK: Cambridge University Press.

Silverberg, S. (in press). Parental well-being and their children's transition to adolescence. In C. Ryff & M. Seltzer (Eds.), *The parental experience in midlife*. Chicago: University of Chicago Press.

Silverberg, S., & Small, S. (1995). *Parental monitoring and adolescent problem behavior across gender, grade, and family structure*. Unpublished manuscript.

Silverberg, S., & Steinberg, L. (1987). Adolescent autonomy, parent-adolescent conflict, and parental well-being. *Journal of Youth and Adolescence, 16,* 293-312.

Small, S., Eastman, G., & Cornelius, S. (1988). Adolescent autonomy and parental stress. *Journal of Youth and Adolescence, 17,* 377-391.

Smetana, J. (1988a). Adolescents' and parents' conceptions of parental authority. *Child Development, 59,* 321-335.

Smetana, J. (1988b). Concepts of self and social convention: Adolescents' and parents' reasoning about hypothetical and actual family conflicts. In M. Gunnar & W. A. Collins (Eds.), *Development during the transition to adolescence: Minnesota symposium on child development* (Vol. 21, pp. 79-122). Hillsdale, NJ: Lawrence Erlbaum.

Smetana, J. (1989). Adolescents' and parents' reasoning about actual family conflict. *Child Development, 60,* 1052-1067.

Smith, C., & Rojewski, J. (1993). School-to-work transition: Alternatives for educational reform. *Youth and Society, 25,* 222-250.

Smollar, J., & Youniss, J. (1989). Transformations in adolescents' perceptions of parents. *International Journal of Behavioural Development, 12,* 71-84.

Spence, J. (1985). Achievement American style: The rewards and costs of individualism. *American Psychologist, 40,* 1285-1295.

Steinberg, L. (1986). Latchkey children and susceptibility to peer pressure: An ecological analysis. *Developmental Psychology, 22,* 433-439.

Steinberg, L. (1989). Pubertal maturation and parent-adolescent distance: An evolutionary perspective. In G. R. Adams, R. Montemayor, & T. P. Gullotta (Eds.), *Biology of adolescent behavior and development* (pp. 71-97). Newbury Park, CA: Sage.

Steinberg, L. (1990). Autonomy, conflict, and harmony in the family relationship. In S. Feldman & G. Elliott (Eds.), *At the threshold: The developing adolescent* (pp. 255-276). Cambridge, MA: Harvard University Press.

Steinberg, L. (1993). *Adolescence* (3rd ed.). New York: McGraw-Hill.

Steinberg, L., & Dornbusch, S. (1991). Negative correlates of part-time employment during adolescence: Replication and elaboration. *Developmental Psychology, 27,* 304-313.

Steinberg, L., Fegley, S., & Dornbusch, S. (1993). Negative impact of part-time work on adolescent adjustment: Evidence from a longitudinal study. *Developmental Psychology, 29,* 171-180.

Steinberg, L., Greenberger, E., Garduque, L., Ruggiero, M., & Vaux, A. (1982). Effects of working on adolescent development. *Developmental Psychology, 18,* 383-395.

Steinberg, L., & Silverberg, S. (1986). The vicissitudes of autonomy in early adolescence. *Child Development, 57,* 841-851.

Steinberg, L., & Steinberg, W. (1994). *Crossing paths: How your child's adolescence triggers your own crisis.* New York: Simon & Schuster.

Surrey, J. (1991). The self-in-relation: A theory of women's development. In J. Jordan, A. Kaplan, J. Miller, I. Stiver, & J. Surrey (Eds.), *Women's growth in connection: Writings from the Stone Center* (pp. 51-66). New York: Guilford.

Torres, A., Forrest, J., & Eisman, S. (1980). Telling parents: Clinic policies and adolescents' use of family planning and abortion services. *Family Planning Perspectives, 12,* 284-292.

Tremper, C., & Kelly, M. (1987). The mental health rationale for policies fostering minors' autonomy. *International Journal of Law and Psychiatry, 10,* 111-127.

Turner, R., Irwin, C., & Millstein, S. (1991). Family structure, family processes, and experimenting with substances during adolescence. *Journal of Research on Adolescence, 1,* 93-106.

Turner, R., Irwin, C., Tschann, J., & Millstein, S. (1994, March). *Autonomous-relatedness and changes in self-esteem during adolescence.* Paper presented at the biennial meetings of the Society for Research on Adolescence, San Diego, CA.

Wallerstein, J., & Blakeslee, S. (1990). *Second chances: Men, women, and children a decade after divorce.* New York: Ticknor & Fields.

Weisner, T., Gallimore, R., & Jordan, C. (1988). Unpackaging cultural effects on classroom learning: Native Hawaiian peer assistance and child-generated activity. *Anthropology and Education Quarterly, 19,* 327-351.

Weithorn, L., & Campbell, S. (1982). The competency of children and adolescents to make informed treatment decisions. *Child Development, 53,* 1589-1598.

White, K., Speisman, J., & Costos, D. (1983). Young adults and their parents: Individuation to mutuality. In H. Grotevant & C. Cooper (Eds.), *Adolescent development in the family: New directions for child development* (pp. 61-76). San Francisco: Jossey-Bass.

Willemsen, E., & Sanger, C. (1991). Statutory emancipation of minors: Use and impact. *American Journal of Orthopsychiatry, 61,* 540-551.

Young, H., & Ferguson, L. (1979). Developmental changes through adolescence in the spontaneous nomination of reference groups as a function of decision context. *Journal of Youth and Adolescence, 8,* 239-252.

Youniss, J., & Smollar, J. (1985). *Adolescent relations with mothers, fathers, and friends.* Chicago: University of Chicago Press.

3. Adolescent Sexual Development

Edward S. Herold
Sheila K. Marshall

Issues such as pregnancy, sexually transmitted diseases, and sexual violence have kept the topic of adolescent sexual behaviors and values salient to policymakers and researchers over the past 20 years. Unfortunately, there has been a tendency to maintain problem-focused research agendas examining these issues. The result has been a paucity of systematic research using developmental frameworks. The difficult task of generating an adequate depiction of adolescent sexual development has been further complicated by the shifting social landscape. For example, one prominent change in the past two decades has been the effect of the acquired immune deficiency syndrome (AIDS). In addition, there has been greater acceptance of sexual relationships outside of marital relationships ("Gallup Poll," 1988), increased nonmarital adolescent childbearing (Newcomer & Baldwin, 1992), and changes in the rates of contraceptive use (Ku, Sonenstein, & Pleck, 1993; Mosher & McNally, 1991).

Is it possible to adequately depict adolescent sexual development? What patterns of sexual behaviors are conducive to healthy sexual development? Research scientists studying adolescent sexual development have an elusive task akin to shooting at a moving target. Indeed, difficulties associated with researching this topic are reflected in the literature. It rarely is grounded in developmental theory, often confuses trends in behaviors with deviance, and frequently neglects social perceptions.

The objective of this chapter is to organize key findings from the literature over the past two decades. This will involve making a clear distinction between trends in social perceptions and behaviors and factors associated with adolescent sexual development. We begin by outlining the trends in sexual behaviors, values, and research emphases over the past two decades. These are followed by a review of key findings from the literature on adolescent sexual development, including patterns of behavior, sexual identity formation, and aberrant sexual experiences. Clarifying the differences between trends and developmental sequences will contribute some distinctions between social change and perceptions of sexual deviance in adolescence.

Last, it is essential to be aware of the role of research and education in influencing the social context in which adolescent sexual development takes place. The emotionally charged topic of adolescent sexual behaviors has been at the center of various social and political movements. These movements influence research and education programs, which in turn affect the lives of adolescents. We end the chapter with a discussion of the methodological difficulties associated with adolescent sexuality research, as well as two conflicting perspectives on sexuality education.

TRENDS FROM THE 1970s TO 1990s

Coital Experience

Compared with the 1970s, research through the early 1990s has found a lower average age of first intercourse and a greater average number of partners among adolescents in the United States (Alan Guttmacher Institute, 1994). Similarly, a national survey of Canadian youth revealed that, by age 16 years, 50% of adolescents had engaged in sexual intercourse, and by age 18, 66% reported having had a coital experience (King et al., 1988).

Furthermore, a national random survey in the United States revealed a narrowing of reported gender differences among younger generations (Laumann, Gagnon, Michael, & Michaels, 1994). The differences between males and females have diminished with an increasing prevalence of earlier sexual activity among European American female adolescents (Newcomer & Baldwin, 1992). In 1971, a national survey of never-married women, aged 15 to 19 years, found that 21% had experienced coitus and 41% of the women aged 18 to 19 years had experienced coitus (Kantner & Zelnik, 1972). In comparison, the 1988 National Survey of Family Growth (Forrest & Singh, 1990) found that more than 50% of 15-year-old to 19-year-old females and 75% of 18-year-old to 19-year-old females reported having experienced sexual intercourse. Males have reported experiencing sexual intercourse at younger ages than have females with 60% of males aged 15 to 19 years reporting intercourse experience and 80% reporting intercourse experience by age 20 years (Sonenstein, Pleck, & Ku, 1991).

In the United States, notable ethnic group differences have been found in age of first intercourse. Surveys over the past two decades have reported that African and Hispanic American teenagers generally begin having sexual intercourse at earlier ages than European American adolescents. Attempts to determine the reasons for ethnic group differences in age at first intercourse have generated considerable debate. The most common hypothesis traces the differences to socioeconomic circumstances. When the effects for socioeconomic indicators are controlled, however, ethnic group differences have been found to persist (Furstenberg, Morgan, Moore, & Peterson, 1987). Recent examination of the role of neighborhood characteristics in ethnic group differences in the sexual activity of female adolescents has revealed that African American and European American female adolescents respond similarly to structural constraints and opportunities with no evidence of an interaction between ethnicity and neighborhood characteristics (Brewster, 1994). Therefore, the potential contextual reasons for ethnic group differences in age of first intercourse remain yet to be fully understood.

The acceptance of coital experience outside marital relationship has increased since the 1970s. Evidence from surveys have shown increasing acceptance of premarital sex in North America over the past 25 years. In 1969, 68% of U.S. citizens thought premarital sex was wrong, but in 1987, 46% of U.S. citizens thought it was wrong ("Gallup Poll," 1988). The proportion saying premarital sex was wrong did increase slightly from 1985 to 1987.

Pregnancy and Contraception

After increasing dramatically during the early 1970s, the teenage pregnancy rate between the late 1970s and the late 1980s in the United States remained stable. Rates then moved upward, and by 1990, about 12% of women between the ages of 15 and 19 years became pregnant (Henshaw, 1994). About one half of adolescent pregnancies result in a live birth, 36% are intentionally aborted, and 14% end in a miscarriage (Zabin & Hayward, 1993). The highest rates of live births occur among the poor in large urban areas of the United States, particularly among minority ethnic groups. Furthermore, the proportion of births to young women who are not married have increased from 15% in 1960 to 66% in 1988 (Newcomer & Baldwin, 1992).

From the 1970s to the 1990s, there was a significant increase in the use of contraceptive methods among adolescents. For example, adolescent males' reports of condom use at first intercourse doubled between 1979 and 1988 from 20% to 54% (Ku et al., 1993). During the same time period, female contraceptive use at first intercourse also increased from 47% to 65% (Mosher & McNally, 1991). The proportion of European American females who reported condom use at first intercourse increased from 24% to 45% and among African Americans, condom use at first intercourse increased from 24% to 32%. Although the condom is most often used at first intercourse, there is a trend for the pill to replace the condom as the most common method of contraception in long-term relationships (Zabin & Hayward, 1993).

Until the AIDS epidemic, the use of condoms by gay males was not investigated. Adolescent gay males are particularly at risk because, in comparison with older gay males, they have more sexual partners and engage in more sexual risk acts (Remafedi, 1987a). In a study of gay and bisexual youths in New York City, 46% of the males consistently used condoms during all anal sex acts and 18% used condoms consistently during all oral sex acts (Rotheram-Borus, Reid, & Rosario, 1994).

Research Emphasis

In the early 1970s, the research emphasis was on sexual intercourse and pregnancy prevention. This changed in the 1980s with the substantial effect of the AIDS epidemic. Funding by many private and federal agencies was directed at social and health behaviors associated with the transmission of the human immunodeficiency virus (HIV). Although AIDS rates for adolescents are low in comparison with other age groups, there is continued concern about HIV transmission because there is a long incubation period of the disease. Indeed, many individuals diagnosed with AIDS in their 20s contracted the HIV as adolescents (Newcomer & Baldwin, 1992).

The threat of AIDS has prompted four new trends in sexual behavior research. First, it facilitated the conducting of research on sexual behavior of adolescents. Prior to AIDS, it was difficult for researchers to obtain samples of high school students to study sexual behavior. Second, AIDS provided a rationale to study behaviors other than vaginal intercourse, especially oral and anal sex practices. Third, groups were studied that had been previously ignored, such as street youth, gay males, and drug users. In particular, there has been a substantial increase in the amount of research focused on gay youth. Last, in response to the widening AIDS epidemic, research has expanded to several other countries. This has led to an increase in cross-cultural comparisons of adolescent sexual behaviors and attitudes.

International Research

In the early 1970s, most of the research on adolescent sexuality was conducted in North America, with a few studies completed in Europe. A North American focus offered a limited perception of the variations in adolescent sexual behavior. Indeed, the emphasis in North America has been on adolescent coitus, the prevention of pregnancy, and the transmission of disease. Cross-cultural research is valuable in demonstrating the diversity of sexual values and patterns of behaviors among adolescents.

In many geographic areas such as Asia and Latin America, sexual behavior patterns for adolescents can be substantially different than for U.S. youth. For example, in the United States, fewer than 1% of male adolescents have paid sex with a female prostitute (Ku et al., 1993). Yet, in countries such as Thailand where prostitution is widespread, most young males' first sexual partner is a prostitute, and many continue to have sexual relationships with prostitutes throughout their adolescence and into adulthood (Muecke, 1990). In contrast, few of the young women in Thailand who are not prostitutes report having engaged in sexual intercourse because of the cultural importance given to female virginity at marriage.

In some African countries, adolescent females have been found to form liaisons with elderly men in exchange for money and other luxuries. The older males will select as partners young females who are in educational institutions and living away from parental control (Adeokun, 1990). One reason given by these males for choosing younger females is their belief that these individuals are less likely to have HIV or other sexually transmitted diseases (STDs); therefore, there is no need to use condoms. One obvious consequence is that this can be a major source of disease transmission to the adolescent girls (Adeokun, 1990).

Much of the research on cultural differences in adolescent sexuality has focused on differences in rates of behavior. Schwartz (1993) has compared the affective reactions of U.S. and Swedish women to their first premarital coitus. He found that U.S. women expressed more negative reactions, and he attributes this to the more conservative norms in the United States. This is consistent with Christensen's (1969) theory of relative consequences that states that in restrictive cultures, where the discrepancy between norms and behavior is greater, the consequences of adolescent sexual behaviors are more negative.

Researchers have also compared adolescent reproductive behaviors across developed countries. The United States has the highest rate of teenage pregnancy of any Western developed nation (Zabin & Hayward, 1993). The lower pregnancy rates in other countries are not due to lower rates of sexual intercourse but are largely attributable to more effective contraceptive use.

In summary, research indicates that over the past two decades, there has been an increasing trend for most individuals to experience first coitus sometime before the end of adolescence. Although adolescent pregnancy rates remain high, they are lower than in the 1970s. This can be largely attributed to the increased use of contraceptives.

General acceptance of sexual intercourse outside of a marital relationship has increased in North America. It is interesting that despite these trends, research on adolescent sexuality since the 1970s has been largely problem based, focusing primarily on sexual intercourse and contraceptive use. This emphasis has generally limited knowledge about adolescent sexuality to a few issues. Traditional research boundaries have been expanded recently in response to concern about AIDS. In particular, researchers have begun to study sexual attitudes and behaviors across cultures. This widened scope of research has clearly been beneficial in demonstrating the diversity of adolescent sexual development patterns.

ADOLESCENT SEXUAL DEVELOPMENT

Adolescent sexuality development involves physical and psychological changes and interpersonal events. Our review of adolescent sexual development literature does not emphasize physical aspects of pubertal development but focuses on the aspects related to psychosocial development. More specifically, this review includes literature that has, since the early 1970s, furthered our knowledge of adolescent sexuality development in the areas of sexual behaviors and sexual identity. Most research on adolescent sexuality development has been conducted in the United States; therefore, this review heavily emphasizes adolescent development within that context and, as such, does not infer universal findings. The evidence presented here does, however, demonstrate the multiple and complex linkages between variables associated with adolescent sexual development.

This section begins with a discussion of the two major paradigms used to explain human sexual development. Each paradigm emphasizes the influence of the social context on adolescent sexual development, a dimension that is highlighted in our review of adolescent sexual behaviors. We then discuss the progression of sexual behaviors that, for most adolescents, begins with self-stimulation and is followed by the establishment of dyadic relationships. It is within intimate dyadic relationships that heterosexual adolescents more often experience first coitus. Key factors that have been examined in relation to this transition are reviewed. We then discuss the contribution of sexual behaviors and intimacy exploration to self-recognition of erotic orientation and sexual identity formation.

Given the rising awareness of aberrant sexual experiences in adolescence, we include literature on sexual abuse, date rape, and prostitution. Although evidence of the effects of these experiences on sexual development is limited, these experiences may have considerable effect on individuals' sexuality and developing capacity for intimate relationships.

Developmental Theory

Unfortunately, research on the psychosocial aspects of adolescent sexuality has not been well grounded in developmental theory. However, as Miller and Fox (1987) have noted, two overarching paradigms have been used to explain human sexuality. Both of these paradigms are helpful in understanding how individual patterns of sexual expression and values develop in conjunction with the values inherent in the social environment.

The first paradigm, emanating largely from Freud (1933, 1953) and his psychoanalytic theory, describes sexuality as a *biological imperative* that unfolds during adolescence. From this perspective, sexuality in adolescence is perceived as needing to be channeled and controlled by individual, interpersonal, and societal restraints. The second paradigm views sexuality as *socially shaped and learned*. This view posits that sexuality is the outcome of "sexual pedagogy" (Miller & Fox, 1987) rather than being internally driven. In addition, sexuality is perceived as variable across social and cultural time and space. Reiss (1967, 1986), Gagnon and Simon (1973), and Gagnon (1990) have provided excellent examples of this social learning and culturally scripted approach to human sexuality.

Both of these paradigms offer invaluable insights into adolescent sexual development; however, independently, these paradigms are incomplete. The social learning paradigm minimizes biological influences on development. The emergent sexuality paradigm presumes that sexual impulses without social controls are out of the control of the adolescent. This comes dangerously close to removing individual agency and responsibility in sexual relations. It is at the interface between these two paradigms that advances in theory and research should be focused (Miller & Fox, 1987). Indeed, Hill (1973) suggested that "the development of sexual behavior must be understood in terms of a complex, but patterned, series of learning experiences super-imposed upon and in interaction with some biological givens" (p. 44).

Masturbation

Masturbation, the sexual self-stimulation of the genitals, is a common sexual practice among adolescents and for many, especially males, provides their first orgasm (Herold, 1984). More adolescent males than females masturbate, with males usually masturbating at earlier ages and more frequently than females (Herold, 1984; Oliver & Hyde, 1993). Many adolescents report feeling guilty about masturbation, and many females report they do not discuss the topic (Herold, 1984).

Adolescent Dyadic Relationship Development

Much of the research on adolescent sexual behavior indicates it is embedded within a relational context (Thornton, 1990; Zelnik, 1983);

however, little is known about the dynamics of adolescent sexual activity within dyadic relationships. Furthermore, extant literature on the dynamics of adolescent sexual relationships generally emphasizes heterosexual couples.

There is evidence of a normative developmental pattern in the sequence of adolescent heterosexual behaviors for European American adolescent heterosexual couples. These couples generally begin with embraces and kissing, move on to fondling, first of breasts, then sex organs, and then engage in more intimate behaviors such as intercourse (Smith & Udry, 1985). It is interesting that African American adolescents in the United States do not follow a similar sequence. Petting behaviors while unclothed were not found to precede intercourse for many African American adolescents (Smith & Udry, 1985). European American and African American adolescents in the United States appear to have different normative expectations regarding heterosexual behaviors (Furstenberg et al., 1987).

Thornton (1990) has studied the relationship between courtship processes and adolescent sexual behaviors and found that adolescents rarely experience sexual intercourse prior to beginning to date, but as they initiate dating, the transition to first coitus unfolds. The speed of the transition to sexual intercourse begins to accelerate once the couple develops a steady dating relationship. The timing of these experiences, however, was found to be related to the age at which adolescents begin to date. Those who began to date at about age 13 years developed steady relationships earlier and continued to date more frequently than those who initiated dating in middle to late adolescence. In addition, those individuals initiating dating earlier had more partners and intercourse more frequently at age 18 years than did those who initiated dating later.

Within heterosexual adolescent relationships, there are gender differences in the attitudes and motivations toward initiating coital activity. It is interesting that the influence of these differences on adolescent intimate relationships has not been fully examined. Young females report being more motivated by love to engage in sexual intercourse, whereas young males report being more motivated by physical desire (Carroll, Volk, & Hyde, 1985). During their initial coital behaviors, it has been found that males report less emotional attachment and commitment (Miller & Simon, 1974; Sorenson, 1973), whereas females are more likely to experience first coitus within what they perceive is a romantic relationship (Zelnik & Shah, 1983).

In response to first coitus, it has been found that males are less likely to experience guilt and more likely to experience satisfaction than are females (Scales & Beckstein, 1982; Sprecher, Barbee, & Schwartz, 1995). Further examination of the contribution to relationship development of these gender differences in attitudes toward sexual intercourse would be useful.

Research in the past 20 years on coital behavior of adolescents demonstrates there has been an increasing detachment of coital activity from marriage (Gagnon, 1990). This is evidenced by the increase in the number of coupled relationships in which there was coital activity and the earlier occurrence of intercourse in the dating relationship. Gagnon suggests that the sexual behaviors in dyadic relationships in adolescence are for the purposes of the relationship and not for the future state of marriage. Unfortunately, love and intimate relationships in adolescence have been given little attention in the literature. This may be due to the stronger problem-focused emphasis in research on adolescent social and sexual relationships. In addition, the strong emotional responses adolescents can experience in relationships are often minimized in importance. Such minimization does not consider the importance of the sincerity and depth of affective responses adolescents experience for each other (Mitchell, 1976) or the importance such intimate relations hold for the development of interpersonal identity formation and later longer-term relationships.

Transition to Coitus

The singular event in adolescent heterosexual behavior that has received more attention than any other research topic is the transition to coitus. The emphasis on coitus has generally been problem driven as researchers addressed the risks of adolescent pregnancy and STD and HIV transmission. From a less problem-driven perspective, there is evidence suggesting many adolescents perceive first coitus as contributing to a self-definition of adult sexual status (Herold, 1984; Hobart, 1975; Whitehurst, 1972). Although first coitus offers risk potentials for adolescents, it can be an important social and psychological transition for many heterosexual adolescents.

Recognizing that the values inherent in the environment influence adolescent sexual expression and values (Hotvedt, 1990), this review of the literature on coital activity in adolescence includes various aspects of the social domains with which adolescents interface. However, given the limited systematic research in this topic area, the extent and direction of effects have generally not been well established. As such, we review the social influences from an ecological perspective, proceeding from community and institutional factors to interpersonal relationships.

Economic resources and the structure of the community in which adolescents live have been found to be associated with adolescents' sexual activity and age of first coital experience. As socioeconomic status decreases, rates of sexual activity increase (Hogan & Kitagawa, 1985; Moore, Simms, & Betsey, 1986). Early research indicated a positive association between living in the context of the inner city and rates of sexual intercourse for adolescents (Clark, Zabin, & Hardy, 1984; Finkel & Finkel, 1975; Zelnik & Kantner, 1980). These associations might be better understood, however, if viewed from the perspective of adolescents. If adolescents are living in economically disadvantaged communities where adult-status behaviors, such as employment, are difficult to attain, sexual activity may be highly valued as a symbol of adult status (Andersen, 1989; Dash, 1989). Recently, researchers examining the influence of community characteristics on sexual activity have found that greater availability of neighborhood economic resources and employment opportunities have been associated with later first coitus among females (Brewster, 1994; Brewster, Billy, & Grady, 1993) and lower risk of impregnation for males (Ku et al., 1993). Furthermore, Brewster (1994) found that these economic constraints and opportunities influenced both African American and European American adolescent females. She suggested that the influence of community characteristics associated with ethnically segregated housing in the United States may account for some of the ethnic differences in the risk of early first intercourse found in other studies.

It is likely that economic constraints and opportunities for employment within the social context contribute to adolescents' values toward educational achievements, plans, and orientations to the future. Findings on the associations between coital activity, education, and aspirations for the future suggest that values toward future employment status inhibit precocious sexual intercourse. Adolescents' expectations of academic achievement have been negatively associated with an early involvement in coitus (Donovan & Jessor, 1985). Similarly, rates of sexual intercourse and educational involvement have been found to be negatively associated (Ohannessian & Crockett, 1993). Furthermore, parents' educational attainment and expectations for their offspring are related to adolescents' school achievement and educational plans, which are inversely related to adolescent engagement in coitus (Miller & Sneesby, 1988). Unfortunately, researchers have often placed orientations and values toward education and future employment plans as existing within the personality of the adolescent. The role of economic and social opportunities and constraints should be considered in assessing these values and their relationships to sexual behavior patterns.

In addition to values associated with education and future status, the values espoused by religious institutions have been found to be associated with adolescents' sexual behaviors. Participation and attendance of adolescents in religion delay initiation of coitus when the church or religious affiliation teaches sexual abstinence (Forste & Heaton, 1988; Herold & Goodwin, 1981; Miller & Olson, 1988; Thornton & Camburn, 1987). Adolescents who belong to religious institutions that prohibit sexual intercourse, however, may engage in sexual behaviors that circumvent coitus. For example, Mahoney (1980) found that religious males moved beyond petting to engage in oral-genital behaviors as a way of gaining sexual experience without losing their technical virginity. The sequence reversal was also observed in females, but the relationship was not as significant.

Family characteristics, interpersonal processes (Miller & Jorgensen, 1988), and parental attitudes (Moore, Peterson, & Furstenburg, 1986) are important influences on adolescents' sexual behaviors, including first coitus. Parental supervision has been associated with the postponement of the initiation of coitus in adolescence (Jessor & Jessor, 1975; Small & Luster, 1994). Adolescents' perceptions of parental supervision have also been negatively associated with initiation of coitus (Hanson, Myers, & Ginsburg, 1987; Hogan & Kitagawa, 1985). The degree of parental control has been found to have a curvilinear relationship with adolescent sexual behavior; adolescent participation in sexual activity was most likely with no parental control, least likely with moderate parental control, and more likely to occur under extreme parental than under moderate control (Miller, McCoy, Olson, & Wallace, 1986).

Research on communication patterns between parents and adolescents suggests that there is little discussion about sex (Fox, 1986; Noller & Bagi, 1985; Walters & Walters, 1980). When discussions occur, it is more often between mothers and female adolescents (Kahn, Smith, & Roberts, 1984; Nolin & Petersen, 1992; Noller & Bagi, 1985). Fathers have been found to report more discomfort talking with their children about sexuality, whereas their offspring have reported that their fathers are less available for discussions (Nolin & Petersen, 1992). When parents engage in discussions about sexuality with their adolescents, the degree of permissiveness toward sexuality has been found to influence the timing of adolescent first coitus. More traditional parental values have been found to be positively associated with delay of their offsprings' first coitus, whereas more permissive parental values have been found to be negatively associated with offsprings' age at first coitus (Miller, McCoy, & Olson, 1986). The degree to which adolescents identify and bond with their parent(s), however, mediates the effect of parental attitudes and reactions to sexual behaviors (DiBlasio & Benda, 1992; Miller & Fox, 1987).

In modern cultures, the extended training period associated with adolescent preparation for economic independence necessitates that much of adolescents' time be spent within the context of peers (e.g., school) and away from supervision of parents. This allows many adolescents to engage in socializing and courtship activities without the supervision of adults. Hence, sexual behaviors in adolescence remain under less control from the family in comparison to preindustrial societies (Barry & Schlegel, 1986; Hotvedt, 1990). Indeed, it has been found that for both males and females, association with peers whom adolescents believe are sexually active has been found to be a much stronger predictor of transition to coitus than parental reaction to sexual behavior or adolescent attachment to parent(s) (DiBlasio & Benda, 1992). Furthermore, adolescents' attitudes toward sexual behavior have also been found to be significantly related to what they either knew friends thought or what they believed friends thought about premarital sexual intercourse (Herold & Goodwin, 1981). Peer influence on sexual values should not be perceived as causal, however, because, as Sack, Keller, and Hinkle (1984) suggest, individuals may select friends with similar sexual values. If individuals are selecting friends with similar sexual values, they may be managing their own affective response to specific sexual behaviors by choosing to construct a peer system reflecting their beliefs.

It is interesting that longitudinal peer network studies examining the influence of peers on sexual behavior show both gender and ethnic differences. Billy and Udry (1985) found evidence that European American adolescent girls were more likely to have intercourse if their friends were sexually experienced. European American male adolescents, rather than being influenced by friends' behavior, appeared to select friends on the basis of prior sexual behavior. In contrast, the sexual behaviors of African American adolescents were not found to be related to friendship connections.

Although associations have been found between adolescent coital behavior and peer and familial influences, the mechanisms underlying these relationships are ambiguous. Some sociologists have suggested that hormones may cause pubertal development, and pubertal development is then socially interpreted as a signal for parental or peer encouragement (or both) of sexual behavior (Gagnon & Simon, 1973; Hardy, 1964). Since the 1970s, Udry and his colleagues have endeavored to test this premise. Unfortunately, the results have been inconsistent. Early results from this work suggested that androgens and social influences provide motivation to engage in sexual behaviors differentially for males and females. Udry, Billy, Morris, Groff, and Raj (1985) found testosterone levels in normal male adolescents to be linked to sexual motivation in both noncoital (including masturbation) and coital behavior. Social influences, measured as the attitudes and behaviors of parents and friends, were not strongly related to coital behavior in males (Udry, 1990). For females, sexual motivation and noncoital sexual behaviors were found to be androgen dependent, but coital behavior was found to be strongly influenced by social processes (Udry, 1990; Udry, Talbert, & Morris, 1986). More recently, Halpern, Udry, Campbell, and Suchindran (1993) replicated and extended earlier work with adolescent boys by using both cross-sectional and longitudinal analyses of the contributions of testosterone and pubertal development to sexual activity. Evidence from this study contradicts previous findings because changes associated with pubertal development were found to predict sexual ideation, noncoital behavior, and transition to coitus. The level of testosterone at initiation of the study predicted age at first coitus. Changes in hormone levels over the 3 years of the study did not predict changes in sexual ideation and noncoital behavior, however. Halpern et al. (1993) note that although the reasons for the discrepancies between studies are not clear, results from the panel design indicate that caution should be taken in interpreting hormone behavior research on adolescents where a single hormone measure has been used.

It appears that, for a portion of the population, there is a pattern of transition to sexual intercourse within adolescence. Early initiation of intercourse, however, can lead to deleterious trajectories of development for adolescents. Also, early intercourse among younger adolescents has been found to be associated with truancy, smoking, and drug use (Costa, Jessor, Donovan, & Fortenberry, 1995; Jessor & Jessor, 1977). Further research is required to fully understand when the transition to coital activity is an aspect of appropriate psychological, social, and sexual development.

Sexual Identity

The primary psychosocial developmental task of adolescence is the consolidation of one's identity, a core aspect of which is a sexual identity. Whereas there has been much discussion of sexual identity formation in adolescence, little empirical research has focused on this topic. As with other areas of adolescent sexuality research, difficulties in obtaining permission by both research ethics committees and parents to study adolescents' sexual identity have impeded research. In addition, there are few measures appropriate for use with adolescents.

The strong emphasis in the literature on the prevention of sexual behaviors (more specifically, coitus) virtually ignores adolescents' developing capacity for intimacy and the need to integrate this with their own sexual responses and gender identities. Bancroft (1989, 1990) has postulated that the principal strands relating to gender identity, sexual response, and the capacity for intimate dyadic relationships develop in parallel during childhood. Bancroft suggests that during adolescence, these strands start to integrate to form the beginning of adult sexuality. Such an integration includes an increasing ability to recognize what is erotically pleasing and displeasing to another and to oneself. As such, sexual exploration is critical to sexual identity formation. Sexual exploration offers adolescents opportunities to integrate their own arousal with learning to care for and respect their partners and attain the physical competence needed to engage in the behaviors (Gagnon, 1990).

Admittedly, there is potential risk for adolescents engaging in sexual behaviors that have both reproductive and psychic consequences. Experimentation in intimacy in the form of sexual behaviors has more often been presumed to have primarily negative consequences (unwanted pregnancy, transmission of STDs) and a lack of positive purpose. The result is that we have gained little understanding of the positive contributions of sexual behaviors to adolescent sexual identity formation. Furthermore, it is possible that the paucity of research on the role of sexual experimentation in adolescence, in particular noncoital behaviors, reflects the unspoken taboo of erotic pleasure in sexual socialization and identity formation (Kleinplatz, 1992). The topic of arousal and desire may present obstacles for researchers and limit interest in research on how sexual identity is developed through the integration of sexual behaviors, sexual response, and interpersonal skills.

Like heterosexual identity formation, little is known about homosexual or bisexual identity formation. It is apparent that of the adolescents who do engage in homoerotic behavior in adolescence, the majority do not continue this behavior into adulthood (Ross-Reynolds, 1982). At the same time, the majority of lesbians and gay men have engaged in heterosexual sex, usually during their adolescence (Bell & Weinberg, 1978; Savin-Williams, 1990). Clearly, adolescence may be a time of experimentation in sexual behaviors without commitment to an enduring sense of identity connected to those behaviors. Indeed, self-recognition as either a heterosexual, bisexual, or homosexual person may be a process of increasing correspondence between one's sexual impulses, attractions, behaviors, and identity (Savin-Williams & Rodriguez, 1993). Unlike heterosexual identity formation, one of the dilemmas facing homosexual and bisexual adolescents in forming sexual identities is the frequent lack of social validation necessary for integration and consolidation of one's commitments, due to the prevalence of heterosexism.

The identity of self as gay does occur for some individuals during adolescence. Indeed, studies indicate that the average age of awareness for males attracted to the same gender was about 13 years and self-designation as gay was between 14 and 21 years of age (Remafedi, 1987b). The average age of awareness of same-gender attraction was found to be 16 years for females, with a self-description as lesbian occurring at about age 21 years (D'Augelli, Collins, & Hart, 1987). As Savin-Williams and Rodriguez (1993) note, however, the process of sexual identity formation is probably a lifelong process. Caution, therefore, should be taken in interpreting the timing of these transitions.

Sexual Violence and
Sexually Aberrant Experiences

In recent years, research on sexually aberrant experiences has increased, revealing findings that suggest that these are important considerations in understanding the development of sexuality during adolescence. However, the associations between sexually aberrant experiences and sexual development in adolescence remain somewhat ambiguous due to the difficulties encountered in researching these topics.

Adolescents can be offenders as well as victims of sexual offenses; however, it is only recently that the seriousness of sexual offenses in adolescence has been given attention in the literature. Unfortunately, as will be demonstrated, research on sexual offenders remains focused on males, obscuring our understanding of sexual violence and the role of gender socialization.

Intrafamilial Sexual Abuse

Intrafamilial sexual abuse occurring prior to, or during, adolescence can precipitate innumerable problematic emotional and behavioral disorders in adolescence (Beitchman et al., 1992; Rickel & Hendren, 1993). It remains unclear, however, whether these problems are directly related to episodes of sexual abuse or associated prolonged exposure to aversive family interactions. In their review of the literature on the long-term effects of childhood and adolescent sexual abuse, Beitchman et al. (1992) found that greater long-term harm was associated with penetration, abuse involving a father or stepfather, and longer duration of sexual abuse. The use of force has also been found to have long-term effects; however, the specific nature of the effects has not been determined. Downs (1993) has suggested that the timing of sexual abuse may affect the severity and form of effects on psychosocial development of abused individuals. Indeed, Beitchman et al. (1992) suggest that there may be a more traumatic effect of postpubertal abuse than prepubertal abuse.

Intrafamilial sexual abuse has been found to be associated with patterns of sexual behaviors in adolescence. Sexual abuse by an adult has been identified as a risk factor for precocious sexual intercourse for females (Small & Luster, 1994; Wyatt, 1989) and males (Small & Luster, 1994). In addition to engaging in sexual relations earlier, adolescent females who have been sexually abused report more sexual partners and briefer sexual relationships than females who have not been sexually abused (Wyatt, 1989). There is also evidence that suggests that revictimization is associated with sexual abuse in childhood (Alexander & Lupfer, 1987; Fromuth, 1986).

Adolescents who engage in prostitution may have a history of intrafamilial sexual abuse. However, there are differences between adolescents who have been sexually abused and engage in prostitution and adolescents who have been sexually abused and do not engage in prostitution. Seng (1989) found that adolescents with a history of sexual abuse who are involved in prostitution are more likely to quit school, frequently run away from home, and abuse drugs and alcohol than sexually abused adolescents not involved in prostitution.

The incidence of past childhood sexual abuse has been associated with an increased risk for becoming offenders of sexual abuse in adolescent males (Becker, 1988; Longo, 1982). The evidence is suggestive and warrants further research, however.

Our review of the literature demonstrates that adolescents who have been sexually abused by family members may be involved in precocious and sometimes deleterious sexual behaviors. It should be understood, however, that sexual abuse is not a prescription for such sexual behaviors. Sexual development is shaped by a multitude of influences. Similarly, there are many factors that affect individuals' response to sexual abuse.

Date Rape

There has been considerable controversy over the incidence of sexual assault in adolescence, including date rape. Determining the actual rates of sexual assault is difficult because most assaults are not reported (McCormick, 1994). Futhermore, there are differences between researchers with regard to the definition of sexual assaults such as date rape. For example, some researchers conceptualize sexual assault as unwanted but not forced sexual experiences (MacKinnon, 1987).

In a national survey by Laumann et al. (1994) of first intercourse experiences, 25% of the women reported that their first intercourse was not wanted but they were not forced to have it, whereas 4% of the women said they had been forced to have intercourse. The most common offenders of unwanted peer sexual contact described by female adolescents are boyfriends, followed by dates, friends, and acquaintances (Small & Kerns, 1993). It has been found that sexually aggressive males are more likely to be hostile to women, use alcohol frequently, and be part of peer groups that view women primarily as sex objects (Muehlenhard, 1995).

Attitudes of older adolescents and young adults toward date rape demonstrate that sexual violence may be part of cultural scenarios. Males and females rate rape justifiability and sex willingness higher in circumstances where the woman initiates the date, goes to the man's apartment, when the man pays for the date, or a combination of these (Muehlenhard, 1988). However, young adult and adolescent males tend to justify forced sex more often than females (Davis, Peck, & Storment, 1993; Muehlenhard, 1988).

Risk factors for unwanted sexual activity among peers in adolescence have been examined by Small and Kerns (1993). They found that females who reported high peer conformity, previous sexual abuse by an adult, excessive alcohol use, and low parental monitoring of their behavior were more vulnerable to unwanted sexual contact. Cumulations of these risk factors place adolescents at greater risk for victimization.

Prostitution

Prostitution is the marketplace for the sale of sex, and a prostitute is an individual who engages in nonmarital sexual activity in exchange for capital (Benjamin & Masters, 1964). Alternatively, sexual slavery is the deception or force of individuals into providing sexual services with no control over financial profits (McCormick, 1994). When adolescents are employed by pimps, the lack of control over income, the use of force, and coercion to remain in the sex trade suggest that many adolescents fall into the category of sexual slavery (McCormick, 1994). The different experiences of males and females suggest that females are more likely to be involved in sexual slavery than males, however. Females are more often controlled by pimps than males; males more often have a freelance status. However, this should not diminish the need for concern over young males' or females' involvement in the sex trade.

There are gender differences in adolescent initiation into prostitution (Campagna & Poffenberger, 1988; Cates, 1989). Adolescent females are more often indoctrinated into the sex trade by pimps and sex traders who introduce them to the use of drugs and alcohol to minimize their resistance (Rickel & Hendren, 1993) and lure them with parental-like support (Caplan, 1984; Ennew, 1986). In addition, the use of violence by pimps undermines the potential empowerment of the female adolescent, further endangering their ability to resist indoctrination (Ennew, 1986). Males are more often introduced to the sex trade through peers on the street (Cates, 1989) or an adult patron (Ennew, 1986). As runaways on the street without financial means, males may learn from peers that prostitution is one way of earning money or gaining a place to stay. For those males who are homosexually oriented, prostitution may be used as a way to gain sexual pleasure with anonymity (Rickel & Hendren, 1993).

Rickel and Hendren's (1993) review of the literature notes that the behavioral characteristics of adolescents involved in prostitution include poor school performance, truancy, quitting school, running away, and use of illegal drugs. Furthermore, a lack of conventional social and emotional support in family relationships (Gray, 1973), strained family relationships, and in some cases, familial sexual abuse (Rickel & Hendren, 1993), a parental history of failed intimate relationships and economic marginality, and a residential neighborhood that provides easy access to initiating prostitution (Longres, 1991) have been associated with adolescent prostitution. This would indicate that various social and familial factors must be taken into consideration in understanding adolescent participation in prostitution.

Sexual Offenses

Sexual offenses in adolescence include sexual assault outside the familial home as well as intrafamilial abuse, such as sibling incest. The seriousness of sexual assaults by adolescents has only recently been given attention in the literature and tends to be focused on male offenders.

The research on attitudes toward date rape and adolescent male sexual aggression that has emerged during the past 20 years (and more specifically within the past 10 years) demonstrates that the social learning of sexual behaviors has serious lifelong implication for males and society (Bolton & MacEachran, 1988). Indeed, the cultural and scientific conceptions that male sexual drive and emotions of anger and rage are constantly at risk of being released by improper sexual display perpetuate the so-called legitimate use of force, victim blaming, and lack of responsibility in sexual conduct (Gagnon, 1990).

Bolton and MacEachran's (1988) review of literature on adolescent sexuality and sexual offenses establishes the serious nature of adolescent male sexual aggression. They report that convicted adolescent male offenders of sexual assaults often have established deviant sexual patterns. Turning to those who experience sexual assaults, one third of the women who reported prior victimization described the offender as male and between the ages of 10 and 19 years of age (Finkelhor, 1979). This would suggest that serious attention needs to be paid to the cultural scripting of sexual aggression and violence in childhood and adolescence.

To summarize, the use of developmental theories in research on the psychosocial aspects of adolescent sexuality has been infrequent. Miller and Fox's (1987) outline of the two paradigms within human sexual development literature is worthy of further attention in ongoing research. Research agendas working at the interface of these paradigms would advance the field of adolescent sexual development.

It has been demonstrated that much of what is known about adolescent sexual behaviors is associated with coital activity. A variety of contextual factors are associated with adolescent transition to first coitus. In addition to interpersonal relations with parents and peers, courtship patterns have also been found to correspond with coital behavior. Indeed, individuals who begin to date in early adolescence experience first coitus earlier than individuals who begin to date in middle to late adolescence. Findings on the association between patterns of courtship and coitus indicate the salience of the association between intimate relationships and sexual behavior in adolescence.

Negative associations between age at first coitus and future vocational status, educational aspirations, and economic constraints for employment may indicate that some adolescents seek validation of adult status through engaging in sexual intercourse or parenthood. It would be beneficial to extend this research and examine adolescents' perspectives toward sexual behaviors and the attainment of adult status under conditions of restricted employment and educational opportunities.

The literature addressing parental socialization of adolescent sexual behavior tends to concentrate heavily on the deterrence of coitus in adolescence. This is problematic because there is an assumption that parents are willing and able to convey specific societal norms that will be received by their adolescent offspring (Trost, 1990). This unidirectional perspective also inadequately represents the parent-adolescent relationship. The increase in incidence of coitus from early adolescence to later adolescence (Sorenson, 1973; Thornton, 1990) demonstrates a significant alteration in the sexual behaviors of many individuals in the second decade of life. A fundamental question that needs to be answered is how parents and offspring negotiate changes in adolescents' sexual behaviors. Indeed, adolescent sexual development ought to be studied within the context of intrafamilial changes.

Much of the research literature appears to assume that parents are opposed to premarital sex and that friendship and peer influences are in opposition to familial influences. Although some parents are opposed to premarital sexual behaviors, some are not. As Trost (1990) notes, social support and social control between adolescents is built on societal values that also exist among adults. Indeed, adolescents and adults both tend to endorse sexual behaviors in loving dyadic relationships and to reject promiscuity. It would be helpful for research and theory to begin to address where family, peer, and friendship values regarding adolescent sexual behavior converge and diverge rather than assuming the values of parents and peers are always in opposition.

The effects of sexually aberrant experiences on adolescent sexual development remain ambiguous, though this area of research warrants continued inquiries. The recent increase in research on date rape has advanced our understanding of the pervasiveness of, and factors associated with, unwanted sexual advances in adolescence. It would be useful to begin to examine the effects of date rape on adolescent sexual development and interpersonal relationships. More specifically, it is important to consider that date rape takes place within the relational context where practice of sexual responsiveness and intimate care for partners has been proposed to occur. In addition, the seriousness of reported male sexual offenses in adolescence (see Bolton & MacEachran, 1988) suggests that further attention to sexual aggressiveness is warranted for both genders.

SEXUALITY EDUCATION

In discussing adolescent sexual development, it is essential to be aware of the role of sexuality education. In the 1970s, a major health concern was that of adolescent pregnancy, and the focus of much sex education was on pregnancy prevention. During the 1980s, concern with the increased rate of STD and HIV transmission led to the establishment of educational programs focused on AIDS prevention.

There is a major political debate over whether educational and service programs to adolescents should be abstinence focused or comprehensive in nature. The intensity of this debate can be seen in the 1995 firing of the Surgeon General of the United States, Joycelyn Elders, for advocating that schoolchildren should be taught about masturbation. Earlier, Elders had been heavily criticized by the conservative right for emphasizing the need to provide comprehensive sexuality education, including condom education, in schools.

Abstinence-based programs, such as *Sex Respect*, use fear-based approaches, strongly discourage adolescent sexual behavior, and do not inform adolescents about methods of contraception except to disparage them (Kantner, 1992). Also, according to Kantner, these programs usually omit important information, contain misinformation, and include a sexist and antichoice bias. Alternatively, comprehensive sexuality programs, as developed by the Sex Information Education Council of the United States, present abstinence as one possible choice but recognize that many adolescents are, or will be, engaging in sexual intercourse. These programs provide strategies for decision making and information on contraceptive technology. An essential aspect of these programs is an emphasis on decision making and communication skills (Kantner, 1992).

A major issue regarding sexuality education is whether or not it produces desired results. The opponents of sexuality education programs claim that they have failed to produce positive results (Whitehead, 1994). On the other hand, some evaluation programs have demonstrated that sexuality programs can have positive results if they go beyond simply providing information and offer relevant skills training, especially in communication. Evaluations of abstinence-only sex education programs have found that they did not delay the timing of first sexual intercourse or reduce its frequency (Christopher & Roosa, 1990). In a review of 23 sexuality programs, Kirby (1994) found that skill-based programs can both delay the age of initiation of first coitus and increase contraceptive and condom use.

When health or birth control clinics are placed in high schools, the effectiveness of pregnancy prevention programs has been found to improve. Indeed, in a high school in South Carolina, the incidence of adolescent pregnancies decreased after the introduction of an integrated sexuality program that included the provision of contraceptive counseling and contraceptive supplies. Unfortunately, when the evaluation program was terminated, including the position of the school nurse, pregnancy rates returned to a higher level (Koo, Dunteman, George, Green, & Vincent, 1994). Research in Baltimore, Maryland, has demonstrated that the presence of a birth control clinic can significantly improve the effectiveness of school pregnancy prevention programs (Zabin, Hirsch, Smith, Street, & Hardy, 1986). Orton and Rosenblatt (1986) have documented a decline in births to adolescents in Ontario, Canada, where both school sexuality education and clinic contraception services are provided in the community.

METHODOLOGICAL ISSUES

One of the most important advances in the field since 1973 has been the integration of social and biological models in understanding adolescent sexual behaviors. In the past, social scientists have been reluctant to consider the possibility of biological bases for sexual behavior (Miller & Fox, 1987; Smith, 1989; Udry, 1990). Since the 1970s, however, Udry and his colleagues have investigated both hormonal and social motivations for sexual involvement in adolescence. These studies have extended our understanding of the differential effects of biological and social influences. However, Halpern and Udry (1992) have demonstrated that radioimmunoassay (RIA) techniques for measuring hormones in plasma and serum share similar validity and reliability issues as behavioral measures. They also found that in comparison to plasma values, saliva values were potentially subject to a great deal of variation. Halpern and Udry suggest ongoing assessment and evaluation of RIA techniques are needed to improve the quality of assessment.

Another major methodological advance over the past two decades has been the increased use of longitudinal research. Longitudinal analyses have been helpful in distinguishing between biological and social influences in sexual behaviors (e.g., Halpern et al., 1993). In addition, this type of research has increased our knowledge of the interrelationships between various nonconventional behaviors (such as early tobacco and alcohol use) and the influence of peer associations on early experience of sexual behaviors (e.g., Costa et al., 1995; Whitbeck, Conger, Simons, & Kao, 1993).

A critical methodological issue is the reliability and validity of adolescents' responses to questions about sexual behavior. Given the emotional sensitivity surrounding the topic of human sexuality, researchers have been concerned about whether adolescents are willing to be truthful regarding their sexual behaviors. However, there is evidence suggesting that reliability is fairly high. In a 3-year longitudinal study, rural adolescents completed a questionnaire on health behaviors in the eighth, ninth, and tenth grades. It was found that 89% of students in eighth grade and 94% in ninth grade who reported having had sexual intercourse gave the same answer in a subsequent year (Alexander, Somerfield, Ensminger, Johnson, & Kim, 1994).

There continues to be a lack of consistency in the use of major concepts in adolescent sexual behavior research. For example, some researchers use the concept of "sexually active" to indicate whether one has experienced sexual intercourse. The difficulty associated with using this conceptualization is that adolescents may sporadically engage in sexual intercourse yet are designated as sexually active. For example, Newcomer and Baldwin (1992) reported that in a study of high school students, 54% had experienced sexual intercourse, but only 39% said they had sex within the past 3 months.

Despite the progress that has been made in the past two decades, sexuality research still carries with it attitudinal constraints that are not experienced by researchers in other areas. This has especially affected the funding of research on adolescent sexuality. For example, Richard Udry and Ronald Rindfuss from the Carolina Population Center at the University of North Carolina were denied funding for a large-scale national study of adolescent sexuality after the project had been approved by National Institute of Child and Human Development (Udry, 1993). The project was canceled by the Secretary of Health and Human Services after it was opposed by organizations that were concerned that the survey results would be used to liberalize public opinion and laws regarding sexual issues. In discussing the cancellation of this project, Udry (1993) emphasized that sex research is considered sensitive at every political level. It is interesting that private funding was secured for this project.

CONCLUSION

Trends in adolescent sexual behaviors over the past two decades and events associated with AIDS demonstrate that the social landscape continues to change. The difficult task of researching adolescent sexual development cannot be accomplished without recognition of changes in the social context. This chapter has outlined some of the changes observed in values and behaviors associated with adolescent sexuality over the past 20 years. Factors associated with adolescent sexual development have been distinguished from these trends.

Researchers have found that premarital sexual coitus is generally accepted by a large portion of the population in North America. Many adults in North America are accepting of premarital sexual intercourse when it takes place within the context of a loving relationship. Furthermore, most individuals experience coitus by the time they reach age 18 or 19 years. A minority of young adolescents under the age of 15 years have experienced coitus, and most likely, intercourse among young adolescents has the potential to be detrimental. Among those aged 13 to 15 years, most have experienced masturbation and some petting. It would be helpful for research to investigate the degree to which adolescent sexual behaviors are consistent with the attitudes of the social context rather than emphasizing coital behaviors as deviant from cultural norms.

Across many cultures, it is expected that adolescents attain the ability to achieve mature, sexually intimate relationships by the end of adolescence. Unfortunately, much of the extant research on adolescent sexual development focuses on the antecedents of coital behaviors and de-emphasizes the relational aspects of adolescent sexual development. It is important to consider processes by which adolescents develop capacities to relate sexually with others. Knowledge of these processes is essential if we are to obtain accurate understanding of issues such as engaging in unwanted sexual behaviors and reasons for nonuse of contraceptives.

We have an abundance of research on the trends and factors related to adolescent coital behavior; however, there is comparatively little research on noncoital behaviors, particularly masturbation. This is unfortunate because it prevents understanding the sexual development of those adolescents who may not engage in coitus, such as gay or lesbian adolescents or those who practice abstinence from coitus before marriage. Furthermore, it would be useful to more fully understand the role of noncoital behaviors in adolescents' development of intimate sexual relations and identity formation.

The intensity of political debates around adolescent sexual behavior continues to influence research and education programs. Within education, proponents of abstinence-based programs believe that they are being successful in motivating youth to abstain from sexual activity. On the other hand, proponents of comprehensive sexuality education believe that the behavioral trends of adolescents are not substantially changing, and by denying adequate education, the sexual difficulties experienced by youth will increase. An important research question stemming from these arguments is how adolescents are responding to the controversy.

REFERENCES

Adeokun, L. (1990). Research on human sexuality in pattern in two countries. In A. Chouinard & J. Albert (Eds.), *Human sexuality: Research perspectives in a world facing AIDS* (pp. 155-172). Ottawa, Ontario: International Development and Research Centre.

Alan Guttmacher Institute. (1994). *Sex and America's teenagers*. New York: Author.

Alexander, C., Somerfield, M., Ensminger, E., Johnson, K., & Kim, Y. (1994). Consistency of adolescent's self-report of sexual behavior in a longitudinal study. *Journal of Youth and Adolescence, 22*, 455-471.

Alexander, P. C., & Lupfer, S. L. (1987). Family characteristics and long-term consequences associated with sexual abuse. *Archives of Sexual Behavior, 16*, 235-245.

Andersen, E. (1989). Sex codes and family life among poor inner city youths. *Annals of the American Academy of Political and Social Science, 501*, 59-78.

Bancroft, J. (1989). *Human sexuality and its problems* (2nd ed.). Edinburgh: Churchill-Livingstone.

Bancroft, J. (1990). The impact of sociocultural influences on adolescent sexual development: Further considerations. In J. Bancroft & J. M. Reinisch (Eds.), *Adolescence and puberty* (pp. 207-216). New York: Oxford University Press.

Barry, H., III, & Schlegel, A. (1986). Cultural customs that influence sexual freedom in adolescence. *Ethnology, 25*, 151-162.

Becker, J. V. (1988). The effects of child sexual abuse on adolescent offenders. In G. E. Wyatt & G. J. Powell (Eds.), *Lasting effects of child sexual abuse* (pp. 193-207). Newbury Park, CA: Sage.

Beitchman, J. H., Zucker, K. J., Hood, J. E., DaCosta, G. A., Akman, D., & Cassavia, E. (1992). A review of the long-term effects of child sexual abuse. *Child Abuse and Neglect, 16,* 101-118.

Bell, A. P., & Weinberg, M. S. (1978). *Homosexualities: A study of diversity among men and women.* New York: Simon & Schuster.

Benjamin, H., & Masters, R. E. L. (1964). *Prostitution and morality.* New York: Julian.

Billy, J. O. G., & Udry, J. R. (1985). Adolescent sexual behavior and friendship choice. *Adolescence, 20,* 21-32.

Bolton, F. G., & MacEachran, A. E. (1988). Adolescent male sexuality: A developmental perspective. *Journal of Adolescent Research, 3,* 259-273.

Brewster, K. L. (1994). Race differences in sexual activity among adolescent women: The role of neighborhood characteristics. *American Sociological Review, 59,* 408-424.

Brewster, K. L., Billy, J. O. G., & Grady, W. R. (1993). Social context and adolescent behavior: The impact of community on the transition to sexual activity. *Social Forces, 71,* 713-740.

Campagna, D. S., & Poffenberger, D. L. (1988). *The sexual trafficking in children.* Medfield, MA: Auburn House.

Caplan, G. M. (1984). The facts of life about teenage prostitution. *Crime and Delinquency, 30,* 68-74.

Carroll, J. L., Volk, K. D., & Hyde, J. S. (1985). Differences in males and females in motives for engaging in sexual intercourse. *Archives of Sexual Behavior, 14,* 131-139.

Cates, J. A. (1989). Adolescent male prostitution by choice. *Child and Adolescent Social Work, 6,* 151-156.

Christensen, H. T. (1969). Normative theory derived from cross-cultural family research. *Journal of Marriage and the Family, 31,* 209-222.

Christopher, S., & Roosa, M. (1990). Evaluation of adolescent pregnancy prevention programs: Is "Just say no" enough? *Family Relations, 39,* 68-72.

Clark, S. D., Zabin, L. S., & Hardy, J. B. (1984). Sex, contraception and parenthood experience and attitudes among urban black young men. *Family Planning Perspectives, 16,* 77-82.

Costa, F. M., Jessor, R., Donovan, J. E., & Fortenberry, J. D. (1995). Early initiation of sexual intercourse: The influence of psychosocial unconventionality. *Journal of Research on Adolescence, 5,* 93-121.

Dash, L. (1989). *When children want children: The urban crisis in teenage childbearing.* New York: Morrow.

D'Augelli, A. R., Collins, C., & Hart, M. M. (1987). Social support patterns of lesbian women in a rural helping network. *Journal of Rural Community Psychology, 8,* 12-22.

Davis, T. C., Peck, G. Q., & Storment, J. M. (1993). Acquaintance rape and the high school student. *Journal of Adolescent Health, 14,* 220-224.

DiBlasio, F. A., & Benda, B. B. (1992). Gender differences in theories of adolescent sexual activity. *Sex Roles, 27,* 221-239.

Donovan, J. E., & Jessor, R. (1985). Structure of problem behavior in adolescence and young adulthood. *Journal of Consulting and Clinical Psychology, 53*, 890-904.

Downs, W. R. (1993). Developmental considerations for the effects of childhood sexual abuse. *Journal of Interpersonal Violence, 8*, 331-345.

Ennew, J. (1986). *The sexual exploitation of children.* New York: St. Martin's.

Feinstein, S. C., & Ardon, M. S. (1973). Trends in dating patterns and adolescent development. *Journal of Youth and Adolescence, 2*, 157-166.

Finkel, M. C., & Finkel, D. J. (1975). Sexual and contraceptive knowledge, attitudes, and behavior of male adolescents. In F. S. Fenstenberg, R. Lincoln, & J. Menken (Eds.), *Teenage sexuality, pregnancy, and childbearing* (pp. 327-335). New York: Alan Guttmacher Institute.

Finkelhor, D. (1979). *Sexually victimized children.* New York: Free Press.

Forrest, J., & Singh, S. (1990). The sexual and reproductive behavior of American women, 1982-1988. *Family Planning Perspectives, 22*, 206-214.

Forste, R. T., & Heaton, T. B. (1988). Initiation of sexual activity among female adolescents. *Youth and Society, 19*, 250-268.

Fox, G. L. (1986). The family context of adolescent sexuality and sex roles. In G. K. Leigh & G. W. Peterson (Eds.), *Adolescents in families* (pp. 177-204). Cincinnati, OH: Southwestern.

Freud, S. (1933). *New introductory lectures on psychoanalysis.* London: Hogarth.

Freud, S. (1953). *A general introduction to psychoanalysis.* New York: Permabooks.

Fromuth, M. E. (1986). The relationship of childhood sexual abuse with later psychological and sexual adjustment in a sample of college women. *Child Abuse and Neglect, 10*, 5-15.

Furstenberg, F., Jr., Morgan, S. P., Moore, K. A., & Peterson, J. L. (1987). Race differences in the timing of first intercourse. *American Sociological Review, 52*, 511-518.

Gagnon, J. H. (1990). The explicit and implicit use of the scripting perspective in sex research. *Annual Review of Sex Research, 1*, 1-43.

Gagnon, J. H., & Simon, W. (1973). *Sexual conduct: The social sources of human sexuality.* Chicago: Aldine.

Gallup Poll shows more Americans say premarital sex is wrong, reversing trend of last 20 years. (1988). *Family Planning Perspectives, 20*, 180-181.

Gray, D. (1973). Turning-out: A study of teenage prostitution. *Urban Life and Culture, 4*, 401-425.

Halpern, C. T., & Udry, J. R. (1992). Variation in adolescent hormone measures and implications for behavioral research. *Journal of Research on Adolescence, 2*, 103-122.

Halpern, C. T., Udry, J. R., Campbell, B., & Suchindran, C. (1993). Testosterone and pubertal development as predictors of sexual activity: A panel analysis of adolescent males. *Psychosomatic Medicine, 55*, 436-447.

Hanson, S. L., Myers, D. E., & Ginsburg, A. L. (1987). The role of responsibility and knowledge in reducing teenage out-of-wedlock childbearing. *Journal of Marriage and the Family, 49*, 241-256.

Hardy, K. (1964). An appetitional theory of sexual motivation. *Psychological Review 71*, 1-18.

Henshaw, S. K. (1994). *U.S. teenage pregnancy statistics.* New York: Alan Guttmacher Institute.

Herold, E. S. (1984). *The sexual behavior of Canadian young people.* Toronto: Fitzhenry & Whiteside.

Herold, E. S., & Goodwin, S. (1981). Adamant virgins, potential nonvirgins and nonvirgins. *Journal of Sex Research, 17,* 97-113.

Hill, J. P. (1973). *Some perspectives on adolescence in American society.* A report prepared for the Office of Child Development, U. S. Department of Health, Education, and Welfare, Washington, D. C.

Hobart, C. W. (1975). Reactions to premarital intercourse. In S. P. Wakil (Ed.), *Marriage, family, & society: Canadian perspectives.* Toronto: Butterworth.

Hogan, D., & Kitagawa, E. (1985). The impact of social status, family structure, and neighborhood on the fertility of black adolescents. *American Journal of Sociology, 90,* 825-836.

Hotvedt, M. E. (1990). Emerging and submerging adolescent sexuality: Culture and sexual orientation. In J. Bancroft & J. M. Reinisch (Eds.), *Adolescence and puberty* (pp. 157-181). New York: Oxford University Press.

Jessor, R., & Jessor, S. (1977). *Problem behavior and psychosocial development: A longitudinal study of youth.* New York: Academic Press.

Jessor, S., & Jessor, R. (1975). Transition from virginity to nonvirginity among youth: A social psychological study over time. *Developmental Psychology, 11,* 473-484.

Kahn, J. R., Smith, K. W., & Roberts, E. J. (1984). *Family communication and adolescent sexual behavior.* Cambridge, MA: American Institute for Research.

Kantner, J. F., & Zelnik, M. (1972). Sexual experience of young unmarried women in the United States. *Family Planning Perspectives, 4,* 8-14.

Kantner, L. (1992). Scared chaste? Fear-based educational curricula. *SIECUS Reports, 21,* 1-15.

King, A., Beazley, R., Warren, W., Hankins, C., Robertson, A., & Radford, J. (1988). *Canada youth and AIDS study.* Kingston, Ontario: Queen's University.

Kirby, D. (1994). Sexuality education: It can reduce unprotected intercourse. *SIECUS Report, 22,* 19-20.

Kleinplatz, P. J. (1992, September). *The erotic experience and the intent to arouse.* Paper presented at the Canadian Research Forum, Picton, Ontario.

Koo, H., Dunteman, G., George, C., Green, Y., & Vincent, M. (1994). Reducing adolescent pregnancy through a school and community based intervention: Denmark, S.C. revisited. *Family Planning Perspectives, 26,* 206-211.

Ku, L., Sonenstein, F. L., & Pleck, J. H. (1993). Young men's risk for behaviors for HIV infection and sexually transmitted diseases, 1988 through 1991. *American Journal of Public Health, 83,* 1609-1615.

Laumann, E., Gagnon, J., Michael, R., & Michaels, S. (1994). *The social organization of sexuality.* Chicago: University of Chicago Press.

Longo, R. E. (1982). Sexual learning and experience among adolescent sexual offenders. *International Journal of Offender Therapy and Comparative Criminology, 26,* 235-241.

Longres, J. F. (1991). An ecological study of parents of adjudicated female teenage prostitutes. *Journal of Social Service Research, 14,* 113-127.

MacKinnon, C. A. (1987). *Feminism unmodified: Discourses on life and law.* Cambridge, MA: Harvard University Press.

Mahoney, E. R. (1980). Religiosity and sexual behavior among heterosexual college students. *Journal of Sex Research, 6,* 97-113.

McCormick, N. B. (1994). *Sexual salvation: Affirming women's sexual rights and pleasures.* Westport, CN: Praeger.

Miller, B. C., & Fox, G. L. (1987). Theories of heterosexual behavior. *Journal of Adolescent Research, 2,* 269-282.

Miller, B. C., & Jorgensen, S. R. (1988). Adolescent fertility-related behavior and its family linkages. In D. Klein & J. Aldous (Eds.), *Social stress and family development.* New York: Guilford.

Miller, B. C., McCoy, J. K., & Olson, T. D. (1986). Dating age and stage as correlates of adolescent sexual attitudes and behavior. *Journal of Adolescent Research, 1,* 361-371.

Miller, B. C., McCoy, J. K., Olson, T. D., & Wallace, C. M. (1986). Parental discipline and control attempts in relation to adolescent sexual attitudes and behavior. *Journal of Marriage and the Family, 48,* 503-512.

Miller, B. C., & Olson, T. D. (1988). Sexual attitudes and behavior of high school students in relation to background and contextual factors. *Journal of Sex Research, 24,* 194-200.

Miller, B. C., & Simon, W. (1974). Adolescent sexual behavior: Context and change. *Social Problems, 22,* 58-75.

Miller, B. C., & Sneesby, K. R. (1988). Educational correlates of adolescents' sexual attitudes and behavior. *Journal of Youth and Adolescence, 17,* 521-530.

Mitchell, J. E. (1976). Adolescent intimacy. *Adolescence, 11,* 275-280.

Moore, K. A., Peterson, J. L., & Furstenburg, F. F. (1986). Parental attitudes and the occurrence of early sexual activity. *Journal of Marriage and the Family, 48,* 777-782.

Moore, K. A., Simms, M. C., & Betsey, C. L. (1986). *Choice and circumstance.* New Brunswick, NJ: Transaction Books.

Mosher, W., & McNally, J. (1991). Contraceptive use at first premarital intercourse: United States, 1965-1988. *Family Planning Perspectives, 23,* 108-116.

Muecke, M. (1990). The AIDS prevention dilemma in Thailand. *Asian and Pacific Population Forum, 4,* 2-27.

Muehlenhard, C. L. (1988). Misinterpreting dating behaviors and the risk of date rape. *Journal of Social and Clinical Psychology, 6,* 20-37.

Muehlenhard, C. L. (1995). *Sexual assault.* Mt. Vernon, IA: Society for the Scientific Study of Human Sexuality.

Newcomer, S., & Baldwin, W. (1992). Demographics of adolescent sexual behavior, contraception, pregnancy, and STD's. *Journal of School Health, 62,* 265-270.

Nolin, M. J., & Petersen, K. K. (1992). Gender differences in parent-child communication about sexuality: An exploratory study. *Journal of Adolescent Research, 7,* 59-79.

Noller, P., & Bagi, S. (1985). Parent-adolescent communication. *Journal of Adolescence, 8,* 125-144.

Ohannessian, C., & Crockett, L. (1993). A longitudinal investigation of the relationship between educational investment and adolescent sexual activity. *Journal of Adolescent Research, 8,* 167-182.

Oliver, M. B., & Hyde, J. S. (1993). Gender differences in sexuality: A meta-analysis. *Psychological Bulletin, 114,* 29-51.

Orton, M., & Rosenblatt, E. (1986). *Adolescent pregnancy in Ontario: Progress in prevention.* Hamilton: Planned Parenthood Ontario.

Reiss, I. L. (1967). *The social context of premarital sexual permissiveness.* New York: Holt, Rinehart & Winston.

Reiss, I. L. (1986). A sociological journey into sexuality. *Journal of Marriage and the Family, 48,* 233-242.

Remafedi, G. (1987a). Adolescent homosexuality: Psychosocial and medical implications. *Pediatrics, 79,* 331-337.

Remafedi, G. (1987b). The healthy sexual development of gay and lesbian adolescents. *SIECUS Report, 17,* 7-8.

Rickel, A. U., & Hendren, M. C. (1993). Aberrant sexual experiences in adolescence. In R. Montemayor, G. R. Adams, & T. P. Gullotta (Eds.), (pp. 141-160). Newbury Park, CA: Sage.

Ross-Reynolds, G. (1982). Issues in counseling the "homosexual adolescent." In J. Grimes (Ed.), *Psychological approaches to problems of children and adolescents* (pp. 55-88). Des Moines: Iowa State Department of Education.

Rotheram-Borus, M., Reid, H., & Rosario, M. (1994). Factors mediating changes in sexual HIV risk behaviors among gay and bisexual male adolescents. *American Journal of Public Health, 84,* 1938-1946.

Sack, A., Keller, J., & Hinkle, D. (1984). Premarital sexual intercourse: A test of the effects of peer group, religiosity, and sexual guilt. *Journal of Sex Research, 20,* 168-185.

Savin-Williams, R. C. (1990). *Gay and lesbian youth: Expressions of identity.* Washington, DC: Hemisphere.

Savin-Williams, R. C., & Rodriguez, R. G. (1993). A developmental, clinical perspective on lesbian, gay male, and bisexual youths. In R. Montemayor, G. R. Adams, & T. P. Gullotta (Eds.), *Adolescent sexuality* (pp. 77-101). Newbury Park, CA: Sage.

Scales, P., & Beckstein, D. (1982). From macho to mutuality: Helping young men make effective decisions about sex, contraception, and pregnancy. In I. Stuart & C. Wells (Eds.), *Pregnancy in adolescence: Needs, problems, and management* (pp. 65-107). New York: Van Nostrand.

Schwartz, I. M. (1993). Affective reactions of American and Swedish women to their first premarital coitus: A cross-cultural comparison. *Journal of Sex Research, 30,* 18-26.

Seng, M. J. (1989). Child sexual abuse and adolescent prostitution: A comparative analysis. *Adolescence, 24,* 665-675.

Small, S. A., & Kerns, D. (1993). Unwanted sexual activity among peers during early and middle adolescence. *Journal of Marriage and the Family, 55,* 941-952.

Small, S. A., & Luster, T. (1994). Adolescent sexual activity: An ecological, risk-factor approach. *Journal of Marriage and the Family, 56,* 181-192.

Smith, E. A. (1989). A biosocial model of adolescent sexual behavior. In G. R. Adams, R. Montemayor, & T. P. Gullotta (Eds.), *Biology of adolescent behavior and development* (pp. 143-167). Newbury Park, CA: Sage.

Smith, E. A., & Udry, J. R. (1985). Coital and non-coital sexual behaviors of white and black adolescents. *American Journal of Public Health, 75,* 1200-1203.

Sonenstein, F., Pleck, J., & Ku, L. (1991). Levels of sexual activity among males in the United States. *Family Planning Perspectives, 23,* 152-158.

Sorenson, R. (1973). *Adolescent sexuality in contemporary America.* New York: World.

Sprecher, S., Barbee, A., & Schwartz, P. (1995). Was it good for you, too? Gender differences in first sexual intercourse experiences. *Journal of Sex Research, 32,* 3-15.

Thornton, A. D. (1990). The courtship process and adolescent sexuality. *Journal of Family Issues, 11,* 239-273.

Thornton, A. D., & Camburn, D. (1987). The influence of the family on premarital sexual attitudes and behavior. *Demography, 24,* 323-340.

Trost, J. E. (1990). Social support and pressure and their impact on sexual behavior. In J. Bancroft & J. M. Reinisch (Eds.), *Adolescence and puberty* (pp. 173-181). New York: Oxford University Press.

Udry, J. R. (1990). Hormonal and social determinants of adolescent sexual initiation. In J. Bancroft & J. M. Reinisch (Eds.), *Adolescence and puberty* (pp. 70-87). New York: Oxford University Press.

Udry, J. R. (1993). The politics of sex research. *Journal of Sex Research, 30,* 103-110.

Udry, J. R., Billy, J. O. G., Morris, N., Groff, T., & Raj, M. (1985). Serum androgenic hormones motivate sexual behavior in boys. *Fertility and Sterility, 43,* 90-94.

Udry, J. R., Talbert, L. M., & Morris, N. (1986). Biosocial foundations for adolescent female sexuality. *Demography, 23,* 217-277.

Walters, J., & Walters, L. H. (1980). Parent-child relationships: A review 1970-1979. *Journal of Marriage and the Family, 42,* 807-822.

Whitbeck, L., Conger, R., Simons, R., & Kao, M. (1993). Minor deviant behaviors and adolescent sexual activity. *Youth and Society, 25,* 24-37.

Whitehead, B. (1994, October). The failure of sex education. *Atlantic Monthly, 274,* 55-80.

Whitehurst, R. (1972). *Losing virginity: Some contemporary trends.* Unpublished manuscript, University of Windsor, Windsor, Ontario.

Wyatt, G. E. (1989). The relationship between child sexual abuse and adolescent sexual functioning in Afro-American and white-American women. *Annals of the New York Academy of Sciences, 528,* 111-122.

Zabin, L., & Hayward, S. (1993). *Adolescent sexual behavior and childbearing.* Newbury Park, CA: Sage.

Zabin, L., Hirsch, M., Smith, E., Street, R., & Hardy, J. (1986). Evaluation of a pregnancy prevention program for urban teenagers. *Family Planning Perspectives, 18,* 119-126.

Zelnik, M. (1983). Sexual activity among adolescents: Perspective of a decade. In E. R. McAnarney (Ed.), *Premature adolescent sexuality and parenthood* (pp. 21-33). New York: Grune & Stratton.

Zelnik, M., & Kantner, J. F. (1980). Sexual activity, contraceptive use and pregnancy among metropolitan-area teenagers: 1971-1979. *Family Planning Perspectives, 12,* 230-237.

Zelnik, M., & Shah, F. K. (1983). First intercourse among young Americans. *Family Planning Perspectives, 15,* 64-72.

4. Adolescence and Intimacy

Judith L. Fischer
Joyce Munsch
Shannon M. Greene

Intimacy in adolescence is important to understand because it high-lights developmental accomplishments, provides links to earlier de-velopment, and previews adult relationships. Views of this construct primarily capture the positive aspects of achieving and maintaining intimacy (Berndt, 1992): being socially competent, feeling accepted, negotiating mutual needs, and establishing connection in a social world. An emerging area of research includes investigations of a dark side to intimacy (Cupach & Spitzberg, 1994; Reis, 1990), such as problem behavior, codependency, and victimization. This chapter provides (a) a historical overview marked by milestones in theory and research on intimacy in adolescence, (b) a summary and synthe-sis of definitional issues surrounding intimacy, (c) a conceptual model focused on adolescence and intimacy, and (d) a review of adolescent intimacy structured by the conceptual model. The major part of the chapter follows the outline suggested by the conceptual framework, identifying (a) predictors and correlates, (b) current contexts, and (c) consequences of intimacy in adolescence. Sugges-tions for future research are interwoven with discussions of the research and conclude the chapter.

HISTORICAL OVERVIEW

During the second decade of the 20th century, influence from American psychology meant that interpersonal concepts such as intimacy were ignored, with the focus instead being on under-standing individual processes such as learning. Strains of modern

AUTHORS' NOTE: Correspondence concerning this chapter may be addressed to Judith L. Fischer, Department of Human Development and Family Studies, Texas Tech University, Lubbock, TX 79409-1162.

life (e.g., geographic mobility, marital disruption), however, generated concern with problems arising from the absence of intimacy, including isolation, loneliness, and alienation. Thus, Gadlin (1977) posited that since 1940, there has been a renewed interest in the concept of intimacy. Concerns have centered around the dialectical tensions between personal independence and human connectedness (see Rawlins, 1992, for elaboration of these tensions in the area of friendship).

Within recent times, two converging camps of theory and research concerned with intimacy have emerged: human development and close personal relationships. In the case of developmentalists, theorists such as Sullivan (1953) and Erikson (1950) have emphasized how a balance between intimacy and isolation fosters the successful transition to adulthood. Both theorists, in fact, view the capacity for intimacy as an essential developmental task for achieving functional adult adjustment and avoiding problems such as isolation. Sullivan (1953) described the importance of "chumships" in childhood for the later development of intimacy. Friendships provide opportunities to develop interpersonal sensitivity, to learn intimacy, to share understanding, and to acquire skills for interpersonal adjustment (Selman, 1980; Youniss, 1980). In Erikson's (1968) view, psychosocial tasks confront the developing person all along the life course (see Franz & White, 1985); however, certain tasks are salient at particular times. In adolescence, identity achievement is a salient task; in young adulthood, intimacy becomes more important and the outcome is consequential—that is, selection of an intimate partner is "for keeps." Furthermore, to the extent that a secure sense of identity has been achieved, then true intimacy with others is possible.

The activities of other developmentalists centered around the publication and widespread use of the intimacy status interview (Orlofsky, Marcia, & Lesser, 1973), which sparked a lively debate over gendered pathways to intimacy achievement as will be discussed. With the development of the Erikson Psychosocial Stages Inventory questionnaire, testing larger numbers of individuals became possible than was feasible with the prior reliance on interview methods (Rosenthal, Gurney, & Moore, 1981). Both questionnaire and interview techniques facilitated social scientists in vigorously investigating the validity of theoretical frameworks and promoting further theorizing around the developmental progression of identity and intimacy in adolescence.

Somewhat paralleling the developmentalists' progress in studying adolescent intimacy was the emergence of the close relationships field (see Kelley et al., 1983). This tradition spawned a focus on identifying general laws that underlie all relationships. Global aspects of relationships became the focus, with intimacy being investigated as a crucial positive dimension (Hinde, 1981). More recently, there has been acknowledgment of this positivist bias that has given priority to topics such as love, romantic attachment, courtship, dating success, and closeness (Duck, 1994). Researchers within this field now seek a greater understanding of the dark side of relationships (Cupach & Spitzberg, 1994) or the challenging aspects of relationships (Duck & Wood, 1995). Topics discussed include but are not limited to (a) developmental delay in achieving intimacy (Fischer, 1981), (b) intimacy failure reflected in loneliness (Boldero & Moore, 1990) and fear of intimacy (Shaver & Hazan, 1988), (c) codependent relationships (Fischer & Crawford, 1992; Fischer, Spann, & Crawford, 1991), (d) negative qualities in social network relationships (Rook, 1990), and (e) premature sexualization of intimacy with attendant risks of early childbearing (Small & Luster, 1994) and sexually transmitted diseases (Koopman, Rosario, & Rotheram-Borus, 1994).

Intimacy is also related to attachment theory, through a concern with how sensitive caregivers respond reliably to infant needs, such as providing a soothing presence under stressful conditions (Reis, 1990). This initial interest in infant attachment processes has been extended to include children and adolescents and, more recently, equivalent processes in adults. The development of adult-level descriptors of attachment styles to reflect internal working models (Bartholomew & Horowitz, 1991; Hazan & Shaver, 1987) has generated a growing body of work on attachment and intimacy. Through the articulation of a link between adolescent and adult intimacy with earlier attachments, there appears to be a promising convergence of interest in adolescent intimacy across the fields of human development and close personal relationships.

DEFINITIONAL ISSUES

Although intimacy is but one quality of human relationships (Hinde, 1981), it serves as a useful intermediate construct for describing relationships in general; moreover, it has stimulated a zeitgeist of interest in understanding close relationships across the lifespan (Chelune, Robison, & Kommor, 1984). Yet, as early as 1981, McCarthy (1981) identified a lack of definitional agreement as a central problem for the field of close relationships. Ironically, approximately a decade later, Register and Henley (1992) described a disturbing divergence in how the term *intimacy* is used, given the use of over 20 substantially different definitions. This lack of consensus led Acitelli and Duck (1987) to conclude that the construct of intimacy had become the proverbial elephant as examined by a blind man.

Definitional confusion poses several problems. For example, such inconsistencies confound instruments and hinder theory construction (Register & Henley, 1992). Furthermore, comparisons across studies become problematic (Helgeson, Shaver, & Dyer, 1987), a critical situation given that intimacy researchers aim to identify rules underlying human relationships. Rather than abandon the elephant, a brief overview of definitions may provide some much-needed clarity. These definitions include (a) processes that reflect intimacy, such as self-disclosure, openness, support, and nonverbal activities and (b) the content of intimacy, such as emotional closeness and feeling cared for by another.

Processes

Self-Disclosure and Openness

Intimacy has traditionally been defined as degree of self-disclosure (Monsour, 1992); this is the most widely accepted definition (Helgeson et al., 1987). However, the mere act of self-disclosure may fail to produce the sense of closeness that generally characterizes intimacy; self-disclosure then represents a process that may lead to the end state of intimacy. Clark and Reis (1988) linked process and outcome by defining intimacy as occurring when "one person expresses important self-relevant feelings and information to another, and as a result of the other's response comes to feel known, validated . . . and cared for" (p. 628). Inherent in this definition is the idea that intimacy constitutes a reciprocal process. Although the authors herald their definition as comprising a broader set of phenomena and process with greater construct and ecological validity than other definitions,

Register and Henley (1992) concluded that such a definition comprises essentially self-disclosure with a twist.

Self-disclosure, or revealing information to another party, is similar to an alternative definition of intimacy: emotional expressiveness or revealing feelings to another. The overlap in these constructs has generally led to their being combined under the rubric of *openness* (Montgomery, 1984). Openness would seem, however, to capture aspects of a particular relationship as well as characteristics of an individual. In other words, intimacy can represent both the capacity of an individual and the actuality of relationship quality. Arguments have arisen supporting one perspective over another (e.g., Weingarten, 1991), when the choice may well depend on the area of interest. For example, developmental questions typically concern the individual's capacity for intimacy. On the other hand, researchers of close relationships often choose topics reflecting interest in the qualities of relationships or the behaviors actually occurring in intimate relationships.

In addition to these concerns, *sexuality* and *intimacy* are sometimes confused, as in the expression "they were intimate," meaning "they had sexual intercourse." Intercourse may or may not include emotional intimacy; thus, sexuality is not a part of the definition of intimacy included in this review (but see Hatfield, Sprecher, Pillemer, Greenberger, & Wexler, 1988; Patterson, 1976).

Support and Nonverbal Activities

Intimacy has also been defined as giving and receiving support (Monsour, 1992). Although correlated with intimacy (Reis, 1990), social support occurs within nonintimate relationships as well (Newcomb, 1990). Similar to self-disclosure, social support would seem instead to describe a process by which an end state of intimacy may arise.

Intimacy has been equated with nonverbal involvement (e.g., Guerrero & Anderson, 1991), reflecting an ethnological perspective. From this perspective, intimacy is viewed as arising from approach versus avoidance forces (Sexton & Sexton, 1982). Here, factors such as physical proximity, eye contact, body orientation, and facial expression are equated with intimacy. Again, these factors describe a process to achieve or maintain intimacy, rather than the content of intimacy itself.

More recently, researchers have turned to participants for information about the meaning of intimacy (Monsour, 1992; Roscoe, Kennedy & Pope, 1987; Waring, Tillman, Frelick, Russell, & Weisz, 1980). This strategy might be thought of as "if we don't know, let's ask them." Yet when participants are asked to describe their intimate relationships, the result is even more definitional confusion. For example, within the field of intimacy, researchers confined prior studies to humans whose relationships were characterized by sustained contact of a typical day-in, day-out nature. Yet when participants described a relationship they considered to be intimate, some included nonhuman relationships (e.g., pets, supernatural beings) or described human relationships of exceedingly brief contact or even limited descriptions to only peak experiences (Register & Henley, 1992).

Content

Last, intimacy has also been defined as emotional closeness, or the extent to which the relationship involves strong, frequent, and diverse causal connections of a positive or negative nature (Kelley et al., 1983). Similarly, the Hillian tradition has conceptualized intimacy as including emotional distance and perceived attachment (e.g., Ellis, 1991; Papini, Roggman, & Anderson, 1991). Such views transform intimacy from a construct with a purely positive valence to one that includes negative processes and end states as well. In fact, evidence by Fischer and Sollie (1986) suggests that separate measures of closeness and distance can be used to advantage. In their research, closeness and distance were negatively related to each other, but the associations of closeness and distance with other variables differed somewhat for each.

In sum, the definitional confusion is far from abating anytime soon; we can conclude that some of the confusion arises from equating the many components that are comprised in the process of achieving or maintaining intimacy (e.g., self-disclosure, openness, nonverbal involvement, social support) with the content of intimacy (e.g., emotional closeness). Furthermore, the question of interest (in this case, adolescent development) shapes the definitional focus on an individual's overall capacity for intimacy—that is, the ability to engage in reciprocal processes that lead to feeling close to another.

OVERVIEW OF THE
CONCEPTUAL MODEL

The conceptual model of this chapter is illustrated in Figure 4.1. The model includes predictors and correlates of intimacy such that intimacy is a central construct of adolescence that has roots in earlier, more distal interpersonal and personal developmental periods (Berndt, 1992; Collins & Repinski, 1994; Erikson, 1968) such as temperament, attachment (Noller, 1994; Shulman, Elicker, & Sroufe, 1994), and identity (Orlofsky et al., 1973). Furthermore, intimacy has concurrent associations with other more proximal constructs that are (a) interpersonal, such as love (Hatfield & Sprecher, 1986; Kingsbury & Minda, 1988; Nelson, Allison, & Sundre, 1992) or relationship quality (Stafford & Canary, 1991) and (b) personal, such as personality, competence (Rice & Mulkeen, 1995), and sex-gender roles (Fischer & Narus, 1981). Current contexts include age-pubertal status and development, gender, cohort-historical period, sociocultural status and ethnicity, and current family. These contexts frame the development of intimacy in multiple ways, as deriving from, reflecting, and influencing salient aspects of the cultural milieu of adolescence. Adolescents of today live in a different world than existed for the adolescents of 10, 20, or 30 years ago. Hill's call to ground research on childhood and adolescence in the actual ecology and experience of young people (Holmbeck & Blyth, 1991) is well founded. Last, the model illustrates that intimacy itself has consequences that are manifested in personal and interpersonal areas that involve both light and dark side issues, such as personal adjustment (Fischer, Sollie, & Morrow, 1986; Gavazzi, Anderson, & Sabatelli, 1993) and coping with stress (Shulman, 1993).

THE CONCEPTUAL MODEL EXAMINED

Predictors and Correlates

The term *predictors* is a shorthand way of describing the distal conditions that lead to the development of intimacy. The task of identifying predictors, preconditions, and causes of intimacy has provoked considerable theoretical and research effort. Generally, these endeavors have focused on two areas: (a) other interpersonal

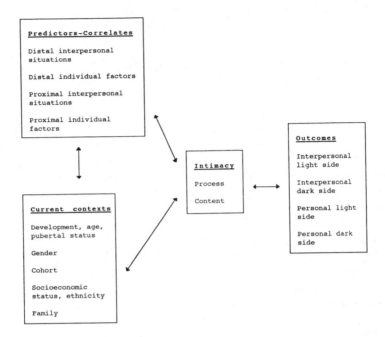

Figure 4.1. Model of Adolescent Intimacy

situations that have provided early experiences with intimacy or fostered the development of interpersonal skills and competencies enhancing the capacity for intimacy and (b) personal developmental task achievement, primarily the successful negotiation of the psychosocial task of identity achievement.

Distal Interpersonal Situations: Attachment

One of the earliest interpersonal relationships that has been linked to later adolescent intimacy concerns the attachment bond of mother and child. Complicating matters are varying terminologies that refer to these attachment bonds; therefore, the terms of each author are used in this review.

According to attachment theory, this bond results in the development of internal working models of relationships, models that are retained in memory and may be reenacted in the person's later relationships; at the very least, these models have implications for the quality of later relationships (Shaver & Hazan, 1988). Three attachment styles—secure, avoidant, and anxious—have been studied with respect to adolescent and preadolescent intimacy. According to Shulman and colleagues (1994), prior secure infant attachments were related to preadolescents (studied in a camp environment) who showed more competence and affection and counted more close friendships than preadolescents in other attachment categories. It is interesting that those with anxious-resistant infant attachments spent as much time with peers as the secure preadolescents; however, they showed lower levels of peer and social competence. The anxious-avoidant young people were characterized by fused relationships at the expense of personal autonomy.

Advantages of those with early secure attachments were seen as well in Noller's (1994) review of her own and other research. The secures had higher intimacy and relationship satisfaction; the avoidants had lower levels of intimacy and emotional intensity, less commitment, and less satisfaction. The anxious-ambivalent indicated high passion, dependence, idealization, and anxiety.

The hypothesis that early attachments are implicated in later adolescent friendships with consequences for intimacy has received some support in the literature and would appear to be a fruitful path for future exploration. An important missing link is understanding the mechanism by which early parent-infant attachment translates into later intimacy in peer relationships. It is possible that the earlier attachments have directly influenced the capacity for intimacy; securely attached infants, for example, might have a foundation (via internal working models) for developing a greater capacity for intimacy in adolescence, whereas less securely attached infants would be hindered in their ability to form later intimate relationships. Alternately, a secure style in infancy may be imitated in adolescent peer attachments, with the early secure attachments providing rewarding conditions that are simply repeated with peers. Certainly, tracing these links across time would help to identify the mechanisms that connect earlier attachments to later intimacy.

Although early attachments are presumed to be related to later peer relationships, changes in the parent-child relationship also are described as important to adolescent intimacy (Allison & Sabatelli, 1988). According to these authors, individuation facilitates identity development with concomitant restructuring of parent-child relations so that intimacy with parents and with peers is allowed. In this sense, the securely attached adolescent finds greater permission for exploration beyond the family boundaries, has the skills and confidence to negotiate these, and hence, enjoys greater intimacy with others. In recent longitudinal research reported by Rice and Mulkeen (1995), however, intimacy with parents showed only minimal interdependence with adolescent-friend intimacy.

Distal Interpersonal Situations: Friendships and Social Networks

In addition to identifying consequences of infant attachments for later relationship qualities and intimacy, research and theory have indicated the importance of friendships to the development of intimacy and psychosocial development in general (Argyle & Henderson, 1984; Bigelow & LaGaipa, 1980; Bukowski, Hoza, & Boivin, 1994; Claes, 1992; Craig-Bray, Adams, & Dobson, 1988; Cristante & Lucca, 1985; Dyk & Adams, 1987; Griffin & Sparks, 1990; Lempers & Clark-Lempers, 1993; Moore & Boldero, 1991; Reisman, 1990). Sullivan's (1953) concept of preadolescent chumship describes this relationship as an opportunity for trying out relationship skills, such as self-disclosure, and for providing consensual validation of the self (Furman & Wehner, 1994). From this base in chumships, the adolescent moves on to early romantic relationships. Collins and Repinski (1994) indicate that the meaning of intimacy differed among younger and older adolescents: For early adolescents, intimacy meant self-disclosure; for older adolescents, intimacy meant feeling accepted, understood, and satisfied. It would appear that early practice in the processes of intimacy may facilitate recognition of the emotional content of intimacy later in adolescence.

Although some researchers view *intimacy* and *friendship* as overlapping concepts (Jones, 1991; Sharabany, 1994b), factor analyses produce two distinct dimensions (Feeney & Noller, 1991; Fischer, 1981). Following factor analyses, Fischer compared relationships that varied on the two dimensions: integrated (high on both), intimate (high on intimacy), friendly (high on friendship), and uninvolved (low on both). She found that young women in high school and college were more often in the intimate category than were men at either grade level. Men in either setting were largely uninvolved. In the Feeney and Noller study, relationship qualities and attachment qualities were factor analyzed with the result that two factors emerged: companionship (friendship) and intimacy (self-disclosure). It is interesting that these two different studies conducted in different decades, on different continents, using different measures found convergence in the identification of friendship and intimacy factors. More research tied to theoretical constructs that follows up this promising lead should be conducted.

Social support variables have been identified as part of intimacy (Reis, 1990) with acknowledgment that the power to hurt another (Vangelisti, 1994) derives from the level of intimacy in the relationship. Nonetheless, Boldero and Moore (1990) found that alleviating loneliness was accomplished by social support among men and positive network appraisals among women. Longitudinal studies would help in the effort to untangle direction of effects in social networks.

A short-term longitudinal study of friendship networks investigated the direction of effects in middle adolescents (Fischer et al., 1986). The investigators examined whether friends helped in the development of personal qualities or whether personal qualities helped with the development of friendships. Overall, it appeared that a particular personal quality, social competence, predicted to later relationship qualities. There were gender differences, however: Boys' later personal qualities were more often predicted from earlier friendship qualities, whereas girls' later friendship qualities were more often predicted from earlier personal qualities. Taken together with other findings on developmental delay in boys' intimacy development (Fischer, 1981; although see also Berndt, 1992, who maintains that boys fail to catch up), it may be that a circular process is operating that brings adolescents to ever-broadening intimacy capacities. For example, friendships help develop the personal qualities, and this occurs earlier for girls than for boys; then, the personal qualities facilitate intimacy with others, again earlier for girls than for boys. Thus, testing boys and girls at the same age would pick up gender-related differences in cycling through this process. Bakken and Romig's (1992) research provided some support for such gender differences; they found that male and female adolescents of the same age (16 years) ranked intimacy components in differing orders: Males ranked control first, then inclusion, then affection; on the other hand, females ranked affection first, then inclusion, and then control components of intimacy.

Regardless of what other factors mediate the development of intimacy, it appeared that earlier levels of a quality were the most prominent predictors of later levels of the quality. For example, Vernberg, Beery, Ewell, and Abwender (1993) provided results from a natural experiment and found that ratings of premove (the adolescents and their families had moved) intimacy and premove companionship predicted to postmove ratings. Fischer et al. (1986) found that the best predictor of later relationship quality was the earlier measure of that relationship quality. Thus, continuity would appear to be important to understanding the development of intimacy in adolescence. However, both the Vernberg et al. and the Fischer et al. studies were conducted over short time spans (6-9 months). Research that employs longer time spans is needed. Rice and Mulkeen's (1995) longitudinal investigation provided a longer time span: Measures were administered in the 8th grade, the 12th grade, and 4 years post-12th grade. Boys reported a greater increase in intimacy from 8th to 12th grade than did girls. However, girls were higher than boys at every time measured. The authors described minimal stability in intimacy with friends over time.

It would be helpful to see studies with intermediate time points (Rice & Mulkeen had assessments at 6th, 7th, 8th, and 12th grades and 4 years post-12th grade, but only the 8th and 12th and 4-years-post findings were reported in this study). Research needs to be attentive not just to continuity as measured by correlations but to discontinuity as well. There may be sudden shifts and jumps in individuals' levels of intimacy that are masked by overall correlational strategies.

Distal Individual Factors:
Temperament and Identity

Individual factors refer to those qualities within the individual that are precursors to or predictors of intimacy in adolescence. An area that could be important to adolescent intimacy development is childhood temperament. The argument is that early temperament difficulties can lead to problems, including rejection by peers, and that affiliation with deviant peers then takes place, with such associations encouraging deviant behavior (Sher, 1994). Research is needed to test this model with respect to adolescent intimacy.

One area that has received an inordinate amount of attention in the literature is the area of identity and intimacy achievement. Much of this research was sparked by Erikson's (1968) model of psychosocial stages of development, which posited that successful completion of one stage was important to the successful negotiation of the next stage. In adolescence, identity tasks are the focus of psychosocial development. Following adolescence, intimacy tasks forge to the forefront. Although identity development is seen as a distal variable because, theoretically, identity achievement precedes intimacy achievement in Erikson's (1968) framework, many of the studies on identity and intimacy have used cross-sectional samples of college students. These cross-sectional studies could be taken as an indication of identity as a current correlate of intimacy. This section reviews the research on the ordering of the constructs of identity and intimacy.

In the past 15 years, research has provided findings inconsistent with Erikson's theorizing, at least with respect to women (e.g., Hodgson & Fischer, 1979). Until recently, with one exception (Fitch & Adams, 1983), the research has been cross-sectional rather than longitudinal, yet better testing of the model would be achieved with longitudinal studies. In preliminary analyses, a recent 9-month longitudinal study found no association between identity and intimacy when family context was taken into account (Bartle, 1994). Despite the paucity of longitudinal designs, the debate has been framed not in terms of testing actual sequencing but in terms of gender (e.g., Mellor, 1989). Females are seen to follow different pathways to intimacy achievement than do males (Hodgson & Fischer, 1979). However, crucial to understanding the findings are the operationalizations of identity and intimacy achievement. Marcia's (1966) development of an identity status interview focused on areas of identity achievement that appeared to relate primarily to issues traditionally important to males: career, politics, and the like. When this interview is employed, those with more advanced identity statuses reported a greater capacity for intimacy (Kacerguis & Adams, 1980). Women's identity and intimacy statuses seemed fused (Schiedel & Marcia, 1985). Later additions to this interview added areas of concern to women, such as sex roles and sexuality (Hodgson & Fischer, 1979, 1981). Most recently, Terrell (1993) proposed that identity achievement requires a component best described as *intimate identity*, or the extent to which the person sees the self as an intimate person.

Included in intimate identity are commitment, shared activities, decision making, sexual involvement, and openness.

In the intimacy status interview developed initially by Orlofsky (Orlofsky et al., 1973), five identity statuses were proposed (i.e., intimate, preintimate, pseudointimate, stereotyped, and isolate). Later, an additional intimacy status, termed *merger status*, was added (Bellen-Smith & Korn, 1986; Tesch & Whitbourne, 1982). Merger status indicated that the identity of one partner was subsumed by a more dominant partner. It was argued that the merger status may be normative for women (Bellen-Smith & Korn, 1986); however, Tesch and Whitbourne (1982) found that in young adulthood, gender differences were not apparent.

It is interesting that struggles with operationalizations of the Eriksonian framework have led researchers to include intimacy issues as part of identity and identity issues as part of intimacy. If the constructs are capable of such stretching, perhaps there are more than measurement issues at work here. Often lost in the discussion of Erikson's psychosocial stages is the original conceptualization of a matrix; that is, although identity is considered the central task of adolescence, it has precursors in earlier stages and reverberates in later stages. Adolescence is the arena in which these aspects come together. The same conditions exist for the intimacy development task of later adolescence and early adulthood: Intimacy issues are reflected in resolutions of earlier conflicts, and they continue as important components of later psychosocial developments. The challenge for researchers is to be true to this more complex patterning of development as reflected in measures and in research questions and to study these issues in younger adolescents.

Proximal Interpersonal Situations:
Communication

Self-disclosure and other communication variables have occupied center stage in the examination of proximal correlates of intimacy. Women tend to be more self-disclosing (Hendrick & Hendrick, 1987; Jones, 1991), particularly at higher levels of intimacy of a topic (Sollie & Fischer, 1985). Cline (1989) argued that gender differences could be accounted for through a cost-benefit analysis. If intimacy is seen as an investment, then men avoid disclosure to maintain control and power in the relationship. Indeed, Bakken and Romig's (1992) research highlighted the primacy of control intimacy among 16-year-old boys.

Proximal Interpersonal Factors:
Love and Loneliness

Another proximal variable that has recently come under scrutiny has to do with love, passionate love, and love styles. Research by Hatfield and Sprecher (1986) indicated that passionate love was correlated with intimacy; nonetheless, these authors argued that it is important for adolescents to develop the skills to turn passionate love into a relationship composed as well of companionate and intimate love. Love styles related to intimacy include a positive association with agape (altruistic love) and a negative association with *ludus* (game-playing love; Sandor & Rosenthal, 1986). In other research on love, intimacy was related to eros (romantic love) as well as *ludus* and agape (Levy & Davis, 1988).

Last, loneliness has been related negatively to intimacy (Boldero & Moore, 1990; Craig-Bray & Adams, 1986; Rotenberg & Whitney, 1992). However, the kinds of measures used seem to regulate the strength of the association. When measures were interview and paper-and-pencil methods, intimacy and loneliness correlated more strongly with each other than when behavior reports were used (Boldero & Moore, 1990).

Proximal Interpersonal Factors:
Kinds of Relationships

Various kinds of relationships may also be characterized differently in terms of intimacy qualities. Parents, peers, same sex, opposite sex, and closest friends are all kinds of relationships that have been examined (Cline, 1989; Sharabany, 1994b; Sollie & Fischer, 1985). According to Cline (1989), there are or can be different working models for different kinds of relationships. Cline found that attachment, caregiving, and affiliation were moderately correlated across four types of relationships (mother, father, closest friend, and romantic partner). Similarly, Sharabany (1994b) reported that intimacy to best friend correlated with intimacy to mother (.66) and to father (.65). Sollie and Fischer (1985) indicated that (a) type of relationship (same sex friendship, opposite sex friendship, and romantic), (b) sex role orientation, and (c) intimacy level of the topic all were significant main effects on self-disclosure. Intimacy of topic interacted with type of relationship and with sex role. There was a greater difference across relationships in levels of self-disclosure at increasing levels of intimacy of the topic.

Proximal Individual Factors: Sex-Gender Roles

Although most of the literature on individual variables has dealt with psychosocial identity, some research has been devoted to other characteristics of the person. In particular, sex-gender roles have received attention. Fischer and Sollie (1986) argued that social roles influenced responses to intimacy needs: Women in a laboratory discussion with intimates and acquaintances of the same or other sex asked more questions of male acquaintances but displayed more active listening and self-disclosure for female acquaintances. Femininity has been positively related to intimacy (Fischer & Narus, 1981). Women who were more androgynous and sex typed indicated more intimacy in their relationships than those who were undifferentiated in their sex role identities. Thus, issues of identity and intimacy are intertwined, and social roles play a large part in how these associations are played out.

Despite the view and evidence that men disclose less, their self-reports of actual expressivity are related to their gender role; for example, the strength aspects of masculinity were related to greater expressivity in men (Narus & Fischer, 1982). In this study, those men identified as more androgynous demonstrated greater expressivity than other men.

The findings of Jones and Dembo (1989) support the contention that it is attitudes and behaviors—the products of socialization—that are important influences on intimate relationships. In their research, significant sex differences favoring females over males for four of eight intimacy scales were found, but sex role group differences were reported for all eight intimacy scales.

Summary

There do not seem to be strong connections across studies of proximal correlates of intimacy; rather, the research seems to have been driven by the interests of the investigators at the time and reflect overlap with definitional issues. A greater sense of direction could be generated by theory-driven research on proximal correlates of intimacy in adolescence. Investigations that examine proximal and distal factors, both personal and interpersonal, are needed to understand better the contributions of each set of factors both singly and in interaction with each other as well as across partners who vary in levels of intimacy. For example, not investigated is the pairing of adolescent partners' working models: What difference does it make to an adolescent with a secure working model to be paired with someone with an insecure working model (see Prager, 1991, and White, Speisman, Jackson, Bartis, & Costos, 1986, for similar research on adults) or for someone with a high propensity to self-disclose to be paired with someone with a low level of self-disclosure? Research can be extended as well to domains not reviewed here, such as personality attributes and experiences of peer victimization or unearned popularity, as well as to associations of variables at different points in time and across time.

Current Contexts

Adolescent intimacy occurs in many important contexts. In this section, development, gender, cohort, socioeconomic status and ethnicity, and family contexts are surveyed.

Development, Age, and Pubertal Status

Developmental issues run through the literature on adolescent intimacy. Such issues appear in the research described earlier that looked at (a) the roots of intimacy in earlier attachment relationships, (b) adolescent intimacy as a precursor of intimacy in later adult relationships, and (c) the sequencing of identity and intimacy.

Additional changes in intimacy occur within the context of the numerous physical, social, and cognitive changes associated with adolescence. Physical changes transform the adolescent's relationships with his or her parents in a number of ways (Paikoff, Brooks-Gunn, & Carlton-Ford, 1991) and bring about an interest in romantic relationships. Changes in cognitive abilities affect the adolescent's understanding of the nature of intimacy, the role of intimacy in friendships, and expectations for reciprocity in the provision of intimacy. Social changes are reflected in the range of targets of intimacy available to the adolescent and nature of the intimate relationships the young person maintains.

It is beyond the scope of this chapter to review the extensive findings on age changes in intimacy, particularly because so many studies examine age in interaction with other variables. Excellent reviews of this topic are available elsewhere (Buhrmester & Furman, 1987; Caffarella & Olson, 1993; Hartup, 1992; Sharabany, 1994a). However, this section highlights some of this body of research.

Investigators have sought to understand developmental changes in conceptions of intimacy (e.g., what a friend is like), expectations for intimate relationships (Bigelow & LaGaipa, 1975; Clark & Ayers, 1993), and qualities or evaluations of intimacy (Clark & Ayers, 1993). Problems created by a lack of definitional clarity are compounded in the developmental study of intimacy because (a) some components of intimacy develop earlier than others (Jones & Dembo, 1989), (b) there are different age patterns depending on which aspect of intimacy is measured, and (c) age and gender interact in complex ways (e.g., Jones & Dembo, 1989; Papini, Farmer, Clark, Micka, & Barnett, 1990). For instance, Sharabany, Gershoni, and Hofman (1981) found little change in intimacy in same-sex friendships from 7th to 11th grades, no age changes for trust and loyalty, and an initial decline followed by an increase in attachment and exclusiveness.

It is important to note that previous research has relied almost exclusively on chronological age as the developmental marker. Only recently has John Hill's interest in the effect of pubertal status on family relations (Steinberg, 1981; Steinberg & Hill, 1978) been applied to aspects of family relationships other than power and status. Recent work on intimacy in the Hillian tradition has examined the relationship of pubertal status and the affective quality of the adolescent-parent relationship (measured as perceived attachment; Papini et al., 1991) and the rate of pubertal change and emotional distance in parent-adolescent relationships (Ellis, 1991). Moving beyond chronological age to consider the effects of variations in physical development on intimacy is a potentially fruitful approach. For example, Simmons and Blyth (1987) found that girls' early pubertal development was a disadvantage for girls' body image but an advantage in terms of increased popularity with the opposite sex. With respect to parents, 6th and 7th graders who looked older were given more independence, but by 10th grade, when the early developers no longer looked different from their peers, there was no difference in independence allowed the girls. With respect to boys, for a short time, early development provided more involvement with the opposite sex. It appeared that they were allowed more independence and were seen as more attractive by the opposite sex than later-developing boys.

Gender

Although gender may be thought of as a characteristic of the person, here we are looking at gender as a context for expectations concerning the development and expression of intimacy. Theoretical and empirical work suggests that men's primary source of meaning and value derives from evidence of their separateness from others and that women interpret experience within a framework of connectedness and caring involvement (Belenky, Clinchy, Goldberger, & Tarule, 1986; Chodorow, 1978; Dinnerstein, 1976; Gilligan, 1982). These authors argue that men's parenting by women involves knowledge of their difference from their primary caregivers. Thus, males organize principles of experience and behavior around separation and difference. Within a context that values men more than women, men attach less importance to connectedness to others. On the other hand, females recognize their similarities with their early caregivers and organize experience and behavior around this similarity and around connection with others. For women, high levels of involvement with others may be a derivative of their relational, connected way of knowing, but for men, shifts in status may require alterations in behavior that confirm personal effectiveness and individuality (Fischer, Sollie, Sorell, & Green, 1989).

A considerable body of adolescent research has found gender differences in intimacy that favor females (Blyth & Foster-Clark, 1987; Coleman, 1974; Douvan & Adelson, 1966; Eder & Hallinan, 1978; Fischer, 1981; Furman & Buhrmester, 1985; Hodgson & Fischer, 1979; Mark & Alper, 1980). These differences have included, but are not limited to (a) differences in expectancy of loyalty and commitment from close friendships, (b) the ordering of concerns about identity and intimacy (reviewed earlier in this chapter), (c) the capacity for intimacy, (d) perceived intimacy in specific relationships (e.g., Furman

& Buhrmester, 1985), and (e) the expression of intimacy. However, other research has failed to find gender differences in intimacy in certain relationships (e.g., Furman & Buhrmester, 1985), in perceived frequency of intimacy (Buhrmester & Furman, 1987), or in regard to certain characteristics (e.g., Hunter & Youniss, 1982). Converging research suggests that males and females have substantially different experiences with intimacy and that these differences arise early in development.

Camarena, Sarigiani, and Petersen (1990) have hypothesized that there may be different gender paths to intimacy. Using separate path analyses for boys and girls to determine the relative contributions of self-disclosure and shared experiences to intimacy (which they defined as emotional closeness), they found that the self-disclosure path to emotional closeness was significant for both boys and girls. When they controlled for self-disclosure, there was no relationship between shared experiences and emotional closeness in girls, although the path remained significant for boys. Camarena et al. concluded that self-disclosure is an important link to emotional closeness for both genders, but shared experiences and activities are an alternative path for boys. These findings highlight not only the idea that males and females have different pathways to achieve intimacy but that the magnitude of gender differences observed depends on what aspects of intimacy processes are operationalized.

Blyth and Foster-Clark (1987) described a social-pressures model that examines the forces that influence gender differences in intimacy (in this case, operationalized as the affective level of the relationship) across a broad set of social relationships. They described both general pressures (e.g., the social acceptability of intimacy for female relationships) and specific pressures (e.g., sexual prohibition against intimacy in certain relationships) that work for and against intimacy in these relationships. Blyth and Foster-Clark concluded that, in general, gender differences became greater as family ties became more distant.

Bukowski and Kramer (1986) used gender socialization processes to try to resolve the inconsistent findings reported in the literature regarding gender differences in friendship conceptions. They maintained that the inconsistencies resulted from a methodology in which girls are asked to describe their friendships with girls and boys to describe their friendships with boys. Bukowski and Kramer suggested that rather than revealing gender differences in conceptions of friendships, responses to such questions may show that both boys and girls have different criteria for the friendships of boys and the friendships of girls. Using fourth and seventh graders, they reported a main effect for sex of character in the vignettes they used but no gender effects, with both boys and girls indicating that intimacy is more likely to distinguish friends from nonfriends among girls than among boys. Whether such differences in beliefs in the role of intimacy in relationships reflect the child's observation of differences in boys' and girls' friendships or whether beliefs about differences and actual differences both reflect underlying cultural prescriptions remains to be answered. Last, another approach to understanding gender differences is illustrated in research by Clark and Ayers (1993) and Munsch and Baier (1995), which posed the question of whether males and females differ in the amount of the discrepancy between what they expect from friendships and what they report actually receiving. Clark and Ayers found that females and adolescents without reciprocated friendships had friendships that failed to provide a level of understanding to meet their expectations. Munsch and Baier found that the discrepancy between adolescents' expectations for the provision of support and the amount of support they later reported actually receiving was significantly greater for females than males for all eight dimensions of support measured. It appears, then, that females may be socialized into having expectations for intimate relationships that are unrealistically high, thereby possibly setting them up for disappointment in intimate relationships.

In a discussion of gender differences, we should not lose sight of the fact that separateness and connectedness are important aspects of development for both men and women. To return to the issue of identity and intimacy, if identity and intimacy are viewed as separate spheres of development, differences in developmental trajectories for males and females are apparent. However, Paul and White (1990) wrote that it is more useful to "conceptualize identity and intimacy as proceeding in a mutually influential way, with forces of socialization and cognitive development operating to make the issues of identity more salient for males and issues of intimacy more salient for females" (p. 384).

Cohort

In recent decades, societal norms have shifted from an emphasis on connectedness to an emphasis on individualism. Moreover, attitudes regarding the role of intimacy and commitment in romantic relationships have changed. There has been encouragement of independence and self-reliance in women by the feminist movement accompanied by increased expectations for men to be "empathic, self-expressive and, generally . . . more intimate" (Paul & White, 1990, p. 385). Researchers need to be aware of such changes and to be sure that the research questions they pose in the future reflect and are sensitive to these changing societal prescriptions (Hill, 1987). Such a view implies that research findings may be bound to the historical context. Future research involving carefully designed replications for emerging cohorts would clarify what findings are stable and what change according to historical periods.

Ethnicity and Socioeconomic Status

Research on intimacy continues to rely primarily on Anglo, middle-class samples, although calls for the need to examine ethnic and cultural differences often appear in the discussion of findings (e.g., Blyth & Foster-Clark, 1987; Clark-Lempers, Lempers, & Ho, 1991; Greene & Grimsley, 1990). The need to give increasing attention to diversity is well illustrated in recent work by Giordano, Cernkovich, and DeMaris (1993) in which they looked at relationships of African American adolescents to their families. They noted that research on African American families has often been based on a compensation argument predicated on the assumption that peer relationships are particularly intimate for African American adolescents because of deficiencies in the family. These researchers found, however, that African American youth scored higher on their measure of family intimacy than European American adolescents. They warned against the dangers of building models of adolescent development without taking race and ethnicity into account.

Cooper (1994) echoed this call to consider cultural variation in research on intimacy but also has discussed the dangers of using race and ethnicity as nominal variables that assume homogeneity of characteristics within each group. Rather, she challenges the field to move beyond "stereotypic, global, and static features of culture by developing multidimensional descriptions of the ecocultural niches of adolescents and their relationships" (p. 81).

Family

Family settings provide an important context for the development of intimacy (Romig & Bakken, 1992). Recent research has focused on the continuity between family and peer relationships. Families are the context in which adolescents develop the relationship competence they in turn bring to peer relationships (Cooper, 1994). However, families also provide different sets of experiences for sons and daughters that play out in friendships and dating relationships (Cooper & Grotevant, 1987). In the discussion of distal interpersonal situations, the parent-child attachment bond was reviewed. In this section, more contemporaneous aspects of families are reviewed, including functional and dysfunctional aspects of the family context.

A large body of literature documents the importance to functional child and adolescent development of parental intimacy, more usually described as parental support, parental warmth (see Peterson & Rollins, 1987), and family cohesion or connectedness (Olson, 1993). In their longitudinal study, Rice and Mulkeen (1995) found adolescent-parent intimacy in 8th grade was significantly related with friend intimacy in young adulthood but not with friend intimacy in either the 8th or 12th grades. Adolescent and parent intimacy in the 12th grade was unrelated to friend intimacy in either the 12th grade or young adulthood. In this study, the current context of the family was not as important to friend intimacy as a more distal, early adolescent context. It is interesting that Rice and Mulkeen reported increases in parent-adolescent intimacy over time, from 8th grade through young adulthood. On the other hand, Olson (1993) reported a large drop in family connectedness in families with a teen (40% connected) compared to families with children (63% connected).

It very well may be that intimacy and connectedness as used in these two studies are assessing differing concepts. An important issue is that the usual measures of intimacy assume linearity with positiveness—that is, increasing levels of intimacy are associated with increasing levels of positive characteristics or outcomes. However, Olson (1993) viewed connectedness as problematic at the extremes of either too little or too much. Too little connectedness implies disengagement in the family and too much connectedness implies enmeshment.

In observational research, Humphrey (1989) has shown that extremes of intimacy can be associated with adolescent eating disorders. Comparing mother-father-adolescent daughter triads in families with normal, anorexic, and bulimic-anorexic daughters, Humphrey found that parents of anorexic girls communicated two messages: nurturant affection but also neglect. Bulimic teens and their families were described as hostilely enmeshed. Normal families were different from both with higher percentages of helping, protecting, trusting, relying on, approaching, and enjoying one another. Connecting these parent-adolescent relationships to adolescent-peer intimacy through studies of eating-disordered and other problem-behavior adolescents would be a next step.

Another area in which there has been research on dysfunctional family intimacy and adolescent and young adult intimacy is the area of child sexual abuse. Lloyd and Emery (1993) summarized this literature by saying, "Interpersonally, female victims report difficulty in close relationships, fear of men, hostility toward their mothers, problems in parenting their own children, marital unhappiness, marital violence, and problems of sexual adjustment in adulthood" (pp. 138-139). These authors also described reports of isolation from friends, teen pregnancy, and early marriage. Thus, the context of inappropriate intimacy with an adult is related to a host of intimacy problems in adolescence and adulthood.

Stafford and Dainton (1994) pointed out the dangers of any kind of stronger bond (or coalition) between a parent and child than between marriage partners. Despite such problems, these authors argue against romanticizing "normal" families:

> Members of normal families routinely fight with each other, ignore each other, disconfirm each other, criticize each other, are rude to each other, and generally treat each other in a manner as heartless as anything experienced in the outside world. (p. 271)

Although this section deals with family contexts, the dating context is very similar, involving close, affectional relations with another. There are positives as well as perils in this context just as there are in the family context. As an example of perils, Marshall's (1994) study of premarital violence reported that more than half of the adolescent and young adult respondents had been violent and more than half had sustained at least one act of violence. Examining the positives of dating relationships should be an important research agenda.

Consequences

With few longitudinal studies, it is difficult to identify accurately the consequences for adolescents of varying trajectories through the achievement of intimacy. This section focuses more on future research possibilities than on past research. It is beyond the scope of this review to include the large number of studies that do not concern adolescent intimacy per se but that relate predictors, correlates, or current contexts to outcomes. The linchpin of this chapter is intimacy, and we have chosen not to review studies that omit more or less explicit, overt aspects of adolescent intimacy.

What does intimacy do for adolescents? An important question has to do with the adolescent's adjustment; for example, does more peer or family support lead to greater adolescent adjustment, psychosocial maturity, or other index of well-being or functionality? Townsend, McCracken, and Wilton (1988) indicated that intimacy was a better predictor than popularity for psychological adjustment. More recently, Gavazzi et al. (1993) reported that the more the support and the less the peer pressure, the better the adolescent's adjustment. Adolescents with the lowest levels of family support had the lowest psychosocial maturity unless they had high levels of peer support. In their short-term longitudinal study, Fischer et al. (1986) found that friend social network qualities predicted later personality for boys but that the opposite was true for girls. Thus, social network ties appeared to have different outcomes depending on gender.

Additional studies on the direction of effects between adjustment and intimacy need to be conducted with longitudinal designs, such as that employed by Rice and Mulkeen (1995). Furthermore, possible differential developmental histories of males and females may need to be taken into account so that boys and girls of different ages as well as similar ages are studied. A cohort-sequential design would be an important contribution to answering this important question.

Reis (1990) is no doubt correct that intimacy problems lead to distress and that intimacy provides a setting not only for beneficent empowerment but also for expressing the darker sides of relationship. On the plus side, intimacy with friends and family helps with coping and stressful situations among females (Shulman, 1993). Such assistance with coping for males has not been seen, although when males need support they turn to their parents (Shulman, 1993).

The dark side of intimacy needs to be examined: the phenomenon of the adolescent broken heart, the consequences of betrayal by a best friend, and so forth are all possible contributors to upset and distress in adolescents' lives (LaFollette & Graham, 1986). Recent essays on enemyship (Wiseman & Duck, 1995), relational transgressions (Metts, 1994), and messages that hurt (Vangelisti, 1994) provide starting points for the further understanding of these phenomena in the intimate relationships of adolescents. The interactions of possible contributors to such distress should also be examined. It may be that more vulnerable adolescents are more affected by the dark side, indeed may even be more frequent victims of the dark side. Losses such as of best friends, romantic partners, and important family members have been implicated in adolescent suicides (DeWilde, Kienhorst, Diekstra, & Wolter, 1994). Greater intimacy with opposite sex romantic partners may lead to some cases of adolescent pregnancy and childbearing. On the other hand, if intimacy promotes greater adjustment and psychosocial maturity, then perhaps it generates greater sexual responsibility on the part of young people. An important research question, then, concerns identifying factors associated with intimacy that lead to beneficial outcomes and emotional closeness versus more harmful outcomes.

Just as there needs to be greater examination of the consequences of the dark side of intimacy, researchers should also broaden the questions asked about the consequences of the light side of intimacy. Adjustment and psychosocial maturity are only a few possible positive benefits to adolescents of greater intimacy. Other positive benefits could be examined, such as altruism, prosocial behavior, opportunities to alter negative working models into more positive and secure ones, and even possible postponement of childbearing.

ADDITIONAL RECOMMENDATIONS
FOR FUTURE RESEARCH

This selected review of literature suggests that the field of intimacy comprises an active and vital area of investigation for understanding close relationships across the life span. Furthermore, the conceptual model suggests a number of possibilities for future research. For example, the model identified cohort, socioeconomic status, and ethnicity as variables to be taken into account; however, the study of adolescent intimacy has rarely included such constructs.

At the most basic level, investigators should continue to work toward greater definitional specificity, a particular concern for developmentalists given that components of intimacy appear to unfold across time. Furthermore, the recent acknowledgment of a dark or negative side to intimacy from researchers of close relationships is viewed as important and as compatible with research from the field of developmentalists. Unaddressed areas in the dark realm include consequences of adolescent romantic relationship dissolution and betrayal by a best friend. Furthermore, we suggest that a balanced approach of examining both negative and positive outcomes would be most beneficial to the understanding of adolescent intimacy.

In addition, an underlying goal is to identify universal principles that explain human relationships; given that historical context shapes these rules, investigators within this field become social historians of sorts, needing to carefully replicate their findings across cohorts as well as to adapt their questions to social changes, such as variations in family type.

Important and still missing theoretical links include information about how parent-infant attachment styles affect subsequent peer and romantic intimacy during adolescence and how the "fit" of working relational models influences intimacy. Researchers will also want to move beyond overly simple variables, such as chronological age, gender, family structure, or ethnicity, to include considerations of how variations in physical development affect intimacy, how gender socialization practices determine expression of intimacy, how family functioning generates consequences and potentials for the next generation, and how cultural differences influence intimacy.

As always, longitudinal designs involving frequent collection of multimethod, multi-informant information would be useful in determining theory-based processes, especially if discontinuous shifts are hypothesized to occur. Such designs would also allow for testing classic theories, such as Erikson's hypothesized complex patterning of psychosocial development.

Given the importance of adolescent intimacy, considerable research remains to be undertaken to advance explanation and empirical findings in this area.

REFERENCES

Acitelli, L. K., & Duck, S. W. (1987). Intimacy as the proverbial elephant. In D. Perlman & S. W. Duck (Eds.), *Intimate relationships* (pp. 297-308). Newbury Park, CA: Sage.

Allison, M. D., & Sabatelli, R. M. (1988). Differentiation and individuation as mediators of identity and intimacy in adolescence. *Journal of Adolescent Research, 3*(1), 1-16.

Argyle, M., & Henderson, M. (1984). The rules of friendship. *Journal of Social and Personal Relationships, 1*(2), 211-237.

Bakken, L., & Romig, C. (1992). Interpersonal needs in middle adolescents: Companionship, leadership and intimacy. *Journal of Adolescence, 15,* 301-316.

Bartholomew, K., & Horowitz, L. M. (1991). Attachment styles among young adults: A test for a four-category model. *Journal of Personality and Social Psychology, 61,* 226-244.

Bartle, S. E. (1994, November). *Longitudinal study of the development of identity and intimacy in college-aged males and females: Preliminary results.* Paper presented at the annual meeting of the National Council on Family Relations, Minneapolis, MN.

Belenky, M. F., Clinchy, B. M., Goldberger, N. R., & Tarule, J. M. (1986). *Women's ways of knowing: The development of self, voice, and mind.* New York: Basic Books.

Bellen-Smith, M., & Korn, J. H. (1986). Merger intimacy status in adult women. *Journal of Personality and Social Psychology, 50*(6), 1186-1191.

Berndt, T. J. (1992). Friendship and friends' influence in adolescence. *Current Directions in Psychological Science, 1*(5), 156-159.

Bigelow, B., & LaGaipa, J. (1975). Children's written descriptions of friendships: A multidimensional analysis. *Developmental Psychology, 11,* 557-585.

Bigelow, B., & LaGaipa, J. (1980). The development of friendship values and choice. In H. Fott, A. Chaptman, & J. Smith (Eds.), *Friendship and social relations in children* (pp. 15-44). New York: John Wiley.

Blyth, D. A., & Foster-Clark, F. S. (1987). Gender differences in perceived intimacy with different members of adolescents' social networks. *Sex Roles, 17*(11/12), 689-718.

Boldero, J., & Moore, S. (1990). An evaluation of de Jong-Giervald's loneliness model with Australian adolescents. *Journal of Youth and Adolescence, 19*(2), 133-147.

Buhrmester, D., & Furman, W. (1987). The development of companionship and intimacy. *Child Development, 58,* 1101-1113.

Bukowski, W. M., Hoza, B., & Boivin, M. (1994). Measuring friendship quality during pre- and early adolescence: The development and psychometric properties of the friendship qualities scale. *Journal of Social and Personal Relationships, 11*(3), 471-484.

Bukowski, W. M., & Kramer, T. L. (1986). Judgments of the features of friendship among early adolescent boys and girls. *Journal of Early Adolescence, 6,* 331-338.

Caffarella, R. S., & Olson, S. K. (1993). Psychosocial development of women: A critical review of the literature. *Adult Education Quarterly, 43,* 125-151.

Camarena, P. M., Sarigiani, P. A., & Petersen, A. C. (1990). Gender-specific pathways to intimacy in early adolescence. *Journal of Youth and Adolescence, 19*(1), 19-32.

Chelune, G. J., Robison, J. T., & Kommor, M. J. (1984). A cognitive interactional model of intimate relationships. In V. J. Derlega (Ed.), *Communication, intimacy, & close relationships*. Orlando, FL: Academic Press.

Chodorow, N. (1978). *The reproduction of motherhood: Psychoanalysis and the sociology of gender*. Berkeley: University of California Press.

Claes, M. E. (1992). Friendship and personal adjustment during adolescence. *Journal of Adolescence, 15*, 39-55.

Clark-Lempers, D. S., Lempers, J. D., & Ho, C. (1991). Early, middle and late adolescents' perceptions of their relationships with significant others. *Journal of Adolescent Research, 6*, 296-315.

Clark, M. L., & Ayers, M. (1993). Friendship expectations and friendship evaluations: Reciprocity and gender effects. *Youth & Society, 24*, 299-313.

Clark, M. S., & Reis, H. T. (1988). Interpersonal processes in close relationships. *Annual Review of Psychology, 39*, 609-672.

Cline, R. J. W. (1989). The politics of intimacy: Costs and benefits determining disclosure intimacy in male-female dyads. *Journal of Social and Personal Relationships, 6*(1), 5-20.

Coleman, J. C. (1974). *Relationships in adolescence*. London: Routledge & Kegan Paul.

Collins, W. A., & Repinski, D. J. (1994). Relationships during adolescence: Continuity and change in interpersonal perspective. In R. Montemayor, G. R. Adams, & T. P. Gullotta (Eds.), *Personal relationships during adolescence* (pp. 7-36). Thousand Oaks, CA: Sage.

Cooper, C. (1994). Cultural perspectives on continuity and change in adolescents' relationships. In R. Montemayor, G. R. Adams, & T. P. Gullotta (Eds.), *Personal relationships during adolescence* (pp. 78-100). Thousand Oaks, CA: Sage.

Cooper, C. R., & Grotevant, H. D. (1987). Gender issues in the interface of family experience and adolescents' friendship and dating identity. *Journal of Youth and Adolescence, 16*, 247-264.

Craig-Bray, L., & Adams, G. R. (1986). Measuring social intimacy in same-sex and opposite-sex contexts. *Journal of Adolescent Research, 1*(1), 95-101.

Craig-Bray, L., Adams, G. R., & Dobson, W. R. (1988). Identity formation and social relations during late adolescence. *Journal of Youth and Adolescence, 17*(2), 173-187.

Cristante, F., & Lucca, A. (1985). Self-perception and perception of peers as regards close-friendship in adolescence: A multivariate investigation. *Archivio di Psicologia, Neurologia e Psichiatria, 46*, 576-593.

Cupach, W. R., & Spitzberg, B. H. (1994). *The dark side of interpersonal communication*. Hillsdale, NJ: Lawrence Erlbaum.

DeWilde, E. J., Kienhorst, C. W. M., Diekstra, R. F. W., & Wolter, W. H. G. (1994). Social support, life events, and behavioral characteristics of psychologically distressed adolescents at high risk for attempting suicide. *Adolescence, 29*, 49-60.

Dinnerstein, D. (1976). *The mermaid and the minotaur: Sexual arrangements and human malaise*. New York: Harper & Row.

Douvan, E., & Adelson, J. (1966). *The adolescent experience*. New York: John Wiley.

Duck, S. (1994). Stratagems, spoils, and a serpent's tooth: On the delights and dilemmas of personal relationships. In W. R. Cupach & B. H. Spitzberg (Eds.),

The dark side of interpersonal communication (pp. 3-24). Hillsdale, NJ: Lawrence Erlbaum.

Duck, S., & Wood, J. (1995). *Confronting relationship challenges* (Vol. 5, Understanding relationship processes series). Thousand Oaks, CA: Sage.

Dyk, P. A. H., & Adams, G. R. (1987). The association between identity development and intimacy during adolescence: A theoretical treatise. *Journal of Adolescent Research, 2*(3), 223-235.

Eder, D., & Hallinan, M. T. (1978). Sex differences in children's friendships. *American Sociological Review, 43,* 237-250.

Ellis, N. B. (1991). An extension of the Steinberg accelerating hypothesis. *Journal of Early Adolescence, 11,* 221-235.

Erikson, E. (1968). *Identity: Youth and crisis.* New York: Norton.

Erikson, E. H. (1950). *Childhood and society.* New York: Norton.

Feeney, J. A., & Noller, P. (1991). Attachment style and verbal descriptions of romantic partners. *Journal of Social and Personal Relationships, 8*(2), 187-215.

Fischer, J. L. (1981). Transitions in relationship style from adolescence to young adulthood. *Journal of Youth and Adolescence, 10*(1), 11-23.

Fischer, J. L., & Crawford, D. W. (1992). Codependency and parenting styles. *Journal of Adolescent Research, 7,* 352-363.

Fischer, J. L., & Narus, Jr., L. R. (1981). Sex roles and intimacy in same sex and other sex relationships. *Psychology of Women Quarterly, 5*(3), 444-455.

Fischer, J. L., & Sollie, D. L. (1986). Women's communication with intimates and acquaintances. *Journal of Social and Personal Relationships, 3,* 19-30.

Fischer, J. L., Sollie, D. L., & Morrow, K. B. (1986). Social networks in male and female adolescents. *Journal of Adolescent Research, 6*(1), 1-14.

Fischer, J. L., Sollie, D. L., Sorell, G. T., & Green, S. K. (1989). Marital status and career stage influences on social networks of young adults. *Journal of Marriage and the Family, 51,* 521-534.

Fischer, J. L., Spann, L., & Crawford, D. W. (1991). Measuring codependency. *Alcoholism Treatment Quarterly, 8,* 87-100.

Fitch, S., & Adams, G. (1983). Ego identity and intimacy status: Replication and extension. *Developmental Psychology, 19,* 839-845.

Franz, C. E., & White, K. M. (1985). Individuation and attachment in personality development: Extending Erikson's theory. *Journal of Personality, 53*(2), 224-256.

Furman, W., & Buhrmester, D. (1985). Children's perceptions of the personal relationships in their social networks. *Developmental Psychology, 21,* 1016-1021.

Furman, W., & Wehner, E. A. (1994). Romantic views: Toward a theory of adolescent romantic relationships. In R. Montemayor, G. R. Adams, & T. P. Gullotta (Eds.), *Personal relationships during adolescence* (pp. 168-195). Thousand Oaks, CA: Sage.

Gadlin, H. (1977). Private lives and public order: A critical view of the history of intimate relations in the United States. In G. Levinger & H. Raush (Eds.), *Close relationships: Perspectives in the meaning of intimacy.* Amherst: University of Massachusetts Press.

Gavazzi, S. M., Anderson, S. A., & Sabatelli, R. M. (1993). Family differentiation, peer differentiation, and adolescent adjustment in a clinical sample. *Journal of Adolescent Research, 8*(2), 205-225.

Gilligan, C. (1982). *In a different voice: Psychological theory and women's development.* Cambridge, MA: Harvard University Press.

Giordano, P. C., Cernkovich, S. A., & DeMaris, A. (1993). The family and peer relations of black adolescents. *Journal of Marriage and the Family, 55,* 277-287.

Greene, A. L., & Grimsley, M. D. (1990). Age and gender differences in adolescents' preferences for parental advice: Mum's the word. *Journal of Adolescent Research, 5,* 396-413.

Griffin, E., & Sparks, G. G. (1990). Friends forever: A longitudinal exploration of intimacy in same-sex friends and platonic pairs. *Journal of Social and Personal Relationships, 7,* 29-46.

Guerrero, L. K., & Anderson, P. A. (1991). The waxing and waning of relational intimacy: Touch as a function of relational stage, gender and touch avoidance. *Journal of Social and Personal Relationships, 8*(2), 147-165.

Hartup, W. W. (1992). Friendships and their developmental significance. In H. McGurk (Ed.), *Childhood social development: Contemporary perspectives* (pp. 175-205). Hove, UK: Lawrence Erlbaum.

Hatfield, E., & Sprecher, S. (1986). Measuring passionate love in intimate relationships. *Journal of Adolescence, 9,* 383-410.

Hatfield, E., Sprecher, S., Pillemer, J. T., Greenberger, D., & Wexler, P. (1988). Gender differences in what is desired in the sexual relationship. *Journal of Psychology & Human Sexuality, 1*(2), 39-52.

Hazan, C., & Shaver, P. (1987). Romantic love conceptualized as an attachment process. *Journal of Personality and Social Psychology, 52,* 511-524.

Helgeson, V. S., Shaver, P., & Dyer, M. (1987). Prototypes of intimacy and distance in same-sex and opposite-sex relationships. *Journal of Social and Personal Relationships, 4*(2), 195-233.

Hendrick, S. S., & Hendrick, C. (1987). Love and sexual attitudes, self-disclosure and sensation seeking. *Journal of Social and Personal Relationships, 4*(3), 281-297.

Hill, J. P. (1987). Research on adolescents and their families: Past and prospect. In C. E. Irwin (Ed.), *Adolescent social behavior & health: New directions for child development* (pp. 13-31). San Francisco: Jossey-Bass.

Hinde, R. A. (1981). The bases of a science of interpersonal relationships. In S. Duck & R. Gilmour (Eds.), *Personal relationships* (Vol. 1, pp. 1-22). New York: Academic Press.

Hodgson, J. W., & Fischer, J. L. (1979). Sex differences in identity and intimacy development in college youth. *Journal of Youth and Adolescence, 8*(1), 37-50.

Hodgson, J. W., & Fischer, J. L. (1981). Pathways of identity development in college women. *Sex Roles, 7*(7), 681-690.

Holmbeck, G. N., & Blyth, D. A. (1991). Introduction. *Journal of Early Adolescence, 11*(1), 6-19.

Humphrey, L. L. (1989). Observed family interaction among subtypes of eating disorders using structural analysis of social behavior. *Journal of Consulting and Clinical Psychology, 57,* 206-214.

Hunter, F. T., & Youniss, J. (1982). Changes in the functions of three relations during adolescence. *Developmental Psychology, 18,* 806-811.

Jones, D. C. (1991). Friendship satisfaction and gender: An examination of sex differences in contributors to friendship satisfaction. *Journal of Social and Personal Relationships, 8*(2), 167-185.

Jones, G. P., & Dembo, M. H. (1989). Age and sex role differences in intimate friendships during childhood and adolescence. *Merrill-Palmer Quarterly, 35*(4), 445-462.

Kacerguis, M., & Adams, G. (1980). Eriksonian stage resolution: The relationship between identity and intimacy. *Journal of Youth and Adolescence, 9,* 117-126.

Kelley, H. H., Berscheid, E., Christensen, A., Harvey, J. H., Houston, T. L., Levinger, G., McClintock, E., Peplau, L. A., & Peterson, D. R. (1983). *Close relationships.* New York: Freeman.

Kingsbury, N. M., & Minda R. B. (1988). An analysis of three expected intimate relationship states: Commitment, maintenance, and termination. *Journal of Social and Personal Relationships, 5*(4), 405-422.

Koopman, C., Rosario, M., & Rotheram-Borus, M. J. (1994). Alcohol and drug use and sexual behaviors placing runaways at risk for HIV infection. *Addictive Behaviors, 19,* 95-103.

LaFollette, H., & Graham, G. (1986). Honesty and intimacy. *Journal of Social and Personal Relationships, 3*(1), 3-18.

Lempers, J. D., & Clark-Lempers, D. S. (1993). A functional comparison of same-sex and opposite-sex friendships during adolescence. *Journal of Adolescent Research, 8*(1), 89-108.

Levy, M. B., & Davis, K. E. (1988). Love styles and attachment styles compared: Their relations to each other and to various relationship characteristics. *Journal of Social and Personal Relationships, 5*(4), 439-471.

Lloyd, S. A., & Emery, B. C. (1993). Abuse in the family: An ecological, life-cycle perspective. In T. H. Brubaker (Ed.), *Family relations: Challenges for the future* (pp. 129-152). Newbury Park, CA: Sage.

Marcia, J. (1966). Development and validation of ego-identity status. *Journal of Personality and Social Psychology, 3,* 551-558.

Mark, E. W., & Alper, T. G. (1980). Sex differences in intimacy motivation. *Psychology of Women Quarterly, 5,* 164-169.

Marshall, L. L. (1994). Physical and psychological abuse. In W. R. Cupach & B. H. Spitzberg (Eds.), *The dark side of interpersonal communication* (pp. 280-311). Hillsdale, NJ: Lawrence Erlbaum.

McCarthy, B. (1981). Studying personal relationships. In S. W. Duck & R. Gilmour (Eds.), *Studying personal relationships* (Personal Relationships, Vol. 1, pp. 23-46). New York: Academic Press.

Mellor, S. (1989). Gender differences in identity formation as a function of self-other relationships. *Journal of Youth and Adolescence, 18*(4), 361-375.

Metts, S. (1994). Relational transgressions. In W. R. Cupach & B. H. Spitzberg (Eds.), *The dark side of interpersonal communication* (pp. 217-240). Hillsdale, NJ: Lawrence Erlbaum.

Monsour, M. (1992). Meanings of intimacy in cross- and same-sex friendships. *Journal of Social and Personal Relationships, 9,* 277-295.

Montgomery, B. (1984). Behavioral characteristics predicting self and peer perceptions of open communication. *Communication Quarterly, 32,* 233-242.

Moore, S., & Boldero, J. (1991). Psychosocial development and friendship functions in adolescence. *Sex Roles, 25*(9/10), 521-536.

Munsch, J., & Baier, M. (1995, November). *Gender differences in a comparison of hypothetical and actual coping.* Poster presented at the meeting of the National Council on Family Relations, Portland, OR.

Narus, Jr., L. R., & Fischer, J. L. (1982). Strong but not silent: A reexamination of expressivity in the relationships of men. *Sex Roles, 8*(2), 159-168.

Nelson, E., Allison, J., & Sundre, D. (1992). Relationships between divorce and college students' development of identity and intimacy. *Journal of Divorce and Remarriage, 18*(3-4), 121-135.

Newcomb, M. (1990). Social support by many other names: Toward a unified conceptualization. *Journal of Social and Personal Relationships, 7,* 479-494.

Noller, P. (1994). Relationships with parents in adolescence: Process and outcome. In R. Montemayor, G. R. Adams, & T. P. Gullotta (Eds.), *Personal relationships during adolescence* (pp. 37-77). Thousand Oaks, CA: Sage.

Olson, D. H. (1993). Family continuity and change: A family life-cycle perspective. In T. H. Brubaker (Ed.), *Family relations: Challenges for the future* (pp. 17-40). Newbury Park, CA: Sage.

Orlofsky, J., Marcia, J., & Lesser, I. (1973). Ego identity status and the intimacy versus isolation crisis of young adulthood. *Journal of Personality and Social Psychology, 27,* 211-219.

Paikoff, R. L., Brooks-Gunn, J., & Carlton-Ford, S. (1991). Effect of reproductive status changes on family functioning and well-being of mothers and daughters. *Journal of Early Adolescence, 11,* 201-220.

Papini, D. R., Farmer, F. F., Clark, S. M., Micka, J. C., & Barnett, J. W. (1990). Early adolescent age and gender differences in patterns of emotional self-disclosure to parents and friends. *Adolescence, 23,* 959-976.

Papini, D. R., Roggman, L. A., & Anderson, J. (1991). Early-adolescent perceptions of attachment to mother and father: A test of the emotional-distancing and buffering hypotheses. *Journal of Early Adolescence, 11,* 258-275.

Patterson, M. L. (1976). An arousal model of interpersonal intimacy. *Psychological Review, 83,* 235-245.

Paul, E. L., & White, K. M. (1990). The development of intimate relationships in late adolescence. *Adolescence, 25,* 375-400.

Peterson, G., & Rollins, B. (1987). Parent-child socialization. In M. Sussman & S. Steinmetz (Eds.), *Handbook of marriage and the family* (pp. 471-507). New York: Plenum.

Prager, K. J. (1991). Intimacy status and couple conflict resolution. *Journal of Social and Personal Relationships, 8*(4), 505-526.

Rawlins, W. K. (1992). *Friendship matters: Communication, dialectics, and the life course.* New York: Aldine de Gruyter.

Register, L. M., & Henley, T. B. (1992). The phenomenology of intimacy. *Journal of Social and Personal Relationships, 9,* 467-481.

Reis, H. T. (1990). The role of intimacy in interpersonal relations. *Journal of Social and Clinical Psychology, 9*(1), 15-30.

Reisman, J. M. (1990). Intimacy in same-sex friendships. *Sex Roles, 23,* 65-82.

Rice, K. G., & Mulkeen, P. (1995). Relationships with parents and peers: A longitudinal study of adolescent intimacy. *Journal of Adolescent Research, 10,* 338-357.

Romig, C., & Bakken, L. (1992). Intimacy development in middle adolescence: Its relationship to gender and family cohesion and adaptability. *Journal of Youth and Adolescence, 21,* 325-328.

Rook, K. (1990). Parallels in the study of social support and social strain. *Journal of Social and Clinical Psychology, 9,* 118-132.

Roscoe, B., Kennedy, D., & Pope, T. (1987). Adolescents' views of intimacy: Distinguishing intimate from nonintimate relationships. *Adolescence, 12*(87), 511-516.

Rosenthal, D. A., Gurney, R. M., & Moore, S. M. (1981). From trust to intimacy: A new inventory for examining Erikson's stages of psychosocial development. *Journal of Youth and Adolescence, 10,* 525-537.

Rotenberg, K. J., & Whitney, P. (1992). Loneliness and disclosure processes in preadolescence. *Merrill-Palmer Quarterly, 38,* 401-416.

Sandor, D., & Rosenthal, D. A. (1986). Youths' outlooks on love: Is it just a stage or two? *Journal of Adolescent Research, 1*(2), 199-212.

Schiedel, D., & Marcia, J. (1985). Ego identity, intimacy, sex role orientation, and gender. *Developmental Psychology, 21,* 149-160.

Selman, R. L. (1980). *The growth of interpersonal understanding: Developmental and clinical analyses.* New York: Academic Press.

Sexton, R. E., & Sexton, V.S. (1982). Intimacy: A historical perspective. In M. Fisher & G. Stricker (Eds.), *Intimacy.* New York: Plenum.

Sharabany, R. (1994a). Continuities in the development of intimate friendships: Object relations, interpersonal and attachment perspectives. In R. Erber & R. Gilmour (Eds.), *Theoretical frameworks for personal relationships* (pp. 157-178). Hillsdale, NJ: Lawrence Erlbaum.

Sharabany, R. (1994b). Intimate friendship scale: Conceptual underpinnings, psychometric properties and construct validity. *Journal of Social and Personal Relationships, 11*(3), 449-469.

Sharabany, R., Gershoni, R., & Hofman, J. E. (1981). Girlfriend, boyfriend: Age and sex differences in intimate friendships. *Developmental Psychology, 17,* 800-808.

Shaver, P. R., & Hazan, C. (1988). A biased overview of the study of love. *Journal of Social and Personal Relationships, 5*(4), 473-501.

Sher, K. J. (1994). Individual-level risk factors. In R. Zucker, G. Boyd, & J. Howard (Eds.), *The development of alcohol problems: Exploring the biopsychosocial matrix of risk* (Research monograph No. 26, pp. 77-108). Rockville, MD: National Institutes of Health.

Shulman, S. (1993). Close relationships and coping behavior in adolescence. *Journal of Adolescence, 16,* 267-283.

Shulman, S., Elicker, J., & Sroufe, L. A. (1994). Stages of friendship growth in preadolescence as related to attachment history. *Journal of Social and Personal Relationships, 11*(3), 341-361.

Simmons, R. G., & Blyth, D. A. (1987). *Moving into adolescence: The impact of pubertal change and school context.* New York: Aldine de Gruyter.

Small, S. A., & Luster, T. (1994). Adolescent sexual activity: An ecological, risk-factor approach. *Journal of Marriage and the Family, 56,* 181-192.

Sollie, D. L., & Fischer, J. L. (1985). Sex-role orientation, intimacy of topic, and target person differences in self-disclosure among women. *Sex Roles, 12*(9/10), 917-929.

Stafford, L., & Canary, D. J. (1991). Maintenance strategies and romantic relationship type, gender and relational characteristics. *Journal of Social and Personal Relationships, 8*(2), 217-242.

Stafford, L., & Dainton, M. (1994). The dark side of "normal" family interaction. In W. R. Cupach & B. H. Spitzberg (Eds.), *The dark side of interpersonal communication* (pp. 259-280). Hillsdale, NJ: Lawrence Erlbaum.

Steinberg, L. (1981). Transformations in family relations at puberty. *Developmental Psychology, 17,* 833-840.

Steinberg, L., & Hill, J. P. (1978). Patterns of family interaction as a function of age, the onset of puberty, and formal thinking. *Developmental Psychology, 14,* 683-684.

Sullivan, H. S. (1953). *The interpersonal theory of psychiatry.* New York: Norton.

Terrell, B. L. (1993). *Intimate identity: Female and male differences.* Unpublished doctoral dissertation. Lubbock: Texas Tech University.

Tesch, S. A., & Whitbourne, S. K. (1982). Intimacy and identity status in young adults. *Journal of Personality and Social Psychology, 43,* 1041-1051.

Townsend, M. A., McCracken, H. E., & Wilton, K. M. (1988). Popularity and intimacy as determinants of psychological well-being in adolescent friendships. *Journal of Early Adolescence, 8,* 421-436.

Vangelisti, A. L. (1994). Messages that hurt. In W. R. Cupach & B. H. Spitzberg (Eds.), *The dark side of interpersonal communication* (pp. 53-82). Hillsdale, NJ: Lawrence Erlbaum.

Vernberg, E. M., Beery, S. H., Ewell, K. K., & Abwender, D. A. (1993). Parents' use of friendship facilitation strategies and the formation of friendships in early adolescence: A prospective study. *Journal of Family Psychology, 7*(3), 356-369.

Waring, E. M., Tillman, M. P., Frelick, L., Russell, L., & Weisz, G. (1980). Concepts of intimacy in the general population. *Journal of Nervous and Mental Disease, 168,* 471-474.

Weingarten, K. (1991). The discourses of intimacy: Adding a social constructionist and feminist view. *Family Process, 30,* 285-305.

White, K. M., Speisman, J. C., Jackson, D., Bartis, S., & Costos, D. (1986). Intimacy maturity and its correlates in young married couples. *Journal of Personality and Social Psychology, 50*(1), 152-162.

Wiseman, J. P., & Duck, S. (1995). Having and managing enemies: A very challenging relationship. In S. Duck & J. T. Wood (Eds.), *Confronting relationship challenges* (Vol. 5, Understanding relationship processes series, pp. 43-72). Thousand Oaks, CA: Sage.

Youniss, J. (1980). *Parents and peers in social development.* Chicago: University of Chicago Press.

5. Identity:
A Multidimensional Analysis

James E. Côté

The study of human identity has proven to be a formidable task. The problems with the concept of identity seem to lie with its promise to explain much about human behavior, but in doing so, the concept takes on a multidimensionality, making it difficult to easily characterize and to arrive at a consensus regarding just what it is. This multidimensionality forms an organizing principle for this chapter in that human identity has social, personal, and psychological manifestations. Accordingly, I will examine some of the most promising approaches in psychology and sociology to understanding how identity is formed in these different dimensions. The product of this examination will be an interdisciplinary analysis currently unavailable in the literature. As such, it will require some readers to delve into unfamiliar territory. However, I believe that only by bringing these disciplines together will we be able to piece together the puzzle of this most interesting facet of human existence: namely, how humans come to define themselves as mature members of their species.

My intention is to leave an archival commentary regarding how far this puzzle has been solved as of the mid-1990s as well as some direction for future research. Because so many literature reviews have been published recently (e.g., Adams, Gullotta, & Montemayor, 1992; Gecas & Burke, 1995; Marcia, Waterman, Mattesson, Archer, & Orlofsky, 1993; Weigert, Teitge, & Teitge, 1986), I will not engage in a detailed survey of the psychological and sociological literatures, and I will not deal with all possible specific topic areas—only those publications most germane to my commentary will be cited. Instead, I will provide a critical analysis that tries to help us surmount the problems that have hindered past attempts to understand fully the multidimensionality of identity formation. Consequently, this chapter constitutes a "treetops" survey that attempts to map the overall forest, rather than trying to count individual trees.

This chapter will be further delimited by a focus on what is perhaps the major obstacle confronting identity research, namely, theorizing social context and coming to grips with issues associated with developmental contextualism (as discussed in the introduction to this volume). To date, more work in psychology has been done on development than context in the area of identity formation; in sociology the reverse is true. As a sociologist, therefore, I will take this opportunity to attempt to link sociological work relevant to the contextual-social side of this issue with work on the developmental-psychological side. To do this, I will introduce and expand relevant sociological formulations, thereby suggesting how various (and changing) macrosocial contexts can affect human development, particularly identity formation during adolescence and youth.

In addition, this chapter will attempt to take stock of John Hill's (1973) reflections on identity research some 20 years ago when this area was still in its infancy. He asked, for example, whether the identity crisis is overestimated, both in prevalence and in developmental significance. And he wondered if we can actually do without the concept of identity, instead using a simpler, more straightforward concept of the self. Last, he deliberated over whether the concept of identity increases our understanding of adolescence. He did not answer these questions; rather, he wrote that "only further analysis of the concept directed toward empirical research" can help us answer them (Hill, 1973, pp. 65-66). I conclude this chapter with reflections on these questions, based on the following critical, interdisciplinary analysis.

THEORETICAL PERSPECTIVES

Disciplinary Differences

Virtually all contemporary formulations of identity have been influenced by Erik Erikson.[1] An obituary following his recent death described Erikson as a psychoanalyst who "profoundly reshaped views of human development," and it notes that his popular recognition peaked during the 1970s from his coining the term *identity crisis* ("Psychoanalyst Coined" 1994, p. E8). Not coincidentally, the social scientific community took increasing interest in the concept of identity during the 1970s; since then, the literature has burgeoned, particularly in psychology and sociology.

132 PSYCHOSOCIAL DEVELOPMENT DURING ADOLESCENCE

The study of identity formation in adolescence and youth has been dominated by psychologists, principally because adolescence has been singled out in psychology as a developmental stage with its own properties (e.g., Davis, 1990; Sprinthall & Collins, 1984). Influenced greatly by Erikson's discussions of ego identity, psychologists have focused on the subjective-experiential dimension of identity. For this reason, most of our knowledge of identity formation in adolescence is restricted to this dimension. We see here that disciplinary differences lie in two areas: (a) assumptions about the nature of adolescence and (b) the dimension of identity deemed important.

With respect to the first difference, whereas psychologists tend to focus on identity in adolescence and youth, sociologists generally apply the identity concept across the life course, not seeing adolescence as a stage intrinsically different from other life stages. Consequently, developmental principles of identity formation during adolescence have not been deemed necessary by most sociologists.[2] Nevertheless, the study of identity in sociology constitutes a large and expanding literature that has implications for identity formation in adolescence and can suggest directions that psychological-developmental approaches to identity might take as they more fully develop the contextual-social component of developmental contextualism.[3]

The second point of divergence of sociology from psychology is one of dimensional focus. For sociologists, the general assumption tends to be that "identity is not the exclusive property of the individual but rather is something that is realized strategically and circumstantially" (Weigert et al., 1986, p. 23) through one's contacts with others. Moreover, although identity is seen to be subjectively constructed by each individual, this is mainly in reference to external circumstances provided by day-to-day interactions, cultural institutions, and social structures. The most recent approach in sociology has been to view identity formation in contemporary society as involving a "life-long reflexive project of self" (Giddens, 1991, pp. 32-33), required by the degree of continual social change. Identity formation thus involves the self negotiating passages through life and reflecting on its actions during these passages. These reflections can then culminate in the creation of stories or narratives that explain past actions (cf. Shotter & Gergen, 1989).

In other words, for many sociologists there is no identity without society, and society steers identity formation while individuals attempt to navigate the passage. (Many psychologists tend to have this the other way around.) Weigert et al. (1986) characterize this when they state the sociological axiom that "social organization is the principle of self-organization, and both together explain social action" (p. 5; cf. Côté, 1993). Accordingly, sociologists tend to be more concerned with general topics related to social and personal identity than with the specific topic of the formation of ego identity.

We can now consider substantive elements of each perspective.

Sociological Perspectives

Two reviews of the sociological approaches to identity can be found in Weigert et al. (1986) and Gecas and Burke (1995); readers are referred to these works for details. I would like to simply draw out here some definitional and typological points that might serve to round out the psychological approach.

Weigert et al. (1986) provide a useful chart of Erikson's influence in stimulating general sociological interest in the concept of identity, tracing how the concept was adopted by five different sociological traditions.[4] It appears that Erikson may have been ahead of his time with many of his sociological observations regarding the changing relevance of identity in relation to Western culture. Indeed, it appears that many of Erikson's midcentury observations about the disruptive effects of social change on identity formation prefigured current sociological concerns regarding modernity and postmodernity. In this context, Weigert et al. (1986) note that the consensus emerged in sociology that the issue of identity is a definitive feature of contemporary life; consequently, identity is now recognized as an organizing theoretical concept and indispensable technical term.

Adding to the background provided by Weigert et al., Gecas and Burke (1995) focus on the use of the concepts of self and identity in sociological social psychology. They provide a useful sociological characterization of identity, as follows:

> Identity refers to who or what one is, to the various meanings attached to oneself by self and other. In sociology, the concept of identity refers both to self-characterizations individuals make in terms of the structural features of group memberships, such as various social roles, memberships, and categories . . . and to the various

character traits an individual displays and others attribute to an actor on the basis of his/her conduct. (p. 42)

This characterization essentially refers to two of the three dimensions of identity that I wish to draw attention to: social identity (as in group memberships) and personal identity (as in character and conduct displays). The term *self*, as used by sociologists, corresponds more closely (but not precisely) to the *identity* to which psychologists refer, although as we will see, psychologists have a more differentiated view of this phenomenon. For Gecas and Burke (1995), the self refers to the process of reflexivity or self-awareness—namely, the "ability to be both subjects and objects to [oneself]. Reflexivity is a special form of consciousness, a consciousness of oneself."

Gecas and Burke (1995) go on to note four general social psychological orientations regarding self and identity. Each of these orientations has different points of emphasis, but they do help map out the multidimensionality of identity. The four orientations are the following

(1) situational, which emphasizes the emergence and maintenance of the self in situated (typically face-to-face) interaction; (2) social structural, which focuses on the consequences of role relationships and other structural features of social groups; (3) biographical-historical, which focuses on the self as a cultural and historical construction; and (4) intrapersonal, focusing on processes within self and personality affecting behavior. (p. 42)

The most recent surge of interest in identity has been among those adopting the biographical-historical approach, particularly "in cultural studies, feminist scholarship, and what has come to be called 'postmodernist' literature on the self" (Gecas & Burke, 1995, p. 44). The type of social analysis preceding postmodern analysis is now referred to as *modernist* analysis.[5] The common theme running through modernist studies is the notion that modernist institutions (especially of the 20th century) create a tension between self and society, resulting in identity confusion, alienation, fragmentation of self, and loss of authenticity among those affected (Gecas & Burke, 1995; Smart, 1993). The postmodernist literature extends these trends to explore new problematic forms of self and identity (of the late 20th century and the future). Gecas and Burke (1995) explain this change as follows:

Postmodern society, with its emphasis on images and illusions and the increasing difficulty in distinguishing the "real" from the "imitation" is viewed as inimical to the maintenance of the bounded, private, centred self striving for agency and authenticity. The postmodern world is saturated with images and simulations to such an extent that the image . . . is viewed as replacing reality. . . . The postmodern self is characterized as decentered, relational, contingent, illusory, and lacking any core or essence. (p. 57)

According to Gecas and Burke, then, the more concrete problems of self in modern society (finding one's authentic self or core) lose their meaning in postmodern society because of the loss of belief that there is a core. Following Gergen (1991), Gecas and Burke (1995) note that in postmodern society, the

emphasis on images and illusions is reflected in greater attention to self-presentation and to style over substance. For that matter, the distinction between the real and presented self, between substance and style, disappears. . . . Fashion and personal appearance increase in importance as central means of creating the self and influencing the definition of the situation. . . . The accentuated emphasis on physical fitness and body shaping is understandable when self and appearance are viewed as the same. (p. 57)

These sociological analyses of identity do not specifically designate adolescence as *the* problematic time of identity formation; rather, the entire life course is now viewed to be problematic in this regard (but see Fornas & Bolin, 1995, and Wallace, 1995, for examples of how these sociological formulations have been applied to adolescence and youth in various countries).[6] As I integrate the various approaches, I will try to show how these formulations are particularly pertinent to adolescence and how the psychological approach can be fruitfully integrated with the sociological one.

Psychological Perspectives

Erikson's influence on the study of identity in adolescence in psychology is widely recognized. (He also influenced psychoanalytic and psychiatric research, but a coherent research tradition has not emerged in those fields.) This influence included the uncontested proposition that the major psychosocial task linking childhood with adulthood involves developing a viable adult identity. Moreover, although Erikson postulated eight interrelated stages of psychosocial development, the identity stage has received the most attention.

With Erikson's focus on psychosocial development, he not only recognized psychological dimensions of identity but social and personal dimensions as well. For Erikson (e.g., 1968), then, psychosocial identity is comprised of three interrelated dimensions: (a) the subjective-psychological dimension, or ego identity as a sense of temporal-spatial continuity and its concomitants; (b) the personal dimension, or a behavioral and character repertoire that differentiates individuals; and (c) the social dimension, or recognized roles within a community. It is important that these components need to come together during the identity stage, and when they do not, or as they are doing so, an identity crisis is evident. Such an identity crisis is characterized by a subjective sense of identity confusion, a behavioral and characterological disarray, and a lack of recognized roles in a community. Accordingly, resolution of the identity stage is facilitated when the three dimensions dovetail: (a) when a relatively firm sense of ego identity is developed, (b) when behavior and character become stabilized, and (c) when community roles are acquired (cf. Côté & Levine, 1987).

Formulated in this manner, we can see how Erikson was able to study a variety of cultures, finding great variation both in how adolescence is structured and the tasks associated with identity formation. It is not widely recognized, however, that he slanted his formulations toward modern American culture (in which he lived as an adult), where resolution of the identity stage is predicated around choice and individuality during a protracted and loosely structured adolescence. For example, in a chapter titled "Reflections on the American Identity," Erikson (1963) wrote:

> The process of American identity formation seems to support an individual's ego identity as long as he can preserve a certain element of deliberate tentativeness of autonomous choice. The individual must be able to convince himself that the next step is up to him and that no matter where he is staying or going he always has the choice of leaving or turning in the opposite direction if he chooses to do so. (p. 286)

The most coherent body of research rooted in Erikson's work on the American identity is based on James Marcia's *identity status* paradigm. This paradigm is well-known, so I will not take the space to explain it fully here.[7] Numerous recent reviews are available, including LaVoie (1994) and relevant chapters in the following recent volumes: Adams et al. (1992), Archer (1994), Kroger (1993a), and Marcia et al. (1993). These reviews reveal that Marcia's elaboration of Erikson's formulations of identity, and subsequent methodological and conceptual elaborations of Marcia's formulations, provide an empirically valid and reliable method of studying how the interplay of choice and commitment affects various dimensions of personality and social behavior, at least among "lower middle to upper middle class ethnic majorities in North America, Northern Europe, and parts of the British Commonwealth" (Marcia, 1989a, p. 402). Antecedent socialization experiences, especially in the family and educational contexts, are also associated with the choice-commitment matrix that embodies the identity statuses (see Marcia, 1993b, pp. 32-35, and Waterman, 1993, pp. 62-67 for up-to-date reviews). The success of this conceptual model in providing verifiable predictions attests to its usefulness in studying certain aspects of Western identity formation, although I believe that a multidimensional understanding of identity formation requires the assessment of more components than those represented by the choice-commitment matrix (e.g., Côté & Levine, 1988, p. 151).

The identity statuses appear to be useful partly because they provide for "a greater variety of styles in dealing with the identity issue than does Erikson's simple dichotomy of identity versus identity confusion" (Marcia, 1980, p. 161). The statuses were originally based on the developmental hypothesis that a "continuum of ego identity based on proximity of an individual to identity achievement . . . [underlies] the statuses" (Marcia, 1967, p. 119). A developmental progression through the statuses was postulated to be a dominant pattern, with identity achievement and identity diffusion as "polar alternatives of status inherent in Erikson's theory," and identity foreclosure and identity moratorium as "roughly intermediate in this distribution" (Marcia, 1966, pp. 551-552). Thus, it appears that the identity statuses were thought of as akin to substages of the identity stage (Côté & Levine, 1988). Revisions to these assumptions have been made, some of which will be discussed (see also Marcia et al., 1993; Waterman, 1988).

EMPIRICAL APPROACHES

Sociological

Sociological approaches to the study of identity have favored more qualitative methodologies and theoretically driven social analysis (see Gecas & Burke, 1995, for discussions of the various methodologies; for examples of primary research, see Becker, Geer, Hughes, & Strauss, 1961; Lynd, 1958; Stryker, 1968; Wheelis, 1958). The most popular *quantitative* instrument is the Twenty Statements Test (TST; Kuhn & McPartland, 1954). Also called the Who Am I? test, subjects are simply asked to provide 20 statements in response to the question, "Who am I?" This measure appears to tap salient features of social and personal identity.

One conclusion drawn from this instrument is that since the 1960s, "there has been a dramatic change in locus of self, a change from conceptualizing oneself in terms of roles and statuses to conceptualizing oneself in terms of affect, desires, and styles of behavior" (Snow & Phillips, 1982, p. 462).[8] In particular, college student samples are becoming less tied to socially defined statuses (e.g., "I am a college student" or "I am Catholic") and are defining themselves in more reflective terms (e.g., "I like rock music"; "I am a happy person"). Zurcher (Wood & Zurcher, 1988; Zurcher, 1977) goes further, arguing that the *mutable self* is emerging as a predominant identity strategy. Similar to the postmodern self discussed earlier, the mutable self is characterized by a highly flexible and autonomous capacity to modify and control self-concepts and to experience the various components of self in varying social contexts. Zurcher believes this versatile identity strategy is adaptive to rapid social change and uncertainty. He also speculates that there is a loose developmental pattern associated with it, at least as it emerges in the college student samples that have been studied. Recent studies confirm the trend toward the mutable self with 80% to 90% of college students in the 1980s adopting reflective identities (compared to about 30% in the 1950s; see Babbitt & Burbach, 1990), suggesting that the TST is a useful instrument for monitoring so-called postmodern trends in identity formation.

Aside from these efforts, identity in adolescence has not been the focus of many quantitative research projects in sociology, so empirical measures that might balance out the context side of development are not to be found in the sociological literature. Many sociologists would argue that identity should simply be a sensitizing concept in any analysis (cf. Blumer, 1969).

Psychological

Kroger (1993b) provides a useful summary of the empirical approaches used in the psychological-developmental study of identity, grouping them into three general approaches. The first assesses resolution of the identity stage (along with the other psychosocial stages postulated by Erikson) with the use of paper-and-pencil measures. This approach was among the earliest but seems to have been largely abandoned. The second exclusively focuses on the identity stage, using paper-and-pencil measures of degree of ego identity. The third is a dimensional approach, out of which the identity status paradigm has emerged, involving some 300 studies (Kroger, 1993b). These studies have examined family nurturance as a predictor of identity status, personality variables associated with each status, and developmental patterns among the identity statuses. The identity statuses have been measured using the original semistructured interview (Marcia, 1964) and paper-and-pencil measures (e.g., Adams, Bennion, & Huh, 1987).

In the past few years, there appears to have been a branching out of research rooted in the identity status paradigm (see especially chapters in Adams et al., 1992). The variant approaches, although committed to the typology of identity statuses, differ according to an emphasis on personal identity and self-actualization (Waterman, 1992), processes underlying identity formation (Grotevant, 1992), and social cognition (Berzonsky, 1992). In addition, the areas or domains of commitment formation have been expanded to increase the relevance and inclusivity of the typology. For example, to be more inclusive of women, premarital intercourse (Marcia & Friedman, 1970) and sex roles (Matteson, 1977) have been added; to include younger samples, dating and friendships were operationalized (Grotevant & Cooper, 1981); to be sensitive to minority groups, ethnicity has been studied (Phinney, 1989); and to understand European samples (specifically Dutch), lifestyle concerns were measured (Bosma, 1985).

These modifications have undoubtedly increased the usefulness and validity of the identity status paradigm and are responsive to the need for better understanding developmental contextualism. As I argue later, however, the heavy conceptual investment in the four-category typology creates difficulties in establishing a model of identity formation that fully applies in all cultures. In particular, the investment in the notion that identity is, or has to be, "achieved" is problematic in certain contexts (see also Côté & Levine, 1988).

DEVELOPMENTAL PATTERNS

As noted earlier, concern with tracing developmental patterns of identity formation has mainly been the purview of psychologists. In contrast, sociologists have tended to approach identity formation as the gradual product of lifelong socialization processes that tend to shape the individual into cultural molds.[9] These two approaches reflect radically different assumptions that make it difficult to reconcile the disciplines. On the one hand, they reflect differing assumptions regarding the nature of adolescence, but on the other hand, they reflect differing views about how humans make their way to maturity (this later difference has been described in terms of the socialization model versus the developmental model by Bush & Simmons, 1981, p. 134). These assumptions about adolescence and maturation dovetail in the following manner: Sociologists tend to view adolescence simply as a different (and often arbitrary) socialization context that provides various forms of cultural conditioning. In this view, individuals change during this period largely as a result of "learning culture," rather than undergoing structural psychic change. Psychologists, on the other hand, tend to view adolescence as a real life stage during which fundamental or structural psychological changes need to take place for maturation to occur. For many sociologists, however, this constitutes a reification of adolescence as it has emerged in Western societies (e.g., Côté, 1994).

Most of the psychological studies of identity formation show that the various subjective components of identity generally increase in strength or salience in predicted ways as certain individuals move toward adult maturity (e.g., Waterman & Archer, 1990). This should not be surprising, though, given that most measures are tied to adult activities, such as career and community commitments. From a structural-development point of view, however, what is more surprising is that the dominant paradigm has not uncovered stronger patterns in this regard. For example, in her review of the identity status literature, Kroger (1993b) notes that whereas the numbers of moratoriums and achievements increase with age in longitudinal studies, "it is noteworthy . . . that large percentages of youths remained foreclosed or diffuse through late adolescence/early adulthood in all of these studies" (p. 10). Based on the identity status paradigm's conceptualization of identity formation, then, it would appear that a significant proportion of the population does not mature to the most advanced levels.

In reference to the longitudinal studies that have examined developmental patterns, Kroger (1993b) notes that "the foreclosure to moratorium to achievement shift [is] . . . the most common pathway of movement" (p. 10). But again, although this may be the most common and desirable pathway among contemporary U.S. youth, it does not seem to describe the development of a majority of young people, given that only between 30% and 40% of college seniors have been classified as being in the identity achievement status (up from about 20% in first year; Waterman, Greary, & Waterman, 1974; Waterman & Waterman, 1971). Moreover, studies of adult populations have found a preponderance of foreclosures (Waterman, 1982) and a minority of achievements (about 20% of fathers of college students, according to Waterman & Waterman, 1975). Although this may not reflect a problem with the conceptualization of how identity is formed for a large proportion of the population, it does raise the issue of whether the identity status paradigm is more prescriptive than descriptive.[10] That is, is this common pathway what the researchers think people ought to do (i.e., form an identity along the choice-commitment matrix), and in conceiving it this way, have they missed what most people actually do?

There also appears to be some question as to whether the identity status paradigm has been shown to be a developmental theory, as originally postulated, in the same way that Piaget or Kohlberg provided theories that describe relatively invariant stages of structural psychic change (cf. LaVoie, 1994). As discussed earlier, the identity statuses were originally postulated in terms of a developmental sequence akin to a series of structural substages of the identity stage. Empirical evidence has not born this out, however, so some assumptions have been revised given the results of a number of empirical studies (e.g., Marcia et al., 1993). This evidence led Waterman (1988) to observe that "there is now general agreement that the identity statuses cannot be ordered along a continuum from a weak to a strong identity. Rather, the identity statuses are a typology, i.e., qualitatively different approaches to the task of identity formation" (pp. 198-199). Elsewhere, he describes the identity status paradigm as "a descriptive model rather than a theory of development, since there are virtually no patterns of identity status change inconsistent with it" (Waterman, 1982, p. 343).

Given that only a minority of the population achieve an identity according to this paradigm, does this mean that most of the adult population does not have an identity? Such a position would be tenable only from a purely psychological perspective based on Western conceptions of self (cf. Baumeister, 1986). From a sociological perspective, everyone has an identity in relation to a social location (even homeless people have social and personal identities). Côté and Levine (1988) were interpreted as charging that the identity status paradigm is elitist for suggesting that there may be an overreliance on the notion that an identity must be achieved to be valid, with the rebuttal that there is a freedom of choice in entering the achievement status (Waterman, 1988; see also LaVoie, 1994; Marcia, 1989a).

Part of the confusion here seems to be with the level of analysis, in that distinctions need to be made among the social, personal, and subjective dimensions of identity. But part of the confusion also seems to stem from basic notions regarding the chain of causation of human behavior. Obviously, identity achievement as formulated with this paradigm involves choice, but even in the simple case of the politics of choice, only in a world of unconstrained choice would identity achievement operate independent of the power and privilege created by social context, particularly in domains such as occupational identity. Clearly, normative and cultural pressures can militate against such unfettered choices, as can a basic lack of awareness that this is what one can, or should, do. As Erikson (1959) wrote, "In America the image of free choice often becomes a dilemma because there are rather definite social and economic mechanisms by which the individual is forced into certain choices" (p. 78).

Others have commented on the question of the developmental relevance of the identity status paradigm. Grotevant (1986) writes that "because there does not appear to be one single developmental sequence for the identity statuses . . . the statuses are less useful than might be desired for making developmental comparisons" (p. 176). Instead, as is now well-known by identity status researchers, development occurs in varying patterns and at different times for different domains. From a contextual point of view, this suggests that contemporary U.S. adolescence involves traveling a long and winding road rather than a straight and narrow path. If we follow the sociological axiom that "social organization is the principle of self-organization" (Weigert et al., 1986, p. 5), then it follows that if the social *institution* of adolescence is complex and disorganized, identity formation among individuals exposed to those institutions will be complex and disorganized as well.

LaVoie (1994) also comments on this problem, noting a "failure to address the mechanisms involved in the transition between statuses even though . . . identity [is recognized] as a developmental process." He also writes that "available data are not supportive of a common structure" that might link possible identity domains, and he concludes that the "structural components of identity are still in question, especially the matter of a deep structure" (pp. 23-26). This observation suggests that we should look to the context of development, rather than only to the inner workings of the individual, to see if there are social influences militating against the formation of a deep structure of identity. More specifically, we need to investigate whether cultural forces are creating a disarray of identity domains and a muddled identity formation. I believe that this is a serious possibility to investigate, particularly in view of sociological works that have alerted us to conditions associated with so-called postmodern society. It may be that the original formulations of the identity status paradigm are more suited to a passing era where it has been more feasible to experience an orderly identity formation based on a continuous underlying identity structure (cf. Gergen, 1991, 1992; Stafseng, 1994). later in this chapter, I present a framework to help evaluate this possibility.

In view of these problems, it seems appropriate to take seriously Snarey, Kohlberg, and Noam's (1983) point that Erikson's identity stage is a *functional phase* defined in terms of both psychic structure and cultural elements. With this in mind, reactions to the identity stage could then be viewed in terms of how cultural contexts, in conjunction with individuals' inner workings of ego identity formation, produce various reactions, some of which become modal or predominant in a culture. In this way, each culture may have its own set or sets of identity statuses that represent modal patterns of identity that can take individuals toward maturity. One obstacle to reconsidering Erikson's notion of the single stage appears to be a tendency to conflate the identity stage with adolescence, including a reification of adolescence based on its U.S.-European manifestations. Adolescence in Western cultures has been unprecedented in terms of how loosely it is structured and how much the individual is given the task of identity construction or the puzzle of identity discovery (cf. Côté & Allahar, 1994). In contrast, other developmental theories (e.g., Piaget's) have not tied themselves so closely to Western adolescence as the main frame of reference for their concepts (see Snarey et al., 1983, for distinctions among structural stages, cultural ages, and functional phases).

This latter approach seems to be a reasonable one for identity status researchers to take, given the weight of empirical evidence. Accordingly, an identity status should not be seen as an exclusive property of an individual, attributable only to inner workings. This sociological position will become clearer, but I will illustrate here with a cross-cultural contrast of a developing country—Western Samoa (Côté, 1994). In this illustration, we also have the benefit of a historical record provided by anthropologist Margaret Mead during the 1920s—one of the few such records regarding non-Western forms of adolescence.

On the question of cross-cultural applications of the identity status paradigm, Samoan culture before contact with the West would be called a *foreclosed society* (Marcia, 1976). However, for Erikson, individuals in all societies should have a generally good sense of ego identity as temporal-spatial continuity if they are effectively supported by their community. In foreclosed societies, such as precontact Samoa, choice-based forms of identity referred to by identity status researchers would not have been common, but it would be culturally inappropriate to have such an individualistic identity (cf. Marcia, 1993a). Instead, my research supports Mead's conclusion that passage through the identity stage was well-structured and orderly for most young people, something that has progressively broken down over the history of contact with the West (Côté, 1994). My point, then, is that instead of the form of ego development associated with identity achievement that helps people function in middle-class urban U.S. environments, individuals in such well-ordered, foreclosed societies are likely to develop other personality strengths that help them function and continue to mature in those environments. In fact, additional ego development was likely to be stimulated as Samoans passed through Erikson's last three psychosocial stages of intimacy, generativity, and integrity. All three of these stages appear to have been well-institutionalized in precontact Samoan culture, and in Erikson's view, the better institutionalized a stage, the more it can nurture ego development (Erikson, 1963).

On the issue of choice, some Western readers may feel that the relative lack of choice in such a society may be stress-producing and an impediment to development for many adolescents in any culture. This may be so for some individuals, but if we use Mead's study as a reference point, it is unlikely that more than a handful of her informants were bothered by it (Côté, 1994). Certainly, there is ample evidence that Samoan child-rearing techniques and cultural conditioning prepared those coming of age for this, by effecting a high degree of conformity-oriented behavior and a low degree of individuated or creative behavior (e.g., Holmes, 1987). Indeed, similar child-rearing techniques prevail in other South Pacific cultures. As Crocombe (1989) argues, in many South Pacific cultures, typical socialization is such that individuals "have been conditioned by their cultures not to 'push' themselves. . . . Much of their cultural conditioning has taught them not to innovate, not to work out their own destiny, not to strive to improve their position" (p. 40). Erikson (1959) touched on this issue in reference to the dilemma of choice being a particular problem in a culture in which there seems to be a great deal of choice. He continued by contrasting choice-oriented and conformity-oriented cultures, noting that they are

> relative matters and we need to examine . . . the specific relationship of choice to conformity in various cultures. Inner identity . . . is a combination of the two; for I cannot feel identical with myself if I do not feel identical with something that has been created and distilled in my culture over a long period. To be firmly told by tradition who one is can be experienced as freedom; while the permission to make original choices can feel like enslavement to some dark fate. (p. 78)

The implications of cultural conditioning for the politics of choice in relation to the identity status paradigm emerge from one of the cross-cultural studies conducted using that paradigm. In New Zealand, Chapman and Nichols (1976) assessed *occupational* identity status among Maori (Polynesian descent) and Pakeha (European descent) high school students. They found that more Maori youth were identity diffused (not committed to an occupation and had not seriously contemplated possible occupations), whereas more Pakeha youth were identity achieved. These findings were interpreted with the assertion that "Maoris typically see occupation as a means of providing the necessities of life and of making it possible to extend hospitality while Pakeha more commonly see occupations as a vehicle to and index of success" (Chapman & Nichols, 1976, p. 65). Noting differing cultural meanings regarding choice and commitment around occupation, Chapman and Nichols argue that the "greater frequency of identity diffusion among Maoris may indicate that this is an adaptive, role-appropriate status for Maoris" (p. 69).

The Chapman and Nichols (1976) study suggests several additional questions. For example, just why might something such as identity diffusion be adaptive for one group and not another? If it is adaptive, certain forms of ego and personal development must be associated with it. What are these and how do they take place? Hence, a specific research question that can be pursued is, "What replaces conscious decision-making as a source of ego development in conformity-oriented cultures?" One avenue to explore in this regard is the guidance the culture may provide the young that makes conscious decision making unnecessary as a stimulus to development. Erikson (1959) alluded to this when he wrote the following:

> Ego identity also rests on the inner continuity between what one was as a child and what one is going to be as an adult. Such inner continuity and sameness are supported by cultural processes so long as they function, with great sagacity. Rites, rituals, and traditions seek to give the individual a sense that, on each stage of his long childhood and apprenticeship, everything occurred in preordained steps, so that he who looks into his future and tests his opportunities will perceive his past stages as adding up to something. (p. 76)

We see from these considerations that when one attempts to apply the identity status paradigm cross-culturally, its implications are undertheorized and underresearched. I believe this is because its conceptual framework refers to inner workings far more than context. Because of this, the paradigm does not provide the theoretical concepts with which to understand the types of ego development that might be linked with specific social and cultural contexts, such as those that are not choice-oriented and self-oriented. In contrast, in Erikson's general theory, people of all cultures can develop a strong sense of ego identity based on role validation and community integration, especially when there is a lack of ambiguity regarding beliefs (cf. Côté & Levine, 1987). In speaking to this general issue, Erikson (1963) wrote that

> even the most "savage" culture must strive for what we . . . call a "strong ego" in its majority or at least in its dominant minority—i.e., an individual core firm and flexible enough to reconcile the necessary contradictions in any human organization, . . . and above all to emerge from . . . infancy with a sense of identity and an idea of integrity. (pp. 185-186)

Recently, Marcia (1993b) commented on this issue by arguing that cross-cultural validity "does not mean identical behavior. Foreclosures in a 'foreclosed' setting ought not to be found behaving exactly like Foreclosures in a setting that encourages moratoria." I agree but do not feel that the following position put forth by Marcia (1993a) takes us out of the conceptual dilemma: "Rather, cross-cultural validity means that, taking into account the processes underlying an identity status, one ought to be able to make verifiable predictions about that status's behavior in a given cultural context" (p. 41). The problem, as Chapman and Nichols's study suggests, is that in many cultural settings, Western-style identity status has little variation—it is almost constant. The question then becomes, "What variation exists with identity formation in, say, a foreclosed setting?" For example, in a conformity-oriented (foreclosed) culture, are there structural changes based on ritualized realignments of identifications (which would be missed and identity formation mislabeled as foreclosed)? These are the types of questions that need to be posed and explored. If we enter a culture with the Western paradigm of choice-driven development, we will not be sensitive to other bases of development (cf. Kroger, 1993b, pp. 11-12).

SOCIAL CONTEXT AND DEVELOPMENT

The issue of how social context affects human development constitutes perhaps the greatest challenge facing researchers. In my view, as should be clear by now, the best way to begin to approach this issue in the area of identity formation is to more clearly delineate the levels or dimensions of identity being explored. This should not only help us to more precisely characterize how social context affects identity in its various forms, but it should also help us avoid confusions and disagreements. For example, important differences may exist at the level of social identity but not ego identity; yet if we use only a global concept of identity, we will not only be imprecise but will be likely to disagree on matters of approach and interpretation.

Kroger (1993b) has noted that research exploring "the roles of culture, social class, ethnicity, and historical ethos . . . [in identity formation] has only just begun" (p. 11).[11] She is referring mainly to developmental-psychological approaches to identity formation, which have tended to undertheorize the social in its broadest sense.[12] Instead, early efforts were devoted mainly to immediate context variables, such as family background and educational settings, as indicated. Interest now appears to have turned to more general issues that have occupied public policy agendas, particularly ethnicity and gender, so I will focus on these issues here. It must be acknowledged from the outset, however, that ethnicity and gender are not social contexts per se. Rather, they are characteristics attributed to individuals that take on particular meanings within socially constructed cultural contexts.

Ethnicity

Initial attempts to study how social contexts affect adolescent development in this area have tended to view the social in terms of demographic-type variables like membership in ethnic groups. However, Phinney and Rosenthal (1992) argue that "ethnic identity . . . [is] a multifaceted, dynamic construct . . . with complex and subtle interactions between different elements of ethnic identity and external forces" (p. 148). They go on to note that simply treating ethnicity as group membership fails to distinguish ethnicity from ethnic identity, confusing the social and psychological dimensions of identity:

> While purporting to measure ethnic identity, researchers simply use ethnic group membership as a variable of interest, without assessing the adolescent's sense of belonging to the group (self-identification), evaluation of his or her group membership (ethnic pride), or any other aspect of ethnic identity. (p. 161)

Clearly, then, the task of assessing social context in relation to something like ethnic identity formation is extremely complex, making it difficult to establish developmental-contextual principles. The difficulties include (a) whether ethnicity or race is related to minority or majority status, (b) whether minority status is disparaged or admired, (c) whether the larger society is assimilationist or multicultural, and (d) how ethnicity and race interact with other factors such as gender (Phinney & Rosenthal, 1992).[13] Accordingly, every adolescent has an ethnicity but its salience is society-dependent as are the combinations and permutations of relations when the social context includes numerous ethnic groups (as in multicultural cities such as Toronto). Moreover, race and ethnicity are more social constructions than genetic realities, suggesting that there are great individual variations in how they are perceived and therefore how they affect the psychological elements of identity.

In terms of psychological reactions to these complexities of social context, researchers are investigating how individuals can move through qualitatively different ways of conceiving of their relationships with other racial-ethnic groups, especially the dominant group(s). These structural changes in ethnic identity formation are often accompanied by dissonance, conflict, and ambivalence (Markstrom-Adams & Beale-Spencer, 1994)—features of the identity crisis that can be difficult to assess empirically.

To cite one concrete illustration of this complexity, it has been noted that certain types of ethnic identity formation may *require* a rejection of the dominant culture. As Markstrom-Adams and Beale-Spencer (1994) note:

> It is precisely those normal, developmentally appropriate processes that make youths painfully aware of the discrepancies in opportunity that the environment holds for them. Thus, their own normal and healthy development . . . leads them to increasingly tune out the larger society to secure self-perceptions as persons of value. (p. 87)

This healthy defensiveness might explain why, for instance, minority youth are no more likely than other adolescents to suffer from low self-esteem. Instead, self-esteem can depend on subjective elements of identity formation that interact with numerous contextual factors associated with family, school, and peers (Phinney & Rosenthal, 1992,

p. 165). On the other hand, certain minority youth may experience lower levels of self-efficacy (Gecas & Burke, 1995).

Understandably, this area is still in search of "a solid theoretical base [that integrates] developmental and social psychological perspectives, together with a consideration of contextual factors" (Phinney & Rosenthal, 1992, p. 166). Research using the dominant psychological perspective (the identity status paradigm) has provided a model by which the outcomes of ethnic identity formation can be studied in terms of the crisis-commitment matrix (e.g., Markstrom-Adams & Beale-Spencer, 1994; Phinney & Rosenthal, 1992). But the starting point for a contextual model, in my view, is to carefully distinguish among the dimensions of identity within a theory that stipulates how macrosocial contexts vary and change and how these varied and changing macrocontexts can affect interactional and subjective-psychological aspects of identity. Readers are referred to several recent reviews of the pioneering attempts to understand the principles involved in ethnic-racial contexts of identity formation (especially Markstrom-Adams & Beale-Spencer, 1994; Phinney & Rosenthal, 1992; Rotheram-Borus & Wyche, 1994).

Gender

The study of gender differences in identity formation seems to have especially suffered from a lack of attention to the distinct levels of identity and to an undertheorizing of the social. Psychologists have focused almost entirely on the subjective aspects of identity formation, often writing as if this is all one needs to know in understanding how males and females might function in the social world. Moreover, as was the case regarding ethnicity, it has been assumed that simple group membership (i.e., being female or male) is all one needs to make predictions, instead of looking at more complex notions such as gender identity (i.e., how much one identifies oneself as male or female, masculine or feminine; see especially, Matteson, 1993; also see Gecas & Burke, 1995, for parallel sociological views). Such simple conceptualizations ignore intragender differences, thereby perpetuating gender stereotypes. Theoretically driven typologies and dimensions characterizing differences among females and differences among males need to be developed and tested to take us beyond this impasse. Several articles have presented models that try to understand intragender differences in a theoretical manner (e.g.,

Côté, 1986b; Hodgson & Fischer, 1981), but little follow-up work has been done in further researching and testing these models.

In addition to these conceptual problems, methodological problems abound. For example, these psychological components of identity have been explored almost entirely among small, nonrandom samples of high school and university students, making it unclear how the research findings might be generalized to larger populations. As such, we do not know how these results are affected by selection factors associated with class, ethnicity, or age,[14] not to mention culture and nationality (i.e., most studies have been done on American samples). Many sociologists view research such as this with a degree of skepticism, seeing it as particularly problematic to undertake an analysis of gender—treating it as *the* master status—when a full analysis must include variables such as race-ethnicity, class, age, culture, and historical era.

To illustrate, it is possible that race is more important for certain dimensions of identity formation than gender, such that depending on their class and age, women of a given race may subjectively experience more in common with men of their own race than with women of another race as they form their sense of identity; moreover, in terms of actual social identity (as per their social location), they may objectively have more in common with their brothers (cf. Brand, 1987; Espin & Gawelek, 1992).[15] Rotheram-Borus and Wyche (1994) refer to this issue in the following manner:

> Some evidence exists that gender and ethnicity interactively influence personality development. . . . It also appears that minority adolescents are socialized into gender roles that differ from those of European-American males and females, . . . and that gender stereotyping is less salient within some ethnic groups than within the European-American group. . . . Because the gender roles of a youth's ethnic group and socioeconomic status will define the context of his or her search to a significant extent, research in this area is greatly needed in the future. (p. 68)

With these caveats in mind, we can now examine the literature that has dominated this area. A survey of the identity status literature on this topic reveals a certain amount of confusion in terms of how to characterize gender differences. The earliest research from the 1970s revealed gender differences that seem to have disappeared during the 1980s. Whether this was due to changing historical circumstances or changing methodologies is not known (Marcia, 1993b), but the general consensus seems to be that among contemporary American high school and college-attending youth, there are no significant differences in how and when females and males form their adult identities. That is, there appears to now be agreement that there are no meaningful differences in the processes by which psychological aspects of identity come together (i.e., the frequencies and subjective meanings of the identity statuses) and when they come together (Archer, 1993; Marcia, 1993b; Waterman, 1993). On the other hand, reliable differences seem to have been identified in terms of the domains or content areas around which identity issues are explored. Archer (1993) summarized these findings as follows:

> Gender differences were found in the domains of sexuality (Waterman & Nevid, 1976), family/career prioritizing (Archer, 1985), and friendship (Thorbecke & Grotevant, 1982), but not on vocation, religious beliefs, sex roles, values, dating, and so forth. In each case of significant gender differences, females have been more likely to be identity achieved or in moratorium and males, foreclosed or diffuse, reinforcing the female self-in-relation expectation. But females have been as likely as males to be self-defined in the intrapersonal domains as well. (p. 85)

In other words, more females studied appeared to be exploring issues related to real life concerns in a world of changing gender roles, thereby increasing the complexity of their identity formation (whereas fewer males appeared to be as concerned with these gender-related issues). As Waterman (1993) put it,

> The task of identity formation is more complex for females than for males in that they endeavor to work out for themselves their goals, values, and beliefs in more domains than do males. Not only do females experience the desire to establish their sense of identity in vocational choice, religious beliefs, political ideology, and sex-role attitudes in the same manner as males, but they engage in more active reflection and decision-making regarding identity in a relational context than do their male counterparts. (p. 62)

This current consensus regarding gender differences in the psychological dimensions of identity appears reasonable but needs to be carefully examined on several grounds. For example, as mentioned earlier, this consensus is based on a few small, selective samples. For sociologists, sample size and the way samples are selected are particularly important if one wants to draw conclusions about whole populations. Moreover, the samples cited by Archer (1993) and Waterman (1993) are often restricted by age to early adolescence to midadolescence, whereas important aspects of gender identity formation often do not take place until early adulthood (and according to Marcia, 1989a, the identity statuses were intended as outcome styles applicable to late adolescence between the ages of 18 to 22). That is, identity formation among contemporary American adolescents is mostly a psychological preparation or anticipation of early adulthood, but it is during early adulthood that this preparation meets social reality, often requiring further formation as an adult social identity is actually adopted (cf. Sexton, 1979).[16]

When a broader perspective is taken, especially to include older women, a somewhat different position is reached, as in a review by Patterson, Sochting, and Marcia (1992), who conclude that gender differences in identity formation are a result of women's greater interpersonal connectedness. They submit that these differences include (a) interpersonal content areas during adolescence, (b) timing in later life (crises after children become sufficiently autonomous), (c) sequencing with other stages (e.g., identity and intimacy being interconnected), and (d) context (identity derived from relationships, which can vary historically). Their conclusions are extensions of Erikson's (1968) postulations, based on their review of empirical evidence, that inner space issues (interpersonal aspects of identity) are more important for women, and outer space issues (vocational and ideological concerns) are more important for men.[17]

It is on these latter issues that the consensus again appears to break down. There appears to be an ambivalence over how to characterize any sources of differences in experiences between men and women. Archer (1992) writes that she is troubled by the intrapersonal-interpersonal methodology because it "is grounded in a traditional Eurocentric perspective" (p. 36).[18] She goes on to give the example of religious beliefs, stating that they have been viewed as intrapersonal, when in fact they are formed in the interpersonal realm. From a sociological perspective, such statements epitomize the failure of the developmental-psychological perspective to appreciate the multidimensionality of identity and its contexts.[19] Religious beliefs are indeed personal and interpersonal, but religious behaviors are generally public, especially in their formalized aspects (e.g., in most religions, most clerics are men, whereas women are proscribed from formal involvement at this level, which produces obvious differences in social identity). As much as people can live in their own psychological worlds in contemporary society, there are still social contextual realities restricting how much this psychic reality can be actualized as they are channeled into various social roles; indeed, belief may be only loosely related to behavior, as is well established in social psychology. Again, the psychological preparations for adult identity undertaken during adolescence may have little to do with the actual social identities arrived at in adulthood.

For these reasons, a position that ignores or denies the relevance of traditional and persistent gender role segregation (de jure and de facto) fails to fully appreciate the relevance of social identity in affecting the overall behavioral repertoire of the individual. This failure becomes glaring when one looks at the actual distribution of roles and division of labor, not only in American society (on which most of this research is based) but in virtually all societies throughout the world and throughout history. Despite progress in equalizing gender roles, there *are* persistent differences in the positions of men and women in American and other Western societies. To underestimate these is to exhibit what has been called a *beta bias*—namely, to underestimate the extent of gender differences (as opposed to the alpha bias, which overestimates certain differences; Hare-Musten & Marecek, 1988).

This problem can be understood by examining how sociologists have approached differences in social identity. When sociologists refer to identity and gender, they often speak of key aspects of social identity and make note of the differential allocation of social roles and the division of labor in a culture. These differences in social identity in the modern era can be understood in terms of a conceptualization that sees women to have been traditionally found mainly in what is referred to as the private sphere and men mainly in the public sphere. Lengerman and Wallace (1985) define these spheres as follows:

> *Public sphere* refers to the complex, bureaucratically organized institutions of modern life: the economy, the state, formal education, organized religion, the professions and unions, the mass media of

communication and entertainment. . . . *Private sphere* refers to the less
formal, emotionally more open networks of social relationships that
coexist with the public sphere: marriage, family, kin, neighborhood,
community, friendship. (p. 107)

They observe that societal power centers lie in this public sphere,
whereas the private sphere exercises less formal power and is heavily
affected by the public one (cf. Lipman-Blumen, 1984). But to the point
at hand, they argue that the "hallmark of the conventional gender
arrangements is that women have restricted access to the public
sphere, whereas men have restricted participation in the private
sphere" (Lengerman & Wallace, 1985, p. 107). Indeed, it is rather
pedestrian to note that much of the women's movement in Western
societies has involved the effort of giving women equal access to the
public sphere as well as encouraging men to take a more active role
in the private one.

Given the relative segregation into separate spheres, it follows that
men and women are traditionally channeled and conditioned to base
their social identities on those roles available to them (Côté & Allahar,
1994). It also follows that more women would define themselves, and
be defined, according to relationships in the private sphere, whereas
men would define themselves, and be defined, according to their
relationships in the public sphere. Over this century, but especially
in the past two decades, there have been radical changes in these
arrangements, with women having considerable access to the public
sphere along with "a searching and critical review of gender arrangements in the private sphere, and fairly energetic efforts to rework
various of those arrangement[s]" (Lengerman & Wallace, 1985, p. 108).
As such, it follows that certain aspects of identity formation have
changed for both men and women but especially those who are
making the effort to cross spheres—and in every Western country
studied so far, more women are doing so than men (e.g., Anderson,
1991).[20]

With these qualifications, we can now reassess the question of the
sources of gender differences in identity. Notwithstanding the conceptual and methodological problems so far identified and based on
the research done largely with American samples, it appears that at
the psychological level there are no differences, or few of significance,
in terms of the processes by which females and males form their sense
of identity. That is, the psychic mechanisms appear to be the same.

At the level of social identity, however, it appears that when males and females are compared as groups (thereby allowing for intragender variation), differences still emerge along the private-public dimension that has dominated modern Western societies, as evidenced by persisting differences in the actual roles assumed in adulthood as well as differential participation in the formal governing institutions.[21]

Last, although not researched widely, gender differences at the level of personal identity are obvious in terms of gender displays of masculinity and femininity in the presentation of self during day-to-day activities (e.g., Goffman, 1976). These displays appear to be nurtured and exaggerated in adolescence by socially produced gender intensification processes (cf. Côté & Allahar, 1994).

When the findings based on the identity status paradigm are reinterpreted in these sociological terms, the differences in domain are understandable in reference to a changing social context by which Western women have gained more access to the public sphere previously dominated by men, and no longer are they as restricted to the private sphere (cf. Marcia, 1993b, p. 39). As a socialization task, therefore, identity formation appears to differ mainly in terms of complexity, with more women than men tackling issues in both spheres as they form their identities. Women who move into the public sphere apparently find it necessary to balance issues associated with both private and public, often negotiating them with significant others as they go along (Kroger, 1983). Moreover, it has been suggested that the pattern seems to involve dealing with the private sphere first, before moving into the public sphere, but this needs to be further examined (Thorbecke & Grotevant, 1982). The majority of men, in contrast, seem to have been less willing to interconnect the public and private, preferring the public; when they do make links, they apparently deal with them as independent issues (Marcia, 1993b; Waterman, 1993).[22] For these reasons, identity formation currently appears to be more complex for those women who attempt to form an identity connected with both the private and public spheres. It also maybe the case that for these nontraditional postadolescent women, timing and sequencing differ from those men and women who pursue their respective traditional spheres (cf. Côté, 1986b; Patterson et al., 1992; Sexton, 1979).[23]

One final point involves a consideration of gender identity. As mentioned earlier, many researchers have turned to studying ethnic identity rather than simple ethnicity because group membership takes on different meanings for different members. Those studying gender might consider following suit.

According to Gecas and Burke (1995), "gender identities are the socially defined self-meanings of masculinity/femininity one has as a male or female member of society and are inherently derived from and tied to social structure" (p. 54). Apparently, consistent differences among the identity statuses have been found on measures of gender identity. For example, in a recent review of the literature, Marcia (1993b) concludes that "across various measures of identity, intimacy, and sex-role typing, the relationships among androgyny, high intimacy, and high identity, as well as between masculinity and identity and femininity and intimacy are fairly well established" (p. 40). If researchers are to persist in examining only the psychological dimension of identity, it seems reasonable that they include a gender identity measure in their research rather than to make blanket generalizations regarding males and females as if they are all the same (see Matteson, 1993, for a detailed discussion of this and related issues). This seems particularly reasonable given that women are now freer in Western societies to be the architects of their own identities more so than in the past, giving rise to possibly greater intragender variation, as gender-role allocation has become less oppressive (cf. Giddens, 1991).

NEW DIRECTIONS: THEORIZING IDENTITY AND CULTURE

Given the importance of understanding the effect of social context on identity formation and the need for a workable, multidimensional conceptual framework, I offer a series of interrelated postulates regarding some broad contextual parameters affecting identity formation. This framework, which integrates sociological and psychological perspectives on identity, speaks to the role of historical ethos and culture in identity formation. It should be noted, however, that these are not developmental postulates per se.

The framework for the culture-identity link (Figure 5.1) is presented as a series of postulates and concepts that build on each other. In the tradition of social theory, this framework should be judged largely as a heuristic middle-range theory (Merton, 1957) whose

	Social Structure	
Premodern →	Early modern → (productive)	Late modern (consumptive)
	Socializing Institutions	
Postfigurative →	Cofigurative →	Prefigurative
	Modal Character Types	
Tradition directed →	Inner directed →	Other directed
	Cultural Ideal of Identity Formation Patterns	
Social identity		
Ascribed →	Achieved (socially) →	Managed
Personal identity		
Heteronomous →	Individuated →	Image-oriented
Ego identity		
Structure		
Foreclosed →	Achieved → (psychologically)	Diffused
Process		
Adopted →	Constructed →	Discovered
	Predominant Motivational Patterns	
Abnormal patterns (negatively sanctioned)		
Anomic crisis →	Perennial crisis →	No crisis
Cultural metaphor (positively sanctioned)		
Identity = role →	Identity = choice →	Identity = image
Emotional control (approach-avoidance sanction)		
Shame →	Guilt →	Shame-anxiety

Figure 5.1. A Framework for the Culture-Identity Link

value lies in its logical consistency, connections with established knowledge, and its empirical correspondence.

The typologies used in this framework are meant as ideal types or abstractions that represent a pure form of a social reality.[24] As such, they are meant to provide simplified models of the cultural patterns that set the standards regarding the possibilities and limitations of social behavior.[25] It must also be noted, however, that more than one pattern can exist in a society, particularly in a pluralistic or multicultural one (although the one used by the dominant group will tend to set the standard). Consequently, there may be fusions among the patterns in a given society and there may be cultural lags, whereby previously predominant patterns persist in certain subcultures, social classes, rural areas, and religious and ethnic-racial subcultures.

It can be seen in the top portion of Figure 5.1 that three levels of analysis are specified vertically. These range from the macrostructural (social structure) through the microinteractional (socializing institutions) to the individual-psychological (modal character types). In addition, three periods of macrostructural change are specified horizontally, producing a three-by-three typology. The periods of macrostructural social change are meant to characterize what has happened over the past several centuries among Western societies and societies influenced by the West. Other sociologists have differing versions of this change, but I believe this typology is defensible on several grounds, as I will argue.

In reference to the level of macrostructure, the distinction between premodern and early modern society constitutes a widely accepted distinction between folk and urban society, a distinction that has been referred to in other terms, such as agrarian versus industrial or Gemeinschaft versus Gesellschaft (e.g., Tonnies, 1887/1955; Wirth, 1938). In Western societies, this transformation was largely completed during the 19th century. The distinction between early modern and late modern is a less accepted one, but my intention here is to focus on what has happened during the 20th century, a period of more rapid social change. I prefer to speak of the early modern period as an era of modernism in which production was a defining feature of social relations. Over this century, however, consumption increased in importance as a defining feature of social relations and identity, with production declining in relative importance as technology has supplanted labor (cf. Giddens, 1991).[26]

Moving to the interactional level, three institutional patterns corresponding to the structural change previously mentioned can be identified with regard to socializing institutions that constitute the action link between culture and the individual. These patterns have already been theorized by Margaret Mead (1970) in her underrecognized book, *Culture and Commitment*. Mead refers to these patterns as figures or models representing three kinds of socialization patterns (cf. Muuss, 1988). The three patterns are *"postfigurative*, in which children learn primarily from their forebears, *cofigurative*, in which both children and adults learn from their peers, and the *prefigurative*, in which adults learn also from their children" (Mead, 1970, p. 1). (Note that her prefixes tend to be counterintuitive—she means *post* to refer to the past, and *pre* to refer to the future; see Muuss, 1988, for a discussion of this formulation.)

To elaborate, associated with premodern societies are postfigurative patterns in which the relations between parents and their offspring are governed by traditional norms that are beyond questioning by either parent or child. The postfigurative pattern is stabilized by the coresidence of three generations and the ascription of adult roles as each generation comes of age.

For Mead, the cofigurative pattern is one in which the intergenerational linkage becomes tenuous, and offspring look to nontraditional sources for their adult identity (e.g., their contemporaries). In this context, there is a fundamental change in the relation between parent and child where the authority of the parent can be questioned and where the child can actually give direction to the parent. For this reason, the eventual adult identity of offspring is no longer taken for granted by either parent or child. Last, in the prefigurative pattern, there is less conception of what the future holds for offspring and the life experiences of parents are of less use to offspring, so their guidance is less highly regarded.

Most germane to our present concerns is Mead's contention that the gap between parents and offspring that opened in the cofigurative pattern is widened in the prefigurative one. In fact, in this type of culture, the young can teach and guide their parents to the point of the parents becoming subservient to them in various ways.[27] In more contemporary sociological language, this leaves those coming of age with the task of becoming the primary architects of their own identities (cf. Giddens, 1991). Such a task often has to be carried out in the midst of internal conflict, confrontations with their parents and parental surrogates, or both. This is especially the case to the extent that offspring reject the content of their early socialization and attempt to replace it with new content (cf. Côté & Levine, 1992). Because of the increasing incoherence of the world for the novitiate and the increasing exploitiveness of that world toward them, this appears an inevitability for many of those now coming of age (cf. Côté & Allahar, 1994).

As we move from the interactional level to the individual-psychological level, it follows that in a given culture, the socializing influence of institutions nurtures certain personality characteristics and therefore favors the development of certain character types. Anthropologists such as Margaret Mead and Ruth Benedict favored this view (e.g., Benedict, 1938; Mead, 1930/1969), but little work has been done since the 1950s. The implication is, though, that character types should be found that represent cultural pressures interacting with human temperaments and dispositions at critical periods in development (cf. Snarey et al. 1993, and the functional phase concept). Moreover, individual differences in character should be distributed around predominant or modal cultural character types (cf. Côté, 1993).

A relevant formulation that has been very influential in sociology comes from David Riesman's (1950) classic, *The Lonely Crowd*. Riesman argues for three character types that coincidentally fit with the structural and interactional patterns identified. He argues that a *tradition-directed* character type characterizes premodern societies, "wherein the important relationships of life [are] . . . controlled by careful and rigid etiquette, learned by the young during the years of intensive socialization that end with initiation into full adult membership" (p. 11). This character type is heteronomous, and "the range of choice . . . is minimal, [so] the apparent social need for an individuated type of character is minimal" (p. 12).

In what correspond to early modern societies, Riesman (1950) notes that *inner-directed* character types emerge as "the principal mode of securing conformity" (p. 14). To counteract the disruptive influences of early industrialization (associated with geographical mobility, urbanization, capital accumulation, and mass production), individuals are socialized with a metaphorical gyroscope that "is implanted early in life by the elders and directed toward generalized but nonetheless inescapably destined goals" (p. 15). Accordingly, parents come to see their offspring as "individuals with careers to make" (p. 17). In this context, inner-directed persons exercise choice and initiative, but the general heading and pattern of acceptable behavior is set before they embark on their careers. The resulting individuality is not a threat to the social and economic order because the person is self-governing, equipped with this gyroscope (or superego, in Freudian terms).

The third character type arises under conditions that resemble late modern society, which was emerging when Riesman (1950) wrote in midcentury. As the means of mass production became mastered and abundance became more taken for granted, the "scarcity" psychology of the inner-directed was supplanted by an "abundance" psychology that gave rise to what he called the *other-directed* character type. Hence, in late modern society, the overproduction that results from technological advances is met with heightened consumerism. In other words, with production problems mastered, a late modern society needs consumption on a large scale, otherwise capital accumulation suffers.

Complementary to mass consumption are mass insecurities regarding whether the right things are done and said. For the population to engage in mass consumption, mass insecurities are necessary in the sense that consumption promises to alleviate anxiety if the right things are consumed.[28] Now, "other people are the problem, not the material environment" (Riesman, 1950, p. 18), and consumption emerges as a way of identifying and maintaining one's loyalties and relationships. Consequently, the other-directed character is sensitive to others—to their opinions and their approval. Riesman uses the metaphor of radar to characterize this orientation, whereby individuals are taught early in life to constantly monitor the social environment to ensure that their consumption patterns (especially in appearance and behavior) conform to the accepted standards of the time and place. The other-directed person strives to meet goals, but those goals can shift, and it is staying in tune with the shifts that are of paramount importance to this character type. We can also see how the prefigurative socialization mechanisms Mead postulated can contribute to other-directedness. That is, with parents providing less guidance and having less influence over their children's identity formation, children will turn to others for direction. To the extent that this becomes culturally conditioned, it should become part of the individual's character.

This typology can help us to organize a number of the identity concepts that have been generated over the past several decades. For example, the term *identity* has been used in many ways to emphasize different facets of human self-definition (cf. Gecas & Burke, 1995). However, the framework suggests the following taxonomy: (a) that the term *social identity* designate the individual's position(s) in a social structure, (b) that the concept of *personal identity* denote the more concrete aspects of individual experience rooted in interactions (and institutions), and (c) that the notion of *ego identity* refer to the more fundamental subjective sense of continuity and sameness that is characteristic of the personality. In this way, these terms need not be in competition with each other. Rather, they can be seen as attempts to map out different facets of the interdisciplinary terrain.

This taxonomy of identity concepts is presented in the middle of Figure 5.1 as a more specific reproduction of the conceptual cross-tabulation of the top portion. In other words, vertically, the representations of identity formation patterns depicted in the middle of the figure are logically linked with the structural, institutional, and character patterns just discussed. And, horizontally, these identity concepts are meant to depict the cultural prototype that is imitated at each period of macrostructural change.

Social identity formation is postulated to differ in each type of society, such that according to the particular cultural prototype, it tends to be *ascribed* in premodern societies, (socially) *achieved* in early modern societies, and *managed* in late modern ones. These terms can be defined as follows: ascribed means assigned on the basis of some inherited status; achieved is used in the sociological sense by which social position is to be accomplished on one's own; and managed means reflexively and strategically fitting oneself into, and maintaining oneself in, a community of strangers by meeting their approval through the creation of the right impressions (cf. Gecas & Burke, 1995). In other words, in premodern society, social identity is largely determined by one's characteristics or attributes (such as race, sex, parents' social status); in early modern society, it is increasingly based on personal accomplishment and material attainment (both of which are ostensibly based on appraisals of merit), whereas in late-modern society, it becomes a matter of impression management, during which identity displays are employed to gain acceptance from others who often have little knowledge of one's social background or accomplishments.

At the interactional level of socializing institutions (i.e., the interpersonal world where culture and individual meet), personal identity is largely *heteronomous*, then *individuated*, and then *image-oriented* as we move through the three types of societies. The heteronomous identity is based on an uncritical acceptance of others' appraisals and expectations, which produces a conformist and mechanical blending into a community; the individuated identity is one that is based on the production of a distinctive personal style and role repertoire by which the person's biography leads to an organic integration into a community; and the image-oriented identity is based on a projection of images that meet the approval of a community, gaining one access so long as the images remain acceptable. Personal identity refers here to interpersonal styles that have been shaped by the actual life experiences of individuals; in a sense, it expresses the culmination of an individual's biography at a given point in time.

Last, at the level of character, two components of ego identity can be classified. In terms of the identity structure studied by identity status theorists, identity *foreclosure* predominates in premodern societies, (psychological) identity *achievement* is the prototypical structure in modern societies, and identity *diffusion* appears to be emerging as the predominant one in late-modern societies, if we follow the framework outlined earlier (cf. Berzonsky, 1993, p. 183). Marcia (1993b) defined identity structure as "how experience is handled as well as . . . what experiences are considered important [by an individual]." In terms of the processes by which identity is formed, premodern society requires its members to *adopt* their identity early in life; in early modern society, people are expected to *construct* their identities as they come of age; and in late modern society, individuals are encouraged to *discover* their identity through experience seeking (continually through the life-course) (cf. Gergen, 1991).

Last, and this is the most tentative portion of the framework, three sets of motivational patterns are represented at the bottom of Figure 5.1. The first refers to what can be called abnormal patterns of identity in the sense that the society would actively discourage such behavior. In premodern society, the anomic identity crisis (refusing to fit into a prescribed niche) would be punished because of the need for conformity and labor among members. In early modern society, the perennial or unresolved crisis would be negatively sanctioned because of the need for motivated and productive workers throughout adulthood. In late modern society, no clear abnormal pattern seems to have emerged, perhaps because it is too early to tell or perhaps because in this era of constantly shifting standards, basically anything goes when it comes to statements of identity. It is also possible that with social control mechanisms becoming looser or less effective as we move through the three types of societies, identity formation is affected in unforeseen ways (cf. Côté, 1994). In view of this, it would seem that not having an identity crisis around certain issues will be increasingly negatively sanctioned, given the need for a flexible, change-oriented population.

The second classification refers to the cultural metaphor that provides the guiding images of identity for a society. In premodern society, one's identity would be largely synonymous with one's adopted roles; in early modern, it should be shaped by one's constructed choices; in late modern society, it appears to be equated with discovered images.

The third classification is adapted from Riesman's (1950) discussion of character types. He argues that each character type has a distinctive "emotional sanction or control" (p. 24) that motivates the individual in approach-avoidance situations. Because the tradition-directed person experiences culture mediated through a small number of individuals on a day-to-day basis, "the sanction for behavior tends to be the fear of being shamed" (Riesman, 1950, p. 24; cf. Côté, 1994, regarding the role of shame in traditional Samoan culture). The inner-directed person is subject to less concrete controls because of independence from family of origin during adulthood but is motivated to conform to parentally derived internalizations out of guilt approach-avoidance.[29] And the other-directed person, who tries to stay tuned with current standards and trends to be sensitive to and please others, is motivated to avoid a sense of anxiety. Borrowing from Giddens (1991), I believe this is more appropriately called *shame anxiety* because the anxiety is about being shamed for not conforming to the latest changes.

This framework appears to provide a starting point from which to theorize the culture-identity link, and I encourage others to critically evaluate it. The chief benefit of such a framework is that it gives identity researchers from all disciplines common reference points from which to anchor concepts and hypotheses in a more cross-culturally and trans-historically sensitive manner.

The framework also has important implications for the identity status paradigm and suggests constructive avenues for advancement of that model. For example, disagreements over whether identity is constructed or discovered are both right, if they are placed in proper cultural context (identity is also adopted). The psychological achievement of identity is also placed in a useful cultural relief, as is the issue of the possible decline in the achieved identity. This issue is important given the apparent preference for identity achievement as a psychological outcome of identity formation (e.g., Archer, 1994). The framework also suggests that identity diffusion will become more commonplace in late modern society in response to socialization pressures encouraging other-directedness and enhanced impression management. Marcia (1989b) recently noted some evidence of an increase in identity diffusion.[30] Studies of large-scale representative samples using paper-and-pencil measures tapping various facets of identity could assess and monitor this.

The postulated increase of diffusion and decrease in achievement as styles of identity formation are accounted for within the framework in the following way: Late modern socialization pressures encourage other-directedness, enhanced impression management, and a desire to discover one's identity through image consumption (cf. Côté & Allahar, 1994). Image consumption has been introduced to successive cohorts throughout this century (especially since midcentury) by various profit-oriented industries via youth cultures and peer cultures. The heightened need to conform during the adolescent period has made it relatively easy for a pattern of image consumption to be introduced that involves an immediate-gratification orientation to enhancing one's physical and experiential self as deemed appropriate by others. Hence, it is now commonplace to adorn the body with various fashions, jewelry, and cosmetics to project particular images that please others while gratifying narcissistic desires, and it is customary to spend great amounts of time in experiences that similarly project images while gaining validation from others, through the consumption of music, mass media, computers and assorted games, and drugs. These all involve image consumption in the sense that illusions are used as a basis for key interactions with others.

The consequence of this as a mass phenomenon is the nurturance of a mass of consumers who have little concern regarding what the future holds and who are receptive to shifting trends and values. Those who reject their (premodern or early modern) culture of primary socialization may be particularly prone to this, given that they are not guided by or act in opposition to the gyroscope discussed by Reisman, thereby losing a basis for inner-directedness. In psychoanalytic terms, this signals an increasing id orientation and a decreasing superego orientation of the personality (cf. Côté, 1993).

The social structural changes associated with late modern society also help explain the disarray in the sequence and timing of transitions through the various identity domains, such that identity formation does not appear orderly for many young people (Kroger, 1993b). It is possible that the assumption of an orderly sequencing and a unitary underlying identity structure is more appropriate to conditions associated with early modern society and the inner-directed character type than with late modern society and its other-directed character types (cf. Stafseng, 1994). In addition, the identification of MAMA cycles (moratorium-achievement—moratorium-achievement) supports the notion that identity is relatively unstable in late modern society, given that some of the most developmentally advanced (according to that model) repeatedly revise their identities during their adulthoods (Stephan, Fraser, & Marcia, 1992).

CONCLUSION

Based on the foregoing critical analysis, I will conclude by attempting to answer the questions raised by John Hill at the beginning of this chapter.

With respect to the issue of whether the identity crisis is overestimated both in prevalence and in developmental significance, it appears that sometimes it is and sometimes it is not. It appears that the crisis-commitment form of crisis studied by the identity status paradigm has been overestimated in two ways: (a) in terms of its developmental significance, in that there is little orderly development, and (b) with regard to its prevalence, given that most of the adult population does not become identity achieved.

The dominance of the identity status has perhaps discouraged the investigation of other forms of the identity crisis, which may be more prevalent and more significant developmentally. For example, crises involving conscious and unconscious conflict resolutions may be more common than the crisis-commitment form, but this has not been thoroughly investigated at this point (see Côté, 1986a, for an operationalization of more conflict-based identity crises). The conflict-based crisis may involve no grand plan and may be more emotional than cognitive (involving ambivalence and resentment) but may still result in a realignment of identifications (cf. Erikson, 1968, 1979).

Yet another type of crisis may be associated with the reflexive project of self discussed by Giddens (1991) and others. This project can be seen as a crisis, especially in relation to identity formation in premodern societies (cf. Mead, 1928, 1969), and appears to be widespread in late modern societies in response to a deficit of meaningful social relations and a surfeit of superficial commodified identity fragments. Given that these conditions can encourage a dissipation rather than an accruing of self in late modern society, the reflexive project may be a poor path to follow in the sense of finding a viable resolution in an adult identity recognized by a stable community of others.

Yet another form of crisis may be so well institutionalized that it goes unnoticed, as in cases where the individual is guided through an identity transformation with community-sanctioned rituals (see Côté & Levine, 1987, for a discussion of various types of crises and stage resolutions).

A little-used quotation from Erikson (1959) helps highlight different forms of identity crisis and their import:

> The identity development of an individual is always anchored in the identity of his group; although through his identity he will seal his individual style. Of individual differences we may often not have the fullest perception. Especially in an alien culture we may see somebody going slowly through an identity crisis, in which conformity seems more emphasized than individuality. This very conformity may keep some aspects of the crisis from verbalization or awareness; only closer study could reveal it. Or the individual's experience may seem entirely submerged in rituals and procedures which seem to exaggerate the horror of individual decision and to offer, as a way out, the narrowest choice of models. *We will not know the nature of this process until we have learned to study its variations* [italics added]. (pp. 105-106)

To return to Hill's question, if we take Erikson's cross-cultural insight and superimpose it on what might be taking place in late modern society, I believe there is a danger in actually underestimating the prevalence and effects of the identity crisis. There is particularly a danger in its more extreme forms being taken as normal and natural aspects of development when they are a response to abnormal social conditions. Readers are reminded that Erikson (1968) originally conceived of the identity crisis when treating war trauma victims and that he drew a parallel between this type of pathology and the experiences of "severely conflicted young people whose sense of confusion is due to a war within themselves" (p. 17). The acceptance of extreme disturbances of identity as normal has been nurtured by the storm and stress model (Côté, 1994; Côté & Allahar, 1994). If we view the identity crisis against a backdrop of history and culture where this transition has normatively involved fitting into an adult role with relative ease, as in the preceding quotation from Erikson, we see that it has most likely taken rather benign and muted forms in the past. So, we should also be alert to the possibility that in late modern societies, forms of the identity crisis are widespread, even pathological and epidemic, when compared to premodern societies. Accordingly, I am wary of attempts to create or force crises as part of an attempt to stimulate development—there may be unintended and disastrous consequences for those individuals unequipped to handle them (Côté & Levine, 1987).

Hill's second question pertains to whether we could actually do without the concept of identity and use perhaps a simpler, more straightforward construct. I think not, because if we were to ignore it, we might then see disruptions in adolescent functioning as normal and natural and be prone to the perils just discussed. In fact, when viewed in terms of the notion of the intergenerational link—that identity formation is the intergenerational glue that holds cultures together—the question arises regarding whether cultural continuity is threatened, that is, whether we are we losing that continuity.[31] This certainly appears to be the case in many developing countries where the young have been culturally disenfranchised by Western influence (Côté, 1994).

As adults lose their conceptions of what the future holds, so do their young, but it becomes particularly difficult for the young to develop a firm sense of ego identity when their own future is uncertain. If we follow Mead's (1970) typology of socializing institutions, a pertinent question has to do with what follows the prefigurative culture. Does unified culture become untenable, and does the cycle begin over again after a breakdown of the identity-culture link? A total breakdown in authority is particularly troublesome inasmuch it sets the stage for arbitrary authority to assert itself by offering certainty in the face of uncertainty. At the risk of sounding melodramatic, certain aspects of late modern society bear a striking resemblance to Aldous Huxley's *Brave New World,* in which identities are managed by an authoritarian state, which predicates individual's identities on a conditioning into simple forms of consumption, production, ingratiation, impression management, and sensory gratification. In this light, I believe we should also be on guard against views that reify or uncritically glorify conditions associated with late modern society as if these conditions are an inevitable and natural unfolding of social evolution.[32]

Last, Hill asked whether the concept of identity increases our understanding of adolescence. Judging by the wealth of attention to the concept of identity, the answer is a resounding yes. This said, I believe it is important that researchers avoid confusing identity formation with adolescence itself. As indicated earlier, adolescence is a variable cultural institution that places different demands on identity formation depending on contemporaneous conditions. Adolescence can take an infinite number of forms, but ego identity is not entirely plastic if you grant that its sine qua non is temporal-spatial continuity. Indeed, the fact that adolescence takes so many forms helps account for the variety of identity crises discussed earlier, especially if we assume that some forms of the identity crisis reflect individual or collective reactions to problematic social contexts. And some of the ways in which adolescence is structured appear to make identity formation more difficult, exacerbating the identity crisis, whereas other structures appear to mitigate this crisis. Perhaps it is my affinity with early modern society, but I believe the heart of this area of study must maintain hold of the notion that the formation of the adult identity is what links generations and preserves the future. It is not necessarily the identity crisis that guards our future; rather, what guards our future is the welcoming of each new generation into the adult community by helping them develop viable, nonexploited identities in that community (cf. Côté & Allahar, 1994).

NOTES

1. See Kroger (1989) for a discussion of five models of identity formation, including Erikson's. See also Chickering's (1969) non-Eriksonian model of vectors of identity development among college students. Chickering's model has been especially popular among those working in university student services and university administrative offices.

2. When these assumptions regarding the fundamental nature of adolescence are translated into psychological terms, the sociological position basically corresponds to the learning theory approach in psychology and the general approach in cultural anthropology—namely, that adolescence is a culturally conditioned period of the life course and it therefore can vary dramatically from one culture to the next (cf. Côté & Allahar, 1994; Sprinthall & Collins, 1984).

3. An objective indicator of the increasing interest in identity can be found with CD-ROM searches of the psychological and sociological literature. A Sociofile search reveals that in 1987, some 568 works referred to the keyword *identity*. This number slowly increased to 703 in 1992, whereas it shot up to 1,367 in 1993 and to 1,922 in 1994. The psychological literature has been more stable, with between 1,000 and 1,100

references per year in PsycLit over the same period. However, the area of social identity increased steadily in PsychLit from 82 references in 1987 to 123 in 1993).

4. According to them, the concept of identity was imported into five different sociological traditions: (a) symbolic interactionism of the Chicago school (which emphasizes the processual and emergent nature of social reality), (b) symbolic interactionism of the Iowa school (which emphasizes the structural and fixed nature of social reality), (c) the sociology of knowledge, (d) structural functionalism, and (e) critical theory (Weigert et al., 1986).

5. Succinct definitions of postmodernity and postmodernism are difficult to provide, but there is now a voluminous literature on these topics (see Smart, 1993, for a review). The term *postmodernity*, however, basically refers to the social conditions that are arising as modernity breaks down or is being rejected. Thus, large-scale modernist institutions based on science, logic, and reason that posit objective realities are seen to be declining in relation to more nonrational, subjective, and relativistic social forms based on individualistic or smaller collective interests. The term *postmodernism* generally refers to those streams of thought that analyze or celebrate these changes. In spite of their currency, many social analysts express a dissatisfaction with these terms (e.g., Gergen, 1991; Giddens, 1991).

6. When the period of adolescence is examined by sociologists, there is a tendency to assume that adolescents face many of the same problems as everyone else in forming and sustaining an identity. The distinctiveness of modern societies lies principally with the marginalization faced by the young—they must make do with fewer resources than adults and construct identities in the face of these circumstances while attempting to separate from their families of origin (Côté & Allahar, 1994). For example, in reaction to an often rejecting and hostile adult world, youth subcultures emerge that provide more meaningful roles on which to predicate identities (e.g., Brake, 1985).

7. Briefly, four identity statuses are studied: identity diffusion, identity foreclosure, identity moratorium, and identity achievement. Operationalized in terms of degrees of conscious choice making and commitments to various identity domains, Diffusions exhibit low levels of choice and commitment; Foreclosures demonstrate low levels of choice but high levels of commitment; Moratoriums present active choice making but incompletely formed commitments; and Achievements express firm commitments after having been through a period of conscious choice making.

8. Turner (1976) postulates a similar movement from the *institutional self* to the *impulsive self*. In the context of identity status research, it is of interest to note his argument that for those who are institutionally oriented, "the self is something attained, created, or achieved, not something discovered" (p. 992). In contrast, the impulsively oriented person discovers the self through a rejection of institutional constraints.

9. The determinism of this position is softened by many sociologists with the view that individuals are capable of resisting cultural and social structural pressures through the exercise of agency. The degree to which this is possible or takes place is taken up in the agency-structure debate (see Collins, 1992, for a critical review).

10. See Waterman and Archer (1990, p. 50) for a discussion of this troublesome issue.

11. The sociological literature has referred to the notion of ethnic identity since the 1960s, emphasizing intergroup conflict (micropolitics and macropolitics), community formation and affiliation, and its roots (whether it is primordial or constructed). See Phinney and Rosenthal (1992) for a review of some of this literature as well as Weigert et al. (1986).

12. It is equally true that sociological approaches have tended to undertheorize the psychological, using all-encompassing concepts such as *the self* rather than a variety of more differentiated ones.

13. The basic assumption behind some attempts to explain nonmainstream identity formation is that discrimination and underprivilege create difficulties for nonmainstream adolescents attempting to make the transition to adulthood (e.g., in the United States and Canada, it is assumed that everyone who is not middle class, Anglo, and male will encounter special or more severe problems or both). Although undoubtedly true in many cases, the overall picture that is emerging reveals far greater complexity than this common sense assumption suggests. For example, see Rotheram-Borus and Wyche (1994) who conclude that "empirical support for . . . lowered expectations for identity achievement among minority group members has been mixed" (p. 67).

14. Given the current prolongation of youth and the accompanying normative delay of entry into adulthood, we need more studies of those in their 20s to see how these developments have affected the various dimensions of identity formation (see Côté & Allahar, 1994, for some work in this area).

15. Similarly, working-class women may experience more in common with their male class counterparts than their middle-class sisters. It should be noted that very little is known about social class differences in identity formation. In the social sciences, social class issues appear to have been eclipsed by the recent interest in gender and ethnicity, in spite of the fact that class *qua* material resources underlies much of the gender and ethnic disparity being debated in the public forum.

16. For example, on the basis of three studies, Archer (1989) concluded that the "minimal finding of gender differences in the processes, domains, or timing of identity activity in these three studies suggests that the traditional theoretical assumptions . . . should be discarded, or at least reconsidered" (p. 136). Maybe so, but the samples in those three studies were restricted in the range of identity formation (the vast majority were either foreclosed or diffused) and in age (subjects were selected from school grades 6 to 12, and one year past high school), limiting the possible variance in the process and timing of identity formation. Clearly, these young women and men have much further to go in confronting the social conditions of contemporary identity formation. Yet this article stands as a strong influence in the current consensus regarding gender.

17. Patterson et al. (1992) do not seem to mean these as absolute "anatomy is destiny" tendencies but rather as tendencies whereby considerable variation exists within and between genders. Yet such formulations suggest unarticulated essentialist assumptions, which in this case seem to be based on the reproductive power of women's bodies (p. 13). Such a position would suggest that innate capacities directly affect identity formation processes, and therefore men and women face differing *epigenetic tasks* during identity formation in adolescence. Certainly, it is now popular

in some circles to speak of women as having certain inherent superior, or even opposite, capacities to men (see Tavris, 1992, for critique of these views).

18. Of course, the identity status paradigm (on which Archer's own work is based) is subject to the same charge of Eurocentrism as is virtually all European-based thought. This type of critique is useful only when it recognizes that all thought has a centrism of some sort and degree, including the very critique itself. Only on the basis of extreme dogmatism could such a postmodern critique be the sole grounds for dismissing a line of thought.

19. Elsewhere, Archer (1993, p. 87) admits that her thinking on gender differences in identity formation is very much in process.

20. Nevertheless, there appears to be a persistence in the belief of the rightness of traditional segregated arrangements, inasmuch as concrete-operational thinking translates what is or has been into what ought to be—taking the descriptive as prescriptive (see Lengerman & Wallace, 1985, pp. 45-46, p. 57, note 5). This type of thinking among the lay public puts pressure on men and women to stay in separate spheres as if it is their rightful place (reinforcing the ideology of gender; cf. Côté & Allahar, 1994), but as Lengerman and Wallace show, it also does not follow logically that to speak of these spheres sociologically is to attempt to relegate men and women to their traditional ones.

21. To cite a well-known real-life example, in spite of 25 years of attempts to equalize gender relations, the Swedish experiment has only been partially successful, especially in getting more than a minority of men to embrace the private sphere to the extent that the majority of women do the public sphere. For details, see Jacobsson and Alfredsson (1993) and Swedish Institute (1992).

22. Sociobiologists may take exception to this, noting that much of the evolutionary history of males has been to dominate the public sphere, whereas for females, it has been to occupy the private. The physiological mechanisms governing choice making in this regard have not been identified, however, and it is difficult to see how this could be conclusively tested against the alternative and more parsimonious explanation that socialization influences produce these choice differentials.

23. See Nava (1992) for an analysis of how great the gap between public and private domains still is for this social task among British youth, especially working-class youth.

24. The use of the *ideal type* is commonly employed as a heuristic devise in sociology. The intention is to specify all of the characteristics of something that would correspond to the perfect case. In actuality, most cases would not exhibit all of the characteristics of the pure case but would vary to differing degrees. This is similar to the diagnostic technique in psychiatry where, say, four of seven symptoms must be present before a diagnosis is given. With only four symptoms, the perfect case is not evident, but the diagnosis is given nevertheless. It is also similar to the way classifications are made by identity status researchers, whereby few cases are pure foreclosures or achievements, for example, but subjects are classified as such anyway.

25. Every culture has ideals that define formal mores, customs, and values, but actual behavior patterns will correspond to these ideals in varying degrees. Thus, there will be predominant patterns of conformity and secondary patterns of deviance. This duality of culture is discussed in Côté (1994).

26. Some scholars prefer to distinguish the modern period from the postmodern one (see Smart, 1993), but I have several reservations for doing so. My main reservation stems from the notion that the transformation from premodern to modern was on a scale far greater than that thought to characterize the transition from the modern to the postmodern era. That is, there was a shift in the basis of social solidarity from one of primary group relations to one of secondary group relations. In secondary group relations, social bonds are more voluntary and based more on rational self-interest, rather than on familial and intergenerational obligation. I do not think that a transition of such a magnitude has taken place in this century, however. Rather, secondary relations seem to have evolved to one of even greater self-interest, but the basis of social solidarity is essentially the same (i.e., contractual). Thus, I speak of the late modern rather than postmodern.

27. A recent incident in Ohio suggests how far this has progressed. In this case, the state acted as an agent of a child, in effect punishing the parent for the child ("Spanker Spanked," 1995). Because the father bruised his son while spanking him with a paddle, the local police spanked the father with the paddle and then destroyed it. The legitimacy of the parent to discipline a child would not be likely to be questioned in a premodern society; in fact, not disciplining has more likely been seen as cruel and negligent as has the act of physically disciplining in late modern society. The fact that the state is involved signifies the extent of the loss of cultural legitimacy of the parent along with the increasing legitimacy of the child.

28. See Ewen (1976) for a discussion of the rise of the advertising industry in the 20th century and its cultivation of insecurities and anxieties to create a sense of need to consume to alleviate the concocted dissonance.

29. That is, one will avoid doing some things (e.g., experiencing certain pleasures at certain times) because one will feel guilty as a result, and one will approach other things (e.g., work) because one will experience guilt if one does not.

30. It is of interest to note that the identity diffusion category bears some resemblance to the impulsive self described earlier. This is particularly important to note if both are becoming more common. It is also interesting that Snow and Phillips (1982) speculate that there may be two types of impulsive self, one that is politicized and one that is self-absorbed. They add that with the former, "self-discovery, self-expression, and self-indulgence function simultaneously as forms of sociocultural protest and avenues to self-renewal," whereas with the latter, "the self becomes a refuge and self-indulgence an end in itself" (p. 474).

31. It is also true that some observers welcome a break in cultural continuity based on conclusions that Western culture has been patriarchal, racist, classist, and so on, but such a break is tied to the increasing anomie of social structure and is not without significant casualties when it comes to matters of individual identity.

32. Granted, it is perhaps too easy to slip into doomsaying when predicting the future. However, although I may be pessimistic in interpreting the implications of current social change, I find many others to be pollyannic in their interpretations. For example, Zurcher (1977) writes that "as many people as possible in our society ought to develop Mutable Selves, and ought to do so as quickly as possible" (p. 237). In a discussion of postmodern theories in sociology, Smart (1993) distinguishes between what can be called optimists and pessimists: The optimists celebrate recent changes and affirm the new status quo, whereas the pessimists believe it should be resisted.

REFERENCES

Adams, G. R., Bennion, L., & Huh, K. (1987). *Objective measure of ego identity status: A reference manual.* (Available from Gerald Adams, Department of Family Studies, University of Guelph, Guelph, Ontario, Canada.)

Adams, G. R., Gullotta, T. P., & Montemayor, R. (Eds.). (1992). *Adolescent identity formation.* Newbury Park, CA: Sage.

Anderson, D. (1991). *The unfinished revolution: The status of women in twelve countries.* Toronto: Doubleday.

Archer, S. L. (1989). Gender differences in identity development: Issues of process, domain and timing. *Journal of Adolescence, 12,* 117-138.

Archer, S. L. (1992). A feminist's approach to identity research. In G. R. Adams, T. P. Gullota, & R. Montemayor (Eds.), *Adolescent identity formation* (pp. 25-49). Newbury Park, CA: Sage.

Archer, S. L. (1993). Identity in relational contexts: A methodological proposal. In J. Kroger (Ed.), *Discussions on ego identity* (pp. 75-99). Hillsdale, NJ: Lawrence Erlbaum.

Archer, S. L. (Ed.). (1994). *Interventions for adolescent identity development.* Thousand Oaks, CA: Sage.

Babbitt, C. E., & Burbach, H. J. (1990). A comparison of self-orientation among college students across the 1960s, 1970s and 1980s. *Youth and Society, 21,* 472-482.

Baumeister, R. F. (1986). *Identity: Cultural change and the struggle for self.* New York: Oxford University Press.

Becker, H. S., Geer, B., Hughes, E. C., & Strauss, A. L. (1961). *Boys in white.* Chicago: University of Chicago Press.

Benedict, R. (1938). Continuities and discontinuities in cultural conditioning. *Psychiatry, 1,* 161-167.

Bennion, L. D., & Adams, G. R. (1986). A revision of the extended version of the Objective Measure of Ego Identity Status: An identity instrument for use with late adolescents. *Journal of Adolescent Research, 1,* 183-197.

Berzonsky, M. D. (1992). A process perspective on identity and stress management. In G. R. Adams, T. P. Gullota, & R. Montemayor (Eds.), *Adolescent identity formation* (pp. 193-215) .Newbury Park, CA: Sage.

Berzonsky, M. D. (1993). A constructionist view of identity development: People as postpositivist self-theorists. In J. Kroger (Ed.), *Discussions on ego identity* (pp. 169-203). Hillsdale, NJ: Lawrence Erlbaum.

Blumer, H. (1969). *Symbolic interactionism: Perspective and method.* Englewood Cliffs, NJ: Prentice Hall.

Bosma, H. A. (1985). *Identity development in adolescents: Coping with commitments.* Groningen, The Netherlands: University of Groningen Press.

Brake, M. (1985). *Comparative youth culture: The sociology of youth culture and youth subculture in America, Britain and Canada.* London: Routledge & Kegan Paul.

Brand, D. (1987). Black women and work: The impact of racially constructed gender roles in the sexual division of labour. *Fireweed, 25,* 28-37.

Bush, D., & Simmons, R. (1981). Socialization processes over the life course. In M. Rosenberg & R. H. Turner (Eds.), *Social psychology: Sociological perspectives.* New York: Basic Books.

Chapman, J. W., & Nicholls, J. G. (1976). Occupational identity status, occupational preference, and field dependence in Maori and Pakeha boys. *Journal of Cross-Cultural Psychology, 7,* 61-72.

Chickering, A. W. (1969). *Education and identity.* San Francisco: Jossey-Bass.

Collins, R. (1992). The romanticism of agency/structure versus the analysis of micro/macro. *Current Sociology, 40,* 77-97.

Côté, J. E. (1986a). Identity crisis modality: A technique for measuring the structure of the identity crisis. *Journal of Adolescence, 9,* 321-325.

Côté, J. E. (1986b). Traditionalism and feminism: A typology of strategies used by university women to manage career-family conflicts. *Social Behavior and Personality, 14,* 133-143.

Côté, J. E. (1993). Foundations of a psychoanalytic social psychology: Neo-Eriksonian propositions regarding the relationship between psychic structure and cultural institutions. *Developmental Review, 13,* 31-53.

Côté, J. E. (1994). *Adolescent storm and stress: An evaluation of the Mead-Freeman controversy.* Hillsdale, NJ: Lawrence Erlbaum.

Côté, J. E., & Allahar, A. L. (1994). *Generation on hold: Coming of age in the late twentieth century.* Toronto: Stoddart.

Côté, J. E., & Levine, C. (1987). A formulation of Erikson's theory of ego identity formation. *Developmental Review, 8,* 273-325.

Côté, J. E., & Levine, C. (1988). A critical examination of the ego identity status paradigm. *Developmental Review, 9,* 147-184.

Côté, J. E., & Levine, C. G. (1992). The genesis of the humanistic academic: A second test of Erikson's theory of ego identity formation. *Youth and Society, 23,* 387-410.

Crocombe, R. (1989). *The South Pacific: An introduction* (5th ed.). Suva, Fiji: University of the South Pacific.

Davis, J. (1990). *Youth and the condition of Britain: Images of adolescent conflict.* London: Athlone.

Erikson, E. H. (1959). Late adolescence. In D. H. Funkenstein (Ed.), *The student and mental health: An international view* (pp. 66-106). Cambridge, MA: Riverside.

Erikson, E. H. (1963). *Childhood and society* (2nd ed.). New York: Norton.

Erikson, E. H. (1968). *Identity: Youth and crisis.* New York: Norton.

Erikson, E. H. (1979). Report from Vikram: Further perspectives on the life cycle. In S. Kakar (Ed.), *Identity and adulthood.* Bombay: Oxford University Press.

Erikson, E. H., & Erikson, K. T. (1957). On the confirmation of the delinquent. *Chicago Review, 10,* 15-23.

Espin, O. M., & Gawelek, M. A. (1992). Women's diversity: Ethnicity, race, class, and gender in theories of feminist psychology. In L. S. Brown & M. Ballou (Eds.), *Personality and psychopathology: Feminist reappraisals* (pp. 88-107). New York: Guilford.

Ewen, S. (1976). *Captains of consciousness: Advertising and the social roots of the consumer culture.* New York: McGraw-Hill.

Fornas, J., & Bolin, G. (Eds.). (1995). *Youth culture in late modernity.* London: Sage.

Gecas, V., & Burke, P. J. (1995). Self and identity. In K. S. Cook, G. A. Fine, & J. S. House (Eds.), *Sociological perspectives on social psychology* (pp. 41-67). Boston: Allyn & Bacon.

Gergen, K. J. (1991). *The saturated self: Dilemmas of identity in contemporary life.* New York: Basic Books.

Gergen, K. J. (1992, November/December). The decline of personality. *Psychology Today*, 59-63.

Giddens, A. (1991). *Modernity and self-identity: Self and society in the late modern age.* Stanford, CA: Stanford University Press.

Goffman, E. (1976). *Gender advertisements.* New York: Harper & Row.

Grotevant, H. D. (1986). Assessment of identity development: Current issues and future directions. *Journal of Adolescent Research, 1,* 175-182.

Grotevant, H. D. (1992). Assigned and chosen identity components. In G. R. Adams, T. P. Gullota, & R. Montemayor (Eds.), *Adolescent identity formation* (pp. 73-90). Newbury Park, CA: Sage.

Grotevant, H. D., & Cooper, C. (1981). Assessing adolescent identity in the areas of occupation, religion, politics, friendship, dating, and sex roles: Manual for administration and coding of the interview. *JSAS Catalog of Selected Documents in Psychology, 11,* 52 (Ms. No. 2295).

Hare-Mustin, R. T., & Marecek, J. (1988). The meaning of difference: Gender theory, postmodernism, and psychology. *American Psychologist, 43,* 455-464.

Hempel, C. G. (1966). *Philosophy of natural science.* Englewood Cliffs, NJ: Prentice Hall.

Hill, J. P. (1973). *Some perspectives on adolescence in American society.* A report prepared for the Office of Child Development, U. S. Department of Health, Education, and Welfare, Washington, D. C.

Hodgson, J. W., & Fischer, J. L. (1981). Pathways of identity development in college women. *Sex Roles, 7,* 681-690.

Holmes, L. D. (1987). *Quest for the real Samoa: The Mead/Freeman controversy and beyond.* South Hadley, MA: Bergin & Garvey.

Jacobsson, R., & Alfredsson, K. (1993). *Equal worth: The status of men and women in Sweden.* Stockholm: Swedish Institute.

Kroger, J. (1983). A developmental study of identity formation among late adolescent and adult women. *Psychological Documents, 13* (Ms. No. 2537).

Kroger, J. (1989). *Identity in adolescence: The balance between self and other.* London: Routledge.

Kroger, J. (Ed.). (1993a). *Discussions on ego identity.* Hillsdale, NJ: Lawrence Erlbaum.

Kroger, J. (1993b). Ego identity: An overview. In J. Kroger (Ed.), *Discussions on ego identity.* Hillsdale, NJ: Lawrence Erlbaum.

Kuhn, M. H., & McPartland, T. S. (1954). An empirical investigation of self-attitudes. *American Sociological Review, 19,* 68-76.

LaVoie, J. C. (1994). Identity in adolescence: Issues of theory, structure and transition. *Journal of Adolescence, 17,* 17-28.

Lengerman, P. M., & Wallace, R. A. (1985). *Gender in America: Social control and social change.* Englewood Cliffs, NJ: Prentice Hall.

Lipman-Blumen, J. (1984). *Gender roles and power.* Englewood Cliffs, NJ: Prentice Hall.

Lynd, H. M. (1958). *On shame and the search for identity.* New York: Science Editions.

Marcia, J. E. (1964). *Determination and construct validation of ego identity status.* Unpublished doctoral dissertation, Ohio State University, Columbus.

Marcia, J. E. (1966). Development and validation of ego identity status. *Journal of Personality and Social Psychology, 3,* 551-558.

Marcia, J. E. (1967). Ego identity status: Relationship to change in self-esteem,'general maladjustment,' and authoritarianism. *Journal of Personality, 35*, 119-133.

Marcia, J. E. (1976). *Studies in ego identity.* Unpublished manuscript.

Marcia, J. E. (1980). Identity in adolescence. In J. Adelson (Ed.), *Handbook of adolescent psychology.* New York: John Wiley.

Marcia, J. E. (1989a). Identity and intervention. *Journal of Adolescence, 12*, 401-410.

Marcia, J. E. (1989b). Identity diffusion differentiated. In M. A. Luszcz & T. Nettlebeck (Eds.), *Psychological development: Perspectives across the life-span* (pp. 289-294). New York: Elsevier North-Holland.

Marcia, J. E. (1993a). The status of the statuses: Research review. In J. E. Marcia, A. S. Waterman, D. R. Matteson, S. L. Archer, & J. L. Orlofsky (Eds.), *Ego identity: A handbook for psychosocial research* (pp. 22-41). New York: Springer-Verlag.

Marcia, J. E. (1993b). Epilogue. In J. E. Marcia, A. S. Waterman, D. R. Matteson, S. L. Archer, & J. L. Orlofsky (Eds.), *Ego identity: A handbook for psychosocial research* (pp. 273-281). New York: Springer-Verlag.

Marcia, J. E., & Friedman, M. (1970). Ego identity status in college women. *Journal of Personality, 38*, 249-262.

Marcia, J. E., Waterman, A. S., Matteson, D. R., Archer, S. L., & Orlofsky, J. L. (Eds.). (1993). *Ego identity: A handbook for psychosocial research.* New York: Springer-Verlag.

Markstrom-Adams, C., & Beale-Spencer, M. (1994). A model for identity intervention with minority adolescents. In S. L. Archer (Ed.), *Interventions for adolescent identity development.* Thousand Oaks, CA: Sage.

Matteson, D. R. (1977). Exploration and commitment: Sex differences and methodological problems in the use of the identity status categories. *Journal of Youth and Adolescence, 6*, 353-379.

Matteson, D. R. (1993). Differences within and between genders: A challenge to the theory. In J. E. Marcia, A. S. Waterman, D. R. Matteson, S. L. Archer, & J. L Orlofsky (Eds.), *Ego identity: A handbook for psychosocial research* (pp. 69-110). New York: Springer-Verlag.

Mead, M. (1928). *Coming of age in Samoa: A psychological study of primitive youth for Western civilization.* New York: Morrow.

Mead, M. (1969). *Social organization of Manu'a* (2nd ed.). Honolulu, HI: Bernice P. Bishop Museum. (Original work published 1930)

Mead, M. (1970). *Culture and commitment.* Garden City, NJ: Doubleday.

Merton, R. (1957). *Social theory and social structure.* New York: Free Press.

Muuss, R. (1988). *Theories of adolescence* (5th ed.). New York: McGraw-Hill.

Nava, M. (1992). *Changing cultures: Feminism, youth and consumerism.* Newbury Park, CA: Sage.

Patterson, S. J., Sochting, I., & Marcia, J. E. (1992). The inner space and beyond: Women and identity. In G. R. Adams, T. P. Gullota, & R. Montemayor (Eds.), *Adolescent identity formation* (pp. 9-24). Newbury Park, CA: Sage.

Phinney, J. S. (1989). Stages of ethnic identity development in minority group adolescents. *Journal of Early Adolescence, 9*, 34-49.

Phinney, J. S., & Rosenthal, D. A. (1992). Ethnic identity in adolescence: Process, context, and outcome. In G. R. Adams, T. P. Gullota, & R. Montemayor (Eds.), *Adolescent identity formation* (pp. 145-172). Newbury Park, CA: Sage.

Psychoanalyst coined identity crisis. (1994, May 13). *The [Toronto] Globe & Mail*, p. E8

Riesman, D. (1950). *The lonely crowd: A study of the changing American character.* New Haven, CT: Yale University Press.

Rotheram-Borus, M. J., & Wyche, K. F. (1994). Ethnic differences in identity formation in the United States. In S. L. Archer (Ed.), *Interventions for adolescent identity development* (pp. 62-83). Thousand Oaks, CA: Sage.

Sexton, L. G. (1979). *Between two worlds: Young women in crisis.* New York: Morrow.

Shotter, J., & Gergen, K. J. (Eds.). (1989). *Texts of identity: Inquiries in social construction.* London: Sage.

Smart, B. (1993). *Postmodernity.* London: Routledge.

Snarey, J., Kohlberg, L., & Noam, G. (1983). Ego development in perspective: Structural stage, functional phase, and cultural age-period models. *Developmental Review, 3,* 303-338.

Snow, D. A., & Phillips, C. I.. (1982). The changing self-orientations of college students: From institution to impulse. *Social Science Quarterly, 63,* 462-476.

Spanker spanked. (1995, February 9). *The [Toronto] Globe & Mail,* p. A2.

Sprinthall, N. A., & Collins, W. A. (1984). *Adolescent psychology: A developmental view.* Reading, MA: Addison-Wesley.

Stafseng, O. (1994). A critique of slippery theories on postmodernity and youth. *Udkast, 22,* 190-210.

Stephen, J., Fraser, E., & Marcia, J. E. (1992). Moratorium-achievement (MAMA) cycles in lifespan identity development: Value orientations and reasoning system correlates. *Journal of Adolescence, 15,* 283-300.

Stryker, S. (1968). Identity salience and role performance: The relevance of symbolic interaction theory for family research. *Journal of Marriage and the Family, 30,* 558-564.

Swedish Institute. (1992). *Equality between men and women in Sweden.* Stockholm: Author.

Tavris, C. (1992). *The mismeasure of woman.* New York: Touchstone.

Thorbecke, W., & Grotevant, H. D. (1982). Gender differences in interpersonal identity formation. *Journal of Youth and Adolescence, 11,* 479-492.

Tonnies, F. (1955). *Community and association.* London: Routledge & Kegan Paul. (Original work published 1887 in German)

Turner, R. H. (1976). The real self: From institution to impulse. *American Journal of Sociology, 81,* 989-1016.

Wallace, C. (1995, July). *How old is young and young is old? The restructuring of age and the life-course in Europe.* Paper presented at Youth 2000: An International Conference, Middlesborough, England.

Waterman, A. S. (1982). Identity development from adolescence to adulthood: An extension of theory and a review of research. *Developmental Psychology, 18,* 341-358.

Waterman, A. S. (1988). Identity status theory and Erikson's theory: Communalities and differences. *Developmental Review, 8,* 185-208.

Waterman, A. S. (1992). Identity as an aspect of optimal psychological functioning. In G. R. Adams, T. P. Gullota, & R. Montemayor (Eds.), *Adolescent identity formation* (pp. 50-72). Newbury Park, CA: Sage.

Waterman, A. S. (1993). Developmental perspectives on identity formation: From adolescence to adulthood. In J. E. Marcia, A. S. Waterman, D. R. Matteson, S. L.

Archer, & J. L. Orlofsky (Eds.), *Ego identity: A handbook for psychosocial research* (pp. 42-68). New York: Springer-Verlag.

Waterman, A. S., & Archer, S. L. (1990). A life-span perspective on identity formation: Developments in form, function, and process. In P. B. Baltes, D. L. Featherman, & R. M. Lerner (Eds.), *Life-span development and behavior* (Vol. 10, pp. 29-57). Hillsdale, NJ: Lawrence Erlbaum.

Waterman, A. S., Geary, P. S., & Waterman, C. K. (1974). Longitudinal study of changes in ego identity status from the freshman to the senior year at college. *Developmental Psychology, 10,* 387-392.

Waterman, A. S., & Waterman, C. K. (1971). A longitudinal study of changes in ego identity status during the freshman year at college. *Developmental Psychology, 5,* 167-173.

Waterman, C. K., & Waterman, A. S. (1975). Fathers and sons: A study of ego identity across two generations. *Journal of Youth and Adolescence, 4,* 331-338.

Weigert, A. J., Teitge, J. S., & Teitge, D. W. (1986). *Society and identity: Toward a sociological psychology.* Cambridge, UK: Cambridge University Press.

Wheelis, A. (1958). *The quest for identity.* New York: Norton.

Wirth, L. (1938). Urbanism as a way of life. *American Journal of Sociology, 44,* 1-24.

Wood, M. R., & Zurcher, L. A., Jr. (1988). *The development of a postmodern self: A computer-assisted comparative analysis of personal documents.* New York: Greenwood.

Zurcher, L. A., Jr. (1977). *The mutable self: A self-concept for social change.* Beverly Hills, CA: Sage.

6. Domains of Adolescent Achievement

Sanford M. Dornbusch
Melissa R. Herman
Jeanne A. Morley

Achievement is usually considered a primitive concept whose definition is unnecessary. We know it when we see it. Yet it requires definition if we are to survey various forms of adolescent achievement. Depending on the perspective from which behavior is viewed, the same level of performance in a particular arena may be seen as high or low in achievement, or it may not even be perceived. These individual characteristics, in turn, may reflect aspects of the social context that cause the individual to value a particular form of achievement more highly and to consider the expenditure of effort worthwhile.

Evaluation of performance using some set of standards is a part of the process of defining certain behaviors as representing an achievement. Evaluation requires a sampling of performances, a system for weighting various aspects of the performances, and the assessment of the performances in terms of a given set of standards (Natriello & Dornbusch, 1984). Standards represent social definitions of that which is acceptable or unacceptable or of high or low quality. Standards may differ among local groups, and there may also be differences between local standards and those of the larger society.

Whether certain adolescent behaviors constitute an achievement, therefore, differs according to the persons doing the evaluation. A set of performances may represent an achievement to one group, a failure to another, be irrelevant for a third group, and not be known to a fourth group. For example, achievements that are known to peers but unknown to parents cannot be viewed by parents as an achievement. The adolescent's own valuing of such an achievement will, accordingly, depend on the relative importance of these two groups. These sets of evaluators are operating as normative reference groups, with the more influential group establishing within the adolescent a conception of the perspective of the generalized other (Mead, 1934).

Groups of evaluators also differ in their willingness to relate current arenas of achievement to highly valued areas of future achievement. For example, compared with parents, peers are more attuned to current problems and standards and are not as likely to be concerned about the consequences of adolescent achievements in adult life. Hartup (1983) argues that there is little disagreement between parents and friends on long-term goals and that discord usually arises over trivial matters and those that relate to status within the family and identity outside the family. Accordingly, if an issue is likely to have long-term consequences, adolescents report that they go to their parents for advice much more frequently than to their peers (Brittain, 1963; Kandel, 1986; Larson, 1972).

The determinants of achievement are not studied by behavioral scientists alone. The determinants are also continuing topics of everyday conversation. Some lay persons emphasize virtue and morality as the basis for achievement, others stress the key role of personal characteristics, and others accent the way in which talented individuals operate as a force in social evolution (Rosen, Crockett, & Nunn, 1969). Regardless of the emphasis, however, everyday discussions of achievement typically portray stable characteristics of the individual as the source of high achievement.

Our emphasis will be on the social forces and structures that influence adolescent achievement. Such an emphasis is appropriate when one considers our current level of ignorance about the sources of the individual factors that lead to achievement and the need for understanding how diverse contexts shape individual achievement (Simonton, 1994). Coleman (1969) puts well the case for examining the social environment within which individual achievement takes place.

> Our knowledge of the individual determinants of achievement, cognitive and affective, . . . is in its infancy. One direction toward developing that knowledge is to move explicitly outside the individual, to the social environment in which achievement occurs. For the social environment, whether in the individual's present or his past, comprises the determinants, not only of achievement, but also of the non-biological individual determinants of achievement: those factors

which we call motivation, values, personality, drive, and even developed abilities. Thus these social factors, acting as determinants of achievement, or as determinants of determinants of achievement, constitute one window through which the process of achievement may be seen, a window which allows a view of the way various elements conjoin to produce a result. (p. v)

THE DOMAINS OF
ADOLESCENT ACHIEVEMENT

One can achieve in every aspect of life, from developing serenity to improving foul-shooting in basketball to learning interpersonal skills. The broadness of our mandate to examine various domains of adolescent achievement has a major positive consequence: We are forced to consider different domains of adolescent functioning and not limit ourselves to schooling and deviance, the adolescent outcomes most frequently studied.

For example, in the Savin-Williams and Berndt's (1990) review of the literature on peer influence, a rough count found 47 references to deviance as a dependent variable and 39 to schooling outcomes. These were, as we expected, the two most frequent dependent variables in previous research on peer influences. The third most frequent dependent variable, a general category combining psychological and social adjustment, was referred to only 21 times. Repeating these analyses using Furstenberg's (1990) review of family influences, we again found a preponderance of references to deviance (25) and schooling (15) as adolescent outcomes, followed by economic resources (9) and sexual activity (7). Thus, deviance and schooling were indeed the most frequently studied adolescent outcomes.

The number of potential domains of achievement in the life space of each adolescent is infinite. The senior author can recall when, from week to week, he knew the rankings of the songs on the Hit Parade. Knowing the popularity and longevity of these songs would, he hoped, give him material for conversation with his friends. In this chapter, we shall not be this idiographic and specific. Instead, we will choose domains of achievement that are broad and yet capture an essential element in the lives of many adolescents, are perceived as significant by most adolescents, and are often objectified in the form of social institutions.

Accordingly, we consider only four domains of achievement in this summary report: academic, extracurricular (including athletic), social, and workplace. There are other potential domains of achievement. For example, the development of emotional autonomy, along with good relations with parents, is a major achievement in adolescence (Steinberg & Silverberg, 1986). Similarly, achieving an appropriate level of restraint in self-regulation is an important component of learning to live independently in society (Feldman & Weinberger, 1994). This issue is adequately addressed elsewhere in this volume (see Chapter 2). We decided to focus on domains in which achievement is less internal and individualistic and more publicly recognized.

The first two domains of achievement—academic and extracurricular—are centered in the school. For adolescents, the school is the major socializing institution outside of the family. Our concern with extracurricular activities reflects research findings that portray schools as more than just academic institutions. Many adolescents focus more on social and extracurricular achievement than on academic achievement during the hours they spend at school (Coleman, 1961; Csikszentmihalyi & Larson, 1984).

The third domain, social, is partially located in the school but also includes relations with peers in the neighborhood. Making friends and having some status within a group of peers is, particularly from an adolescent point of view, a crucial achievement. Because acceptance by peers is viewed by adolescents as so important (Eskilson & Wiley, 1987), the values of peers have a major influence on adolescent efforts to achieve. All other things being equal, what peers value is likely to be what the adolescent values.

The final domain, workplace, is an increasingly common arena in adolescent development. Among U.S. adolescents, most will work part-time for pay at some time during their high school years (Greenberger & Steinberg, 1986). What they learn, as well as the energy and time they expend on the job, can affect their achievement in other domains.

These four domains, though far from exhaustive, do cover important aspects of adolescent life. They are sufficiently comprehensive so as to cover many of the developmental tasks of adolescence, and they are sufficiently restricted so as to permit a relatively brief survey of diverse forms of adolescent achievement.

FIVE QUESTIONS ABOUT
ADOLESCENT ACHIEVEMENT

The discussion of adolescent achievement in diverse domains enables us to consider questions that are too seldom addressed.

1. Because adolescence is typically viewed as preparation for adulthood, how does the vision of the adult future shape the perceptions and behavior of adolescents and their significant others?
2. How do differences in the social context, including socioeconomic status and ethnicity, affect adolescent perceptions and behaviors within each domain?
3. How does the individual adolescent's level of achievement in a particular domain lead to changes of perceptions and behaviors in that domain?
4. Across domains, how does achievement in a specific domain affect achievement in other domains?
5. Across domains, what are the similarities and differences in the predictors and consequences of adolescent achievement?

Given our limited time, knowledge, and space, we cannot hope to provide definitive answers to any of these questions. Yet discussion of these cross-cutting questions may stimulate research that will not be limited to adolescents' academic performance and deviance. Too little research has sought to understand adolescent achievement across several domains. Let us then embark on an unusual voyage across adolescent domains of achievement.

THEORIES OF ACHIEVEMENT

Psychological Theories

Current psychological theories about the factors underlying human achievement stress the cognitive processes by which active human agents select their domains of potential achievement and decide how much effort to invest in each. The three most important psychological perspectives, each of which is applicable to adolescent achievement, are *attribution theory, self-efficacy theory,* and *expectancy-value theory.*

Weiner's work on attributions (Weiner, 1985; Weiner et al., 1971; Weiner, Russell, & Lerman, 1979) focused attention on the interpretation of outcomes. Continued effort for achievement in an arena depends on the actor's perception of the causes of success or failure in previous attempts to achieve in that arena. If an adolescent attributes a failure to low ability (which is stable and uncontrollable), the response to that failure is likely to determine future behavior more than would an attribution to effort (which is unstable and controllable). Attribution theory has emphasized how expectancies for future success, based on emotional attributions for past success and failure, affect future efforts to achieve.

Bandura's (1977, 1986, 1989) work on efficacy expectations has also had a major influence on research on achievement. What arenas are chosen for achievement, the effort that will be expended, and the willingness to persist toward a goal have all been shown to be influenced by the actor's beliefs that he or she can effectively do the tasks that lead to desired outcomes.

Although both attribution and self-efficacy theories agree that the perceived value of a prospective achievement is important, empirical research in these two traditions usually assumes a high valuation of the goal and focuses on expectancies for individual success in attaining that goal. By contrast, expectancy-value theories, particularly in the work of Eccles and her colleagues (see Wigfield & Eccles, 1992), emphasize the factors that affect the individual's valuing of goals as well as the expectations that the goals can be achieved.

Expectancy-value research on children incorporates the insights of previous investigators (Wigfield & Eccles, 1992). Eccles et al. (1983) built on previous research and theory on values (Atkinson, 1957, 1964, 1966; Feather, 1982, 1988; Rokeach, 1979). Eccles stressed the attainment value of the task (Battle, 1965, 1966), the intrinsic enjoyment or interest in the task (Deci, 1975), the importance or utility of the task for future goals (Deci & Ryan, 1980; Harter, 1981), and the emotional costs and effort in investing in a particular task.

Expectancy-value theory provides a useful perspective in examining adolescent achievement across diverse domains, for the theory includes factors affecting both the valuing of a specific goal and the expectation of attaining that goal. It is our belief that different factors, sometimes value related and sometimes expectancy related, will be prominent in each domain. Thus, our survey will attempt to use the expectancy-value perspective to understand differences among domains in the factors leading to adolescent achievement.

Although the psychological approaches that we have summarized view each individual as living in a context that shapes personal beliefs and behaviors, the psychological emphasis is primarily on individual differences. Although Eccles (1984), for example, has shown how expectancy-value theories can help to explain gender differences in achievement of children and adolescents, sociological and social psychological perspectives are more directly oriented to the understanding of group differences in achievement. Let us briefly review some of those perspectives using the ecological scheme of classification suggested by Bronfenbrenner and Crouter (1983).

Sociological and
Social Psychological Theories

At the exosystem level, the development of the adolescent is affected by environments in which adolescents themselves do not participate (Bronfenbrenner, 1986). For example, the parental world of work and the parental network of contacts influence the life of the adolescent through differences in household wealth and social capital, respectively. The exosystem extends even further, beyond the family's contacts to the wider society. We note the power of culturally pervasive beliefs and behaviors in shaping adolescent perceptions and behaviors.

For example, within educational institutions, three approaches at the exosystem level help in understanding gender, ethnic, and social class differences in academic achievement. First, stereotype vulnerability (Steele, 1992) inserts into the minds of members of disadvantaged groups a fear of impending failure, confirming the wider society's negative view of their group's ability to perform in the academic domain. Second, expectation states in the classroom, associated with the perception of a unidimensional order of ability among students, produce status problems that reinforce tendencies for low interaction and poor academic performance among those labeled as less competent (Cohen, 1993). Third, a general tendency toward the reproduction of inequality (Bowles & Gintis, 1976) provides unequal resources that give more educational opportunity to advantaged groups of children and adolescents and less to members of disadvantaged groups.

At the mesosystem level, specific contexts shape the behavior of most participants and create a climate in which various forms of achievement are hindered or encouraged (Bronfenbrenner, 1986). Specific neighborhoods (Jencks & Mayer, 1988) and schools (Coleman, 1961; Kilgore, 1991) are examples of contexts that shape values and expectations for achievement. The world of the adolescent is not sharply limited so that the youth participates in only one developmental context at a time. Too often, researchers limit themselves to a single context, studying, for example, the school or the home or the peer network. The senior author would like to provide a personal example: When he began to study the effect of the home environment on school performance, most of his colleagues in the School of Education forcefully expressed their disapproval of his examining the relation between behaviors in these disparate contexts. His study was funded only after a group of school superintendents and principals expressed their strong support. The boundary of the school is not fixed at the playground fence. What happens at home affects adolescent effort and achievement at school. And what happens at school may change the relations between parents and adolescents. At the mesosystem level, achievement in one context can affect achievement in another.

Last, at the microsystem level, social psychological processes operate within specific groups and organizations. For example, comparison and normative reference groups operate to set different standards for achievement within different peer groups, classrooms, and schools (Cohen, 1962). Socialization processes are also at work in different settings—not only in schools and families but also in friendship groups (Maccoby, 1966). And there are the omnipresent processes of evaluation operating as powerfully in small groups of peers as in formal relations between teacher and student (Natriello & Dornbusch, 1984).

Our inclusion of this brief summary of psychological, sociological, and social psychological perspectives does not imply that we will be able to test directly their utility for understanding adolescent achievement. Rather, we have discussed these approaches because they have shaped our descriptions of the precursors and consequences of achievement in different domains and contexts. They provide the lenses as we focus on several domains of adolescent achievement.

ACADEMIC ACHIEVEMENT

Achievement in the academic domain is a function of the standard used for the assessment of performance. Grades, for example, are a relatively public measure of academic performance used by parents and others to assess the quality of the adolescent's performance. How high should grades be to be satisfactory? At a low level, getting grades high enough to be eligible for participation in athletics may be the goal. At a slightly higher level, passing enough courses to graduate from high school may be seen as adequate. Students aspiring to attendance at 4-year colleges or universities will have much higher standards for academic achievement. Last, those students who aspire to admission to selective colleges and universities will have the highest standards.

But grades are not given in a vacuum. There are enormous differences in the standards used by different schools and different teachers. Because schools use relative standards for grading, those that differ in their socioeconomic composition are likely to differ in the absolute standards for a specific grade (Ianni, 1989). So widespread are the differences in the meaning of an A or B grade that selective colleges and universities give substantial weight to performance on standardized achievement tests, such as those of the College Entrance Exam Board (SAT) or the American College Testing Program (Ciompi, 1993). Performance on such tests is a second public measure of academic achievement.

There are other kinds of achievement, however, that are not so easily measured and, hence, not as public. A student who has considerable intrinsic interest in a particular subject may get joy from the mastery of specific topics. That same student, nevertheless, may not be viewed by teachers as achieving in a course because evaluation typically assesses the performance of more routine and objective assignments. For example, Nobel laureates Albert Einstein and Richard Feynman, bored by traditional instruction, were not always perceived by teachers as high achievers on assigned tasks (Feynman, 1985; White, 1993).

The level of achievement differs dramatically depending on the context as well as on the aspirations of the students and their families. A grade of B may represent an outstanding achievement in some families and be a grave disappointment in others.

When we discuss academic achievement in this paper, we refer either to above-average performance in terms of a national standard or to high performance in terms of a local standard. Such an image of achievement necessarily emphasizes public aspects of achievement to the exclusion of more private and personal aspects, such as exceeding a personal goal in an academic subject. In this chapter, high achievement will usually be assessed in terms of a local standard. We will specifically note those occasional instances when a national standard is employed.

In modern industrial society, adolescence is typically viewed as a period between childhood and adulthood that is preparation for the future. Schooling, for example, is typically viewed as anticipatory socialization for adult occupational roles (Williams, 1969). In nonindustrial societies, vocational training takes place within the family. But with a complex society composed of tens of thousands of occupations, the educational system assumes the task of vocational preparation. The institution of schooling has to some extent replaced the educational role of the family and assumed the central place in training for future occupations.

Limiting ourselves to modern industrial society, nearly all adolescents expect to work in a paid occupation as adults. In the first half of the 20th century, middle-class female adolescents often saw the future primarily in terms of marriage and a family. Today, the emphasis on occupational futures is almost as great among adolescent females as among males. In a survey of high school students, more than 70% viewed learning in high school as primarily a means toward an occupational goal. Learning for its own sake was the goal of only a minority of students (Harris, 1976).

In addition to the perceived link between schooling and occupational attainment, there is another factor affecting student willingness to expend effort when faced with obstacles to academic achievement. Looking at the motivational processes of those students who did well in school compared with those who did less well, Henderson and Dweck (1990) noted the importance of the relation between student beliefs and coping patterns. Those students who held an incremental theory of intelligence, believing that they could develop intelligence through learning, continued vigorous efforts when faced with obstacles. Those who viewed intelligence as an entity (fixed trait) were more vulnerable, seeing every setback as a sign of a stable internal problem.

Mastery-oriented children (Ames & Archer, 1988; Elliott & Dweck, 1988), believing in an incremental view of intelligence, hold to their objectives and try various learning strategies when challenged by failure. On the other hand, in accordance with attribution theory, patterns of learned helplessness and lack of control lead to anxiety and lack of persistent effort. In studies controlling for previous level of achievement, students who felt intelligence was a fixed entity got poorer grades than did students holding an incremental perspective on intelligence (Henderson & Dweck, 1990). The apparent devaluation of school achievement by some students, even though the wider society values academic performance highly, may be a product of low confidence and the belief that intelligence is a fixed entity (Henderson & Dweck, 1990). Furthermore, it is noteworthy that students who do poorly in high school do not value school less. They and their parents value academic performance just as much as high-performing students (Ritter, Mont-Reynaud, & Dornbusch, 1993).

Thus, achievement in the domain of academics appears to be largely a function of the future utility of the accomplishment. Few adolescents claim to find intrinsic enjoyment in their academic efforts. Nevertheless, despite the evidence of a generally high valuation of academics, low expectancies for success often inhibit the pursuit of academic achievement.

Academic achievement is not simply a result of individual ability combined with motivation. Many other factors, in particular institutional forms and processes, play an important role in determining achievement.

Stratification within secondary schools, through systems of curriculum tracking and ability grouping, is widespread in the United States and abroad (Kerckhoff, 1986; Oakes, Gamoran, & Page, 1992). Tracking is premised on an ideology of individual differences. Paradoxically, individual differences in academic achievement are themselves a product of track placement (Dornbusch, 1994). Curricular tracking produces inequalities in educational experiences and opportunities for students who are placed at different tiers of this hierarchy. Students in the lower tracks have less access to science laboratories and guidance services, fewer material resources in the classroom, and teachers who are usually lower in ability and experience. Furthermore, these low-track students are expected to learn less and expend less effort compared with students in higher tracks (for reviews, see Gamoran & Berends, 1987; Oakes et al., 1992).

Tracking matters, because it forms the contexts within which adolescent school achievement occurs. In our own studies of tracking (Dornbusch, 1994), we found that students with higher eighth-grade math test scores using national standards do not get high grades in their math and science courses in high school when assigned to the low track. When assigned to the lower track, such students do less work and sink to the level of their course mates. Using the other students in the low-track class as a comparison reference group, students of high ability reduce their level of effort. These high-ability students in lower tracks are not challenged to excel. For example, they report their courses are easy, and they do less homework in those courses than in high-track courses (Ball, 1981; Oakes, 1985; Rosenbaum, 1976).

Location in the tracking system mediates parental and peer influences on educational aspirations of adolescents. Those in the higher track will be likely to aspire to college regardless of parental desires, whereas those in the lower track tend to aspire to college only when parents are favorable toward higher education. Peer influences on aspirations to attend college show a similar pattern of dependence on track location of the adolescent. Such differences in aspirations influence expectations and achievement in school.

Looking just at students who had both high educational expectations and high levels of ability in mathematics, Dornbusch (1994) found that about one fourth of African Americans and Hispanic Americans and one tenth of non-Hispanic Whites and Asian Americans were not taking the courses in math and science required for admission to 4-year colleges. Schools overestimate their ability to assess ability, and numerous students are misassigned. Even sadder, students and their families are often unaware of track placement and its consequences (Useem, 1992). Lacking information about what is happening in high school and how that will affect their child's postsecondary educational opportunities, many parents, especially those of low social class or minority status, are unable to pressure schools to redress these misassignments. When individuals are placed at a level below their academic potential, the entire society, as well as the individual, suffers from the loss of skill and economic productivity.

Institutional effects on academic achievement among adolescents interact in sometimes unanticipated ways with individual and developmental effects. Simmons and Blyth (1987) have shown that the structural change of adding middle schools and junior high schools prior to high school hindered the academic achievement of a substantial proportion of adolescent girls. Because pubertal development occurs earlier among females, girls are more likely than boys to experience puberty at the same time as they leave elementary school to move to a middle or junior high school. Compared with staying in an elementary school for 8 years, the additional stress brought on by changing schools earlier has negative effects on adolescent females' academic achievement, effects that often last as girls move on to high school. The larger the number of stressful events, the more likely the adolescent will experience various indicators of maladjustment (Ge, Lorenz, Conger, Elder, & Simons, 1994).

In the early stages of adolescence, earlier pubertal development (ahead of age-mates) has positive effects for boys but not for girls. The increased height and strength of boys lead parents and teachers to have higher expectations for their educational performance. Yet among females, early puberty has no clear effect on others' educational expectations (Duncan & Dornbusch, 1982). Perhaps this finding is a product of adults' differential views of courtship, marriage, and fertility among males and females. The societal vision of the future for adolescent females, compared with that for adolescent males, less clearly focuses on educational achievement and later occupational success. The effects of such differences in social reactions on the internal world of the adolescent should become an important element in the scientific study of adolescence (Adams, Day, Dyk, Frede, & Rogers, 1992; Lerner, 1992).

In addition to the institutional effects of schools, there are several nonschool contexts within which adolescent academic achievement is shaped. There have long been studies of the strong relations between a family's socioeconomic status and ethnicity and student academic performance, aspirations, and achievement. These studies emphasized differences associated with social class, ethnicity, and family structure. But these are "status addresses," and only recently have studies sought to determine the processes that underlie such status differences. Let us give examples of such processes. Authoritative parenting, more frequent among middle-class parents, is associated with higher adolescent grades in school (Steinberg, Lamborn, Dornbusch, & Darling, 1992). Too-early autonomy, understandably found more often among single-parent families, is associated with lower grades (Dornbusch et al., 1985). The high academic performance of Chinese students is explained in part by the parental emphasis on teaching in the home (Chao, 1994). Studies of parental behavior have shown a lamentable inability to explain much of the variation in school performance among Asian American students (Dornbusch, Ritter, Leiderman, Roberts, & Fraleigh, 1987), and that failure may be due to the cultural limitations of the predominantly White middle-class models of child and adolescent development used by U.S. researchers. As a final example, we would note the extent to which African American parenting patterns, with resulting low school performance of adolescents, reflect poverty more than a distinct cultural tradition (McLoyd, Jayaratne, Ceballo, & Borquez, 1994).

Beyond the context of the family, the community context, as well as the context of the student body of the school, plays a role in academic achievement. Kandel and Lesser (1970) showed that the higher the socioeconomic status of the school, the larger the proportion of students at each status level who are planning to continue their education. The social class of the parents, however, is a much stronger indicator of college aspirations than is community socioeconomic status (Jencks & Mayer, 1988).

The ethnic makeup of a community also appears to mediate parental influences on academic achievement. Dornbusch, Ritter, and Steinberg (1991) found that parental advantages, such as college graduation of the parents and being in a two-natural-parent household, were not associated with better school performance of African American and non-Hispanic White adolescents who live in a heavily minority community. Yet African American and non-Hispanic White parents who lived in predominantly non-Hispanic White communities were able to pass on their family advantages. Some aspects of the community, or of the school response to the community, are clearly depressing school achievement in minority areas. The minority groups are more affected by such processes because a higher proportion of minority families live in these areas.

Thus, our analysis of the literature on academic achievement suggests an increasing awareness of the importance of context and of the interrelation of variables at the individual, group, and institutional levels. U.S. secondary schools provide a diverse set of contexts and standards within which adolescents achieve academically. That diversity is partly a function of variation in the nature of the communities from which the schools draw their students, but it also reflects differences in school organization. The development of middle schools and junior high schools has placed an additional stressor on adolescent females, whereas tracking has dramatically restricted the potential achievement of students assigned to the lower tracks. Such assignments do not merely reflect differences in ability but have an independent and powerful influence on middle-ability students who are misassigned to lower-level courses.

In addition to these contextual factors, motivational forces at the individual level play a role in fostering academic achievement. Students typically perceive the main purpose of secondary education to be attainment of a better job as an adult, finding the details of their course work neither interesting, relevant, nor intrinsically motivating. With respect to motivation, student belief in the incremental development of intelligence and skills is related to the expenditure of greater effort in school and overcoming obstacles to academic achievement.

EXTRACURRICULAR ACHIEVEMENT

The domain of extracurricular achievement includes participation in diverse forms of school activities that are not part of the curriculum. Extracurricular activities take place at the school and are part of the larger school organization, even though they are, by definition, outside of the realm of academic achievement. In our discussion of extracurricular achievement, we will not consider community, athletic, and religious activities that take place outside of the school.

Extracurricular activities can be divided into two broad categories: athletics and other noncurricular activities. These other activities include performing arts, clubs, and student government. Recruitment into athletic activities at the school level is very different from recruitment into other extracurricular activities and, as we shall see, is related in different ways to other domains of achievement.

What is achievement in the domain of extracurricular activities? In the athletic realm, the first level of achievement is "making the team." To be listed as one of the school's representatives is a source of pride and accomplishment. Once on a team, playing time becomes the crucial indicator of achievement. Of those who play most of the time, there are sometimes a few individuals who are labeled "stars."

The size of a school has a major effect on the probability of an individual student achieving athletically. In a small high school, a much higher proportion of those wishing to play on a team will have the opportunity. Because interscholastic leagues are organized by size of student enrollment, a student who could not make first string at a large school might be a star in league competition among smaller schools.

More than any other domain of achievement that we discuss, athletic achievement is publicly announced and heralded. Information about athletic achievement is disseminated throughout the school and community in many ways. For instance, athletes wear their team jackets, schools hold pep rallies, trophies are prominently displayed, and victories are hailed on the public address system in the school and in local newspapers.

For other extracurricular activities, achievement is public but typically not as widely disseminated. The first standard of achievement is membership in an activity. Students who participate in numerous clubs and activities to "pad" their college applications are asked by college admissions officers to document the depth and range of involvement in such activities (Ciompi, 1993). In performing arts and student government, on the other hand, hierarchies are present and recognized. Those who occupy the highest offices or play leading roles receive public recognition of their contribution to the activity. As was true in athletics, the smaller the size of a school, the higher the probability that an individual student will be able to point to achievement in other extracurricular activities. Extracurricular achievement, then, involves both participation and publicly recognized excellence in a given activity or sport.

Extracurricular achievement is primarily a function of the intrinsic enjoyment and immediate prestige of the accomplishment. The adolescent perception of the future utility of extracurricular activities can also be an important influence. Although the value of extracurricular achievement may be an impetus for many adolescents, expectancies for success are also important.

As in other domains, those who believe that their talents can be developed through practice will persevere in the face of difficulties. In addition, those students who have low expectations for success in terms of making the football team or winning the class election will tend to devalue the achievement for themselves (Henderson & Dweck, 1990; Rotella, 1980).

Coleman's (1961) influential work on the adolescent society stressed the much greater emphasis on athletic performance in U.S. high schools than would be expected on the basis of the utility of athletics for adult futures. In large measure, this emphasis on athletic performance is based on the symbolic importance of athletic teams for the schools they represent. Athletic teams are often the only aspect of school life that is widely discussed and observed by members of the larger nonschool community.

Occupational achievement is extremely valued in U.S. society (Williams, 1969). For those adolescents who are stars, extracurricular activities, usually considered a source of fun and exercise, are often transmuted into preparation for an adult career. For the majority of students, however, participation in extracurricular activities is unrelated to future occupational goals. Among the stars, appraisal of future success in acting or sports is often unrealistic. For example, more current college football and basketball players expect to play in the National Football League or National Basketball Association than there are total players in those two leagues (American Institutes for Research [AIR], 1988).

The adolescent's vision of the future utility of athletics is shaped by ethnicity and gender. The social structure of opportunity in this country presents limited occupational opportunities that are visible to low-status adolescents. Hence, minority students choose more risky paths to high-paying jobs (Merton, 1968). In the second half of the 20th century, although institutional and personal discrimination hindered occupational achievement for adult African American males, numerous African Americans in the United States and Canada achieved prominent success in professional athletics. The vision of the future for African American athletes in high school is accordingly weighted toward athletic careers. Feeding this trend is the overrepresentation of African Americans on Division I football and basketball teams and their greater likelihood of being the stars of those teams (AIR, 1988).

Being female, by contrast, does not often inspire dreams of adult careers in athletics. Although there has been a considerable increase in the importance of women's sports at the high school and college level, there are only limited opportunities for female star athletes to become professionals at their sport. In addition, the athletic achievements of males are given almost universal acclaim, whereas there is some denigration of women athletes by those who see female athletic performance as violating gender stereotypes (Engel, 1994).

Within the domain of extracurricular activities, achievement in athletics sometimes has different predictors and consequences than does achievement in other extracurricular activities. Context plays a key role in this domain. Though extracurricular achievement is often highly valued by adolescents, its value is mediated by expectations for success and by the ethnic and gender context. As indicated earlier, when members of an ethnic group perceive few options for adult occupational success, they are more likely to invest heavily in extracurricular activities that may have occupational payoffs. For example, early in the 20th century, the sport of boxing was dominated by Irish Americans and Jewish Americans. Their participation in this brutal sport that brings success to very few was a function of their perception that success in more conventional occupations was unlikely. As the number of avenues for occupational success increased for those of Irish and Jewish descent, members of these groups no longer viewed boxing as a reasonable option. Today, boxing is dominated by new groups who perceive their legitimate occupational aspirations as blocked, such as Hispanic Americans and African Americans. In similar fashion, we can predict that more young women will devote themselves to sports when those sports are perceived as likely to provide economic reward.

SOCIAL ACHIEVEMENT

In the social realm, adolescence is characterized by increased age segregation and reduced contact with adults. Cross-cultural evidence suggests that the salience of the peer group in adolescence is greater for boys than for girls (Schlegel & Barry, 1991). Although relations with parents and other adults are central in early childhood, the importance of friendships with peers gradually increases with age. Both adolescents and adults view the development of friendships with peers as a vital task of adolescence. With parents, they seek approval and guidance on educational and career goals, but with peers, they engage in self-disclosure and share interpersonal problems. With friends, adolescents feel they are understood and can express themselves more fully (Savin-Williams & Berndt, 1990; Youniss & Smollar, 1985).

Social achievement is a multifaceted concept. Most adolescents measure achievement in this domain in terms of the number and quality of their friendships, and researchers have seldom distinguished between number and quality (Savin-Williams & Berndt, 1990). To some adolescents, the overall social prestige of their group of friends is also a necessary element in social achievement—to be friends with members of the highest status group is a sign of true social success. Nevertheless, feeling integrated into some peer group, even one that is not prestigious, is seen as a form of adolescent social achievement by members of those groups. For those adolescents who are located in an acceptable niche, peer groups provide an adaptive context in which to negotiate adolescence (Brown, 1990).

Although standards of interpersonal achievement vary from individual to individual, social achievements remain public performances. Typically, a student's peers know who his or her friends are and how prestigious those friends are in the school or neighborhood context. A specific set of peers may use unusual standards for social achievement and actively denigrate other groups of peers. Yet even adolescents who do not aspire to membership in the higher status groups know how their social achievements will be evaluated by their peers (Brown & Lohr, 1987; Coleman, 1961).

Peer groups often function as normative reference groups for adolescents. Indeed, adolescents may be influenced by peer groups to which they do not belong but to which they aspire. The influence of peer groups is partially a product of the time spent with peers. In a typical week, high school students spend twice as much time with peers as with adults (Savin-Williams & Berndt, 1990). Dornbusch (1987) found that adolescents, faced with conflict between parental and peer norms, are more influenced by the group that they believe will learn which choice they have made. The lesser amount of time spent with parents compared with peers leads to greater peer influence on behavior, despite adolescents' continuing to value parental approval more than peer approval.

Despite the emphasis on a monolithic youth culture, researchers have found multiple youth cultures (Brown, 1990), and they have found that peer groups often support the values of the adult society. The prevalence of battles between the youth culture and the values of adults is exaggerated (Ianni, 1989).

The studies of adolescent susceptibility to peer influence have produced two major findings that help to explain the unwillingness of many adolescents to follow the lead of their peers. First, Constanzo (1970) found susceptibility to peer influence decreases as adolescents increase confidence in their social skills. Social achievements reduce the power of peers over the adolescent. Second, the inclination to follow the lead of friends is much weaker when the peer group is moving toward antisocial activities (Cusick, 1973).

In the long term, adolescent social achievement has as its major consequence the development of social skills. Although being socially adept precedes success in the interpersonal realm as much as it is a consequence of it, some refining and learning of social skills do arise in peer interactions. Indeed, just as was true in the academic domain for intelligence, students who held an incremental view of personality (rather than viewing it as a fixed entity) were more likely to engage in a mastery-oriented pattern when faced with mild social rejection (Goetz & Dweck, 1980). In the social domain, as in other domains, developing the appropriate skills requires sustained motivation and effort, and that, in turn, depends on making appropriate attributions.

Some adolescents, like some adults, attribute success and failure in the social realm to internal, relatively stable characteristics, such as shyness or physical attractiveness. Those who believe personal skills to be stable, especially those who hold low expectations for social success, will decrease the value they place on achievement in the social domain. For most adolescents, the value of social attainment remains high. Many also find considerable intrinsic enjoyment in their friendships with peers. The extent to which social achievement is both enjoyable and possible helps determine its value in the eyes of adolescents.

Social achievement, then, is both the acquisition of social skills and the development of friendships. Those who achieve in this domain in high school should continue to find interpersonal success because of their skills, their social confidence, their image of personality, and their use of the networks they developed as adolescents.

An adolescent's visions of the future may affect the value he or she places on social achievement. U.S. emphasis on long-term goals, such as adult occupational attainment, leads to a diminished emphasis by adults on the social achievements of adolescents. Despite the importance of social skills for later participation in bureaucracies and professions, social achievement among adolescents is not perceived as a major influence on occupational achievement. For example, the massive bibliography on interpersonal competence developed by Spitzberg and Cupach (1989) has no references to the effects of social skills on occupational success, mentioning only that communication skills are highly valued in the business world. Such lack of attention to adult occupational achievement may be one reason that social achievement is so seldom studied longitudinally.

The empirical research on adolescent social achievement seeks to analyze adolescent social life in terms of the characteristics of either individual relationships or the social structure of crowds. Studies of friendship pairs have typically stressed the number of social relationships during adolescence. By contrast, the social support literature on friendship suggests that outcomes are more a function of the quality of relationships than of their quantity (Cohen & Willis, 1985). The intimacy of friendships increases as children enter early adolescence (Berndt, 1981; Douvan & Adelson, 1966; Youniss & Smollar, 1985), and more intimate relationships are viewed by adolescents as sources of social support (Berndt & Perry, 1990). Adolescent friendships not only differ in their intensity, but many are unstable and not reciprocated. Epstein (1986) found that reciprocated friendships were more likely to be stable. We need studies of the effects of the stability and reciprocity of friendships on long-term adolescent outcomes (Savin-Williams & Berndt, 1990).

As adolescents develop, they have increasing opportunities to encounter peers with diverse characteristics. Yet during the adolescent period, friends become more similar to each other, especially if the relationship is reciprocal and stable (Epstein, 1989). In part, similarity among friends is a product of selection, for adolescents seek relationships that are familiar and conflict-free (Savin-Williams & Berndt, 1990). Billy and Udry (1985) note that the similarity in values between adolescents and their friends is often misinterpreted as the product of peer influence. Their studies of sexual behavior indicate that approximately half of the observed similarities are the product of selecting like-minded friends.

Larger groupings of friends, called *crowds*, form a part of the social structure within schools and neighborhoods. Whereas cliques refer to a group characterized by close relationships, crowds are larger reputation-based collectives. Unlike Coleman (1974), Brown, Eicher, and Petrie (1986) did not find that the most popular adolescents valued crowds more than did less elite groups of students. For most adolescents, affiliation with peer groups and crowds is more typically a way station in their development, between early identification with family and self-identity as an individual.

Though enormously influential, Coleman's (1961) results have been considerably revised by other researchers. In contradiction to Coleman, the importance of crowd affiliation declines with age (Brown et al., 1986). Younger adolescents were concerned about membership in a crowd, emphasizing its ability to provide emotional and instrumental support, foster friendships, and facilitate social interaction. In contrast, older adolescents felt that established friendship networks obviated the need for crowds and expressed dissatisfaction with their conformity demands. Not surprisingly, adolescents who said they were central members of a crowd were likely to place more importance on crowd membership than did those on the periphery or in no crowd at all.

Adolescents develop their social ties in a specific context, and that context affects their social development. For example, Entwisle (1990) reports that small secondary schools enhance personal development and social behavior among adolescents. The social context also interacts with pubertal development. Compared with normal or late maturers, early maturing girls in Sweden are more likely to drink and be sexually active only when their social network includes older friends (Magnusson, 1988).

In conclusion, the increasing salience of social patterns and skills during adolescence has led to a continuing debate on the extent to which peer values conflict with parental goals for their children. That peers operate as normative reference groups for adolescents is clear, but more recent research has produced an image of multiple youth cultures, most of which are supportive of adult values.

The development of social skills is enhanced when the adolescent has a conception of that skill as incremental, subject to change, and a product of effort. Social skills in children have been related to developmental outcomes in adolescence, such as delinquency, mental health, academic adjustment, and social status (Spitzberg & Cupach, 1989). We deplore the lack of longitudinal research on the effects of social skills on achievement in adulthood. In part, this deficiency is the product of problems of conceptualization and measurement of social skills, but in addition, it is a lack of recognition of their fundamental importance in an increasingly complex set of work institutions.

ACHIEVEMENT IN THE WORKPLACE

Approximately 70% to 85% of U.S. high school students work for pay at some time while attending high school, with a somewhat lower proportion among minority females (D'Amico, 1984). If one adds summer employment, almost all adolescents have some work experience before graduating from high school (Hamilton & Powers, 1990). Thus, achievement in the realm of employment is a significant experience for many teenagers.

The workplace has become, like the school, family, and peer group, a major part of the teenage world in the United States. Other countries discourage active participation in the workplace among adolescents who are still in school. The high proportion of U.S. teenagers who work while going to school is a relatively recent phenomenon. Prior to the 20th century, about 70% of all adolescent males and 35% of adolescent females worked full-time. It was only after the 1930s and the passage of child labor laws that more U.S. adolescents were in school than in the workplace. And it is only since the 1940s that adolescent students took part-time jobs in large numbers. Most of these jobs were in retail and service occupations, which became common in the United States and Canada earlier than in the rest of the industrial world (Reubens, Harrison, & Rupp, 1981). Starting in the 1950s, employment rates for boys and girls in high school have become increasingly similar (Mortimer, Finch, Owens, & Shanahan, 1990).

Rates of labor force participation are much higher for students 16 years and older than for those under 16 (Greenberger & Steinberg, 1986). Furthermore, younger adolescents tend to work shorter hours. Among high school sophomores in the High School and Beyond sample, males averaged about 15 hours per week of employment and females averaged about 10 hours per week. Among high school seniors, the males and females worked an average of 21 hours and 18 hours, respectively. How is this heavy investment in work possible for full-time high school students in the United States? An undemanding school curriculum (the average U.S. high school student in 1980 spent less than one hour per week on homework) and a post-secondary education system that accepts students with poor academic backgrounds provide an opportunity for millions of adolescents in the United States to combine work and school (Lewin-Epstein, 1981). The rates of adolescent labor force participation are much lower in Canada, Sweden, and especially Japan, where the demands of school are more rigorous (Reubens et al., 1981).

The high proportion of U.S. teenagers who work part-time makes it important that the nature of their jobs be somewhat fulfilling and educational. Proponents of adolescent work had hoped that participation in the workplace would increase adolescents' contact with their elders, provide meaningful work experience, and help them adopt adult perspectives (National Commission on Youth, 1980; National Panel on High Schools and Adolescent Education, 1976; President's Science Advisory Committee Panel on Youth, 1973). Researchers, though, have noted that many adolescents spend their time almost exclusively with other adolescents (Greenberger & Steinberg, 1986). In fact, most adolescents are not even supervised by adults in their jobs but by other adolescents (Greenberger & Steinberg, 1986)! Observations of teenagers on the job showed that for 78% of their working hours, they were not near any adult. Only 12% of their time on the job was spent near an adult supervisor. Nor did teenagers develop ties with adults as mentors or confidants. Over 90% of all teenage workers reported no contacts at all outside of work with those adults they met in the workplace (Greenberger & Steinberg, 1986). Such age segregation keeps adolescents from learning about adult roles.

Nor does teenage work improve relations with adults in the family. Ianni (1989) found that adolescent work seems to diminish the number of family interactions and the quality of parent-adolescent relationships. But Manning (1990) found that the relation of disagreements to hours of employment varied by topic. She reported that youths who work more hours had fewer disagreements with parents about school and family and more disagreements about curfews and were less carefully monitored by their parents.

Greenberger and Steinberg (1986) conclude that, over the past century, the conditions of work for U.S. adolescents have become steadily less likely to produce constructive outcomes. The decline of apprenticeships and the discontinuity between adolescent jobs and adult occupations mean that teenage workers are not getting trained for adult roles (Gillis, 1981). Adolescent work in the United States does not resemble the apprenticeship system that has been so successful in West Germany. In a partnership between companies and the German government, adolescents there are able to learn skilled trades while continuing their education (Hamilton, 1990). By contrast, in the United States, almost half of all high school seniors with jobs are working in food service or as store clerks (Lewin-Epstein, 1981). Whereas adolescents often used to work in skilled trades, in factories, or on farms, those three types of employment combined are now held by only 13% of employed seniors in the United States (Greenberger & Steinberg, 1986).

Although teenage employment probably produces both positive and negative results, research to date shows little firm evidence that youth employment has long-term positive consequences. Mortimer and Finch (1986) found that by 5 years after graduation, any benefits due to work experience, such as the increased wages after graduation reported by Meyer and Wise (1982), had already faded. Greenberger and Steinberg (1986) found that, when adolescents worked 20 hours or more per week, outcomes were far more likely to be negative than when teens invested only a few hours per week in part-time work. Indeed, many working adolescents developed cynical attitudes toward work and were dishonest on the job (Greenberger & Steinberg, 1986). Still, the majority of female high school graduates, looking back at their early work experience, felt that it had fostered the development of personal responsibility (Hamilton & Powers, 1990).

Although experts often find that teenage employment has negative correlates, the rates of employment indicate that adolescents find value in work. The typical adolescent job in the service sector is unrelated to future occupational aspirations and thus generally unaffected by the adolescent's vision of the future. For adolescents, the primary value of employment is short-term: the paycheck. It is this paycheck, rather than any intrinsic enjoyment of the work or view of its utility for the future, that guides the pursuit of work. Thus, teens whose parents provide them with an ample allowance are unlikely to seek employment. It is interesting, though, that middle-class adolescents are more likely than poor adolescents to get part-time employment, and they use their earnings primarily for personal expenditures. Middle-class youth also start work at an earlier age than those less advantaged (Mortimer et al., 1990).

The earnings of most teenagers are not added to the family's coffers nor to savings for long-range goals but instead, buy clothing and pay for entertainment and discretionary purchases (Bachman, 1983). Only a small minority of teenage workers give a substantial proportion of their pay to their parents or save for further education, and only 1% give all of their pay to their family (Steinberg & Dornbusch, 1991; Steinberg, Fegley, & Dornbusch, 1993). There is little long-term value in the typical service sector job, either in socialization for future occupational roles or in contact with adults who might mentor the adolescent. In addition, the discontinuity between adolescent and adult employment suggests that there is probably little link between performance in these jobs and expectations for performance in later employment.

Workplace achievement is public achievement. Both the adolescent's being employed and the purchases made with his or her earnings are generally known, but the meaning of achievement in the workplace depends heavily on social context. Among adolescents, particularly those in lower socioeconomic groups, simply getting a job is an achievement. To the surprise of many adults, more middle-class adolescents and more non-Hispanic Whites work while in high school than African American and Hispanic American students, who are far more likely to seek work than to get work (Greenberger & Steinberg, 1986). In part, adolescent difficulties in getting part-time jobs are a result of the decline of low-skill jobs available near communities populated by minorities and members of low socioeconomic groups (Wilson, 1987). In addition, adolescents in lower socioeconomic groups have fewer ties to adult job holders and, thereby, are disadvantaged in the search for jobs (Garanovetter, 1973). Middle-class adolescents are more likely to have the cultural capital that makes getting employment easier, a factor that helps in reproducing existing inequalities. For instance, these teenagers may be better dressed and more articulate than their lower-class counterparts. Although middle-class adolescents are better at getting jobs, lower-class adolescents are more likely to seek employment. This suggests that the value of the achievement is high and that low expectations for success do not hinder the effort too much.

There is little information on minority youth employment. It is possible that both the immediate effect and the long-term consequences of adolescent employment will differ greatly by social class and by ethnic group. To fully understand the meaning of workplace achievement for all adolescents, we need more research that takes the context of employment into account.

There is also a need for more longitudinal studies of adolescents in the workplace. The most influential study, Greenberger and Steinberg's (1986), found some conflicting results when comparing longitudinal and cross-sectional results. Still, we can conclude that adolescent employment is typically unrelated to future occupations or adult mentoring. Immediate monetary compensation is the main reward of adolescent work.

INTERRELATIONS AMONG DOMAINS

Now that we have discussed the four domains of adolescent achievement, we turn our attention to the interrelations among the domains. We report some central findings on the relations between each pair of domains. It is of theoretical and practical importance to assess the relation between achievement in disparate domains. If high achievement in one domain leads to low achievement in another, then the overall image of adolescent achievement is of choices that must be made. If, on the other hand, achievement in one domain tends to be associated with achievement in another, then encouragement for adolescent achievement as a whole is an appropriate strategy. Because the bulk of the literature on adolescent achievement does not encompass diverse domains, our task is novel and will, we hope, lead others to reflect on the long-term empirical connections between the domains of adolescent achievement.

ACADEMIC AND EXTRACURRICULAR ACHIEVEMENT

How is achievement in the academic domain related to extracurricular achievement? One answer to that question comes from a comparison of the academic achievement of students who participate in extracurricular activities with that of students who do not participate. It may also be useful to compare the academic outcomes of students who participate in different activities. Although some research suggests that nonathletic activities are associated with higher grades than athletic ones and that participation itself is related to higher grades (Bender, 1978; Landers & Landers, 1978), there is some indication that controlling for initial academic ability and social class renders such effects negligible (Hauser & Leptow, 1978). The contexts in which students attempt achievement in each domain also influence the interaction between domains. In examining these issues, we will include some findings relating to participation in extracurricular activities in college. Although the respondents will not all be adolescents, analysis at the college level adds to our understanding of the relation between academic and athletic achievement among adolescents.

Coleman's (1961) main contribution in *The Adolescent Society* was to stress the influence of the context on different domains of adolescent achievement. The value assigned to athletic achievement or academic achievement in a specific school shaped the effort of the students at that school. In addition to the institutional context of the school, there may be effects of such contexts as ethnicity or socioeconomic status. For example, it is widely believed that, in a context of high reward for achievement in the athletic domain, there is a relative decline in the emphasis on academics within the African American male population.

Coleman implied that the pursuit of athletic achievement distracted students from academics despite the fact that his own data showed higher grade point averages (GPAs) for outstanding athletes than for the student body as a whole (Rehberg, 1969). Since the publication of *The Adolescent Society*, there have been many attempts both to confirm and to disprove Coleman's theory with empirical research. For example, Feltz and Weiss (1984) showed that boys who participated in athletics had GPAs that were significantly higher than average. In comparison to a matched sample of non-athletes, however, the academic advantage of athletes was not significant (Feltz & Weiss, 1984).

Coleman's (1961) view of athletics as an alternative to academics implied that the social system in high school delegitimates academic activities and favors athletic pursuits. For example, a greater percentage of boys would prefer to be remembered for their athletic prowess (41%) rather than for their academic achievement (31%; Coleman, 1961). Freisen's (1968) study of Canadian youth reported similar criteria for popularity in high school, but Freisen found that students would rather be remembered for academic achievement than for athletic prowess. In other words, students knew the norms of the popular crowd but failed to endorse them. A decade after Coleman, Eitzen (1976) found that although the students he studied were just as enthusiastic about sports as the earlier group, males who wished to be remembered for their athletic skills made up only 25% of his sample compared with 45% who favored academics. In contrast, Thirer and Wright (1985) found that males in the 1980s emphasized the importance of achievement in athletics more than in academics.

Lueptow and Kayser (1973) conducted a longitudinal study that concluded that differences in academic interest between athletes and non-athletes were due to the initial dissimilarity of the two groups, not to the socialization effects of athletic participation. The relative strength of their longitudinal design suggests that earlier cross-sectional studies had too hastily assumed that athletic achievement caused devaluation of academics. Hauser and Lueptow (1978) later found that high-participant, high-status athletes were better students than non-athletes at the starts of their high school careers, but they slipped from this advantaged position over the course of high school—especially during their sport's season. According to Steinberg (1988), the academic advantage that early investigators found among athletes was mostly a result of individual characteristics that led them into sports, rather than something gained through extracurricular participation. Where differences did exist between participants and nonparticipants, they were most noticeable among those already less disposed toward educational achievement. The continuing controversy surrounding Coleman's original thesis that athletic participation causes academic devaluation suggests that this area needs further study.

There have been a few attempts to contrast the relative effects of athletics and other extracurricular activities on academic achievement. In one example, Bender (1978) found a tendency toward slightly lower correlations between grades and athletic participation than between grades and participation in performing arts or clubs. Landers and Landers (1978) compared Scholastic Aptitude Test (SAT) scores of high school senior athletes who had participated in leadership or service activities to those of athletes who had not participated in such activities. They found that those students who participated only in sports scored significantly lower on the SAT than those who also did other extracurricular activities.

McNeal (1995) found that athletic participation did a much better job of preventing students from dropping out of high school than did participation in any other activities. Participation in performing arts showed only a tendency to reduce dropping out, but this may be because performing arts students were initially less inclined to drop out. McNeal did not explore the connection between extracurricular participation and better academic performance.

Schools are not just places where students take courses. Adolescents see the school as the center of their social lives (Coleman, 1961). Participation in extracurricular activities further connects students to each other and to significant adults (coaches and teachers). The slight positive effect of extracurricular participation on academic achievement for low achieving students may be a function of the connection to the school that these activities provide. Unfortunately, lower-track students report being discouraged by both peers and teachers from participating in extracurricular activities (Rosenbaum, 1976).

Several researchers have studied the differences in academic aspirations between athletes and non-athletes. Athletes from families of lower socioeconomic status whose parents did not encourage them to go to college and who performed poorly in school had higher educational aspirations than did non-athletes of the same background. This result, for white student athletes only, appeared to be the result of association with other college-oriented youth (Picou, 1978).

Spady (1970, 1971) found that students in extracurricular activities who had low grades and high status among peers had higher educational aspirations. Thus, lower-ability students whose peer status is enhanced by extracurricular participation may be more likely to strive for higher education, yet they may also be more likely to find their expectations dashed by the reality that they are not prepared (financially or intellectually) for college-level work (Steinberg, 1988).

For those who do make it to college, there is a similar set of connections between athletic and academic achievement. Shapiro (1984) argued that college athletics has a positive influence on the educational attainment of student athletes because the graduation rates of athletes were found to be higher than or comparable to those of the general student population. However, college student athletes typically have a much stronger support network of teammates, coaches, special academic advisers, tutors, and financial aid. This assistance constitutes a large advantage for student athletes in terms of staying in school (although it may not improve their grade point averages), and it is likely to account for their higher graduation rates.

Adler and Adler (1985) found that most athletes entered college with optimistic goals and attitudes about their academic careers but that their social and academic experiences as student athletes led them to become progressively detached from academics. As a result, they made pragmatic adjustments, abandoning their earlier aspirations and expectations, and resigned themselves to inferior academic performance.

Football and basketball players at the college level were more likely than other student athletes to have academic difficulties, in spite of being more likely to attend educational skill-building courses and to report greater access to other educational resources (e.g., tutors and academic advisers) (AIR, 1988). African American football and basketball players were especially likely to have these academic difficulties. These African American athletes reported that being involved in athletics made it harder to get the grades they are capable of, to study for exams, to keep up with course work, and to prepare for class. Among male football and basketball players who regarded earning a degree as a most important goal, 15% of the non-African Americans and more than 30% of the African Americans had a GPA below C (AIR, 1988). These athletes in major sports were failing in a domain that they deemed very important.

Male football and basketball players from nationally ranked college sports programs performed less well than players from less successful teams on almost every measure of academic performance (AIR, 1988). This ranking of athletic programs can be seen as a proxy for investment in and commitment to athletic achievement, with corresponding lower investment and commitment to academic achievement. Players in these top-ranked programs are more likely than those in the other programs to feel that it is difficult to be regarded as serious students by professors, to keep up with course work, and to get the grades they are capable of getting (AIR, 1988).

Student athletes as a whole have slightly lower cumulative grades in college than do students in other extracurricular activities, but they are not very different on other dimensions of academic performance. The two groups have the same level of satisfaction with their academic performance (AIR, 1988). The evidence indicates that athletic participation in college, particularly with the major investment of time and energy required by top-ranked sports programs, is associated with lower levels of academic achievement.

A well-designed study by Ratcliff (1995) at the National Center for Postsecondary Teaching, Learning, and Assessment produced similar results. They matched athletes and non-athletes of the same math and reading ability before the freshman year of college. Both groups were tested again at the end of the freshman year; the non-athletes were found to have improved significantly more than the athletes.

For males in some sports, reading comprehension and math scores actually decreased over the course of the freshman year. This research suggests that too intense a focus on one domain of achievement (extracurricular athletics) can have a negative effect on academic achievement.

In sum, evidence on the relation between academic and extracurricular achievement is mixed. There has not been convincing evidence of a causal relation between the two domains. The relatively few attempts to contrast athletics to other extracurricular activities in terms of its association with academic achievement have suggested that other extracurricular activities are more positive than athletics. Research on athletic achievement indicates a more negative correlation to academic achievement at the college level than at the high school level. More research is particularly needed to study the effects of race, ethnicity, and gender on the relation between academics and extracurricular activities.

The previous research, much of it a generation old, tended to examine only final outcomes, as opposed to the processes underlying the development of extracurricular and academic orientations. Longitudinal studies are required, and the variables to be included should range across social linkages, relations to the family, and social contexts.

ACADEMIC AND
SOCIAL ACHIEVEMENT

The relation between peer influences and academic achievement is complex. First, the relation between individual adolescents and their peers is clearly reciprocal, with each influencing the other. Second, peer influences are not monolithic. Peers have differing relationships toward academics in different contexts, and attempts to paint peers as consistently anti-academic seem to be oversimplistic.

James Coleman (1961) found that adolescents reported that getting good grades was relatively low on the list of prerequisites for being in the elite social crowd, although the importance of academics varied with the community context. Coleman saw a consistent tendency for adolescent society to devalue academic achievement, influencing adolescents to reduce their academic effort and interest. Faris

(1961) similarly reported that an informal culture existed among adolescents that defined study as unpleasant and unimportant and reduced aspirations for learning. This perspective from the 1960s is supported by a more recent study. Ratcliff (1995) compared fraternity and sorority members with independent students of the same math and reading ability prior to the freshman year of college. The researchers found that membership in sororities and fraternities had a negative effect on reading and math scores compared with freshmen who were not members of such organizations. This research suggests that too intense a focus on the social domain can have a negative effect on academic achievement.

Many researchers, especially those who have demonstrated significant subgroup differences within crowds of adolescents (Brown, 1990; Cohen, 1979), have taken issue with Coleman's monolithic image of the adolescent culture. Furthermore, several studies, including Coleman's, found that although achieving high grades was never a means of achieving social success, the members of high prestige social groups had above-average grades (Brown, 1990; Coleman, 1961; Steinberg, 1988). Ethnographic evidence about high school crowds suggests that academic orientation is an important differentiating factor between crowds, with some strongly oriented toward academic success, others strongly against it, and many neutral (Buff, 1970; Cusick, 1973; Larkin, 1979; Varenne, 1982). Thus, depicting the relation between school performance and social prestige as purely negative is inaccurate (Brown, 1990). In addition, a survey of the research literature on interpersonal skills concluded that they are generally associated with academic adjustment (Spitzberg & Cupach, 1989). A longitudinal study of an extreme group of highly withdrawn French Canadian children found that they had poor school achievement and lower self-perceptions of their academic abilities 6 years later during adolescence (Moskowitz & Schwartzman, 1989).

Similarity between the academic performance of friends has been cited as evidence for the influence of peers on academic achievement. Nevertheless, academic orientation has been shown primarily to predate peer relationships and may be the basis for initiating friendships (Cohen, 1983; Epstein, 1983; Kandel, 1978). In addition to this initial similarity, though, there is evidence that over the course of a school year, friends' academic attitudes and achievements grow slightly more alike (Epstein, 1983; Kandel, 1978). Thus, it is not surprising that adolescents with academically high-achieving friends do better in school than those with low-achieving friends (Steinberg, 1988).

Coleman's (1961) conclusion that academic achievement works against social achievement has inspired several studies of the difficulties that adolescents face as they choose to focus on one or more domains for achievement (Faune, 1984; Golden & Cherry, 1982; Ishiyama & Chabassol, 1985; Schneider & Coutts, 1985). The results were inconsistent, with some finding that high school students feared academic success because of anticipated peer reactions (Ishiyama & Chabassol, 1985) and others finding high positive correlations between GPA and peer status (Faunce, 1984). Clasen and Brown (1985) found that pressure from peers to achieve in academics was generally strong throughout high school. The strength of this relation differed significantly by crowd, with "jocks" and "populars" reporting much more pressure to do well in school than "toughs" and "druggies."

Ethnographic research suggests that some ethnic or racial minority adolescents may face peer norms that particularly discourage academic achievement as a value of the majority culture (Fordham & Ogbu, 1986; Gibson, 1982; Labov, 1982). Although these studies found that many adolescents cut back on academic effort in the face of peer pressure, other adolescents continued to achieve but engaged in efforts to hide their academic achievements from peers (Fordham & Ogbu, 1986; Fuller, 1984). This conflict between peer norms and academic achievement can be very stressful (Fordham & Ogbu, 1986). It is hard to be an adolescent, eager for acceptance by peers, and have those peers jeer at high academic performance as a sign of having sold out to the majority culture. Although these conflicts have been demonstrated particularly among members of ethnic minorities, even students in all-White schools who are labeled "brains" suffer from peer rejection (Brown, Lohr, & Trujillo, 1983; Coleman, 1961).

A very different aspect of the relation between academic and social achievement is the influence of institutional academic arrangements on social interaction. Curriculum tracking in schools—channeling students into objectively distinct instructional groups—creates a within-school status hierarchy. Some students are formally recognized as better and more capable than others (Oakes, 1987). Survey and ethnographic research shows quite clearly that there are marked differences between ability groups and curriculum tracks in social as well as academic domains (for reviews, see Gamoran & Berends, 1987; Oakes et al., 1992).

Tracking is detrimental to the social prestige of lower-track students. Students are more likely to choose friends who take the same classes they do. Students who are in the lower track are more likely to be high in societal deviance and low in social prestige within the school. Accordingly, each student in the lower track is more likely to have friends who are deviant and low in social prestige. Furthermore, the subculture of students in the lower tracks supports antagonism toward teachers and school, leading to an alternative structure of values and rewards that hinders academic achievement (Hargreaves, 1967).

Oakes's (1985) study of the effects of tracking showed that students in low-track classes, more than those in the high tracks, felt that other students in their classes were unfriendly to them. They also experienced more hostile interactions in their classes. Trust, cooperation, and even good will among students are far less characteristic of classes in the low track than classes in the high track (Oakes, 1985).

Steinberg (1988) sums up the interaction between these domains well:

> On balance, most peers seem to encourage academic success (as opposed to failure), but are suspicious of outstanding achievement and intolerant of those who flaunt their scholastic accomplishments. Although students may need to struggle against the norms of their friends or their crowd, there is a choice of peer associates, and most students are able to align themselves with peers who share their academic interests and aspirations. (p. 23)

ACADEMIC AND
WORKPLACE ACHIEVEMENT

There are a few positive findings relating achievement in school and the workplace. For instance, those teens who are employed for less than 20 hours a week, compared with those not working at all, are less likely to drop out of school (D'Amico, 1984), and those adolescents who worked only a few hours per week had higher grades than those who did not work at all (Steinberg & Dornbusch, 1991).

On the whole, though, employment seems to interact negatively with academic achievement. Greenberger and Steinberg (1986) found that, before getting a job, adolescents who later worked more than 20 hours per week were typically disengaged in school. However, taking on a job for more than 20 hours per week further disengaged adolescents from school (Steinberg & Dornbusch, 1991). Employed adolescents spent less time on homework, were absent from school or tardy more often, and cut class more (Greenberger & Steinberg, 1986). Analyses of the Youth in Transition Study found that, 5 years after high school, males who had worked during high school had lower GPAs, less positive academic self-concepts, lower educational and occupational aspirations, and lower educational attainments than those who had not worked (Mortimer & Finch, 1986). Those who were employed longer when in high school were more disadvantaged. Marsh (1991) found similarly discouraging correlates of youth employment, but his analysis did highlight one positive relationship: Among those few adolescents who worked to save for college, the work experience was positively correlated with grades, honors, homework, attendance, and educational aspirations (Marsh, 1991). Once in college, however, Ratcliff (1995) found that women and minority students who had off-campus jobs during college were 36% more likely to drop out of school than members of the same groups who did not have jobs.

The empirical evidence suggests that the immediate consequences of employment for school outcomes are curvilinearly related to the number of hours that the adolescent works. Having a job can be positive, but as working hours increase, adolescent educational and occupational aspirations diminish (Finch & Mortimer, 1985). Other research concurs that long work hours during the school year are associated with both lower investment and lower performance in school (Steinberg & Dornbusch, 1991). Although evidence about the effects of hours of work on high school grades is somewhat mixed, Greenberger and Steinberg (1986) have noted that the decline in grades attributable to adolescent employment is small—in part because teenagers seek to maintain their grades by carefully selecting courses that require less time and effort.

Thus, findings about the relation between these domains is consistent and straightforward. Workplace achievement is generally associated with lower academic achievement and aspirations.

EXTRACURRICULAR
AND SOCIAL ACHIEVEMENT

Research on the interaction of social and extracurricular achievement is very limited. Most of what we know about the relation of these domains comes from the AIR (1988) study of college athletics and extracurricular activities. Nevertheless, we can point to several suggestive findings for younger adolescents.

There has been some research on gender differences in the relation between extracurricular achievement and social status. Among junior high students, Eder and Parker (1987) found that adolescents who participated in extracurricular activities increased their visibility among peers and influenced their membership in elite peer groups. Among males, the emphasis was on athletic competition, whereas females focused more on appearance and the management of emotions. At the high school level, when asked to identify the most desirable roles, males identified outstanding student and outstanding athlete, whereas females indicated outstanding student and member of a leading peer group (Chandler, 1990). These gender differences suggest that athletic prowess is perceived by males as crucial in their social order, whereas females see social status as separate from any particular extracurricular domain.

At the college level, the relation between extracurricular and social achievement is different for athletics than for other activities. Student athletes reported that social interactions were more difficult than did those participating in other extracurricular activities. Fewer student athletes (35%) than students in other extracurricular activities (61%) reported it was easy for them to be liked by others for just being themselves (AIR, 1988). Student athletes also reported it was harder to talk with others about their personal problems and concerns (AIR, 1988).

Not surprisingly, college students tend to develop friendships with, and spend time with, others who share their extracurricular interests. There were not significant differences between athletes and those in other extracurricular activities in terms of the proportion who spent most of their time with friends from their extracurricular activities (AIR, 1988).

African American athletes are in a special situation. Those African American football and basketball players on college campuses with very few African American undergraduates were more apt to feel different from other students, to feel they lacked control over their lives, and to feel isolated from other students than were their counterparts on campuses where the percentage of African American undergraduates was higher.

On campuses with low enrollments of African American students, African American football and basketball players reported racial isolation and considerable racial discrimination. They, accordingly, reported high anxiety and depression. They found it harder to talk about their personal problems than did African American players at predominantly African American schools. At predominantly White schools, African American football and basketball players found it more difficult to get to know other students and to be liked by others than did African Americans in other extracurricular activities.

Extracurricular achievement serves primarily as a context within which adolescent social achievement operates. Extracurricular activities, including athletics, often serve to form friendship groups and can offer evidence of achievements that give social capital to adolescents. Limited evidence suggests that the relation between extracurricular and social achievement is positive among junior high and high school students. This relation probably does not change at the college level. Yet in terms of football and basketball achievement, college students appear to suffer socially as a result of their athletic achievements. In the major revenue-producing sports (men's basketball and football), the college athlete's world becomes more isolated and segregated. The exclusive focus on athletic achievement leads to a reduction in social contacts and a sense of isolation. Last, in the context of predominantly White colleges and universities, the social difficulties of African American athletes are particularly extreme.

EXTRACURRICULAR AND
WORKPLACE ACHIEVEMENT

Part-time employment tends to reduce participation in all forms of extracurricular activities, including athletics (Greenberger & Steinberg, 1986; Marsh, 1991). Marsh (1991) found that increased commitments in one sphere of activity, such as work, are likely to result in reduced commitments in other spheres, such as extracurricular and social activities. Although work for adolescents is often portrayed as a means of gaining adult perspectives and maturity, researchers note that other arenas of development are correspondingly sacrificed (Greenberger & Steinberg, 1986). Indeed, adolescents reported their most positive moods when participating in arts, hobbies, and sports, whereas they were most likely to wish to be doing something else while on a part-time job. They recognize the primary reward of the job as income rather than intrinsic pleasure or growth (Csikszentmihalyi & Larson, 1984). Older girls who worked longer hours were less satisfied with their lives than those who worked less—perhaps, in part, because longer hours preclude participation in extracurricular activities (Yamoor & Mortimer, 1990). Thus, there is a negative correlation between achievement in the workplace and in extracurricular activities.

SOCIAL AND
WORKPLACE ACHIEVEMENT

The relation between achievement in the realm of paid employment and social achievement is largely unquantified. Many proponents of youth employment have argued that one of its benefits would be to weaken the "troublesome youth culture" (Timpane, Abramowitz, Bobrow, & Pascal, 1976). Yet recent research has suggested that youth employment actually strengthens the social culture that proponents had hoped to erode (Greenberger & Steinberg, 1986).

In general, employed adolescents have less close relationships with peers (Steinberg, Greenberger, Garduque, Ruggiero, & Vaux, 1982). As the previous section indicated, these adolescents have little time to be involved in extracurricular activities, a major arena of social interaction. Thus, adolescents who achieve in the workplace may suffer socially as a result.

Yet among female high school graduates who did not intend to attend college, Hamilton and Powers (1990) found that almost half felt their work experience had enhanced their social development. For these young women, work experience had taught them to be more tolerant and cooperative and to deal with people of varied backgrounds.

Employment in the typical adolescent job in retail and service settings provides ample opportunity to continue socializing with other adolescents after school. The topics of conversation on the job are "precisely those over which 'youth culture' opponents have expressed concern: clothing, dating, popularity, purchases" (Greenberger & Steinberg, 1986, p. 200). Youth culture may also be supported by the spending patterns of adolescents who are employed. Having the money to buy socially valued items may increase the status of employed adolescents among their peers.

Research by Ruggiero, Greenberger, and Steinberg (1982) found that occupational deviance (stealing from work, cheating on time cards, etc.) was most common when adolescents described their work environment as positive socially. Ruggiero et al. suggest that "illicit behavior in the workplace serves to validate membership in the youth culture" (Greenberger & Steinberg, 1986).

Thus, workplace achievement seems to promote certain types of social achievement that are not considered desirable by society. Social achievement appears generally to be inhibited by employment. It is suggestive that work during the summer, when there may be no conflict between work and school, contributes positively to social self-concept (Marsh, 1991). Also, as previously mentioned, older girls who worked longer hours were less satisfied with their lives, and this may result from having less time for valued social activities (Yamoor & Mortimer, 1990). Further research is needed, though, to compare the social achievements outside the workplace of those who work with those who do not.

DISCUSSION AND IMPLICATIONS

There is an expected order of achievements in the life course. Adolescence is generally perceived as a time of preparation for adult life, and the central domain of adult achievement is increasingly occupational. Thus, the academic, extracurricular, social, and work domains are appropriately given major emphasis as one discusses the important tasks of adolescent development. But an excessive investment of time and energy in any of these domains can operate to reduce achievement in the other domains. For example, an interpretation of the somewhat negative relations between achievement in the workplace and achievement in the other three domains is that heavy doses of part-time employment during adolescence are improperly placed in the life course. When achievement in the workplace is invested with high inputs of effort and time, there is a corresponding disruption in those other domains of achievement that are more typically associated with adolescence. Similarly, the negative relations between fraternity or sorority participation and academic achievement and the negative relation between the most demanding athletic programs and academic performance of athletes illustrate the same point. Although research has not demonstrated it, it is likely that extreme and exclusive involvement in academic pursuits will also lead to reduced achievement in other domains.

There are also differences in the perceived time scales of the domains of achievement. Social achievement is viewed mainly through its immediate consequences. Adults often perceive workplace achievement as developing a work ethic and the skills and habits needed for future occupational achievement. For the adolescents, the reality of workplace achievement is an increase in immediate discretionary income.

Extracurricular achievement is usually a source of immediate intrinsic pleasure. For some, however, who are leaders in athletics or in other extracurricular activities, excellence signifies the potential for later occupational achievement. Athletics is viewed as professional preparation for male students who feel that other opportunities are closed to them. Success in other extracurricular activities may be viewed as an aid to getting into selective colleges. Last, academic achievement is generally perceived as preparation for adult occupations. Academic achievement is viewed positively among both adolescents and adults. It is interesting that, though investments in academic efforts increase stress for the adolescent, this stress is typically ignored. Ultimately, it is the long-term consequences of academic success that make it a positive achievement despite the stress. The effect of achievement in these domains, then, ranges from immediate enjoyment to investment in a long-term future.

The power of context has been demonstrated repeatedly as we have examined various domains. The contexts that change the relations between variables are numerous: ethnicity, social class, size and type of school, and the organization of the curriculum. For example, within a single school, tracking can produce different contexts for both academic and social achievement. Too seldom have we been able to report on the effect of community context on adolescent development because the community is rarely defined as the small residential area that is perceived as the adolescent's neighborhood.

Our analysis of the interrelations of achievement in pairs of domains typically found mixed results. One explanation of these complex relations is that they are markedly dependent on their contexts. When context has so large an influence, the magnitude and direction of relations between achievement in two domains is less likely to be stable.

Last, adolescent achievement is determined in large measure by the subjective perceptions of the adolescents. Research based on the perspectives of attribution theory and mastery learning indicates that the beliefs of the adolescent, who is an active agent in perceiving current efforts and situations, help create an atmosphere of perseverance and achievement in all four domains.

We found particularly striking the lack of longitudinal studies that track individual achievements during adolescence and observe their consequences as individuals move into adulthood. Too often, the study of adolescent development has limited itself to the adolescent years. There is a desperate need for determining what achievements, at what times, for which adolescents, in what contexts are most likely to produce various forms of adult achievement.

The previous research, some of it a generation old, tended to examine only final outcomes, as opposed to the processes underlying the development of extracurricular and academic orientations. Longitudinal studies are required, and the variables to be included should range across the domains of adolescent development. The approach taken by Ratcliff (1995) and his associates at the National Center for Post-Secondary Teaching, Learning, and Assessment is particularly encouraging. Their research included all four domains of achievement, and it examined the effect of achievement in each of three domains (social, work, and extracurricular) on academic achievement. Equally important is the longitudinal nature of the study, comparing students who were of equal academic ability before they engaged in certain activities during the following year. Although the study used academic achievement as the only dependent measure, measures of achievement in other domains were at least included as independent variables. We urge longitudinal research, beginning at the high school or junior high level, that simultaneously examines all four domains of achievement. It is important to measure how the domains affect each other and to consider their long-term effects on adolescent and adult outcomes.

Even as we urge the simultaneous analysis of the four domains of achievement and their interrelations, we feel it is important to consider the effects of these achievements on other types of outcomes. In particular, outcomes such as level of deviance and psychological maladjustment will vary with achievement in combinations of the four domains. Last, as our knowledge in these areas develops, it will be important to consider the effects of ethnic, gender, and socioeconomic contexts on the interrelations of adolescent achievements.

REFERENCES

Adams, G. R., Day, T., Dyk, P. H., Frede, E., & Rogers, D. R. B. (1992). On the dialectics of pubescence and psychosocial development. *Journal of Early Adolescence, 12*, 348-365.

Adler, P., & Adler, P. A. (1985). From idealism to pragmatic detachment: The academic performance of college athletes. *Sociology of Education, 58*, 241-250.

American Institutes for Research. (1988). *Report #1: Summary results from the 1987-1988 national study of intercollegiate athletes.* Palo Alto, CA: Author.

Ames, C., & Archer, J. (1988). Achievement goals in the classrooms: Students' learning strategies and motivation processes. *Journal of Educational Psychology, 80*, 260-267.

Atkinson, J. W. (1957). Motivational determinants of risk taking behavior. *Psychological Review, 64*, 359-372.

Atkinson, J. W. (1964). *An introduction to motivation.* Princeton, NJ: Van Nostrand.

Atkinson, J. W. (1966). Motivational determinants of risk taking behavior. In J. W. Atkinson & N. T. Feather (Eds.), *A theory of achievement motivation* (pp. 11-31). New York: John Wiley.

Bachman, M. G. (1983). Premature affluence: Do high school seniors earn too much? *Economic Outlook on the USA, 10*, 64-67.

Ball, S. J. (1981). *Beachside comprehensive: A case-study of secondary schooling.* New York: Cambridge University Press.

Bandura, A. (1977). Self-efficacy: Toward a unifying theory of behavioral change. *Psychological Review, 84*, 191-215.

Bandura, A. (1986). *Social foundations of thought and action: A social cognitive theory.* Englewood Cliffs, NJ: Prentice Hall.

Bandura, A. (1989). Human agency in social cognitive theory. *American Psychologist, 44*, 1175-1184.

Battle, E. (1965). Motivational determinants of academic task persistence. *Journal of Personality and Social Psychology, 2*, 209-218.

Battle, E. (1966). Motivational determinants of academic competence. *Journal of Personality and Social Psychology, 4*, 534-642.

Bender, D. S. (1978, March). *Extracurricular activities and achievement orientation of adolescent males and females.* Paper presented at the annual meeting of the American Educational Research Association, Toronto.

Berndt, T. J. (1981). Relations between social cognition, non-social cognition, and social behavior: The case of friendship. In J. H. Flavell and L. D. Ross (Eds.), *Social cognitive development: Frontiers and possible futures* (pp. 176-199). Cambridge, UK: Cambridge University Press.

Berndt, T. J., & Perry, T. B. (1990). Distinctive features and effects of early adolescent friendships. In R. Montemayor, G. R. Adams, & T. P. Gullotta (Eds.), *From childhood to adolescence: A transitional period?* (pp. 269-290). Newbury Park, CA: Sage.

Billy, J. O. G., & Udry, J. R. (1985). Patterns of adolescent friendship and effects on sexual behavior. *Social Psychology Quarterly, 48*, 27-41.

Bowles, S., & Gintis, H. (1976). *Schooling in capitalist America.* New York: Basic Books.

Brittain, C. V. (1963). Adolescent choices and parent-peer cross-pressures. *American Sociological Review, 28*, 385-391.

Bronfenbrenner, U. (1986). Ecology of the family as a context for human development: Research perspectives. *Developmental Psychology, 22*(6), 723-742.

Bronfenbrenner, U., & Crouter, A. (1983). The evolution of environmental models in developmental research. In P. Mussen (Ed.), *Handbook of child psychology* (Vol. 1). New York: John Wiley.

Brown, B. B. (1990). Peer groups and peer cultures. In S. Feldman & G. Elliott (Eds.), *At the threshold* (pp. 171-196). Cambridge, MA: Harvard University Press.

Brown, B. B., Eicher, S. A., & Petrie, S. (1986). The importance of peer group ("crowd") affiliation in adolescence. *Journal of Adolescence, 9*, 73-96.

Brown, B. B., & Lohr, M. J. (1987). Peer-group affiliation and adolescent self-esteem: An integration of ego-identity and symbolic-interaction theories. *Journal of Personality and Social Psychology, 52*, 47-55.

Brown, B. B., Lohr, M. J., & Trujillo, C. (1983, April). *Adolescent peer group stereotypes, member conformity and identity development.* Paper presented at the biennial meeting of the Society for Research in Child Development, Detroit, MI.

Buff, S. A. (1970). Greasers, dupers, and hippies: Three responses to the adult world. In L. Howe (Ed.), *The white majority.* New York: Random House.

Chandler, T. J. L. (1990). The academic all American as vaunted adolescent role-identity. *Sociology of Sport Journal, 7*, 287-293.

Chao, R. K. (1994). Beyond parental control and authoritarian parenting style: Understanding Chinese parenting through the cultural notion of training. *Child Development, 65*, 1111-1119.

Ciompi, K. (1993). *How colleges choose students.* New York: College Entrance Exam Board.

Clasen, D. R., & Brown, B. B. (1985). The multidimensionality of peer pressure in adolescence. *Journal of Youth and Adolescence, 14*, 451-468.

Cohen, B. P. (1962). The process of choosing a reference group. In J. H. Criswell, H. Solomon, & P. Suppes (Eds.), *Mathematical methods in small group processes* (pp. 101-118). Stanford, CA: Stanford University Press.

Cohen, E. G. (1993). Dismantling status hierarchies in heterogeneous classrooms. In J. Oakes (Ed.), *New educational communities: Schools and classrooms where all children can be smart* (National Society for the Study of Education Handbook, Vol. 94). Chicago: National Society for the Study of Education.

Cohen, J. (1979). High school cultures and the adult world. *Adolescence, 14,* 491-502.

Cohen, J. (1983). Commentary: The relationship between friendship selection and peer influence. In J. L. Epstein & N. Karweit (Eds.), *Friends in school.* New York: Academic Press.

Cohen, S., & Willis, T. A. (1985). Stress, social support, and the buffering hypothesis. *Psychological Bulletin, 98,* 310-357.

Coleman, J. S. (1961). *The adolescent society.* New York: Free Press.

Coleman, J. S. (1969). *Research for tomorrow's schools: Disciplined inquiry for education.* New York: Macmillan.

Coleman, J. S. (1974). *Relationships in adolescence.* Boston: Routledge & Kegan Paul.

Constanzo, P. R. (1970). Conformity development as a function of self-blame. *Journal of Personality and Social Psychology, 14,* 366-374.

Csikszentmihalyi, M., & Larson, R. (1984). *Being adolescent.* New York: Basic Books.

Cusick, P. A. (1973). *Inside high school.* New York: Holt, Rinehardt, & Winston.

D'Amico, R. (1984). Does employment during high school impair academic progress? *Sociology of Education, 57,* 5-12.

Deci, E. L. (1975). *Intrinsic motivation.* New York: Plenum.

Deci, E. L., & Ryan, R. M. (1980). The empirical exploration of intrinsic motivation processes. In L. Berkowitz (Ed.), *Advances in experimental social psychology* (Vol. 13, pp. 39-80). New York: Academic Press.

Dornbusch, S. M. (1987). Individual moral choices and social evaluations: A research odyssey. In E. J. Lawler & B. Markovsky (Eds.), *Advances in group processes: Theory and research* (Vol. 4, pp. 271-307). Greenwich, CT: JAI.

Dornbusch, S. M. (1994). *Off the track.* Presidential address to the Society for Research on Adolescence, San Diego, CA. (Available from Stanford M. Dornbusch, Sociology Department, Stanford University, Building 120, Stanford, CA 94305-2047)

Dornbusch, S. M., Carlsmith, J. M., Bushwall, S. J., Ritter, P. L., Leiderman, H., Hastorf, A. H., & Gross, R. T. (1985). Single parents, extended households, and the control of adolescents. *Child Development, 56,* 326-341.

Dornbusch, S. M., Ritter, P. L., Leiderman, P. H., Roberts, D. F., & Fraleigh, M. J. (1987). The relation of parenting style to adolescent school performance. *Child Development, 58,* 1244-1257.

Dornbusch, S. M., Ritter, P., & Steinberg, L. (1991). Community influences on the relation of family statuses to adolescent school performance: Differences between African Americans and non-Hispanic Whites. *American Journal of Education, 99,* 543-567.

Douvan, E., & Adelson, J. (1966). *The adolescent experience.* New York: John Wiley.

Duncan, P., & Dornbusch, S. M. (1982). Educational correlates of early and late sexual maturation in adolescence. *Journal of Pediatrics, 100,* 633-637.

Eccles, J. S. (1984). Sex differences in achievement patterns. In T. Sonderegger (Ed.), *Nebraska symposium on motivation* (Vol. 32, pp. 97-132). Lincoln: University of Nebraska Press.

Eccles, J. S., Adler, T. F., Futterman, R., Goff, S. B., Kaczala, C. M., Meece, J. L., & Midgley, C. (1983). Expectancies, values, and academic behaviors. In J. T. Spence (Ed.), *Achievement and achievement motivation* (pp. 75-146). San Francisco: Freeman.

Eder, D., & Parker, S. (1987). The cultural production and reproduction of gender: The effect of extracurricular activities on peer-group culture. *Sociology of Education, 60,* 200-213.

Eitzen, S. (1976). Sport and social status in American public secondary education. *Review of Sport & Leisure, 1,* 139-155.

Elliott, E. S., & Dweck, C. S. (1988). Goals: An approach to motivation and achievement. *Journal of Personality and Social Psychology, 54,* 5-12.

Engel, A. (1994). Sex roles and gender stereotyping in young women's participation in sport. *Feminism and Psychology, 4,* 439-448.

Entwisle, D. R. (1990). Schools and the adolescent. In S. Feldman & G. Elliott (Eds.), *At the threshold.* Cambridge, MA: Harvard University Press.

Epstein, J. L. (1983). The influence of friends on achievement and affective outcomes. In J. L. Epstein & N. Karweit (Eds.), *Friends in school.* New York: Academic Press.

Epstein, J. L. (1986). Friendship selection: Developmental and environmental influences. In R. C. Mueller & C. R. Cooper (Eds.), *Process and outcome in peer relationships* (pp. 129-160). New York: Academic Press.

Epstein, J. L. (1989). The selection of friends: Changes across the grades and in different school environments. In T. J. Berndt & G. W. Ladd (Eds.), *Peer relationships in child development* (pp. 158-187). New York: John Wiley.

Eskilson, A., & Wiley, M. G. (1987). Parents, peers, perceived pressure, and adolescent self-concept: Is a daughter a daughter all of her life? *Sociological Quarterly, 28*(1), 135-145.

Faris, R. E. L. (1961). Reflections on the ability dimension in human society. *American Sociological Review, 26,* 835-843.

Faunce, W. (1984). School achievement, social status, and self-esteem. *Social Psychology Quarterly, 47,* 3-14.

Feather, N. T. (1982). Human values and the prediction of action: An expectancy-value analysis. In N. T. Feather (Ed.), *Expectations and actions: Expectancy-value models in psychology* (pp. 263-289). Hillsdale, NJ: Lawrence Erlbaum.

Feather, N. T. (1988). Values, valences, and course enrollment: Testing the role of personal values within an expectancy-value framework. *Journal of Educational Psychology, 80,* 381-391.

Feldman, S. S., & Weinberger, D. A. (1994). Self-restraint as a mediator of family influences on boys' delinquent behavior: A longitudinal study. *Child Development, 65,* 195-211.

Felson, R. B. (1986). Reference groups and self-appraisals of academic ability and performance. *Social Psychology Quarterly, 49,* 103-109.

Feltz, D., & Weiss, M. (1984). The impact of girls' interscholastic sport participation on academic orientation. *Research Quarterly for Exercise and Sport, 55,* 332-339.

Feynman, R. P. (1985). *"Surely you're joking, Mr. Feynman!": Adventures of a curious character.* New York: Norton.

Finch, M. D., & Mortimer, J. T. (1985). Adolescent work hours and the process of achievement. In A. C. Kerckhoff (Ed.), *Research in sociology of education and socialization* (Vol. 5, pp. 171-196). Greenwich, CT: JAI.

Fordham, S., & Ogbu, J. U. (1986). Black students' school success: Coping with the burden of "acting white." *Urban Review, 18,* 176-206.

Friesen, D., (1969). Academic-athletic-popularity syndrome in the Canadian high school society, *Adolescence,* (Vol. 3, pp. 39-52).

Fuller, M. (1984). Black girls in a London comprehensive school. In M. Hammersley & P. Woods (Eds.), *Life in school: The sociology of pupil culture.* New York: Open University Press.

Furstenburg, F. (1990). *Coming of age in a changing family system at the threshold: The developing adolescent.* S. Shirley Feldman & Glen R. Elliott (Eds.), (pp. 147-170). Cambridge, MA: Harvard University Press.

Gamoran, A., & Berends, M. (1987). The effects of stratification in secondary schools: Synthesis of survey and ethnographic research. *Review of Educational Research, 57,* 415-435.

Ge, X., Lorenz, F. O., Conger, R. D., Elder, G. H., & Simons, R. L. (1994). Trajectories of stressful life events and depressive symptoms during adolescence. *Developmental Psychology 30, 4,* 467-483.

Gibson, M. (1982). Reputation and respectability: How competing cultural systems affect students' performance in school. *Anthropology and Education Quarterly, 13,* 3-27.

Gillis, J. R. (1981). *Youth and history.* New York: Academic Press.

Goetz, T. E., & Dweck, C. S. (1980). Learned helplessness in social situations. *Journal of Personality and Social Psychology, 39,* 249-255.

Golden, G., & Cherry, F. (1982). Test performance and social comparison choices of high school men and women. *Sex Roles, 8,* 761-772.

Granovetter, M. S. (1973). The strength of weak ties. *American Journal of Sociology, 78,* 1360-1380.

Greenberger, E., & Steinberg, L. D. (1986). *When teenagers work: The psychological and social costs of adolescent employment.* New York: Basic Books.

Hamilton, S. F. (1990). *Apprenticeship for adulthood.* New York: Free Press

Hamilton, S. F., & Powers, J. L. (1990). Failed expectations: Working-class girls' transition from school to work. *Youth and Society, 22*(2), 241-262.

Hargreaves, D. H. (1967). *Social relations in a secondary school.* London: Tinling.

Harris, M. L. (1976). *Student effort in high school as a product of the perceived links between work and school.* Unpublished doctoral dissertation, Stanford University, Stanford, CA.

Harter, S. (1981). A model of mastery motivation in children: Individual differences and developmental change. In W. A. Collins (Ed.), *Minnesota symposium on child psychology* (Vol. 14, pp. 215-255). Hillsdale, NJ: Lawrence Erlbaum.

Hartup, W. W. (1983). Peer relations. In E. M. Hetherington (Ed.), *Handbook of child psychology* (Vol. 4, pp. 103-196). New York: John Wiley.

Hauser, W. J., & Lueptow, L. B. (1978). Participation in athletics and academic achievement: A replication and extension. *Sociological Quarterly, 19,* 304-309.

Henderson, V. L., & Dweck, C. S. (1990). Motivation and achievement. In S. Feldman & G. Elliott (Eds.), *At the threshold.* Cambridge, MA: Harvard University Press.

Ianni, F. A. J. (1989). *The search for structure: A report on American youth today.* New York: Free Press.

Ishiyama, F. I., & Chabassol, D. J. (1985). Adolescents' fear of the social consequences of academic success as a function of age and sex. *Journal of Youth and Adolescence, 14,* 37-46.

Jencks, C., & Mayer, S. (1988). *The social consequences of growing up in a poor neighborhood.* Unpublished manuscript, Northwestern University, Center for Urban Affairs and Policy Research, Evanston, IL.

Kandel, D. B. (1978). Homophily, selection, and socialization. *American Journal of Sociology, 84,* 427-438.

Kandel, D. B. (1986). Processes of peer influence in adolescence. In R. K. Silbereisen, K. Eyferth, & G. Rudinger (Eds.), *Development as action in context* (pp. 203-277). Berlin: Springer-Verlag.

Kandel, D. B., & Lesser, G. S. (1970). School, family, and peer influences on educational plans of adolescents in the United States and Denmark. *Sociology of Education, 43,* 270-287.

Kerckhoff, A. C. (1986). Effects of ability grouping in British secondary schools. *American Sociological Review, 51,* 842-858.

Kilgore, S. B. (1991). The organizational context of tracking in schools. *American Sociological Review, 56,* 189-203.

Labov, W. (1982). Competing value systems in the inner-city schools. In P. Gilmore & A. Glathorn (Eds.), *Children in and out of school: Ethnography and education.* Washington, DC: Center for Applied Linguistics.

Landers, D. M., & Landers, D. M. (1978). Socialization via interscholastic athletics: Its effects on delinquency and educational attainment. *Sociology of Education, 51,* 299-303.

Larkin, R. W. (1979). *Suburban youth in cultural crisis.* New York: Oxford University Press.

Larson, L. E. (1972). The influence of parents and peers during adolescence: The situation hypothesis revisited. *Journal of Marriage and the Family, 36,* 123-138.

Lerner, R. M. (1992). Dialectics, developmental, contextualism, and the further enhancement of theory about puberty and psychosocial development. *Journal of Early Adolescence, 12,* 366-388.

Lewin-Epstein, N. (1981). *Youth employment during high school.* Washington, DC: National Center for Education Statistics.

Lueptow, L. B., & Kayser, B. D. (1973). Athletic involvement, academic achievement, and aspiration. *Sociological Focus, 7,* 24-36.

Maccoby, E. E. (1966). *The development of sex differences.* Stanford, CA: Stanford University Press.

Magnusson, D. (1988). *Individual development from an interactional perspective: A longitudinal study.* Hillsdale, NJ: Lawrence Erlbaum.

Manning, W. D. (1990). Parenting employed teenagers. *Youth and Society, 22*(2), 184-200.

Marsh, H. W. (1991). Employment during high school: Character building or a subversion of academic goals? *Sociology of Education, 64,* 172-189.

McLoyd, V. C., Jayaratne, T. E., Ceballo, R., & Borquez, J. (1994). Unemployment and work interruption among African American single mothers: Effects on parenting and adolescent socioemotional functioning. *Child Development, 65,* 562-589.

McNeal, R. B. (1995). Extracurricular activities and high school dropouts. *Sociology of Education, 68,* 62-81.

Mead, G. H. (1934). *Mind, self, and society from the standpoint of a social behaviorist.* Chicago: University of Chicago Press.

Merton, R. K. (1968). Social structure and anomie. In R. K. Merton (Ed.), *Social theory and social structure*. New York: Free Press.

Meyer, R. H., & Wise, D. A. (1982). High school preparation and early labor force experience. In R. B. Freeman & D. A. Wise (Eds.), *The youth labor market problem: Its nature, causes, and consequences* (pp. 277-348). Chicago: University of Chicago Press.

Mortimer, J. T., & Finch, M. D. (1986). The effects of part-time work on self-concept and achievement. In K. M. Borman & J. Reisman (Eds.), *Becoming a worker* (pp. 66-89). Norwood, NJ: Ablex.

Mortimer, J. T., Finch, M. D., Owens, T. J., & Shanahan, M. (1990). Gender and work in adolescence. *Youth and Society, 22*(2), 201-224.

Moskowitz, D. S., & Schwartzman, A. E. (1989). Painting group portraits: Studying life outcomes for aggressive and withdrawn children. *Journal of Personality, 57*(4), 723-746.

National Commission on Youth. (1980). *The transition of youth to adulthood*. Boulder, CO: Westview.

National Panel on High Schools and Adolescent Education. (1976). *The education of adolescents*. Washington, DC: Government Printing Office.

Natriello, G., & Dornbusch, S. M. (1984). *Teacher evaluative standards and student effort*. New York: Longman.

Oakes, J. (1985). *Keeping track: How schools structure inequality*. New Haven: Yale University Press.

Oakes, J. (1987). Curriculum inequality and school reform. *Equity and Excellence, 23*, 8-14.

Oakes, J., Gamoran, A., & Page, R. N. (1992). Curriculum differentiation: Opportunities, outcomes, and meanings. In P. W. Jackson (Ed.), *Handbook of research on curriculum* (pp. 570-608). New York: Macmillan.

Picou, S. J. (1978). Race, athletic achievement, and educational aspiration. *Sociological Quarterly, 19*, 429-438.

President's Science Advisory Committee Panel on Youth. (1973). *Youth: Transition to adulthood*. Chicago: University of Chicago Press.

Ratcliff, J. L. (1995). *Realizing the potential: Improving postsecondary teaching, learning, and assessment*. University Park, PA: National Center for Post-Secondary Teaching, Learning, and Assessment.

Rehberg, R. A. (1969). Behavioral and attitudinal consequences of high school interscholastic sports: A speculative consideration. *Adolescence, 4*, 69-88.

Reubens, B. G., Harrison, J. A. C., & Rupp, K. (1981). *The youth labor force 1945-1995: A cross-national analysis*. Totowa, NJ: Allanheld, Osmun.

Ritter, P. L., Mont-Reynaud, R., & Dornbusch, S. M. (1993). Minority parents and their youth: Concern, encouragement, and support for school achievement. In N. F. Chavkin (Ed.), *Families and schools in a pluralistic society* (pp. 107-119). Albany: State University of New York Press.

Rokeach, M. (1979). From individual to institutional values with special reference to the values of science. In M. Rokeach (Ed.), *Understanding human values* (pp. 47-70). New York: Free Press.

Rosen, B. C., Crockett, H. J., & Nunn, C. Z. (Eds.). (1969). *Achievement in American society*. Cambridge, MA: Schenkman.

Rosenbaum, J. E. (1976). *Making inequality: The hidden curriculum of high school tracking.* New York: John Wiley.

Rotella, R. J. (1980, April). *Psychological processes for achieving and coping with stress in sports.* Paper presented at the Preconvention Symposium of the National Association for Sport and Physical Education Sport Psychology.

Ruggiero, M., Greenberger, E., & Steinberg, L. D. (1982). Occupational deviance among first-time workers. *Youth and Society, 13,* 423-448.

Savin-Williams, R. C., & Berndt, T. J. (1990). Friendship and peer status. In S. Feldman & G. Elliott (Eds.), *At the threshold.* Cambridge, MA: Harvard University Press.

Schlegel, A., & Barry, H. (1991). *Adolescence: An anthropological inquiry.* New York: Free Press.

Schneider, F., & Coutts, L. (1985). Person orientation of male and female high school students: To the educational disadvantage of males? *Sex Roles, 13,* 47-63.

Shapiro, B. J. (1984). Intercollegiate athletic participation and academic achievement: A case study of Michigan State University student-athletes, 1950-1980. *Sociology of Sport Journal, 1,* 46-51.

Simmons, R. G., & Blyth, D. A. (1987). *Moving into adolescence: The impact of pubertal change and school context.* New York.

Simonton, D. K. (1994). *Greatness: Who makes history and why.* New York: Guilford.

Spady, W. G. (1970). Lament for the letterman: Effects of peer status and extracurricular activities on goals and achievement. *American Journal of Sociology, 75,* 680-702.

Spady, W. G. (1971). Status, achievement, and motivation in the American high school. *School Review, 79,* 379-403.

Spitzberg, B. H., & Cupach, W. R. (1989). *Handbook of interpersonal competence research.* New York: Springer-Verlag.

Steele, C. M. (1992, April). Race and the schooling of Black Americans. *Atlantic Monthly,* 68-78.

Steinberg, L. D. (1988). *Noninstructional influences on high school student achievement: The contributions of parents, peers, extracurricular activities, and part-time work.* Unpublished manuscript.

Steinberg, L. D., & Dornbusch, S. M. (1991). Negative correlates of part-time employment during adolescence: Replication and elaboration. *Developmental Psychology, 27,* 304-313.

Steinberg, L. D., Fegley, S., & Dornbusch, S. M. (1993). Negative impact of part-time work on adolescent adjustment: Evidence from a longitudinal study. *Developmental Psychology, 29*(2), 171-180.

Steinberg, L. D., Greenberger, E., Garduque, L., Ruggiero, M., & Vaux, A. (1982). Effects of working on adolescent development. *Developmental Psychology, 18,* 385-395.

Steinberg, L., Lamborn, S. D., Dornbusch, S. M., & Darling, N. (1992). Impact of parenting practices on adolescent achievement: Authoritative parenting, school involvement, and encouragement to succeed. *Child Development, 63,* 1266-1281.

Steinberg, L. D., & Silverberg, S. (1986). The vicissitudes of autonomy in adolescence. *Child Development, 57,* 841-851.

Stevens, C. J., Puchtell, L. A., Ryu, S., & Mortimer, J. T. (1992). Adolescent work and boys' and girls' orientations to the future. *Sociological Quarterly, 33*(2), 153-169.

Thirer, J., & Wright, S. D. (1985). Sport and social status for adolescent males and females. *Sociology of Sport Journal, 2,* 164-171.

Timpane, M., Abramowitz, S., Bobrow, S., & Pascal, A. (1976). The development of concepts of social structure: Social convention. In J. Glick & K. A. Clarke-Steward (Eds.), *The development of social understanding* (pp. 25-107). New York: Gardner.

Useem, E. L. (1992). Middle schools and math groups: Parents' involvement in children's placement. *Sociology of Education, 5,* 263-279.

Varenne, H. (1982). Jocks and freaks: The symbolic structure of the expression of social interaction among American senior high school students. In G. Spindler (Ed.), *Doing the ethnography of schooling.* New York: Holt, Rinehart, & Winston.

Weiner, B. (1985). An attributional theory of achievement motivation and emotion. *Psychological Review, 92,* 548-573.

Weiner, B., Frieze, I., Kukla, A., Reed, L., Rest, S., & Rosenbaum, R. M. (1971). *Perceiving the causes of success and failure.* Morristown, NJ: General Learning Press.

Weiner, B., Russell, D., & Lerman, D. (1979). The cognition-emotion process in achievement-related contexts. *Journal of Personality and Social Psychology, 37,* 1211-1220.

White, M. (1993). *Albert Einstein.* New York: Simon & Schuster.

Wigfield, A., & Eccles, J. S. (1992). The development of achievement task values: A theoretical analysis. *Developmental Review, 12,* 265-310.

Williams, R. M. (1969). Achievement and success as value orientations. In B. C. Rosen, H. J. Crockett, & C. Z. Nunn (Eds.), *Achievement in American society* (pp. 13-17). Cambridge, MA: Schenkman.

Wilson, W. J. (1987). *The truly disadvantaged.* Chicago: University of Chicago Press.

Yamoor, C. M., & Mortimer, J. T. (1990). Age and gender differences in the effects of employment on adolescent achievement and well-being. *Youth and Society, 22*(2), 225-240.

Youniss, J., & Smollar, J. (1985). *Adolescent relations with mothers, fathers and friends.* Chicago: University of Chicago Press.

7. Cognitive Socialization in Adolescence: Critical Period for a Critical Habit of Mind

Daniel P. Keating
Doris K. Sasse

Our understanding of the developmental sources and pathways of adolescent thinking has grown substantially in recent years (Keating, 1980b, 1990a). Several features of this knowledge growth are especially salient. First, as in many other areas of cognitive science, we have developed a stronger appreciation for the role of context in the development of adolescent thinking. Of particular note is the insight that context is not merely an afterthought in the process of cognitive structuring but, in fact, becomes embedded in structure over the course of development. This is reflected in a range of outcomes, most prominently perhaps in the observation of domain specificity in cognitive achievements (Keating & Crane, 1990; Matthews & Keating, 1995).

A second and related phenomenon is the growing recognition of the fundamental effect of noncognitive features of adolescent development on the growth of thinking. The role of emotions and social relationships increasingly is seen as central to the understanding of cognitive development throughout the life span, and adolescence is no different in this respect. Our metaphor of cognition as entirely or principally structural or skill-based is yielding to a perspective that emphasizes the developmental integration of these various facets (Keating, 1996).

A third clear trend in the work on adolescent thinking is to take account of essential contextualism and developmental integration by embedding core research questions in more real world or applied contexts. In contrast to an earlier strategy to look for the most abstract or decontextualized examples of adolescent thinking, many contemporary researchers are finding a richer field of inquiry in the examination of these fundamental questions by studying them as they emerge in everyday contexts.

232

One way of capturing the central tendency of these salient features is to identify and explore the fundamental dynamics among biological, cognitive, and psychosocial development. The centrality of this dynamic interplay and the necessity of an eventual synthesis were anticipated in the work of an earlier generation of adolescent theorists (e.g., Hill, 1988; Hill & Palmquist, 1978). One major obstacle to studying these dynamics has been their daunting complexity, but new analytic and conceptual tools have made this approach ripe for exploration at this time (Keating, 1996).

In this paper, we sketch one critical development during the adolescent years, the development of a critical habit of mind. We have been exploring the integrative potential of viewing core cognitive developments as habits of mind—rather than merely as structures, schemes, or abilities—to capture the effect of contexts, psychosocial factors, and real-world constraints (Keating, 1996; Keating & Crane, 1990; Keating & MacLean, 1988; Matthews & Keating, 1995). The core developmental process by which habits of mind emerge is through cognitive socialization, which in turn acknowledges the fundamentally social nature of all cognitive activity (Bruner, 1986; Vygotsky, 1978).

The central question posed in this paper, then, is whether and in what respects we should regard adolescence as a critical period for the development of a critical habit of mind. The major context in which we examine this question is that of the school, although outside-of-school effects need also to be examined. We start with the widespread concern that schools are not effective agents of cognitive socialization in the development of a critical habit of mind.

CRITICAL THINKING IN SCHOOLS

In the current wave of concern about the quality of education in our schools, one of the most pervasive themes is the virtual absence of serious thinking that occurs there. Although expressed in diverse ways, the picture that emerges is both coherent and troubling. Much has been made of the failure of students to develop proficiency in many basic skills, such as literacy or mathematical competence, but perhaps even more striking, it seems that they are acquiring less than minimal competence in the ability to think seriously, rationally, or critically.

Students are docile, compliant, and without initiative. For many, the basic neglect of intellectual stimulation is so severe as to make secondary education an educational fraud, . . . [an] almost wholesale neglect of the intellect. (Lazerson, 1986, pp. 38-39)

Studies on the outcome of schooling show that although elementary skills are improving, higher-level processes are being acquired less well. In mathematics, there appears to be an increase in the performances associated with basic skill and computation but little improvement and even a reported decline in mathematical understanding and problem solving. The evidence is reiterated in science education. (Glaser, 1984, p. 94)

Skills in learning, reasoning, and general problem solving . . . are neglected by the schools. (Chipman & Segal, 1985, p. 1)

In spite of persistent injunctions that schools ought to teach reasoning, problem-solving, critical thinking, and creative use of the mind, many studies confirm the conspicuous absence of attention to these goals in classrooms. (Newmann, 1990a, p. 41)

Given the historically articulated mission of schooling, these conclusions—and the list could easily be expanded virtually ad infinitum—constitute a rather daunting indictment of contemporary educational practice. It is noteworthy that this indictment does not rest solely on the evaluation of student performance in test situations. It is supported as much or more by recent observational studies of typical activities in the schools (Goodlad, 1983; Newmann, 1990b; Powell, Farrar, & Cohen, 1985; Sizer, 1985)—and in many college classrooms (Boyer, 1987).

Though these conclusions may be stated more or less starkly, there seems to be reasonable consensus about their validity. Converging evidence—from formal evaluations of student performance, from detailed observations of classroom activities, and from the informal experiences of many teachers in secondary and higher education—establishes a convincing and substantive basis for these claims. Not for the first time in our history, the discrepancy between hopes for schools and everyday reality has led to disappointment. Facing this sharp division between articulated goals and actual practice, we are impelled to seek its sources. The list of candidates to account for the absence of serious thinking in contemporary schooling, however, is a long one:

Research suggests that the failure to emphasize higher order thinking may be due—at least in US schools—to several obstacles: difficulties in defining higher order thinking and in evaluating student performance in "thinking"; class size and teaching schedules that prevent teachers from responding in detail to students' work; curriculum guidelines and testing programs that require coverage of vast amounts of material; students' apparent preferences for highly structured work with clear, "correct" answers; and teachers' conceptions of knowledge that emphasize the acquisition of information rather than interpretation, analysis and evaluation. (Newmann, 1990a, p. 41)

The lack of a clear definition is revealed in the array of terminology to identify what seems to be a core concept of thinking. Different observers may use different criteria to describe thinking, whether these criteria are latent or manifest. Even a partial list of the headings under which studies of these activities are indexed conveys some sense of the problem: abstraction, analogy, causation, cognition, creativity, critical thinking, explanation, formal thought, generalization, inferential thinking, intellect, logic, problem solving, questioning, reasoning, reflective thinking, thoughtfulness.

The level of observation is another difficulty. If the focus is on individual student performance on tasks or tests, the manifestations of thinking may overlap little with its manifestation in classroom discourse. For example, recent attempts to apply the principles and findings from cognitive science and developmental psychology to problems of education have often focused on programs of direct instruction rather than on typical educational practice. Thus, considerable work is needed to bridge the gaps among analyses of the individual student, analyses of instruction, and analyses of actual classroom social interaction (Bransford, Arbitman-Smith, Stein, & Vye, 1985; Keating, 1990b; Newmann, 1990a, 1990b).

A critical review of the evidence may help to identify which of these sources are most likely to be remedied. In this regard, it is helpful to conceive of each level as posing a potential constraint or barrier to the exercise of serious thinking. Simply stated, high school students may not engage much in serious thinking because (a) they are developmentally unprepared to do so, (b) they have not been adequately instructed in how to do so, (c) the everyday practices of schooling—more broadly defined than direct instruction—do not support them in doing so, or (d) external influences override schools' attempts to support such thinking. It is not necessary, of course, to presume a single cause from among these possibilities.

Consider then a construct of *critical thinking,* by which is meant cognitive activity that involves transformation of knowledge rather than mere application of simple algorithms or known routines and invokes a notion of guided, purposeful thinking. Making even the first distinction can be difficult, at times. In one study, we found that many college students in an advanced mathematics class who had demonstrated full competence in the application of a ratio-proportion algorithm in a paper-and-pencil pretest were unable to apply this knowledge to the judgment of geometrically regular concrete objects (Keating & Crane, 1990). The definition of critical thinking, then, is always a contingent one, relative to the developmental level of the individual. This becomes crucial in our subsequent discussion of the relationship between critical thinking and everyday school practices. The second notion, purposefulness, has a long history in education (Dewey, 1910), although it is the feature that seems most frequently lost in everyday school activities.

Within this category, several further distinctions are helpful. Some justification is required for adding to the already heavy burden of taxonomies and schemes present in the literature on thinking. Many existing taxonomies have as a primary focus the careful subdivision of tasks or tests on the basis of individual or group differences in performance. Though this perspective allows for greater control in the interest of the internal validity of the scheme, it may yield less external validity—that is, the understanding of everyday cognitive activities in the schools (Keating, 1996; Keating & MacLean, 1987; Morrison, Lord, & Keating, 1984). Thus, the grouping used here is based both on educational applicability and research evidence of similarity.

These are rather broad criteria, of course, and any rational clustering rests on a priori theoretical perspectives. To begin, let us posit three broad groupings under the heading of critical thinking: (a) conceptual flexibility, (b) reflective thinking, and (c) cognitive self-regulation. As will become evident, it is inappropriate to regard these as independent of each other; instead, they are more likely to be evinced as integrated features of purposeful attempts to use one's intellect.

Conceptual Flexibility

As in the case of each of the main groups within critical thinking, there are a number of manifestations of conceptual fluency. Most generally, it is the activity whereby connections are made among initially differing aspects of a concept—as in the generation of related concepts or ideas, the comparison of different ideas, or the application of a particular concept to novel content. Each of these comprises several areas of research and theoretical attention.

Divergent Thinking

The generation of related concepts or ideas has been discussed in numerous ways. One perspective is that of *divergent thinking*, in which the individual produces as many associations to a stated object as possible. Though originally believed useful as an index of a variety of skills—originality or creativity, for example—the research seems to show rather conclusively that measures of this construct principally assess ideational fluency, that is, the rate, frequency, or total quantity of ideas produced (Keating, 1980a; Kogan, 1983; Wallach, 1970, 1985). It seems clear on both empirical and theoretical grounds that ideational fluency is perhaps a necessary but is by no means a sufficient condition for creative thought (Keating, 1980a). As traditionally assessed, ideational fluency of this sort is alogical or associationist. It does, however, deserve to be associated with the notion of critical thinking, in that it typically requires going beyond the information given (Bruner, 1973). Critical thinking includes more than just sequential, linear cognitive activities. Based on the best current evidence, however, it is wise to be wary of educational programs whose only focus is open-ended generation of ideas; as noted below, the integration of these cognitive activities with other, more reflective ones is essential.

Analogical Thinking

A different kind of generativity—more systematic and methodical—is captured by the notions of *analogy, generalization,* and *inference.* Here, the generation of a novel idea is extracted from the relationships among existing, well-stated propositions or concepts.

In these activities, the problem presented is to generate the most essential or most useful concept that provides an organization for several seemingly different concepts.

Closely related to generalization are the notions of comparison and analogy. It is similar in that the focus is on the relationships between or among concepts, but it does not require the discovery of a unifying concept. Rather, it is a means of systematically exploring both similarities and differences between two or more propositions, concepts, or even events. The ubiquitous essay question prelude, "Compare and contrast . . ." is a familiar example. A more thoroughly researched topic under this heading is analogical reasoning. Many intelligence tests have items of this sort: A : B : : C : D (read "A is to B as C is to D"), in which the test taker is presented with several options for D. Indeed, many of the direct instructional programs that attempt to enhance thinking focus precisely on items of this type (Bransford et al., 1985).

When specific options are presented, the student must compare the relationship between A and B and map it onto the C to D relationship (Sternberg, 1977). It is interesting that this becomes a more challenging task as we move from more discrete toward more ill-defined material (e.g., comparing geometric figures versus comparing verbal concepts; Keating, 1984). When options are not presented at all—an open-ended analogy—the task is more similar to what we mean by analogy in everyday cognitive activity, but the difficulties in developing precise psychological theories of such reasoning are greater than for building models of the more bounded test-type analogies.

To illustrate this, consider a simple example discussed by Bransford et al. (1985, p. 145): "Bee is to honey as cow is to _____." If a series of options is presented that includes the answer "milk," even young children have little difficulty. But, as Bransford et al. note, they may solve it through pure association. Cow and milk are commonly paired, and picking it from the list of choices may require no critical thinking at all. Imagine, however, that we present no options to choose among. Students who generate the response "milk" would likely be viewed as having accurately completed the comparison. Though not eliminating the possibility of pure association, the chance is reduced because other words are also paired with cow in everyday language, and the student would have had to generate the correct one. But now, consider the response "cud." From the perspective of the human, the obvious answer is "milk," as a food produced by or through each animal. From the perspective of the cow (or the biologist seeking to understand the cow), "cud" is as good a comparison to "honey" as is "milk" for several reasons—both are partially processed nutrients available for subsequent use.

This example illuminates several important points. First, it is crucial when thinking about thinking to be as explicit as possible. Though several kinds of thinking have been described, they in fact are quite different activities. Second, there is little empirical support for the belief that by training for one of them—say, geometric analogies when the options from which to choose are presented—we are increasing students' critical thinking in general. The ability to engage in this cognitive activity in the context of meaningful content is more central to critical thinking.

Given the Western epistemological bias (especially among academics) for abstract, as opposed to concrete, conceptualizing (Hogan, 1982; Keating & MacLean, 1988), a word of caution is in order here. As teachers, we are frequently surprised by students' seeming inability to generate the connections among even obviously (to us) related constructs. Thus, it is not surprising that we focus on the benefits of abstraction or generalization rather than the risks. But clearly, abstractions are only as good as they are useful in practice. All abstractions need to be tested against some practical reality—if only an artificially constructed experimental reality—before we can evaluate them. Standing alone, such abstractions, generalizations, or inferences, even though systematically generated, are of no more inherent value for productive thinking than the alogical ideational fluency.

Applying Algorithms

A third type of conceptual fluency can be described as the application of an algorithm to some novel content. As noted above, it is important to exclude the routine application of well-learned procedures to familiar content, even though such routines are often nontrivial. Automatizing basic procedures, such as word decoding or numerical calculation, are probably essential to freeing attentional capacity for critical thinking (Keating, 1984; Manis, Keating, & Morrison, 1980; Miller, Perlmutter, & Keating, 1984), but once automatized, they are not usefully regarded as critical thinking. On the other hand, the ability to apply an existing algorithm even to closely related content is not always easy (Keating & Crane, 1990). It makes sense to regard this latter activity as essential to critical thinking, both because it cannot be taken for granted and because of its obvious utility.

Reflective Thinking

This notion is likely to be closer to the core of what most people regard as critical thinking and has been identified as such for many years (Dewey, 1910). Whereas conceptual flexibility is essential for generating new ideas and new applications for existing ideas, reflective thinking is essential for systematically evaluating them. Analogies, for example, may be either right or wrong. Other than determining their respective validity, there is nothing to distinguish the relative value of "Evolution is like an ascending ladder" versus "Evolution is like a spreading bush." Both are perfectly appropriate analogies; the former, however, is wrong on the evidence (Gould, 1990). There are several important research areas that can be subsumed under a notion of reflective thinking.

Formal Logic

The variety of topics under this heading comprise perhaps the most thoroughly researched questions in adolescent development (Inhelder & Piaget, 1958; Keating, 1980b, 1990a, 1990c; Piaget, 1972). Indeed, notions such as *deductive logic, formal reasoning, logical thinking, scientific thinking,* and *syllogistic reasoning*—and related terms—are for many theorists virtually synonymous with the concept of critical thinking or even intelligence per se. Clearly, the system of formal logical reasoning is highly and justifiably regarded as central to critical thinking in many domains. As well, the apparent lack of such formal thinking skills in adolescents—and adults—has been viewed as a fundamental developmental constraint on their ability to think critically (Kuhn, Amsel, & O'Loughlin, 1988).

Despite the apparent centrality of formal thinking within the broader construct of critical thinking, it would be a mistake to assume that skill in formal logic is always transferable across domains of knowledge. To qualify as critical thinking, these logical skills must be available for use in contexts other than the specific one in which they may have been acquired. Otherwise, they are more akin to routine algorithmic or procedural knowledge (Ceci, 1990; Keating, 1990c; Keating & Crane, 1990).

Second, the productive value of formal logic cannot always be assumed. It is important to recognize that the validity of the outcomes of thought does not inhere in the methods that generated them, even if the methods have demonstrated broad historical success. This is true even in relatively more "closed" knowledge systems like mathematics (Keating, 1974; Kline, 1980) or physics (Feyerabend, 1975). It is always the case that theories need to be tested against practice for validation. In this sense, critical thinking is always linked to meaningful activity. The absence of such links can undermine attempts to educate for critical thinking.

This poses greater difficulties for the human sciences as compared with the natural sciences (Keating & MacLean, 1988). In the latter case, the validity criterion is typically self-evident: The bridge stands or falls; the plane flies or does not. What is the criterion for answers to more open questions, such as those concerning personal growth, interpersonal interaction, or social organization? In these cases, the question of values can never justifiably be set aside; however generated, solutions to such questions are validated or legitimized with respect to the consensus of those who live with the consequences (Habermas, 1979; Keating & MacLean, 1988).

The implications of these caveats are important for educational attempts to enhance critical thinking. An emphasis on logical method per se at the expense of content may be counterproductive (Keating, 1980a). Not only may such skills fail to generalize (Glaser, 1984), they may come to be regarded as a substitute for truly critical thinking. This risk seems to be even greater in the human sciences, especially in social studies and history. In these areas especially, an open discourse seems to be essential to the acquisition of critical thinking (Newmann, 1985, 1990a). Assuming the validity of a particular logic is likely to run counter to attempts at open discourse (Gilligan, 1982; Hogan, 1982).

Informal Reasoning

Relative to the amount of research devoted to the development of more formal reasoning, there has been less attention paid to the development of critical thinking in practical or social settings. Although there is some research on the development in adolescence of social and interpersonal reasoning, the empirical evidence seems to suggest considerable overlap with more formal logic (e.g., Keating, 1990a; Keating & Clark, 1980). Given a recent resurgence of interest in questions of social and practical intelligence (Gardner, 1983; Selman, 1980) and given the obvious importance of developing critical thinking in these domains, this can be clearly marked as an area in need of considerably more research. One finding that seems likely to endure is that reasoning is intimately connected both to content and context (Ceci, 1990; Kuhn et al., 1988; Nisbett, Fong, Lehman, & Cheng, 1987).

Skepticism

A different but quite important sense of critical thinking seems more properly viewed as an orientation toward intellectual questions rather than a formal system or set of skills. It is the concept of a *critical perspective or attitude* (Schrag, 1988). Too often, the connotation of a critical attitude is largely or entirely negative and is a block to creativity (Keating, 1980a). Although skepticism and a questioning of basic assumptions can become negative or even nihilistic, in isolation, they remain fundamental to critical thinking. Chandler (1987) has made a cogent case that the emergence of a skeptical epistemological stance in interaction with other aspects of adolescent development—particularly identity issues—raises some potential hazards for healthy psychological development. The distinction between constructively critical thinking and a wholly negative skepticism is important to bear in mind, especially when designing educational interventions.

This, too, is a less researched topic than others reviewed here, largely because of the relative difficulty of operationalization. One possible empirical route is found in the related topic of perspective taking. The ability and perceived necessity to view an issue from a variety of perspectives other than one's own is a hallmark of critical thinking, especially for questions in domains such as interpersonal relationships (Selman, 1980) or social organization (Haan, Smith, & Block, 1968).

Cognitive Self-Regulation

As described above, conceptual flexibility can be viewed as a generative feature of critical thinking and reflective thinking as an evaluative one. Deploying these cognitive resources appropriately to particular problems seems to require also an executive function. Given a specific problem to solve or topic to understand, some selection and organization of the cognitive activities described is needed. It is a critical component of critical thinking, however, and seemingly undervalued in psychological and educational assessment and in classroom discourse. Again, it is useful to make a distinction between more and less systematic versions of this aspect of critical thinking.

Comprehension Monitoring

The more systematic version has been described with terms such as *inquiry, information gathering, questioning,* and *independent comprehension.* Perhaps the most investigated topic in this category is the systematic extraction of information from text, including such topics as metacognition, metacomprehension, and comprehension monitoring (Brown, 1981; Brown, Bransford, Ferrara, & Campione, 1983; Campione & Armbruster, 1985). Here, one key notion is that students need to acquire skills in knowing what they do not know and to seek additional or clarifying information from the text. A variety of instructional programs have attempted to enhance the acquisition of this skill (Campione & Armbruster, 1985). The active engagement of the student in integrating his or her knowledge with the information of the text clearly qualifies such thinking as critical and as different from merely rote or literal comprehension of isolated factual information.

The systematic acquisition of information in situations beyond written textual material has been less thoroughly investigated. This notion of guided inquiry, however, is central to much of the research on expertise and expert systems (Chi, Glaser, & Rees, 1982; Glaser, 1984). A key difference between experts and novices appears to be that experts engage in a far more organized search for information about the problem at hand. In turn, this more organized search rests heavily on a more articulated knowledge base, which permits a more systematic cognitive representation of the problem space. Such inquiry, whether in text or nontext situations, may well be available even to nonexperts. Whether it is a learnable general skill or instead, an orientation, attitude, or other "noncognitive" aspect of thinking is a question to which we will return below.

Curiosity

The less systematic search for information is more akin to the notion of *curiosity*. Nearly all the research on information seeking in adolescents and adults has been carried out in the context of well-structured problems. Much of the literature on scientific discovery, however, suggests that an important starting point is often an unguided or loosely guided set of observations about interesting phenomena. Given the educational emphasis on convergent solutions of well-structured problems and on methodical—versus open-ended—inquiry and comprehension, it is unsurprising, even trite, to note that this form of critical thinking is rare indeed in schools (Newmann, 1985, p. 10). When student and teacher accountability are almost wholly tied to performance on highly structured tests and tasks (Frederiksen, 1984), the spirit of curiosity may well be dimmed.

Recurring Themes

Several central themes have emerged for the analysis of possible constraints on critical thinking among adolescents. First, and especially relevant to empirical research on these questions, is the degree to which critical thinking can more usefully be considered as a general ability or instead, as necessarily tied to specific domains of content knowledge. Second, there is a question, perhaps even more fundamental, as to whether the metaphor of "skill" is in fact the most appropriate one (Schrag, 1988). Acceptance of the skill metaphor has a number of important implications both for psychological models of thinking and for educational practice addressed to its enhancement. Third is the issue of whether it is helpful to regard the various aspects of thinking as relatively more independent (and perhaps hierarchical) or more interdependent, even integrated (Keating, 1996).

These recurring themes—generalizability of critical thinking, thinking as a skill versus an orientation, and the independence versus interdependence of aspects of critical thinking—are closely related to each other. Understanding their operation in the schooling context, and hence their implications for the practice of schooling, provides a sound opportunity for knowledge building about developmental theory and applications.

CONSTRAINTS ON
CRITICAL THINKING

Adolescent Thinking

In many ways, it may seem that the most straightforward answer to our key question—Why is there so little evidence for critical thinking among high school students?—resides in the adolescents themselves. If the cognitive developmental level of the students is inadequate to support the types of critical thinking just described, then the disquiet of observers of the high school scene may be misplaced. Indeed, there have been calls for the reduction of cognitive demands of schooling, especially in early adolescence, because students may not be developmentally ready for such engagement (Epstein, 1978; Toepfer, 1979).

Superficially at least, there seems to be evidence for this view, at least in the case of logical thinking. Across many studies of formal operational thinking, for example, the highly robust finding is that half or more of the adolescent (and adult) population fails to demonstrate such thinking on the frequently used Piagetian tasks (Keating, 1980b; Kuhn et al., 1988). This has been interpreted by some as reflecting, for adolescents, biological limitations linked to brain development (Epstein, 1974).

In previous reviews (Keating, 1988, 1990a), we have analyzed the psychological and physiological evidence for recommending the withholding of challenging cognitive material in early adolescence. The conclusion is straightforward: "The practice of revising curriculum to lessen the cognitive challenges for preadolescents and early adolescents while educators await some specific ... maturation is *not* supported by the best available data" (Keating, 1990a, p. 63).

Indeed, based on a consideration of the available evidence, there are good reasons to believe that adolescence is a critical period for the development of critical thinking.[1] Consider first some of the key cognitive achievements of adolescence (Keating, 1990a): (a) an increase in automaticity of basic processes, which frees cognitive resources for other concerns; (b) a far greater breadth of content knowledge across many domains; (c) an increased ability to maintain different representations of knowledge simultaneously, permitting new combinations of that knowledge; (d) an increase in the spontaneous use of cognitive strategies and procedures; and (e) a new appreciation of the relativity and uncertainty of knowledge. In sum, the adolescent is well positioned to engage in each of the major activities that subsume critical thinking—generation, evaluation, and execution.

One should not assume that these developments are automatic for adolescents nor that they will automatically coalesce into critical thinking. Developmental acquisitions in childhood underlie these gains, and if basic skills and knowledge have not been acquired, then the outlook for critical thinking is bleaker. As well, there is no guarantee that these accomplishments will indeed become integrated in the necessary fashion (Eylon & Linn, 1988; Keating, 1990a; Keating & Crane, 1990; Kuhn et al., 1988; Linn & Songer, 1991).

But critical thinking does not rest on skills alone. It is as much an orientation or a habit of mind as a set of skills (Keating, 1990b, 1996; Schrag, 1988). There are several potential developments in adolescence that seem essential to the formation of a critical habit of mind. First, there is an apparent focusing of interest on particular topics that is shown in an increased differentiation of abilities during adolescence. Although a critical habit of mind is in many ways general across domains, the actual application of critical thinking is to specific questions or issues. Adolescents show an increasing concentration on particular areas, and thus, the potential for such focus.

Second, adolescents begin to reveal more independence of thinking, as in other arenas of developing autonomy. This is no doubt connected to the increasing recognition of the uncertainty and relativity of knowledge. If all answers are not fixed and eternal, then one's own opportunity to understand them is opened up. As noted, this can emerge into a rejection of critical thinking in the form of skepticism— that is, the denial of the possibility of knowledge or understanding.[2]

Third, adolescents often display considerable emotional investment in philosophical issues, such as the nature of knowledge (epistemology) or the essence of justice (moral philosophy). This emotional investment, if nurtured, becomes an important component of the critical habit of mind, which requires commitment as well as cognitive skills.

These developments are of course linked to other important changes in adolescence (Keating, 1990a). Of particular importance are processes of individuation and separation from parental figures and identity issues related to this. Coming to view oneself as a separate and independent person is a long-term challenge through adolescence and into young adulthood; the commitments that define the self during this period tend to endure.

It may be useful to articulate more clearly the ways in which the perspective outlined here builds on prior work on adolescent thinking (Keating, 1980b, 1990a). An earlier focus on precise specification of the purely logical distinctions between children and adolescents, between younger and older adolescents, or between adolescents and young adults has given way to a broader perspective that includes a variety of significant changes in thinking that occur from the onset of adolescence until the transition to adulthood. There are a number of reasons for this shift: (a) the difficulty in ascribing changes in thinking entirely to changes in underlying logical structures, (b) the strong effects of both context and content in the operation of thinking in everyday life, (c) the lack of clear demarcations in performance between various age groups, and (d) the demonstrated importance of noncognitive factors (motivation, self-perception, emotion, personality, social interaction) in cognitive activity.

The move away from strict stagelike models does not imply a move away from the recognition of important qualitative shifts in thinking across this age range. Such qualitative shifts are apparent in both broad age trends and in individual developmental pathways. What appears to be emerging in contemporary research is an attempt to embed the specific cognitive shifts in a larger picture that integrates them with developments in other key domains. This theoretical and methodological effort, which we have referred to as *developmental integration*, requires us to address the complexity entailed by examining cognition in its full context. From this integrative perspective, the key cognitive shifts noted earlier—increasing breadth of knowledge, the ability to maintain and compare competing representations, the greater spontaneous use of strategies to deal with complexity, the recognition of relativity—can be viewed as significant contributors to an enhanced capacity for critical thinking. To move that capacity toward an attained capability, however, requires substantial support from cognitive socialization environments.

For a host of reasons, then, adolescence can be viewed as a critical period for the development of critical thinking and a critical habit of mind. Adequate external support for this development is essential, however. If the problem is not beyond our control due to developmental limitations, then it makes sense to look elsewhere. If critical thinking is possible for adolescents but not much present in contemporary schooling, one may justifiably doubt the degree of support it receives. We need to look to the educational practices relevant for critical thinking.

EDUCATION FOR CRITICAL THINKING

The resurgence of educational interest in critical thinking has provoked an expanding research effort. Three major aspects of this research are central here. First, observational studies on thinking in the typical secondary school classroom have, as noted earlier, documented the paucity of such thinking. In response to this, a second line of research has examined educational interventions to teach thinking through direct instruction, as a set of skills to be acquired. The third, more recent approach has been to examine the features of regular teaching activity that tend to encourage critical thinking. A brief review of these latter two efforts are in order.

Teaching Thinking:
Direct Instruction

Nearly all the programs for direct educational intervention on thinking skills are appropriately categorized as aiming at the enhancement of procedural knowledge. The typical hope is that by developing problem-solving heuristics with a particular type of material—usually not tied to any particular subject matter content—that students will be enabled to employ these skills in a wide range of specific content domains. If such transfer were to be convincingly demonstrated, it would make a strong counterargument to Glaser's (1984) specificity position.

In reality, convincing evidence of this sort has not been forthcoming, at least not yet (see reviews by Bransford et al., 1985; Campione & Armbruster, 1985; Chance, 1986; Nickerson, Perkins, & Smith, 1985). In many cases, there is little formal evaluation of any sort. Where careful evaluations have been done, the criteria are typically the students' performance on materials exactly the same as, or very much like, the training materials. Though this may be a necessary first step in the evaluation process, it is weak evidence of a strong claim (the general enhancement of thinking).

The next and crucial step of transfer to quite different kinds of content is the natural litmus test. The criteria may be hard to specify, but without this information, the issue is reduced to how effectively particular programs "teach to their own tests."

This is a serious concern, if the early research on expert knowledge systems is borne out (Chi et al., 1982; Keating, 1990b; Keating & Crane, 1990). That is, if content knowledge and procedural knowledge are inevitably intertwined, then programs of direct instruction in general thinking may be misguided at a rather basic level. The pattern in these training programs is often reminiscent of the creative thinking programs popular not so long ago. In those as well, the target criterion became enhanced test performance rather than real-world creativity, and the focus became isolated from research on what is necessarily a large and complex question (Keating, 1980a). For purposes of development, what we would need instead is a better understanding of the acquisition of well-integrated operational and content knowledge structures (Keating & MacLean, 1988).

There is another important feature of cognitive activity, most broadly termed *metacognition*, that has similarly been the focus of direct instructional efforts. Although it is the case that the ability or inclination to monitor one's own cognitive activity (for consistency, for gaps in information that need to be remedied, for checking the accuracy of some procedural application, and so on) can easily be categorized as part of critical thinking, as noted earlier, it is less clear that efforts to enhance this independently will be very successful. At the simplest level, they may reduce to mere exhortations to students to "THINK!" More elaborate attempts to enhance metacognitive activity have encountered some of the same difficulties as (and sometimes overlap conceptually with) programs for direct instruction of thinking processes. Specifically, individuals often have difficulty transferring such skills to any content outside of that in which it was first learned (Brown et al., 1983; Cavanaugh & Perlmutter, 1982).

One might even imagine the possibility that a focus on such activities could be counterproductive early in the learning process, by drawing conscious attention to activities that might better be left alone to proceed toward automaticity. In this sense, metacognition may be a luxurious epiphenomenon of the already accomplished expert: Once a difficult skill or domain has been mastered, attention can be given over to whether or not the system is operating smoothly.

A second kind of monitoring is much more problematic for cognitive developmental theories of any kind. If we conceive of thinking in general as purposeful and goal directed (Vygotsky, 1978) and critical thinking even more consciously so, then we are compelled to recognize that the goals of the test taker may not be those of the test giver, and the goals of the student may not be the same as those of the teacher. This intrusion of the individual's own goals, motivations, and commitments opens the floodgates on our typically closed-system models of thinking, learning, and teaching. It may yet prove the case that many of the constraints on critical thinking are not exclusively cognitive but derive instead from questions of motivation and goals (Dweck, 1986).

Teaching Thinking: Classroom Thoughtfulness

Several conclusions can be drawn from the analyses above. First, there is no evidence to argue for fundamental developmental limitations on adolescents' ability to think critically. Second, the promise of generalizable benefits from direct instruction in thinking skills has yet to be realized, and there are sound reasons to suspect that such a skill instruction approach may be inadequate, even inappropriate. Third, there is some evidence from the emerging literature on expertise that significant advances in the development of critical thinking may rest instead on an integrated model that focuses on conceptual flexibility, reflective thinking, cognitive self-regulation, and domain-specific knowledge. What these conclusions suggest is that we need to turn our attention more clearly toward the practices of general instruction in schools to consider the ways in which they support or hinder the acquisition of an integrated functioning of critical thinking—and how they might be altered so as to become more supportive.

This is obviously a tall order, if one judges from the current reviews of everyday schooling (Goodlad, 1983; Sizer, 1985). Much of the school day seems to be occupied with nonacademic, nonintellective content. What content there is, is often presented in disconnected packets of information from which rote recall or rote application is all that is expected.

What then are the constraints in everyday schooling that inhibit the emergence of critical thinking? First, it is quite clear that the test-driven demands for accountability affect both teachers and students dramatically. As Frederiksen (1984) has pointed out, this test bias has come to affect what is considered legitimate within school curricula. If key aspects of critical thinking are devalued by not being assessed for any reason that counts, then teachers are less likely to demand it of students. Students, in turn, learn what is and is not important in the eyes of the school and the community. The elaborate credentialing system of education is designed partly as a social force to motivate students to acquire necessary skills. By failing to denote critical thinking as necessary—because we don't test for it, and it is only the test scores that are used for purposes of accountability— such activity tends to disappear from school.

Second, there are many reasons to believe that the development of critical thinking rests squarely on the availability of ample amounts of relevant discourse (Glaser, 1984; Keating & MacLean, 1988; Newmann, 1985; Vygotsky, 1978). "Interactive inquiry methods are powerful tools for teaching thinking in the context of subject matter" (Glaser, 1984, p. 101). But adequate opportunity for real discourse is hard to come by in high schools. There are many other demands on teachers, both for nonacademic supervision and for coverage of the academic material likely to be needed by students on tests. To be successful, such discourse or interactive inquiry must be finely tuned to the actual developmental level of the students. It "requires that a teacher be continually vigilant and keep in mind the particulars of each student's thinking" (Glaser, 1984, p. 101).

With even average class sizes, this is a daunting task, especially when the developmental levels within any given classroom may vary quite markedly. If, as seems likely, different approaches are called for at different phases of acquisition, the complexity increases geometrically. Organizational rearrangements that would dramatically reduce class size, at least for some reasonable proportion of the school day, could be expected on the basis of current research to accomplish a great deal for the enhancement of critical thinking (Bennett, 1987).

When such discourse focuses on topics such as social studies or history, additional problems are encountered (Newmann, 1985). For a truly open, critical discourse, the recognition that knowledge is "problematic and tentative" (Newmann, 1985, p. 10) is essential. This viewpoint, however, runs counter to the socially appointed role as an authority that is imposed on teachers.

Thus, a host of factors conspire to limit discourse, and discourse seems essential to the development of critical thinking as elaborated here. This presents an important challenge to researchers and educators.

One potentially productive route is to study teachers who are able to create an effective classroom climate for discourse, despite the constraints. To the extent that those skills might be acquired by others, changes within the present framework might be possible. Newmann (1990a, 1990b) and his colleagues (McCartney & Schrag, 1990; Onosko, 1990; Stevenson, 1990) have reported a research program to identify the features of effective educational situations for critical thinking, with a focus on the notion of classroom thoughtfulness.

The pattern of empirical findings that differentiate more from less thoughtful lessons observed in the research coincides with a view of critical thinking as an integrated activity rather than an isolated skill (Newmann, 1990b). More thoughtful classes were those in which teachers gave careful consideration to the quality of the students' discussion and challenged them to justify and clarify their assertions and in which teacher-centered discussion rather than lecture, recitation, or unguided discussion predominated. In these classes, students were more likely to be engaged, to generate original points, and to make germane comments.

It should be noted, however, that the classrooms observed were selected in part for their commitment to the enhancement of higher-order thinking. In more representative samples, it may be the case that less subtle distinctions would obtain. It is noteworthy that there was considerable variability even among this selected sample.

Identifying the features of classrooms that enhance thoughtfulness is of course only the first step. Institutionalizing the identified desirable features is also necessary. A closer examination of the organizational and systemic factors that reinforce the current framework is then required to discover the constraints on institutional change. The accelerating level of dissatisfaction now evident may provide a rare historical opportunity to propose and enact such changes.

Distributed Cognition

One potentially valuable approach is to take the idea of thinking as a social activity even further, using the concept of knowledge building that arises from a cumulative discourse (Bereiter & Scardamalia, 1993, 1996). From this perspective, the ability of the individual to participate effectively in a learning community is a hallmark of a critical habit of mind (Keating, 1995, 1996). Such participation requires independent thought and action as well as group collaboration and is focused on the building of knowledge about a meaningful topic rather than the acquisition of transmitted knowledge and skills. It may well be that participation in well-structured learning communities, supported by the new information technologies, will provoke more widespread acquisition of critical habits of mind. Realizing such changes will require substantial rethinking and restructuring of school activities, but such transformational change is likely to be necessary for success in the information age (Keating, 1995).

One of the key goals in efforts to establish effective learning communities—whether supported by emerging information technologies or by more traditional means—should be to enhance effective participation by all members of society. There is overwhelming evidence that for traditional measures of educational achievement, less powerful groups in society, whether defined by social class, gender, culture, or ethnicity, have fared less well (Keating, 1990a). Without specific attention to these traditional divisions, it is likely that access to full participation in the kinds of learning communities that can promote critical thinking will yield similar divisions. On the other hand, the freedom to develop critical thinking by shifting the focus from knowledge transmission (which has an inherent authority structure) to knowledge building (which can accommodate a broader participatory structure on what counts as knowledge) represents a historic opportunity for far greater inclusiveness (Keating, 1996). Realizing this potential requires that we gain a better theoretical and empirical grasp both of the fundamental nature of cognitive activity and of the socialization environments in which it can prosper.

COGNITIVE SOCIALIZATION
OUTSIDE SCHOOL

Last, it is important to note that schools do not present the sole opportunities for, nor the sole barriers to, critical thinking. Aspects of the larger culture conspire as well to instantiate and reinforce a noncritical perspective in all of us, and adolescents are clearly not immune from these influences (Keating, 1990a).

Consider two salient aspects of contemporary society that have received critical attention: mass media, and television in particular, and the social organization of modern urban centers. Adolescents watch television for many hours per week and are exposed to thousands of advertisements annually (Keating, 1990a). The goal of advertising, of course, is to move products, and rarely do they appeal to our skills in critical analysis to do so. Indeed, they are typically designed to overcome critical thinking—by overwhelming decision-making capacities with endless and usually irrelevant criteria, by using an accelerated presentation rate to defeat reflective thinking, and by using sophisticated techniques to link products with strong emotions and desires. This is stiff competition, even for the most effective teachers.

The world experienced by North American and most Western adolescents outside school and beyond television is also increasingly narrow. The notion of meaningful discourse in public spaces has largely yielded to a mix of shopping mall cultures and isolated residential enclaves (Powell et al., 1985; Sennett, 1991). Opportunities for adolescents to observe or engage in critical discourse are rare, and shifting cultural patterns have contributed to this.

These and other identifiable social and technological changes make it clear that there are substantial challenges to our capacity for developing critical thinking more widely in the population. But such developments are fundamental to the building of a learning society that can adapt to and meet the rapidly evolving circumstances of contemporary life (Keating, 1995, 1996).

Thus, even major reform in the schools cannot be expected to carry the full weight of generating or preserving the habit of critical thinking. But this circumstance does make the school even more important as an arena in which it is possible for students to acquire the ability and the disposition to think and to be empowered by that acquisition. Understanding the nature of adolescent thinking, and how it develops in all its complexity, is fundamental to that accomplishment.

NOTES

1. In this context, the term *critical period* does not have the formal meaning that it does in ethology—that is, the only period during which a particular behavior can be established (e.g., imprinting in ducklings). Rather, we use it in the more general sense

of a developmentally sensitive period during which particular structures and habits are relatively easier to acquire and after which such acquisitions, although not impossible, are more difficult and less likely.

2. It is important to distinguish between *criticism* and *skepticism* because they are often confused. In our use of the terms, critical thinking is aimed at the production of knowledge and understanding through deep questioning and a desire to get to the root of the matter. It is thus closely connected with a search for knowledge based on principles rather than on isolated facts, assumptions, or unexamined biases. Skepticism is, instead, the negation of knowledge, taking to an extreme the claim that because knowledge is never final, there is no such thing as knowledge. Although closely aligned in colloquial use—the critic and the skeptic seem to have much in common—the goals are quite different. In fact, skepticism is philosophically more akin to fundamentalism, in that they both appeal to absolutes.

REFERENCES

Bennett, S. (1987). *New dimensions in research on class size and academic achievement.* Madison, WI: National Center on Effective Secondary Schools.

Bereiter, C., & Scardamalia, M. (1993). *Surpassing ourselves: An inquiry into the nature of expertise.* La Salle, IL: Open Court.

Bereiter, C., & Scardamalia, M. (1996). Rethinking learning. In D. Olson & N. Torrance (Eds.), *Handbook of education and human development: New models of learning, teaching, and schooling* (pp. 485-513). Cambridge, MA: Basil Blackwell.

Boyer, E. (1987). *College: The undergraduate experience in America.* New York: Harper & Row.

Bransford, J. D., Arbitman-Smith, R., Stein, B. S., & Vye, N. J. (1985). Improving thinking and learning skills: An analysis of three approaches. In J. W. Segal, S. F. Chipman, & R. Glaser (Eds.), *Thinking and learning skills* (Vol. 1, pp. 133-206). Hillsdale, NJ: Lawrence Erlbaum.

Brown, A. L. (1981). Metacognition and reading and writing: The development and facilitation of selective attention strategies for learning from texts. In M. L. Kamil (Ed.), *Directions in reading: Research and instruction.* Washington, DC: The National Reading Conference.

Brown, A. L., Bransford, J. D., Ferrara, R. A., & Campione, J. C. (1983). Learning, remembering, and understanding. In P. H. Mussen (Ed.), *Handbook of child psychology* (4th ed., Vol. 3, pp. 77-166). New York: John Wiley.

Bruner, J. S. (1973). *Beyond the information given.* New York: Norton.

Bruner, J. S. (1986). *Acts of meaning.* New York: Cambridge University Press.

Campione, J. C., & Armbruster, B. B. (1985). Acquiring information from texts: An analysis of four approaches. In J. W. Segal, S. F. Chipman, & R. Glaser (Eds.), *Thinking and learning skills* (Vol. 1, pp. 317-359). Hillsdale, NJ: Lawrence Erlbaum.

Cavanaugh, J. C., & Perlmutter, M. (1982). Metamemory: A critical reexamination. *Child Development, 53,* 11-28.

Ceci, S. J. (1990). *On intelligence . . . More or less.* Englewood Cliffs, NJ: Prentice Hall.

Chance, P. (1986). *Thinking in the classroom: A survey of programs.* New York: Teachers College Press.

Chandler, M. (1987). The Othello effect: Essay on the emergence and eclipse of skeptical doubt. *Human Development, 30,* 137-159.

Chi, M. T. H., Glaser, R., & Rees, E. (1982). Expertise in problem solving. In R. J. Sternberg (Ed.), *Advances in the psychology of human intelligence* (Vol. 1, pp. 7-75). Hillsdale, NJ: Lawrence Erlbaum.

Chipman, S. F., & Segal, J. W. (1985). Higher cognitive goals for education: An introduction. In J. W. Segal, S. F. Chipman, & R. Glaser (Eds.), *Thinking and learning skills* (Vol. 1, pp. 1-19). Hillsdale, NJ: Lawrence Erlbaum.

Dewey, J. (1910). *How we think.* Boston: Heath.

Dweck, C. S. (1986). Motivational processes affecting learning. *American Psychologist, 41,* 1040-1048.

Epstein, H. T. (1974). Phrenoblysis: Special brain and mind growth periods. *Developmental Psychology, 7,* 207-216.

Epstein, H. T. (1978). Growth spurts during brain development. In J. Chall & F. Mirsky (Eds.), *Education and the brain* (NSSE Yearbook, Pt. 2, pp. 343-371). Chicago: University of Chicago Press.

Eylon, B., & Linn, M. C. (1988). Learning and instruction: An examination of four research perspectives in science education. *Review of Educational Research, 58,* 251-301.

Feyerabend, P. (1975). *Against method.* London: New Left Books.

Frederiksen, N. (1984). The real test bias: Influences of testing on teaching and learning. *American Psychologist, 39,* 193-202.

Gardner, H. (1983). *Frames of mind: The theory of multiple intelligences.* New York: Basic Books.

Gilligan, C. (1982). *In a different voice.* Cambridge, MA: Harvard University Press.

Glaser, R. (1984). Education and thinking: The role of knowledge. *American Psychologist, 39,* 93-104.

Goodlad, J. I. (1983). *A place called school: Prospects for the future.* New York: McGraw-Hill.

Gould, S. J. (1990). *Wonderful life.* New York: Norton.

Haan, N., Smith, M. B., & Block, J. H. (1968). The moral reasoning of young adults: Political-social behavior, family background, and personality correlates. *Journal of Personality and Social Psychology, 10,* 183-201.

Habermas, J. (1979). Communication and the evolution of society (T. McCarthy, Trans.). boston: Beacon Press.

Hill, J. P. (1988). Adapting to menarche: Familial control and conflict. In M. R. Gunnar & W. A. Collins (Eds.), *Development during the transition to adolescence: 21st Minnesota symposium on child development* (pp. 43-77). Hillsdale, NJ: Lawrence Erlbaum.

Hill, J. P., & Palmquist, W. J. (1978). Social cognition and social relationships in early adolescence. *International Journal of Behavioral Development, 1,* 1-36.

Hogan, R. (1982). Reaction: Biases in theories of development. In F. M. Newmann & C. E. Sleeter (Eds.), *Adolescent development and secondary schooling.* Madison: Wisconsin Center for Education Research.

Inhelder, B., & Piaget, J. (1958). *The growth of logical thinking from childhood to adolescence.* New York: Basic Books.

Keating, D. P. (1974). The study of mathematically precocious youth. In J. C. Stanley, D. P. Keating, & L. H. Fox (Eds.), *Mathematical talent: Discovery, description, and development* (pp. 23-46). Baltimore: Johns Hopkins University Press.

Keating, D. P. (1980a). Four faces of creativity: The continuing plight of the intellectually underserved. *Gifted Child Quarterly, 24,* 56-61.

Keating, D. P. (1980b). Thinking processes in adolescence. In J. Adelson (Ed.), *Handbook of adolescent psychology* (pp. 211-246). New York: John Wiley.

Keating, D. P. (1984). The emperor's new clothes: The "new look" in intelligence research. In R. J. Sternberg (Ed.), *Advances in the psychology of human intelligence* (Vol. 2, pp. 1-47). Hillsdale, NJ: Lawrence Erlbaum.

Keating, D. P. (1988). *Adolescents' ability to engage in critical thinking.* Madison, WI: National Center for Effective Secondary Education.

Keating, D. P. (1990a). Adolescent thinking. In S. S. Feldman & G. R. Elliott (Eds.), *At the threshold: The developing adolescent* (pp. 54-89). Cambridge, MA: Harvard University Press.

Keating, D. P. (1990b). Charting pathways to the development of expertise. *Educational Psychologist, 25,* 243-267.

Keating, D. P. (1990c). Structuralism, deconstruction, reconstruction: The limits of reasoning. In W. F. Overton (Ed.), *Reasoning, necessity, and logic: Developmental perspectives* (pp. 299-319). Hillsdale, NJ: Lawrence Erlbaum.

Keating, D. P. (1995). The transformation of schooling: Dealing with developmental diversity. In J. Lupart, A. McKeough, & C. Yewchuck (Eds.), *Schools in transition: Rethinking regular and special education* (pp. 119-139). Toronto: Nelson.

Keating, D. P. (1996). Habits of mind for a learning society: Educating for human development. In D. Olson & N. Torrance (Eds.), *Handbook of education and human development: New models of learning, teaching, and schooling* (pp. 461-481). Cambridge, MA: Basil Blackwell.

Keating, D. P., & Clark, L. V. (1980). Development of physical and social reasoning in adolescence. *Developmental Psychology, 16,* 23-30.

Keating, D. P., & Crane, L. L. (1990). Domain-general and domain-specific processes in proportional reasoning. *Merrill-Palmer Quarterly, 36,* 411-424.

Keating, D. P., & MacLean, D. J. (1987). Cognitive processing, cognitive ability, and development: A reconsideration. In P. A. Vernon (Ed.), *Speed of information-processing and intelligence* (pp. 239-270). Norwood, NJ: Ablex.

Keating, D. P., & MacLean, D. J. (1988). Reconstruction in cognitive development: A post-structuralist agenda. In P. B. Baltes, D. L. Featherman, & R. M. Lerner (Eds.), *Life span development and behavior* (Vol. 8, pp. 283-317). Hillsdale, NJ: Lawrence Erlbaum.

Kline, M. (1980). *Mathematics: The loss of certainty.* New York: Oxford University Press.

Kogan, N. (1983). Stylistic variation in childhood and adolescence: Creativity, metaphor, and cognitive styles. In P. H. Mussen (Ed.), *Handbook of child psychology* (4th ed., Vol. 3, pp. 630-706). New York: John Wiley.

Kuhn, D., Amsel, E., & O'Loughlin, M. (1988). *The development of scientific thinking skills.* San Diego, CA: Academic Press.

Lazerson, M. (1986). Review of "A Study of High Schools." *Harvard Educational Review, 56,* 37-48.

Linn, M. C., & Songer, N. B. (1991). Cognitive and conceptual change in adolescence. *American Journal of Education, 99*(4), 379-417.

Manis, F. R., Keating, D. P., & Morrison, F. J. (1980). Developmental differences in the allocation of processing capacity. *Journal of Experimental Child Psychology, 29,* 156-169.

Matthews, D. J., & Keating, D. P. (1995). Domain specificity and habits of mind: An investigation of patterns of high-level development. *Journal of Early Adolescence, 15*, 319-343.

McCartney, C., & Schrag, F. (1990). Departmental and school leadership in promoting higher-order thinking. *Journal of Curriculum Studies, 22*, 529-543.

Miller, K., Perlmutter, M., & Keating, D. P. (1984). Cognitive arithmetic: Comparison of operations. *Journal of Experimental Psychology: Learning, Memory, and Cognition, 10*, 46-60.

Morrison, F. J., Lord, C. A., & Keating, D. P. (1984). Applied developmental psychology. In F. Morrison, C. Lord, & D. Keating (Eds.), *Applied developmental psychology* (Vol. 1, pp. 1-19). New York: Academic Press.

Newmann, F. M. (1985). The radical perspective on social studies: A synthesis and critique. *Theory and Research in Social Education, 13*, 1-18.

Newmann, F. M. (1990a). Higher order thinking in teaching social studies: A rationale for the assessment of classroom thoughtfulness. *Journal of Curriculum Studies, 22*, 41-56.

Newmann, F. M. (1990b). Qualities of thoughtful social studies classes: An empirical profile. *Journal of Curriculum Studies, 22*, 253-275.

Nickerson, R. S., Perkins, D. N. & Smith, E. E. (1995). The teaching of thinking. Hillsdale, NJ: Erlbaum.

Nisbett, R. E., Fong, G. T., Lehman, D. R., & Cheng, P. W. (1987). Teaching reasoning. *Science, 237*, 625-631.

Onosko, J. J. (1990). Comparing teachers' instruction to promote students' thinking. *Journal of Curriculum Studies, 22*, 443-461.

Piaget, J. (1972). Intellectual evolution from adolescence to adulthood. *Human Development, 15*, 1-12.

Powell, A. G., Farrar, E., & Cohen, D. K. (1985). *The shopping mall high school: Winners and losers in the educational marketplace.* Boston: Houghton Mifflin.

Schrag, F. (1988). *Thinking in school and society.* London: Routledge & Kegan Paul.

Selman, R. L. (1980). *The growth of interpersonal understanding.* New York: Academic Press.

Sennett, R. J. (1991). *Conscience of the eye.* New York: Knopf.

Sizer, T. (1985). *Horace's compromise: The dilemma of the American high school.* Boston: Houghton Mifflin.

Sternberg, R. J. (1977). *Intelligence, information processing, and analogical reasoning: The componential analysis of human abilities.* Hillsdale, NJ: Lawrence Erlbaum.

Stevenson, R. B. (1990). Engagement and cognitive challenge in thoughtful social studies classes: A study of student perspectives. *Journal of Curriculum Studies, 22*, 329-341.

Toepfer, C. F. (1979). Brain growth periodization: A new dogma for education. *Middle School Journal, 10*(3), 20.

Vygotsky, L. (1978). Mind in society: The development of higher psychological processes. In M. Cole, V. John-Steiner, S. Scribner, & E. Souberman (Eds.), *Mind in society: The development of higher psychological processes.* Cambridge, MA: Harvard University Press.

Wallach, M. A. (1970). Creativity. In P. H. Mussen (Ed.), *Carmichael's manual of child psychology* (3rd ed., Vol. 1 pp. 1211-1272). New York: John Wiley.

Wallach, M. A. (1985). Creativity testing and giftedness. In F. D. Horowitz & M. O'Brien (Eds.), *The gifted and talented: Developmental perspectives* (pp. 99-123). Washington, DC: American Psychological Association.

8. Puberty:
The Interplay of Biological and Psychosocial Processes in Adolescence

Sucheta D. Connolly
Roberta L. Paikoff
Christy M. Buchanan

Pubertal development is often considered the most clear demarcation of the transition from childhood to adolescence (Brooks-Gunn & Reiter, 1990; Buchanan, Eccles, & Becker, 1992; Hill, 1980, 1983; Paikoff & Brooks-Gunn, 1990a, 1990b, 1991; Petersen & Taylor, 1980). Considered a "primary developmental change" (Hill, 1980), pubertal development has been of major interest to researchers in adolescent psychology because the changes of puberty have been linked to a wide variety of social, relational, emotional, and cognitive factors in adolescence (Brooks-Gunn, Graber, & Paikoff, 1994; Buchanan et al., 1992; Holmbeck, in press; Laursen & Collins, 1994; Paikoff & Brooks-Gunn, 1991). In this chapter, we initially review what is known about pubertal development (primarily in Western cultures) from historical and conceptual perspectives. In addition, we provide some discussion of different methodologies and designs used to investigate aspects of pubertal development and their links to psychosocial functioning. We examine some of the challenges of studying puberty and related limitations of the current research. This overview of the major issues in defining and studying puberty provides a framework to compare and contrast the research reviewed. For the major portion of this chapter, we discuss evidence to date for links between pubertal development and psychosocial functioning, briefly reviewing aspects of affective experience; attentional behaviors; aggression,

AUTHORS' NOTE: The authors' work on this chapter is supported by the National Institute of Mental Health (Grant #MH50423) and by a William T. Grant Faculty Scholar Award to the second author. We wish to thank Ninfa Sarabia for her assistance with reference preparation, Grayson Holmbeck, Teresa Jacobsen, and the editors for their thoughtful comments on earlier versions of this chapter.

delinquency, and behavior problems; sexual behavior; and familial relationships. Other, more extensive, reviews have been completed recently in many of these areas (see especially Brooks-Gunn et al., 1994; Brooks-Gunn & Paikoff, 1993; Brooks-Gunn & Reiter, 1990; Buchanan et al., 1992; Holmbeck, in press; Holmbeck, Paikoff, & Brooks-Gunn, in press; Paikoff & Brooks-Gunn, 1991; Petersen et al., 1993); thus, we primarily restrict ourselves to summaries of what is known in each of these areas. Last, we conclude by discussing the role that contextual and individual factors may play in understanding links between pubertal development and psychosocial functioning and provide our suggestions for the important next steps with regard to work in this field.

PUBERTY IN ADOLESCENT DEVELOPMENT:
DOMINANT HISTORICAL PERPSECTIVES

Researchers have historically been interested in the link between the physical and emotional changes of adolescence and especially puberty. Hall (1904) saw pubertal changes as negative and stressful for the adolescent, with adolescence itself a period of "Sturm und Drang," or storm and stress. Similarly, Anna Freud (1966) characterized puberty as a period of overwhelming libidinal drives and anxiety, due to upsurges in hormones. Hormonal changes were speculated to account for the sexual and instinctual transformations posited to occur at puberty (Buchanan et al., 1992; Paikoff & Brooks-Gunn, 1990a, 1990b). Pubertal onset was also hypothesized to result in a revivification of oedipal wishes, with the associated rebelliousness presumed to be a part of normal development. It is a common popular belief today that puberty marks the onset of raging emotions and negative mood swings that can spiral out of control.

John Hill (1973) and other researchers have questioned whether this storm-and-stress model of early adolescence is an accurate one, but this long-held view of normal adolescent development as a tumultuous period has been difficult to change despite the fact that many research studies do not support it (Brooks-Gunn, 1989; Buchanan et al., 1992; Hauser & Bowlds, 1990; Holmbeck & Hill, 1988; Offer & Schonert-Reichl, 1992). For example, Offer and his colleagues have examined normal adolescent development across diverse populations and found that the majority of teenagers (approximately 80%)

do not experience turmoil or psychological disturbance but rather show good coping and a smooth transition through this phase of life (Offer & Boxer, 1991). These findings are bolstered by Hauser and Bowlds's (1990) review of the literature, where similar rates of maladjustment or difficulties (e.g., 20%) are reported, and continuity across developmental phases is emphasized. Thus, our best estimates suggest that approximately 20% of the adolescent population experience adjustment difficulties and that many of the same 20% also experienced adjustment difficulties as children. Many of these individuals will continue to experience adjustment difficulties during their adult years. In addition, although puberty is often remembered negatively by parents who are asked to reflect back on the experience, recent studies of adolescents at the time of menarche and spermarche describe both positive and negative feelings (Brooks-Gunn & Reiter, 1990).

What becomes interesting and important, then, is understanding the various factors that influence pubertal status, timing of puberty, and the links between pubertal and psychosocial functioning. By doing so, we can elucidate normative patterns of variation as well as understand individual cases in which psychosocial or adjustment difficulties occur *for the first time* in adolescence and in which prior adjustment difficulties are resolved during the adolescent years.

A MULTIDIMENSIONAL
DEFINITION OF PUBERTY

John Hill (1973) cautioned against defining puberty as a discrete event but instead emphasized that biological and physical factors interact with psychosocial variables and together influence the development of the individual adolescent. In keeping with the foresight of John Hill and the viewpoint of current researchers, we define and examine puberty as a multifaceted process that includes multiple overlapping events, ranging from the biological processes of hormonal and physical changes to the physical and social changes that are visible to others. In addition, the pattern of synchrony or asynchrony of these interdependent processes needs to be considered.

In this chapter, *pubertal status* is defined as the stage of pubertal development reached by the adolescent based on physical, hormonal, and sex characteristics. The studies examined here have assessed pubertal status with a wide range of measurements that include (a) Tanner staging or other scales based on observable physical and sex characteristics; (b) peak height velocity, skeletal age, or skeletal growth; and (c) presence or absence of menarche. The *timing* of puberty is defined relative to adolescent age and peer group. In this chapter, we discuss early and late maturers who still fall within the normal range of reaching various pubertal milestones but do not devote excessive time to the clinical conditions or disorders of puberty (e.g., overly precocious or overly delayed puberty).

The endocrinological changes of puberty mark the maturation of a process that begins during gestation. By midgestation, the hypothalamic-pituitary unit responsible for pubertal development is fully developed and functional (Rosenfield, 1991). At birth in females, without the inhibition of maternal estrogens, gonadotropins rise and the ovary functions at a pubertal level for a few months, though this is not readily apparent physically (Rosenfield, 1991). After this initial surge, follicle-stimulating hormone (FSH), luteinizing hormone (LH), and sex steroids are suppressed to a very low level until late childhood, when the endocrinological changes of puberty actually begin. In the male fetus, gonads develop and begin to secrete androgens. These hormones ultimately result in the development of male internal and external sex organs (Brooks-Gunn & Reiter, 1990).

The earliest signs of adrenarche occur in normal boys and girls between 6 and 8 years of age and are defined by the increased secretion of dehydroepiandrosterone (DHEA), dehydroepiandrosterone sulfate (DHEAS), and other androgens by the adrenal gland. Adrenocorticotropic hormone (ACTH) and other adrenal-stimulating hormones enhance androgen production, but the cause of adrenarche remains unclear. Adrenarche is followed by the development of axillary and pubic hair, body odor, facial skin oiliness, acne, and by a transient acceleration of bone growth and maturation (Kletter & Kelch, 1993; Parker, 1991). Between 6 and 9 years of age, gonadotropin secretion gradually increases and is referred to as *gonadarche*, with reactivation of the hypothalamic-pituitary-gonadotropin-gonadal axis. Adrenarche precedes gonadarche by approximately 2 years, and the processes seem to be independent of one another (Rosenfield, 1991).

Puberty is initiated by maturation of the central nervous system (CNS) centers that lessen neural restraint and allow pulsatile secretion of gonadotropin-releasing hormone by the hypothalamus during sleep. This CNS maturity corresponds better to pubertal bone age than chronological age and is also closely tied in with body mass, or metabolic level, and nutrition. CNS maturity stimulates the pituitary gonadotrope to secrete LH and FSH (Rosenfield, 1991). There is an increased responsiveness of the gonads to the nocturnal, pulsatile secretion of FSH and LH and eventually, increased secretion of gonadal hormones, such as testosterone in the testes and estrogen in the ovaries.

The physical changes of puberty have been well described in the literature (Marshall & Tanner, 1970; Tanner, 1971; Tanner, Whitehouse, & Takaishi, 1966). The adolescent growth spurt is one of the most visible signs of adolescent development. The velocity of growth in height approximately doubles for a year or more, with a peak velocity of height averaging about 10.5 centimeters a year (cm/yr) in boys and 9.0 cm/yr in girls, with a standard deviation of about 1.0 cm/yr. Though the absolute age at which this peak velocity is reached can differ, as a group, girls consistently reach their peak approximately 2 years before boys. There also is a spurt in muscle growth that coincides with the skeletal growth spurt and, similarly, girls peak earlier (Tanner, 1971; Tanner et al., 1966).

Along with the physical changes in skeletal and muscular growth during puberty are the physical changes that signal maturation of the reproductive system (primary sexual characteristics, such as genitalia and ovaries) and further differentiation between the sexes (secondary sexual characteristics, such as facial hair and breast development). The age at which the various events begin and end is quite variable for boys and girls, as diagrammed in Figure 8.1, but the sequence of events is much less variable than the age at which the events occur (Tanner, 1971). In boys, the first physical sign of pubertal sexual development is increased growth of the testes and scrotum, followed closely by slight growth of the pubic hair, and followed, on average, in 1 year by the spurts in height and penis growth. The first ejaculation of seminal fluid follows in about another year; it takes approximately 3 years to pass from the first acceleration of genital growth to adult male genitalia but can take as long as 4.7 years. Axillary hair appears when pubic hair is reaching Tanner stage 4 and is accompanied by the beginning of facial hair growth in boys (Brooks-Gunn & Reiter, 1990; Tanner, 1971).

In girls, breast budding (thelarche) is the first physical sign of pubertal development. Pubic hair development (pubarche) follows

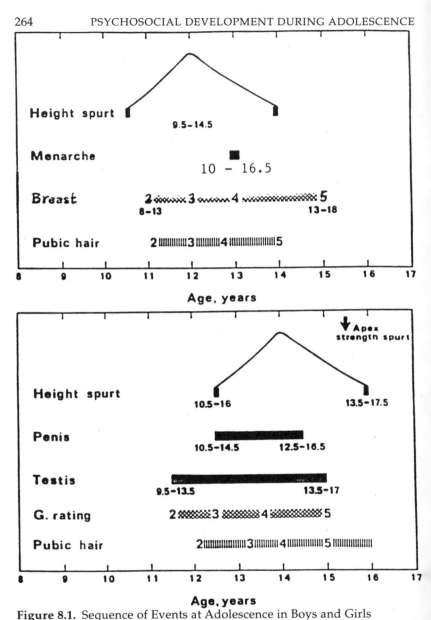

Figure 8.1. Sequence of Events at Adolescence in Boys and Girls

SOURCE: Marshall and Tanner (1970). Reprinted by permission
NOTE: The average boy and girl are represented. The range of ages within which each event
charted may begin and end is given by the figures placed directly below its start and finish.
"G." refers to the rating of genital development or genital stage.

soon after this in most girls, but in one fifth to one third of girls, pubic hair development precedes breast budding (Brooks-Gunn & Reiter, 1990; Tanner, 1971). Axillary hair usually appears about a year later than pubic hair and passes through similar stages as pubic hair development (Rosenfield, 1991). The uterus and vagina develop at the same time as the breasts, with enlargement as well of the labia and clitoris. Menarche (the onset of menses) occurs at 12.7 years on an average in North American girls and about 2.3 years (SD 1.0) after breast development begins (Rosenfield, 1991). Menarche almost invariably follows peak height velocity and occurs during deceleration of height growth. The early menstrual cycles are often irregular and approximately half of them are ovulatory in the first 2 years. Most girls establish menstrual regularity by 2 years after initial menarche (Rosenfield, 1991; Tanner, 1971).

There is a great degree of variability in how quickly boys and girls pass through the stages of puberty and in the closeness with which various events are linked together (Brooks-Gunn & Reiter, 1990; Petersen & Taylor, 1980; Tanner, 1971). In girls, the period of time it takes to proceed from the onset of pubertal physical development to maturation can be anywhere from 1.5 to 6 years. In boys, the genitalia may take from 2 to 5 years to pass from Tanner stage 2 to stage 5 and still be within the normal range. In addition, the timing of events relative to one another is also variable. For most girls, menarche occurs when breast and pubic hair are in stage 4 of their development, but it occurs 10% of the time for girls in stage 5 of breast and pubic hair growth and less often in stage 2 or stage 1 of pubic hair growth (Tanner, 1971). Why certain individuals have tighter linkage between various pubertal events is not clear, but it may be dependent on the group of hormones that controls each event and how they are integrated (Rosenfield, 1991; Tanner, 1971).

Extremes in variation of pubertal timing result in either precocious or overly delayed puberty. Precocious puberty in girls is defined as the first sign of breast development before age 7.5 years, sexual pubic hair before age 8.5 years, and menses before age 9.5 years (Rosenfield, 1991). Precocious puberty is less common in boys than girls, and in boys, is defined by the appearance of secondary sex characteristics prior to the age of 9 years (Kletter & Kelch, 1993). This pubertal prematurity can be caused by early reactivation of the hypothalamic-pituitary hormonal axis responsible for sexual maturation (complete or true precocious puberty) or due to a disturbance outside this axis (incomplete or pseudoprecocious puberty) that results in autonomous secretion of sex steroids, androgens, or gonadotropins (Kletter & Kelch, 1993; Rosenfield, 1991). In true precocious puberty (TPP), pubertal maturation is complete, with a full range of hormonal secretion, and secondary sex characteristics are appropriate for the sex of the child (isosexual). In pseudoprecocious puberty, pubertal maturation is incomplete, with early sexual development influenced by androgens or estrogens but not both; secondary sexual characteristics may or may not be isosexual (Rosenfield, 1991). In boys without treatment for precocious puberty, final adult height was decreased, even though these boys had tall stature during childhood (Kletter & Kelch, 1993).

Less attention has been paid to overly delayed puberty than to precocious puberty in the psychological or clinical literatures, perhaps reflecting cultural concerns (e.g., emphasis on early puberty as a potential problem, given links to sexual and reproductive maturity, whereas delayed puberty is seen as potentially desirable, especially for girls). From a medical standpoint, overly delayed puberty is a more complex phenomenon and less clearly encapsulated. For example, if an adolescent girl has never menstruated (primary amenorrhea) and comes to the clinician at a chronologic age when all her peers have menstruated, the first step is to determine if she is pubertal or prepubertal in regard to her hormonal and physical development. Her pubertal status (e.g., pubertal or prepubertal) leads to two different sets of differential diagnoses. Other considerations in the work-up of disorders of delayed puberty, such as amenorrhea, include low or normal FSH levels, adequate estrogenization, bone age, nutritional status, degree of physical activity, stress level, genetic syndromes, and other physiologic disorders in anatomy or function of internal and external genital structures (Rosenfield, 1991). As a rule of thumb, girls who have menstruated at least once but have not established regular cycles by 2 years after menarche need further medical investigation (Rosenfield, 1991; Tanner, 1971). Boys are evaluated for delayed puberty when there is a lack of secondary sex characteristics by 14 years or sexual maturation has not been completed within 4.5 to 5 years of onset (Kletter & Kelch, 1993). The differential diagnosis of delayed puberty in boys is divided into those disorders with low or normal serum gonadotropin concentration and those with high serum gonadotropin concentrations (Kletter & Kelch, 1993).

It becomes clear from this discussion of the biological aspects of pubertal development that adolescents may mature earlier or later than their peers without falling outside the normal range physiologically. However, the psychosocial implications of an adolescent's pubertal status and timing within this normal range of development are not as well defined. John Hill (1973) noted that two adolescents of the same chronological age but with different pubertal timing may be exposed to a very different set of internal stimuli and external stimuli (in terms of the reactions of others), which could result in behavioral consequences that persist into adulthood. In recent years, adolescent research has explored this and other related hypotheses. Next, we will examine contextual factors in the occurrence of puberty as well as the role of context in understanding the meaning of puberty to the adolescent. Then, the methods used to measure the associations between pubertal development and psychosocial adjustment will be discussed, major studies of associations between puberty and psychosocial functioning will be reviewed, and last, we will focus on the implications of this work for future studies in the area.

Context and Pubertal Change

John Hill (1973) described a theory of development across the life cycle in which behavior at any one point was a function of interrelations between personal and situational variables. The effects of gender, ethnicity or race, and social class (situational variables) are considered briefly in relationship to the significant biological and developmental changes (person variables) of puberty already discussed.

The pubertal height spurt is affected by a number of factors. The average age at which the peak height velocity is reached is probably more dependent on characteristics and circumstances of the group studied than the height of the peak (Tanner, 1971). In moderately well-off British or North American boys, the peak is, on average, 14 years, and in girls, it is 12 years, with a standard deviation of 0.9 years in both cases. This accounts for the observation that girls are often taller than boys of the same age in early adolescence. With a similar spurt in muscle growth, there is a period from approximately 12.5 to 13.5 years when girls, on the average, have larger muscles than boys of the same age (Tanner, 1971). It is important to note that girls are much earlier in their pubertal sexual development at the point of maximum skeletal growth, whereas many boys reach mature genitalia at their maximum growth.

During the past 100 years, there has been a secular trend for children to become progressively larger at all ages. This trend is more striking than differences between socioeconomic classes in Europe and America. Together with the greater height in children, there is a smaller upward trend in adult height, and final height is being reached at an earlier age. Most of the trend toward greater size in children reflects a more rapid maturation; only a minor part reflects a greater ultimate size. Earlier maturation is reflected by the trend toward earlier age at menarche, with decreases of between 3 to 4 months per decade since 1850 in average-income sections of Western Europe (Tanner, 1971). Multiple factors are involved in this secular trend, including better health care and increased income, but better nutrition is the major one (Brooks-Gunn & Reiter, 1990). When Asian and African populations as well as other ethnic groups who have adequate nutrition and possibly similar socioeconomic status to the Europeans mentioned are studied, the age at menarche and overall maturational timing seems to be the same (Brooks-Gunn & Reiter, 1990; Tanner, 1971). Individuals in different cultures may differ in important ways, however, regarding their attributions of the meaning of puberty as a whole, as well as to specific pubertal events.

Context and the Meaning of Puberty

The physical changes of puberty are public (e.g., visible to others) as well as private (internal) and signal for the individual and society a transition into another phase of life. In many nonindustrialized societies, the transition is from childhood into the workforce, marriage, and parenthood. In many industrialized nations, there is an intermediate period of adolescence, due to educational trends that delay entry into the full responsibilities of the adult world. Pubertal events have been given different meanings across different cultures, and this results in a range of cultural expectations regarding pubertal status and timing. For example, puberty is marked by ceremony in many cultures in which the community participates in a traditional ritual that celebrates the passage from childhood to adulthood (Brooks-Gunn & Reiter, 1990). In developed societies, popular portrayals in the literature on menarche paint a generally negative picture of puberty as a crisis for girls (Brooks-Gunn, 1984, 1989). Early physical maturity, and especially early timing of menarche, are often viewed as bad and embarrassing developments, with a focus on the negative consequences of puberty. This crisis model of puberty in girls has been challenged, and instead, the developmental and social aspects of puberty have been considered along with the effects of education of adolescents about pubertal changes. For example, Brooks-Gunn and her colleagues have developed a framework for understanding puberty in a social setting and found that negative reports of symptoms in postmenarcheal girls in grades 7 to 12 are associated with their being unprepared for menarche, being early to mature, and receiving information from sources perceived as negative (Brooks-Gunn & Reiter, 1990; Brooks-Gunn & Ruble, 1982; Ruble & Brooks-Gunn, 1982). This refutes earlier theories that the onset of puberty or menarche alone triggers negative feelings in most girls.

Unfortunately, there is much less research examining the pubertal experience in boys (Gaddis & Brooks-Gunn, 1985). Girls are more likely to receive information through school and the community about menarche than are boys about ejaculation. Boys are much less likely to discuss the ejaculation experience with parents and peers, other than in joking, than girls are to discuss menarche. In boys, positive feelings may be stronger than negative feelings at puberty (Gaddis & Brooks-Gunn, 1985), although very little is known.

Last, much of the normative research on pubertal processes has been conducted with middle-class to upper-middle-class European American children (Paikoff & Brooks-Gunn, 1991; Spencer & Dornbusch, 1990). Given the differences in meaning of other social experiences (see, e.g., Ogbu's work [1978] on educational values or Jarrett's [1995] work on values and strategies for social mobility in poor communities), it seems likely that pubertal changes evoke different reactions within different subcultures of Western society, based both on ethnicity and on social resources. As data on normative developmental processes extend to include individuals of diverse social and ethnic groups, our knowledge regarding similarities and differences in the meaning of puberty, as well as links to psychosocial adaptation, will be enhanced. Several such studies are already in progress (Huston, Garcia Coll, & McLoyd, 1994; Sagrestano, Parfenoff, Paikoff, & Holmbeck, 1995; Spencer & McLoyd, 1990).

MEASUREMENT AND DESIGN ISSUES
IN THE STUDY OF PUBERTAL PROCESSES

The study of pubertal development and its links to psychosocial adjustment was limited until recently by inadequate technology for measuring pubertal changes. Thus, although the dominant historical theoretical hypotheses regarding puberty directly implicated hormonal changes, until recently, measurement of hormone change in a normally developed population was not possible. Instead, investigators relied on measures of physical maturational status (e.g., physician, parent, or self Tanner ratings) or answers to questions regarding particular pubertal events, such as growth spurt or menarche. These studies were problematic in that the storm-and-stress hypothesis could not be directly addressed. In addition, the complexity of puberty as a multifaceted, multileveled series of biological and social events resulted in numerous possible types of measurements from numerous different sources (Buchanan et al., 1992; Paikoff & Brooks-Gunn, 1990a, 1990b; Paikoff, Buchanan, & Brooks-Gunn, 1991). Use of different sources and measures of pubertal change often make it difficult to interpret and to draw conclusions from a series of related findings.

The past 10 to 15 years, however, have witnessed a rapid growth in laboratory studies on the effects of pubertal hormones on psychological and social development, due largely to technological changes that have made such work feasible (Brooks-Gunn & Warren, 1989; Buchanan et al., 1992; Inoff-Germain et al., 1988; Nottelmann, et al., 1987; Olweus, Mattsson, Schalling, & Low, 1988; Paikoff & Brooks-Gunn, 1990a, 1990b; Susman, Dorn, & Chrousos, 1991; Udry, Billy, Morris, Groff, & Raj, 1985; Udry & Talbert, 1988). In addition to providing more direct tests of storm-and-stress hypotheses, use of hormonal measures and methods adds another layer of methodological problems to the area of pubertal development (Paikoff, Buchanan, & Brooks-Gunn, 1991).

Because puberty is a process involving multiple events and sequences over time (Buchanan et al., 1992; Hill, 1973, 1980; Paikoff, Buchanan, & Brooks-Gunn, 1991), the difficulties of measurement are, for the most part, encompassed in the need to transform this process into discrete, measurable incidents. As mentioned earlier, despite relative similarities in sequences of pubertal events across individuals, onset and tempo can vary dramatically within a normal range. In addition, links between levels of these processes (e.g., between hormonal changes and secondary sex characteristic maturation), although clearly causal in nature, do not appear to be linear and are not well understood; thus, it is difficult to examine them in conjunction with one another (Brooks-Gunn & Reiter, 1990; Tanner, 1971). Therefore, in current research, it is sometimes the case that a series of pubertal events or incidents must be considered simultaneously. More often, researchers have chosen to isolate a specific aspect of pubertal development and to study its links to psychosocial functioning in relative isolation from other interlocking events. It has become clear in the course of this work that such isolated studies (although critical initially both for instrument and construct refinement) will not serve to elucidate our understanding of pubertal development and its links to psychosocial functioning and that more integrative studies of puberty are necessary. Such studies will probably need to involve multiple assessments of different types and levels of pubertal events over time, in samples large enough to ensure statistical power in specific subgroups, to capture gender and ethnicity differences (Paikoff, Buchanan, & Brooks-Gunn, 1991). Thus, the necessary studies are often considered cost prohibitive—a major barrier to the completion of work in this area.

Along with the source of information, investigators have to decide on the specific measurement used by the rater to assess pubertal status and who will be the source of information. This can range from actual Tanner staging by a physician (Brooks-Gunn & Warren, 1989; Duncan, Ritter, Dornbusch, Gross, & Carlsmitt, 1985; Inoff-Germain et al., 1988), self-report Tanner staging based on pictures and line drawings (via Brooks-Gunn & Warren, 1985; Udry & Morris, 1985; Paikoff, Brooks-Gunn & Warren, 1991), or scales such as the Petersen Pubertal Development Scale (PDS; Petersen, Crockett, Richards, & Boxer, 1988), to parental report of observed physical changes or Tanner staging (Gargiulo, Attie, Brooks-Gunn, & Warren, 1987) and researcher extrapolations from height and weight alone (Blyth et al., 1981; Jones & Bayley, 1971; Petersen, Sarigiani, & Kennedy, 1991; Scerbo & Kolko, 1994). It is difficult to compare studies that assess pubertal status in different ways, but a few pubertal measures have been compared. When ratings of pubertal status using Tanner criteria were compared across different raters (adolescents, parents, and health care personnel) and across various stages of puberty, adolescent and parent ratings fell adequately within one stage of the examiner rating, but exact accuracy was not shown (Dorn, Susman,

Nottelmann, Inoff-Germain, & Chrousos, 1990). Adolescent self-rating was closer to examiner rating than parent rating, especially for girls, and overall there was less accuracy in both self and parent ratings at later stages of puberty. Dorn et al. (1990) also suggest that the degree of discrepancy between perceived and actual (based on a health care assessment) pubertal stage is worth examining to see if there is a relation between this discrepancy and developmental or adjustment problems.

Defining menarche and distinguishing menarcheal onset data from data regarding the onset of puberty have also not been consistent in the adolescent literature. Many studies use presence or absence of menarche, or age at menarche, as the primary assessment of pubertal status or timing, despite the wide range of ages within which menarche may begin and despite its relatively late occurrence in puberty. As shown in Figure 8.1, the normal range for menarche covers ages 10 to 16.5 years. Assessing menarche alone, without regard for the process of pubertal development as a whole, reduces consideration of other factors that may interact with menarche to play a critical role in the targeted behavior or psychosocial outcome being studied.

The degree of integration and the appropriateness of particular measurement choice for any one study will have to be made based on the question or questions that most drive the investigator's work. For example, if the investigator is interested in general issues of pubertal physical maturation, then global ratings of pubertal status may be adequate. However, if the investigator's hypothesis focuses on a specific pubertal event, then detailed measurements that specifically consider that event within the continuum of pubertal development should be selected. When the proposed investigation deals largely with expectations or attributions of child, parent, or others regarding pubertal events, self or other report measures of event(s) may be the most appropriate methodology choice. If an investigator is interested in expectations or attributions regarding timing of maturation as opposed to occurrence of pubertal events, measures of perceived timing may be most appropriate. It is important to consider the parameters of late and early pubertal maturation in any given study that sets out to examine pubertal timing-behavioral relationships.

For the majority of investigators interested in the study of puberty and its links to psychosocial functioning, some aspect of the investigation revolves around the association between biological aspects of pubertal changes and psychosocial functioning, making the need for different levels of behavioral measurement all the more important. Hormone-behavior relationships, as well as relationships between psychosocial functioning and pubertal status and timing, can be significantly affected by the source of the psychosocial or behavioral rating. For example, the adolescent may be a better rater of internalizing behaviors, whereas teachers and parents may be better raters of externalizing behaviors (Achenbach, McConaughy, & Howell, 1987; Thurber & Hollingsworth, 1992). Scerbo and Kolko (1994) found that staff members may notice disruptive behaviors more readily and parents may notice mood or internalizing behaviors more readily than clinical staff in structured settings with many children. The results of many of the studies in this chapter examining psychosocial functioning depend on the specificity and sensitivity of the symptom scales, behavioral ratings, and conflict assessments used to quantify and diagnose mental health. The child and adolescent psychiatric literature suggests that a syndrome or diagnosis may not be as sensitive an indicator of psychosocial functioning as specific symptoms described by their severity (Kruesi, Rapport, Hamburger, Hibbs, & Potter, 1990), variability, or both (Scerbo & Kolko, 1994) when examining the relationship between hormone levels and behavior. This measurement issue regarding psychosocial functioning may also hold true in the definition of symptoms that do not characterize a disorder but fall within a range of normal psychological functioning during pubertal development.

Issues of research design also become important and are accentuated where hormonal variables are of interest. The benefits of longitudinal designs are clear, and where hormonal variables are of interest, such studies should begin in middle childhood (ages approximately 6-9 years) to capture *initial* hormonal changes. Such complex and long-term work is often difficult to justify to funding sources and problematic for young investigators in need of clearly interpretable outcome data for publication, tenure, and promotion. It is also difficult to sustain participation of subjects over time, given the invasiveness of hormonal measures. Such pragmatic issues can clearly influence the type and amount of work done within this area.

The timing and frequency of measurements of hormones and other pubertal events are other important issues for consideration in longitudinal research designs as well, particularly where hormonal variables are concerned (Buchanan et al., 1992; Paikoff, Buchanan, & Brooks-Gunn, 1991). Hormonal concentrations vary by time of day and, later in puberty, by time within cycle for girls; thus, attention to specificity in timing of hormone data collection is required for interpretation of hormonal data within a given study and across studies. Because so little is known regarding links between hormones and psychosocial functioning, timing of assessments and aggregation of data have varied widely across studies (e.g., some investigators have examined mean level differences in hormone levels across groups of adolescents; some have focused on variability within adolescents across a day or week) making review and interpretation difficult (Buchanan et al., 1992; Paikoff, Buchanan, & Brooks-Gunn, 1991). The same difficulties can emerge when considering timing of psychosocial and behavioral measurements. For example, Scerbo and Kolko (1994) suggested that staff ratings conducted daily may be more reliable or accurate measures of current disruptive behavior, whereas teacher and parent ratings collected once at the onset of their study may reflect perceptions of the child over a longer period of time and thus more accurately reflect long-standing traits, such as internalizing behavior.

In summary, issues of measurement continue to be problematic within the field of research examining links between pubertal development and psychosocial functioning, due to the nature of the pubertal process as well as continued concern over the most appropriate measurement and design strategies to elucidate the pubertal process itself and its links to psychosocial functioning. The most helpful way to reduce these measurement problems may be to have multiple investigators across sites collaborate on a series of studies and recommendations for particular measurements of puberty dependent on context. From our perspective, we make the following preliminary suggestions to open such a dialogue: (a) Where measurement of pubertal status is of interest, appropriate instruments may vary by gender, ethnicity, and social class. Whereas studies of European American middle-class girls have found Tanner stage drawings to be most useful (Brooks-Gunn & Warren, 1985; Udry & Morris, 1985), other studies suggest that boys are more likely to overrepresent their pubertal stage using these drawings relative to their parents or physicians (Miller, Tucker, Pasch, & Eccles, 1988), and parents tend to underrepresent their sons' pubertal stage, especially at later stages of puberty (Dorn et al., 1990). Preliminary evidence from a study of urban African American children living in poverty found parental ratings of pubertal status (using the PDS) were most reliable for boys, whereas both PDS and Tanner staging were reliable for girls (Sagrestano et al., 1995). Thus, investigators may wish to consider issues of culture, ethnicity, and gender in adoption of an appropriate measure of pubertal status. (b) Where issues of pubertal timing of particular events are preferable, items must be event specific, and timing categories should be coded based on either national or subpopulation norms. Where perception of puberty is of primary interest, questionnaire or more open-ended interview or projective data may be most appropriate.

LINKS BETWEEN PUBERTAL AND PSYCHOSOCIAL DEVELOPMENT ACROSS THE ADOLESCENT YEARS

The psychological and social importance of pubertal status and timing has been studied extensively, especially among young girls. In particular, the following factors have received emphasis: affective experiences; attentional behaviors; aggression, delinquency, and other problem behaviors; sexuality; and social relationships, particularly with family. We now provide a brief review of these areas, focusing primarily on physical changes of puberty (though also including data on hormonal changes), in part because so many recent and extensive reviews of the hormonal literature are already available (see Brooks-Gunn, Graber, & Paikoff, 1994; Buchanan et al., 1992; Paikoff & Brooks-Gunn, 1990a, 1990b). Most studies described in this section used self-report measures of pubertal status on various pubertal indexes.

Puberty and Affective Experiences

Links between puberty and affective experiences have been a major focus of research on puberty and psychosocial functioning. In particular, moods and mood lability, depressive affect, irritability, anxiety and worry, self-esteem, and body image have been examined.

Moods and Mood Lability

This group of studies is most directly assessing storm and stress as an outcome; the most recent studies in this area integrate the full hypothesis, as discussed earlier in the theories of Freud and others, by including hormonal assessments and linking them to mood lability. Overall, there is some evidence that variability of mood may be greater in more developed boys and girls (Susman, Nottelmann, & Blue, 1983), but there is at least as much evidence that there is no significant relationship (Buchanan, 1991; Crockett & Petersen, 1987; Miller, 1988). However, when absolute levels of various moods were assessed over a month's time and the variability of these moods was computed, pubertal girls did show more intense and variable negative mood states than prepubertal girls (Buchanan, 1991; Miller, 1988). Comparing studies on this topic is difficult because specificity of mood measurements varies.

With regard to hormonal research, Buchanan (1989) found a significant association between FSH (measured by urine samples) and mood variability over 1 month in girls 9 to 10 years old, but the direction of the association was variable (Buchanan et al., 1992). More studies are needed to replicate and clarify this finding.

Another group of studies has examined associations between puberty and depressed affect. The majority of studies in girls showed no significant association between pubertal status and depressed affect (Buchanan et al., 1992). When pubertal timing is considered, however, late maturing girls tend to show less depressed affect and early maturers more depressed affect over time (Buchanan et al., 1992). Depressed affect was more often associated with negative events among premenarcheal girls than postmenarcheal girls (Baydar, Brooks-Gunn, & Warren, 1989).

A few studies have examined the relationship between pubertal status and depressed affect in boys, with mixed results and no clear trend (Buchanan et al., 1992; Crockett & Petersen, 1987; Dorn, Crockett, & Petersen, 1988; Susman et al., 1983). Only one study addressed pubertal timing in boys, finding that late maturers reported more sad affect (Nottelmann, Susman, Blue, et al., 1987). Thus, contrary to the results with regard to girls' pubertal timing, late maturing boys have been found to report more sad affect than early maturing or on-time boys (Nottelmann, Susman, Inoff-Germain, et al., 1987).

In the adult hormone literature, low concentrations of estrogen have been associated with depressive symptoms, whereas higher concentrations of estrogen have been associated with more positive mood (Buchanan et al., 1992). The adolescent studies examining hormones and depressive affect, however, have had more complex and more variable results.

One National Institute of Health group collected morning blood samples from boys and girls 9 to 14 years old and found a positive relationship in boys between low gonadal activity and more sad affect on a one-time self-image assessment (Susman et al., 1985; Susman et al., 1991; Susman et al., 1987) and a negative relationship when happiness was measured over 5 days (Nottelmann et al., 1985). Using repeated measures of mood over several days, Eccles et al. (1988) reported a weak relationship between positive mood in boys and lower LH concentrations for a younger age group (boys 11-12 years old). Scerbo and Kolko (1994) found a positive relationship between depressed mood and basal cortisol (gathered by salivary sample in 37 clinic-referred boys, 7-14 years old, with disruptive behavior diagnoses). These findings held for parent report only, not for staff or teacher ratings. Again, specificity of measurement and length of study may have an effect on findings as well as pubertal stages (early versus late adolescence) covered by the study (Buchanan et al., 1992).

The National Institute of Health group found low levels of DHEAS and high-for-age FSH related to more depressive affect or behavior (or both) in girls (Buchanan et al., 1992). Sad affect in girls was associated with high testosterone and cortisol concentrations 1 year later (Susman et al., 1991). Studies at the Educational Testing Service (ETS) included girls' (10 to 14 years old) blood samples drawn once in late afternoon to measure hormones. The ETS group (Brooks-Gunn & Warren, 1989; Paikoff, Brooks-Gunn, & Warren, 1991; Warren & Brooks-Gunn, 1989) reported a positive association between estradiol and depressive affect (Buchanan et al., 1992). Eccles et al. (1988) found a positive relationship between estrogen and positive mood over 1 month in girls 9 to 10 years old. Paikoff, Brooks-Gunn, and Warren (1991) and Susman et al. (1991) both found that preexisting depression predicted later depression better than hormone levels.

This review suggests that there is relatively inconsistent evidence on the role of pubertal factors in depressive and other negative affective experiences. There were no clear trends in boys due to the contrasting results in the very few studies that included them. A single study on timing in boys, however, suggested late maturing boys experienced sadder affect. Pubertal status appears to exert a small but consistent effect on depressive affect, such that initial hormonal changes increase depressive affect in girls. Pubertal timing also may affect depressive affect, with later-maturing girls experiencing less depressive affect. Both of these findings, however, are relatively small in magnitude, particularly when compared with prior affective experiences. Thus, one of the more important findings in this area underscores the importance of understanding continuity over time in negative affective experiences. We know very little about how puberty or other factors during the preadolescent and young adolescent years may influence (or, in fact, be influenced by) particular developmental trajectories and the continuation of or deviation from them.

Irritability

The few studies that have examined the relationship between irritability and pubertal status and timing vary in their definition of *irritability*, making their results difficult to compare (Buchanan et al., 1992). In eighth-grade girls, late pubertal girls were less irritable than midpubertal or postpubertal girls, suggesting a phase-specific relationship (Dorn et al., 1988). Girls with true precocious puberty (TPP) did more sulking, crying, and whining than controls (Sonis et al., 1985). Effects of pubertal timing on boys' irritability have not been considered. More studies examining irritability and puberty are needed.

The Sonis et al.'s (1985) study with girls diagnosed with TPP has some special considerations. The girls with TPP had a younger age range (6 to 11 years) than other studies examining puberty. It is not clear if the results here reflect pubertal status alone, abnormally early pubertal maturation relative to chronologic age and peers (timing), psychological and emotional development more characteristic for chronologic age versus pubertal age, or most likely, some combination of these factors (Buchanan et al., 1992). A variety of matched control groups for girls and boys with TPP that considers these variables may allow us to learn more from this special group of children and adolescents.

A limited number of studies examining hormones and irritability in adolescents suggest a positive association between hormone concentrations and irritability in boys (Buchanan et al., 1992; Eccles et al., 1988; Olweus, Mattsson, Schaling, & Low,1980). Again, these studies examined different target symptoms or behaviors and may be measuring very different aspects of the broader definition of irritability, making it difficult to draw any conclusions across studies.

Anxiety and Worry

A few studies have considered anxiety and worry in relation to pubertal status and timing. There may be a positive association between anxiety and pubertal stage in boys and early maturation in boys and girls (Buchanan et al., 1992; Jones & Bayley, 1971; Peskin, 1967; Sonis et al., 1985; Stone & Barker, 1939; Susman et al., 1991). The existing studies do not report a consistent relationship between hormones and anxiety in adolescents (Olweus et al., 1980; Olweus et al., 1988; Susman et al., 1991; Susman et al., 1987). Buchanan et al. (1992) explained these contrasting results with positive relations between adrenal androgens and anxiety in early adolescent boys and diminished adrenal androgen influence on anxiety later in puberty. There was no direct examination of pubertal status in these studies.

Self-Consciousness,
Self-Esteem, and Body Image

The understanding of the development of self-concepts and self-feelings during adolescence remains a murky area (Brooks-Gunn & Paikoff, 1992; Harter, 1983, 1990; Wylie, 1979). Differentiating between self-concept and self-esteem and self-image and body image have been particularly problematic; thus, these topics are considered together in this section. Also in this section, pubertal status is often assessed by menarcheal status in girls and peak height velocity in boys.

A few studies have considered associations between pubertal status and self-consciousness with no consistent trends in boys or girls (Buchanan et al., 1992). Ruble and Brooks-Gunn (1982) found that in postmenarcheal seventh- and eighth-grade girls, those who felt unprepared for menarche reported more self-consciousness than girls who felt prepared, with no such relationship in earlier or later grades studied. This may suggest a time-limited phase of vulnerability. In contrast, there were no associations over time between puberty and self-consciousness when pubertal status and timing were considered in other studies including boys and girls (Blyth et al., 1981; Simmons & Blyth, 1987; Simmons, Blyth, & McKinney, 1983).

Numerous studies have examined pubertal status and timing and its relationship to self-esteem and perceived competence in girls.

Garwood and Allen (1979) found that postmenarcheal girls had higher self-concept and better overall adjustment on a clinical self-concept scale with no difference on a counseling scale. In contrast, Simmons, Blyth, Van Cleave, and Bush (1979) followed girls longitudinally from sixth to seventh grade and found puberty was not related to overall self-esteem. Girls who had started to menstruate and also begun to date had lower self-esteem, however, especially after the transition to junior high school. Simmons, Burgeson, Carlton-Ford, and Blyth (1987) found similar results; however, cumulative change and life transitions, including pubertal change, had negative effects on self-image. This longitudinal study is exceptional in that pubertal status was considered in relation to behaviors of interest over separate points in time (Buchanan et al., 1992). More pubertally advanced girls had lower self-images in another study (Tobin-Richards & Kavrell, 1984), and this effect on self-image was influenced by weight, satisfaction with weight, body image, peer relationships, and athletic involvement. The studies in this section suggest an interaction between various factors, including pubertal status, may influence self-esteem in girls (Buchanan et al., 1992). In studies considering pubertal timing, early maturation was positively associated with body image in boys and negatively associated, but less consistently, in girls. Late maturation was negatively associated with self-image in boys with no clear trend in girls for global self-image (Buchanan et al., 1992; Duncan et al., 1985; Gargiulo et al., 1987; Nottelmann, Susman, Blue, et al., 1987; Simmons & Blyth, 1987; Simmons et al., 1983; Tobin-Richards, Boxer, & Petersen, 1983).

A few studies have focused on boys' body image, self-esteem, and pubertal factors (Blyth et al., 1981; Mussen & Jones, 1957). The results of these studies correspond with some of the studies discussed earlier about boys and girls that showed a trend toward a more positive body image and self-image in early maturing boys as compared to late maturing boys, though longitudinal evidence on this issue is more mixed (Buchanan et al., 1992; Peskin, 1967).

Flaming and Morse (1991) responded to the paucity of studies that examine what boys experience emotionally as they go through the physical changes that occur with puberty by conducting a qualitative research study using the method of grounded theory with a sample of Anglo-Canadians who were at least 15 years old. Their findings indicated that pubescent boys are frequently embarrassed about the changes they are experiencing, and they used several strategies to avoid or deal with the embarrassment. For example, boys began comparing themselves with other boys to establish that they were maturing in a normal fashion. The slower the physically observable changes occurred, the more abnormal the adolescent perceived himself to be and the more embarrassment felt by the boy. Although the boys reported being educated that maturational timing varied significantly, this did not reduce the perception of being abnormal. These observations concur with the association between more negative body image and self-image in late maturing boys described earlier, though it is difficult to directly compare qualitative and quantitative data.

The associations between self-consciousness and hormones at puberty have not been examined. Lower perceived competence and lower self-image, especially in regard to social relationships and coping, were associated with high adrenal androgens in boys and high FSH in girls (Buchanan et al., 1992). When Nottelmann, Cutler, and Chrousos (1986) followed the rate of change in hormones for 1 year, higher self-image scores were associated with higher rates of change in hormone levels, regardless of direction.

In addition to affective experience, other internalizing behaviors for girls have been considered in relationship to pubertal development. Killen et al. (1992) examined the association between stage of pubertal development (using self-reported Tanner stage and body mass index) and eating disorder symptoms, based on structured diagnostic interviews with sixth- and seventh-grade girls. Girls of similar ages manifesting eating disorder symptoms were more developmentally advanced by Tanner staging (stage 4 or 5). The study recommended that an assessment of pubertal status be included in psychiatric risk studies of young adolescents. Graber, Brooks-Gunn, Paikoff, and Warren (1994) followed adolescent girls longitudinally over an 8-year period to examine eating problems, using the EAT-26, an abbreviated version of the Eating Attitudes Test (EAT; Garner & Garfinkel, 1979). The adolescent pattern of eating problems over young and midadolescence was associated with earlier pubertal maturation (defined by self-reported age at menarche) and higher percentage of body fat, among other factors. These longitudinal findings also suggest that early age at menarche and advanced pubertal status are risk factors for episodic as well as chronic eating problems.

It is difficult to draw firm conclusions from the results of these studies that examined the relationship between puberty and a variety of affective experiences and internalizing behaviors because there were either contrasting results or just too few studies looking at the same affective experience. It has been difficult to define a given affective experience with good specificity across studies; similar interpretive problems exist with regard to pubertal status and timing. Despite these reservations, it appears that in boys, early pubertal maturation or timing is associated with a better body image (strong association) and better self-image and that later maturation is associated with sadder affect. In contrast, there is a trend toward less positive affective experiences overall for earlier-maturing girls, especially in regard to body image. It is not clear, however, if these associations persist over time. Advanced pubertal status and early age at menarche may be risk factors for episodic as well as chronic eating problems. When studies examining pubertal status results alone (not timing) are considered, there is no clear trend in girls, but initial hormonal changes may increase depressive affect in girls. Also, there may be a phase-specific relationship between self-concept and postmenarcheal status. Hormone studies showed that lower self-image was associated with high adrenal androgens in boys and high FSH in girls, with similar results for perceived competence. Other hormonal study results were not as consistent.

Puberty and Attentional Behaviors

In this section, we review data within the general domain of attentional behaviors, including data on energy or activity level, restlessness or concentration, and impulsivity.

Energy or Activity Level

Several cross-sectional studies have examined energy level and pubertal status and timing and suggest there may be a relationship between increasing pubertal status and lower energy levels in boys and girls (Buchanan, 1991; Buchanan et al., 1992; Sonis et al., 1985; Susman et al., 1983). The results are conflicting and complex, however, and androgens and estrogens do not appear to have the consistently positive relationship to activity level in adolescents as they seem to in adults (Buchanan et al., 1992).

Restlessness, Concentration, and Impulsivity

Overall, the associations between puberty and attentional behaviors, including energy level, restlessness, concentration, and impulsivity, suggest that pubertal status in girls may be related to greater restlessness and poorer concentration (Buchanan, 1991; Buchanan et al., 1992; Sonis et al., 1985; Stone & Barker, 1939). Impulse control may increase at menarche in a phase-specific, short-term fashion, but this finding needs to be replicated (Petersen & Crockett, 1985, 1986). In the same study, late maturing girls had better impulse control than early maturing or on-time girls.

The few hormone studies on this topic suggest that estrogen in girls and adrenal androgens in boys show negative relations with impulsivity in early puberty, but testosterone effects may become more significant in boys later in puberty (Buchanan et al., 1992). One study over 1 month reported a positive relationship between FSH concentrations and variability in restlessness in girls (Buchanan, 1989).

It is currently difficult to draw any firm conclusions due to the small number of studies in this section and their often contrasting results. The popular belief that adolescents negotiating the changes of puberty consistently have increased attentional difficulties has not been shown to date, however.

Puberty and Aggression, Delinquency,
and Other Behavior Problems

Aggression, behavior problems, and delinquency have also been examined with regard to pubertal status and timing. With regard to pubertal status, inconsistent results have once again been the rule. Nottelmann, Susman, Inoff-Germain, et al. (1987) found a negative relationship between pubertal development and externalizing (delinquent, aggressive, cruel) behavior for girls. In contrast, higher Tanner stage (Paikoff, Brooks-Gunn, & Warren, 1991) and menarche (Simmons & Blyth, 1987; Simmons et al., 1983) showed a positive relationship to behavior problems in girls; no similar relationships between pubertal status and behavior problems were reported for boys. Menarcheal status in girls interacted with negative life events: When negative events were present, premenarcheal girls showed more behavior problems than postmenarcheal girls and without negative events, postmenarcheal girls showed more behavior problems (Brooks-Gunn, Warren, & Rosso, 1988). These findings suggest that considering the interaction between various factors along with pubertal status may help us understand the complexity of relationships to behavior problems and may help to understand conflicting results between studies (Buchanan et al., 1992).

Several studies have examined pubertal timing in girls and reported a positive association between early maturation and deviant or externalizing behavior (Magnusson, 1988; Magnusson, Stattin, & Allen, 1985; Sonis et al., 1985). The possible interaction between earlier or greater exposure to deviant peers and deviant behavior in early maturing girls deserves further study (Silbereisen, Petersen, Albrecht, & Kracke, 1989).

A number of studies have focused on pubertal timing in boys in relation to aggression and behavioral difficulties. Overall, similar to the trend in girls, these studies found early maturing boys to have more behavioral problems in these areas (Duncan et al., 1985; Mussen & Jones, 1957; Peskin, 1967). This agreement between the studies is notable because they used very different measures of pubertal status or timing as well as very different assessments of aggressive behavior (Buchanan et al., 1992).

Several laboratories have looked at hormones and their associations with adolescent aggression and problem behavior. Normal adolescent boys and delinquent boys showed a positive association between testosterone levels and aggression scores. In the normal groups, the association was stronger when the aggression was provoked (Mattsson, Schalling, Olweus, Low, & Svensson, 1980; Olweus et al., 1980, 1988). The difference in testosterone between the normal and delinquent groups was in the expected direction but not significant (Buchanan et al., 1992). More recently, Scerbo and Kolko (1994) found similar results with observed aggression in a group of 37 boys and 3 girls aged 7 to 14 years who were clinic-referred with disruptive behavior diagnoses. These findings held for staff report only. Cortisol was not found to significantly moderate this relationship. It is important that race was considered, and there were no significant differences between African American and Caucasian boys for salivary testosterone-aggression relationship. However, larger sample sizes might be needed for adequate power to test ethnicity differences. In contrast, aggression was not significantly related to testosterone for boys in another group of studies that found low sex steroids and high adrenal androgens associated with behavioral difficulties in boys (Buchanan et al., 1992).

In girls, there were no consistent results regarding hormones and aggression, especially when studies controlled for pubertal status (Buchanan et al., 1992; Eccles et al., 1988; Nottelmann, Susman, Inoff-Germain, et al., 1987; Paikoff, Brooks-Gunn, & Warren, 1991). Udry and Talbert (1988) found that testosterone was positively related to a cluster of personality attributes in boys and girls that included an aggressive style, with girls showing greater differences in personality dimensions with smaller differences in testosterone than boys.

Overall, there were associations in both directions between pubertal status and externalizing behaviors in girls but a clear trend in regard to pubertal timing with early maturing girls showing more deviant behavior and more contact with deviant peers than late maturing or on-time girls. In boys, there were no associations reported for pubertal status and externalizing behaviors, but there was a trend similar to girls' toward more behavior problems in early maturing boys. Hormonal evidence is more clear and consistent regarding testosterone and the adrenal androgens for boys than in any associations for girls.

Puberty and Sexuality

In most reviews, sexuality and links to pubertal factors are considered as an aspect of delinquency and problem behavior. We separate this section from earlier ones to reinforce notions that psychosexual development should be considered in terms of normative process rather than as a problem behavior (Brooks-Gunn & Paikoff, 1993; Paikoff, in press; Paikoff & Brooks-Gunn, 1994). Outside of the studies linking maturational timing to sexuality as part of a cluster of problem behaviors, there is little evidence regarding this link in the current literature. We have assumed that maturational status influences motivation and interest in sexual activity and that timing of puberty is linked as well; however, few investigators have explicitly addressed this issue. Critical research in this area should involve integration of basic developmental process in the understanding of sexuality as a normative developmental process in and of itself (Paikoff, 1995).

The hormonal effects at puberty are better understood when placed within a continuum of sexual development. The studies in adult males have looked at androgen effects in normal and hypogonadal men. Hypogonadal men showed a dose-related response in sexual interest to changes in androgen levels, whereas there was no such relationship between testosterone levels and sexual behavior in normal men (Udry, 1988). Udry concluded that there appears to be a ceiling effect for androgens so that normal adult males are beyond the point of additional androgen effects despite individual variance in androgens. Udry (1988) also described that adult females are sensitive to testosterone at low levels that do not lead to a response in males, and androgens have been positively correlated to sexual interest and behavior in women.

Prepubertal girls and boys have similar levels of testosterone, but during puberty, girls' levels double, whereas boys' levels increase by 10 to 20 times (Udry, 1988). Despite these differences, pubertal females are more sensitive than males to the same changes in testosterone levels (Udry & Talbert, 1988). Udry and his colleagues present the most direct research addressing the relationships between these pubertal hormones and adolescent sexual behavior, motivations, and coital activity (Udry, 1988; Udry & Billy, 1987; Udry et al., 1985; Udry, Talbert, & Morris, 1986). Androgens strongly influenced the sexual motivation and sexual behavior, including coitus, of adolescent European American males, with free testosterone the most significant hormonal predictor of sexual behavior (Udry et al., 1985). This effect remained significant when pubertal status and age were considered. A similar study in adolescent European American females showed a significant relationship between the adrenal androgens (free testosterone, DHEA, DHEAS, and androstenedione) and sexual motivations and noncoital sexual behavior. Coital behavior in girls was primarily differentiated by social control processes, not hormones (Udry & Billy, 1987; Udry et al., 1986).

Puberty and Family Relationships

Many studies have examined the associations between pubertal status and timing and family relationships. In contrast to the previous sections, which measured internalizing and externalizing behaviors related to an individual, this group of studies sets out to assess behavior within the context of a relationship. In contrast to prior sections, pubertal status also seems to play as strong or stronger a role in these associations as pubertal timing. The studies examining pubertal status in girls showed a trend toward more problems between the adolescent and her family at menarche: Garwood and Allen (1979) included African American and European American girls, and Hill (1988) included parents through observation of family interactions.

Pubertal timing was considered in several studies that included girls. Hill and colleagues (Hill & Holmbeck, 1987; Hill, Holmbeck, Marlow, Green, & Lynch, 1985a; Holmbeck & Hill, 1991) reported short-term perturbations between mothers and daughters around menarche, with potentially longer-lasting perturbations if the girl was an early maturer (based on age at menarche). Similarly, early maturing girls reported more conflict (Savin-Williams & Small, 1986). Independence from parents was also positively related to early maturation and menarche, with a weakening of this relationship in later puberty (Simmons & Blyth, 1987; Simmons et al., 1983). It is not clear, however, if this independence would create more or less conflict in the family. In contrast, Paikoff, Brooks-Gunn, and Carlton-Ford (1991) found that mothers of early maturing daughters perceived less family conflict than did those with on-time or late maturing daughters. Steinberg (1987a) found increased pubertal development, but not timing, predicted conflict with mothers. Paikoff, Brooks-Gunn, and Carlton-Ford (1991) suggested that short-term increases in conflict between adolescents and their parents during and shortly after the pubertal period decreased postpubertally, accounting for the discrepancies across studies.

The bulk of studies in this area have included both boys and girls and evaluated the effect of pubertal status on family relationships. Overall, there is a trend toward increased conflicts and difficulties with pubertal maturation, but this effect is somewhat dependent on the stage of puberty (Anderson, Hetherington, & Clingempeel, 1989; Buchanan et al., 1992; Inoff-Germain et al., 1988; Paikoff & Brooks-Gunn, 1991; Steinberg, 1988, 1989). Anderson et al. (1989) showed fewer such associations in their longitudinal analysis, however. Clingempeel, Colyar, Brand, and Hetherington (1992) assessed the effects of parents' marital transition (e.g., divorce) and pubertal status on grandparent-grandchild relationships. Using parent, child, and grandparent report, they concluded that in grandfather-granddaughter relationships, higher pubertal status resulted in less involvement, whereas in grandsons' relationships with both grandparents, greater change in physical development resulted in more involvement and greater perceived closeness. Several studies reported phase-specific results that suggest higher family conflict in the *transpubertal* (midpuberty) phase (Buchanan et al., 1992; Papini & Savage, 1987; Papini & Sebby, 1988).

John Hill was a part of nearly all the studies that focused on boys (as well as many of the studies on girls) in considering associations between pubertal status and family relationships (Hill & Holmbeck, 1987; Hill, Holmbeck, Marlow, Green, & Lynch, 1985b; Steinberg, 1981; Steinberg & Hill, 1978). Again, the resulting family conflicts and problems seem to depend on the stage of pubertal development or growth (especially peak of pubertal growth) and may be temporary or phase-specific (especially early or midpuberty). Pubertal timing for boys was assessed in only a few studies with mixed results: Early timing predicted conflict with mothers (Steinberg, 1987a) and late timing was associated with more conflict (Savin-Williams & Small, 1986).

Only a few studies have examined hormones and conflictual behavior in the family during adolescence. These few studies suggest some association between increasing hormone concentrations and conflicts in the family at puberty. Some researchers question which one increases first: hormones or conflicts (Buchanan et al., 1992). Inoff-Germain et al. (1988) found estrogen and androstenedione in girls were positively related to anger and aggression toward their parents, and in boys, higher LH and DHEA and lower DHEAS predicted more anger and aggression toward parents. More arguments between children and their parents, more emotional autonomy, less cohesion between children and fathers, and lower frequency of calm family discussions were associated with higher testosterone concentrations in 11-year-olds to 16-year-olds, especially for boys (Steinberg, 1987b).

Overall, research has revealed a trend toward increased conflicts and difficulties in family relationships during puberty in boys and girls. This conflictual period appears to be a short-lived phase, however, that peaks during puberty and declines postpubertally. The results of numerous studies in this section depended on the pubertal status (growth, development, or both) of the child when target behaviors were assessed. Of the studies that considered pubertal timing, there was a weak trend toward increased or longer-lasting conflicts for early maturing girls but mixed results in boys.

In a recent review of behavioral conflict during adolescence, Laursen and Collins (1994) report the results of a meta-analysis finding no (or very consistent but very small) effects of puberty on parent-adolescent conflict. The Laursen and Collins (1994) results are influenced in part by their more specific definition of conflict than has been true in previous studies and, in part, by the examination of these effects without consideration of the possible role of demographic, individual, and social factors as mediators or moderators of associations between puberty and family relationships. This last point is a critical one. It underscores where research in this field needs to go to move our knowledge forward: Consideration of potential moderators or mediators of associations between puberty and family relationships is critical for integration of context and developmental change within the same design, to better understand development over time.

CONCLUSIONS AND
FUTURE IMPLICATIONS

In reviewing the literature on puberty and its effects on psychosocial functioning, we are struck by the lack of meaningful improvements and movements in our knowledge since the early 1990s when the last major reviews of this literature were completed (Brooks-Gunn & Reiter, 1990; Buchanan et al., 1992; Paikoff & Brooks-Gunn, 1990a, 1990b). Due to the lack of new empirical evidence, recent articles on this topic have chosen to develop conceptual models rather than conduct more traditional reviews (Brooks-Gunn et al., 1994). Given the current volume's focus on the life, work, and interests of John Hill, we have chosen to review the major findings in puberty and psychosocial functioning, despite the dearth of new evidence. Thus, in our concluding remarks, we recap our summaries of the literature we have reviewed and discuss reasons why new evidence has not been forthcoming. Last, we speculate on what is needed for further growth in knowledge and understanding regarding the pubertal process and its effect on psychosocial functioning.

It appears that aspects of the pubertal process may affect depressive affect, self-esteem and body image, aggression and delinquency, sexuality, and family relationships but that these effects are likely to be small relative to other contextual factors (such as individual and family history). In each of these areas except for family relationships, it appears likely that pubertal *timing* (either perceived or actual) is more likely to be associated with aspects of psychosocial functioning than pubertal *status*. For family relationships, pubertal status may be as important as or more important then pubertal timing. Hormonal links have been found in each of these areas as well; however, in our opinion, only in aggression and sexuality are these links reported consistently at a meaningful level for interpretation across studies. In many of the other areas reviewed (e.g., moods and mood lability, energy level, irritability), there is simply not enough evidence to draw firm conclusions regarding the role of puberty in explaining psychosocial adaptation.

After an initially promising series of studies in the late 1980s and early 1990s, little additional work has been conducted viewing pubertal processes as a multifaceted series of events occurring over time. We suspect that this is the result of several different factors. First, as stated, many of the major studies of pubertal process have reported consistent but relatively small effects of puberty on psychosocial adaptation. Whereas some might argue that this alone is reason enough for the scaling back of pubertal research, we feel strongly that these results do not yet serve to clarify whether (a) pubertal processes exert only a small effect on psychosocial adaptation or (b) the effects of pubertal processes on psychosocial adaptation are moderated by a series of important demographic, individual, and social factors that studies have not fully explored (Holmbeck, in press). Brooks-Gunn et al. (1994) presented a relatively complex and thorough series of models integrating hormonal, pubertal, and psychosocial factors with regard to affective expression (and, more specifically, depressive affect) and noted that little evidence has been collected that addresses the most complex models illustrated. For example, studies have seldom collected longitudinal data on multiple biological and social measures that allow us to look at transactions between biological and social systems in understanding development and adaptation during adolescence (Brooks-Gunn et al., 1994). We believe addressing those models is critical to the determination of both the level and the nature of associations between pubertal processes and psychosocial adaptation.

As previously described by Holmbeck and colleagues (Holmbeck, in press), the results in studies of the associations between pubertal processes and family relationships are representative of the types of results possible when hidden moderator effects are present; that is, null findings or small effect sizes are likely when moderators are present but uninvestigated. Thus, we feel it is at least as possible that these more complex processes are at work as that nothing, or very little, is there. We encourage the field to pursue and investigate these more complex models, in the tradition of John Hill (1980, 1983, 1988).

As a corollary of the need for more complex models involving moderator effects, future studies will require far more sophisticated research designs and statistical analyses than have been required in the past. Concerns regarding statistical power as well as statistical significance have come to the forefront of research designs. As described earlier under methodological issues, such designs will be cumbersome both in terms of investigator and other personnel time and demands and in terms of sample recruitment and repeated measurements. Thus, conducting such work requires extensive time and extensive funding, both of which are difficult to come by in current academic times.

In addition to concerns regarding the extensiveness of funding required to investigate these issues, some tacit concerns regarding the role of pubertal processes in psychosocial adaptation may influence the dearth of studies in this arena as well. In particular, given the restricted levels of federal funding available as well as the clear priority of funding intervention research and basic research on "intervenable" variables, many investigators may shy away from work on pubertal and other biological processes in association with psychosocial adaptation because biological factors are considered less intervenable than other individual and social factors. From our perspective, in part adapted from Hill's (1983) framework and research agenda for the study of adolescence, pubertal processes, when examined from a moderated effects model, may be critical to our understanding of development during adolescence. Knowledge about the parameters of influence of pubertal processes and other biological factors during the adolescent years may assist in improving our research and intervention designs for promoting adolescent mental health and preventing mental health problems during adolescence. For example, if we find that gender moderates the effects of pubertal processes on depressive affect, we may be able to use these results both to target at-risk populations for adolescent depression and to design programs that address adolescent needs better, both in terms of education regarding pubertal processes and in coverage of affective experiences surrounding pubertal processes.

Thus, despite the difficulties involved in conducting work that seriously examines the contribution of pubertal processes in understanding psychosocial adaptation during early adolescence, there is a clear need for work examining these complexities from both applied and basic research perspectives. Indeed, a luncheon arranged at the most recent meetings of the Society for Research on Adolescence expressly to discuss biological issues in adolescence was extremely well attended by investigators at various stages of their careers (C. M. Buchanan & R. L. Paikoff, personal communication, February, 1994). Given such interest, we have high hopes for the next generation of studies examining pubertal processes and their links to psychosocial adaptation.

REFERENCES

Achenbach, T. M., McConaughy, S. H., & Howell, C. T. (1987). Child/adolescent behavioral and emotional problems: Implications of cross-informant correlations for situational specificity. *Psychological Bulletin, 101,* 213-232.

Anderson, E. R., Hetherington, E. M., & Clingempeel, W. G. (1989). Transformations in family relations at puberty: Effects of family context. *Journal of Early Adolescence, 9,* 310-334.

Baydar, N., Brooks-Gunn, J., & Warren, M. P. (1989). *Determinants of depressive symptoms in adolescent girls: A four year longitudinal study.* Princeton, NJ: Educational Testing Service.

Blyth, D. A., Simmons, R. G., Bulcroft, R., Felt, D., Van Cleave, E. F., & Bush, D. M. (1981). The effects of physical development on self-image and satisfaction with body-image for early adolescent males. *Research in Community and Mental Health, 2,* 43-73.

Brooks-Gunn, J. (1984). The psychological significance of different pubertal events to young girls. *Journal of Early Adolescence, 4*(4), 315-327.

Brooks-Gunn, J. (1989). Pubertal processes and the early adolescent transition. In W. Damon (Ed.), *Child development today and tomorrow* (pp. 155-176). San Francisco: Jossey-Bass.

Brooks-Gunn, J., Graber, J. A., & Paikoff, R. L. (1994). Studying links between hormones and negative affect: Models and measures. *Journal of Research on Adolescence, 4,* 469-486.

Brooks-Gunn, J., & Paikoff, R. L. (1992). Changes in self-feelings during the transition towards adolescence. In H. R. McGurk (Ed.), *Childhood social development: Contemporary perspectives* (pp. 63-97). Hove, UK: Erlbaum.

Brooks-Gunn, J., & Paikoff, R. L. (1993). Sex is a gamble, kissing is a game: Adolescent sexuality, contraception, and pregnancy. In S. Millstein, A. C. Petersen, &

E. Nightingale (Eds.), *Promotion of healthy behavior in adolescence* (pp. 180-208). New York: Oxford.

Brooks-Gunn, J., & Reiter, E. O. (1990). The role of pubertal processes. In S. S. Feldman & G. R. Elliott (Eds.), *At the threshold: The developing adolescent* (pp. 16-53). Cambridge, MA: Harvard University Press.

Brooks-Gunn, J., & Ruble, D. N. (1982). The development of menstrual-related beliefs and behaviors during early adolescence. *Child Development, 53,* 1567-1577.

Brooks-Gunn, J., & Warren, M. P. (1985). Measuring physical status and timing in early adolescence: A developmental perspective. *Journal of Youth and Adolescence, 14,* 163-189.

Brooks-Gunn, J., & Warren, M. P. (1989). Biological and social contributions to negative affect in young adolescent girls. *Child Development, 60,* 40-55.

Brooks-Gunn, J., Warren, M. P., & Rosso, J. T. (1988). *The impact of pubertal and social events upon girls' problem behavior.* Princeton, NJ: Educational Testing Service.

Buchanan, C. M. (1989, April). *Hormone concentrations and variability: Associations with self-reported moods and energy in early adolescent girls.* Poster presented at the biennial meeting of the Society for Research on Child Development, Kansas City, MO.

Buchanan, C. M. (1991). Pubertal status in early-adolescent girls: Relations to moods, energy, and restlessness. *Journal of Early Adolescence, 11,* 185-200.

Buchanan, C. M., Eccles, J. S., & Becker, J. B. (1992). Are adolescents the victims of raging hormones: Evidence for activational effects of hormones on moods and behavior at adolescence. *Psychological Bulletin, 111,* 62-107.

Clingempeel, W. G., Colyar, J. J., Brand, E., & Hetherington, E. M. (1992). Children's relationships with maternal grandparents: A longitudinal study of family structure and pubertal status effects. *Child Development, 63,* 1404-1422.

Crockett, L. J., & Petersen, A. (1987). Pubertal status and psychosocial development: Findings from the early adolescence study. In R. M. Lerner & T. T. Foch (Eds.), *Biological-psychosocial interactions in early adolescence* (pp. 173-188). Hillsdale, NJ: Lawrence Erlbaum.

Dorn, L. D., Crockett, L. J., & Petersen, A. C. (1988). The relations of pubertal status to intrapersonal changes in young adolescents. *Journal of Early Adolescence, 8,* 405-419.

Dorn, L. D., Susman, E. J., Nottelmann, E. D., Inoff-Germain, G., & Chrousos, G. P. (1990). Perceptions of puberty: Adolescent, parent, and health care personnel. *Developmental Psychology, 26,* 322-329.

Duncan, P. D., Ritter, P. L, Dornbusch, S. M., Gross, R. T., & Carlsmith, J. M. (1985). The effects of pubertal timing on body image, school behavior, and deviance. *Journal of Youth and Adolescence, 14,* 227-235.

Eccles, J. S., Miller, C. L., Tucker, M. L., Becker, J., Schramm, W., Midgley, R., Holmes, W., Pasch, L., & Miller, M. (1988, April). Hormones and affect at early adolescence. In J. Brooks-Gunn (Chair), *Hormonal contributions to adolescent behavior.* A symposium conducted at the second biennial meeting of the Society for Research on Adolescence, Alexandria, VA.

Flaming, D., & Morse, J. M. (1991). Minimizing embarrassment: Boys' experiences of pubertal changes. *Issues in Comprehensive Nursing, 14,* 211-230.

Freud, A. (1966). *The ego and the mechanisms of defense* (Rev. ed.). New York: International Universities Press.

Gaddis, A., & Brooks-Gunn, J. (1985). The male experience of pubertal change. *Journal of Youth and Adolescence, 14,* 61-69.

Gargiulo, J., Attie, I., Brooks-Gunn, J., & Warren, M. P. (1987). Girls' dating behavior as function of social context and maturation. *Developmental Psychology, 23,* 730-737.

Garner, D. M., & Garfinkel, P. E. (1979). The eating attitudes test: An index of the symptoms of anorexia nervosa. *Psychological Medicine, 9,* 1-7.

Garwood, S. G., & Allen, L. (1979). Self-concept and identified problem differences between pre- and postmenarcheal adolescents. *Journal of Clinical Psychology, 35,* 528-537.

Graber, J. A., Brooks-Gunn, J., Paikoff, R. L., & Warren, M. P. (1994). Prediction of eating problems: An 8-year study of adolescent girls. *Developmental Psychology, 30,* 823-834.

Hall, G. S. (1904). *Adolescence: Its psychology and its relations to physiology, anthropology, sociology, sex, crime, religion, and education* (Vol. 1). Englewood Cliffs, NJ: Prentice Hall.

Harter, S. (1990). Adolescent self and identity development. In S. S. Feldman & G. R. Elliott (Eds.), *At the threshold: The developing adolescent* (pp. 352-387). Cambridge, MA: Harvard University Press.

Hauser, S. T., & Bowlds, M. K. (1990). Stress, coping and adaptation. In S. S. Feldman & G. R. Elliott (Eds.), *At the threshold: The developing adolescent* (pp. 388-413). Cambridge, MA: Harvard University Press.

Hill, J. P. (1973). *Some perspectives on adolescence in American society.* A report prepared for the Office of Child Development, U. S. Department of Health, Education, and Welfare, Washington, DC.

Hill, J. P. (1980). *Understanding early adolescence: A framework.* Chapel Hill: University of North Carolina, Center for Early Adolescence.

Hill, J. P. (1983). Early adolescence: A research agenda. *Journal of Early Adolescence, 3,* 1-21.

Hill, J. P. (1988). Adapting to menarche: Familial control and conflict. In M. R. Gunnar & W. A. Collins (Eds.), *Development during the transition to adolescence: 21st Minnesota symposium on child development* (pp. 43-77). Hillsdale, NJ: Lawrence Erlbaum.

Hill, J. P., & Holmbeck, G. N. (1987). Disagreements about rules in families with seventh-grade girls and boys. *Journal of Youth and Adolescence, 16,* 221-246.

Hill, J. P., Holmbeck, G. N., Marlow, L., Green, T. M., & Lynch, M. E. (1985a). Menarcheal status and parent-child relations in families of seventh-grade girls. *Journal of Youth and Adolescence, 14,* 301-316.

Hill, J. P., Holmbeck, G. N., Marlow, L., Green, T. M., & Lynch, M. E. (1985b). Pubertal status and parent-child relations in families of seventh-grade boys. *Journal of Early Adolescence, 5,* 31-44.

Holmbeck, G. N. (in press). A model of family relational transformations during the transition to early adolescence: Parent-adolescent conflict and adaptation. In J. A. Graber, J. Brooks-Gunn, & A. C. Petersen (Eds.), *Transitions through adolescence: Interpersonal domains and context.* Hillsdale, NJ: Lawrence Erlbaum.

Holmbeck, G. N., & Hill, J. P. (1988). Storm and stress beliefs about adolescence: Prevalence, self-reported antecedents, and effects of an undergraduate course. *Journal of Youth and Adolescence, 17,* 285-306.

Holmbeck, G. N., & Hill, J. P. (1991). Conflictive engagement, positive affect, and menarche in families with seventh-grade girls. *Child Development, 62,* 1030-1048.

Holmbeck, G. N., Paikoff, R. L., & Brooks-Gunn, J. (1995). Parenting adolescents. In M. Bornstein (Ed.), *Handbook of parenting.* Vol. 1. (pp. 91-118). Hillsdale, NJ: Lawrence Erlbaum.

Huston, A., Garcia Coll, C., & McLoyd, V. (1994). Children and poverty: Issues in contemporary research. *Child Development, 65,* 275-282.

Inoff-Germain, G., Arnold, G. S., Nottelmann, E. D., Susman, E. J., Cutler, G. B., & Chrousos, G. P. (1988). Relations between hormone levels and observational measures of aggressive behavior of young adolescents in family interactions. *Developmental Psychology, 24,* 129-139.

Jarrett, R. L. (1995). Growing up poor: The family experiences of socially mobile youth in low-income African-American neighborhoods. *Journal of Adolescent Research, 10,* 111-135.

Jones, M. C., & Bayley, N. (1971). Physical maturing among boys as related to behavior. In M. C. Jones, N. Bayley, J. W. MacFarlane, & M. P. Honzik (Eds.), *The course of human development* (pp. 252-257). Waltham, MA: Xerox.

Killen, J. D., Hayward, C., Litt, I., Hammer, L. D., Wilson, D. M., Miner, B., Taylor, C. B., Varady, A., & Shisslak, C. (1992). Is puberty a risk factor for eating disorders? *American Journal of Diseases in Children, 146,* 323-325.

Kletter, G. B., & Kelch, R. P. (1993). Disorders of puberty in boys. *Adolescent Endocrinology, 22,* 455-477.

Kruesi, M. J. P., Rapoport, J. L., Hamburger, S., Hibbs, E., & Potter, W. Z. (1990). Cerebrospinal fluid monoamine metabolites, aggression, and impulsivity in disruptive behavior disorders of children and adolescents. *Archives of General Psychiatry, 47,* 419-426.

Laursen, B., & Collins, W. A. (1994). Interpersonal conflict during adolescence. *Psychological Bulletin, 115,* 197-209.

Magnusson, D. (1988). *Individual development from an interactional perspective: A longitudinal study.* Hillsdale, NJ: Lawrence Erlbaum.

Magnusson, D., Stattin, H., & Allen, V. L. (1985). Biological maturation and social development: A longitudinal study of some adjustment processes from mid-adolescence to adulthood. *Journal of Youth and Adolescence, 14,* 267-283.

Marshall, W. A., & Tanner, J. M. (1970). Variations in the pattern of pubertal changes in boys. *Archives of the Diseases of Childhood, 45,* 13.

Mattsson, A., Schalling, D., Olweus, D., Low, H., & Svensson, J. (1980). Plasma testosterone, aggressive behavior, and personality dimensions in young male delinquents. *Journal of the American Academy of Child Psychiatry, 19,* 476-490.

Miller, C. L. (1988). Pubertal development in early adolescent girls: Relationships to mood, energy, restlessness, and certainty about self. *Dissertation Abstracts International, 49,* 1967B. (University Microfilms No. 88-12, 948)

Miller, C. L., Tucker, M. L., Pasch, L., & Eccles, J. S. (1988, March). *Measuring pubertal development: A comparison of different scales and different sources.* Poster presented at the biennial meeting of the Society for Research on Adolescence, Alexandria, VA.

Mussen, P. H., & Jones, M. C. (1957). Self-conceptions, motivations, and interpersonal attitudes of late and early-maturing boys. *Child Development, 28,* 243-256.

Nottelmann, E. D., Cutler, G. B., Jr., & Chrousos, G. P. (1986). Hormone level, physical maturity, and psychological adjustment. In B. A. Hamburg (Chair), *Biology and behavior at puberty*. Symposium conducted at the first biennial meeting of the Society for Research on Adolescence, Madison, WI.

Nottelmann, E. D., Inoff-Germain, G., Susman, E. J., & Chrousos, G. P. (1990). Hormones and behavior at puberty. In J. Bancroft & J. M. Reinisch (Eds.), *Adolescence and puberty* (pp. 88-123). New York: Oxford University Press.

Nottelmann, E. D., Susman, E. J., Blue, J. H., Inoff-Germain, G., Dorn, L. D., Loriaux, D. L., & Cutler, G. (1987). Gonadal and adrenal hormone correlates of adjustment in early adolescence. In R. M. Lerner & T. T. Foch (Eds.), *Biological-psychosocial interactions in early adolescence* (pp. 303-323). Hillsdale, NJ: Lawrence Erlbaum.

Nottelmann, E. D., Susman, E. J., Inoff-Germain, G., Cutler, G., Loriaux, D. L., & Chrousos, G. P. (1987). Developmental processes in early adolescence: Relations between adolescent adjustment problems and chronological age, pubertal stage, and puberty-related serum hormone levels. *Journal of Pediatrics, 110*, 473-480.

Nottelmann, E. D., Susman, E. J., Inoff-Germain, G. E., Dorn, L. D., Cutler, G. B., Loriaux, D. L., & Chrousos, G. P. (1985). *Hormone level and adjustment and behavior during early adolescence*. Paper presented at the annual meeting for the Advancement of Science, Los Angeles.

Offer, D., & Boxer, A. M. (1991). Normal adolescent development: Empirical research findings. In M. Lewis (Ed.), *Child and adolescent psychiatry: A comprehensive textbook* (pp. 266-278). Baltimore: Williams & Wilkins.

Offer, D., & Schonert-Reichl, K. A. (1992). Debunking the myths of adolescence: Findings from recent research. *Journal of the American Academy of Child and Adolescent Psychiatry, 31*, 1003-1014.

Ogbu, J. U. (1978). *An ecological approach to the study of school effectiveness*. Paper prepared for the School Organization and Effects Conference, National Institute of Education, Washington, DC.

Olweus, D., Mattsson, A., Schalling, D., & Low, H. (1980). Testosterone, aggression, physical and personality dimensions in normal adolescent males. *Psychosomatic Medicine, 42*, 253-269.

Olweus, D., Mattsson, A., Schalling, D., & Low, H. (1988). Circulating testosterone levels and aggression in adolescent males: A causal analysis. *Psychosomatic Medicine, 50*, 261-272.

Paikoff, R. L. (1991). Shared views in the family during adolescence. *New Directions for Child Development, 51*.

Paikoff, R. L. (1995). Early heterosexual debut: Situations of sexual possibility. *American Journal of Orthopsychiatry, 65*(3), 389-401.

Paikoff, R. L., & Brooks-Gunn, J. (1990a). Associations between pubertal hormones and behavioral and affective expression. In C. S. Holmes (Ed.), *Psychoneuroendocrinology: Brain, behavior and hormonal interactions* (pp. 205-226). New York: Springer-Verlag.

Paikoff, R. L., & Brooks-Gunn, J. (1990b). Physiological processes: What role do they play during the transition to adolescence? In R. Montemayor, G. R. Adams, & T. P. Gullotta (Eds.), *Advances in adolescent development: Vol. 2. The transition from childhood to adolescence* (pp. 63-81). Beverly Hills, CA: Sage.

Paikoff, R. L., & Brooks-Gunn, J. (1991). Do parent-child relationships change during puberty? *Psychological Bulletin, 110,* 47-66.

Paikoff, R. L., & Brooks-Gunn, J. (1994). Psychosexual development across the life span. In M. Rutter, D. F. Hay, & S. Baron-Cohen (Eds.), *Development through life: A handbook for clinicians* (pp. 558-582). Oxford, UK: Blackwell.

Paikoff, R. L., Brooks-Gunn, J., & Carlton-Ford, S. (1991). Effect of reproductive status changes on family functioning and well-being of mothers and daughters. *Journal of Early Adolescence, 11,* 201-220.

Paikoff, R. L., Brooks-Gunn, J., & Warren, M. P. (1991). Effects of girls' hormonal status on depression and aggression over the course of one year. *Journal of Youth and Adolescence, 20,* 191-215.

Paikoff, R. L., Buchanan, C. M., & Brooks-Gunn, J. (1991). Methodological issues in the study of hormone-behavior links at puberty. In R. M. Lerner, A. C. Petersen, & J. Brooks-Gunn (Eds.), *Encyclopedia of adolescence* (pp. 508-512). New York: Garland.

Papini, D. R., & Savage, C. L. (1987). *Grade, pubertal status, and gender related variations in conflictual issues among adolescents.* Paper presented at the biennial meeting of the Society for Research in Child Development, Baltimore, MD.

Papini, D. R., & Sebby, R. A. (1987). Adolescent pubertal status and affective family relationships: A multivariate assessment. *Journal of Youth and Adolescence, 16,* 1-15.

Papini, D. R., & Sebby, R. A. (1988). Variations in conflictual family issues by adolescent pubertal status, gender and family member. *Journal of Early Adolescence, 8,* 1-15.

Parker, L. N. (1991). Adrenarche. *Endocrinology and Metabolism Clinics of North America, 20*(1), 71-83.

Peskin, H. (1967). Pubertal onset and ego functioning. *Journal of Abnormal Psychology, 72,* 1-15.

Petersen, A. C., Compas, B. E., Brooks-Gunn, J., Stemmler, M., Ely, S., & Grant, K. E. (1993). Depression in adolescence. *American Psychologist, 48*(12), 155.

Petersen, A. C., & Crockett, L. (1985). Pubertal timing and grade effects on adjustment. *Journal of Youth and Adolescence, 14,* 191-206.

Petersen, A. C., & Crockett, L. (1986). Pubertal development and its relation to cognitive and psychosocial development in adolescent girls: Implications for parenting. In J. B. Lancaster & B. A. Hamburg (Eds.), *School-age pregnancies and parenthood* (pp. 147-175). Hawthorne, NY: Aldine.

Petersen, A. C., Crockett, L., Richards, M., & Boxer, A. (1988). A self-report measure of pubertal status: Reliability, validity, and initial norms. *Journal of Youth and Adolescence, 17,* 117-134.

Petersen, A. C., Sarigiani, P. A., & Kennedy, R. E. (1991). Adolescent depression: Why more girls? *Journal of Youth and Adolescence, 20,* 247-271.

Petersen, A. C., & Taylor, B. (1980). The biological approach to adolescence: Biological change and psychological adaptation. In J. Adelson (Ed.), *Handbook of adolescent psychology* (pp. 117-155). New York: John Wiley.

Rosenfield, R. L. (1991). Puberty and its disorders in girls. *Endocrinology and Metabolism Clinics of North America, 20*(1), 15-42.

Ruble, D. N., & Brooks-Gunn, J. (1982). The experience of menarche. *Child Development, 53,* 1557-1566.

Sagrestano, L. M., Parfenoff, S. H., Paikoff, R. L., & Holmbeck, G. N. (1995). *Conflict and pubertal development in low income urban African American adolescents: Links to experiences in sexual possibility situations.* Unpublished manuscript.

Savin-Williams, R. C., & Small, S. A. (1986). The timing of puberty and its relationship to adolescent and parent perceptions of family interactions. *Developmental Psychology, 22,* 342-347.

Scerbo, A. S., & Kolko, D. J. (1994). Salivary testosterone and cortisol in disruptive children: Relationship to aggressive, hyperactive, and internalizing behaviors. *Journal of the American Academy of Child and Adolescent Psychiatry, 33,* 1174-1184.

Silbereisen, R. K., Petersen, A. C., Albrecht, H. T., & Kracke, B. (1989). Maturational timing and the development of problem behavior: Longitudinal studies in adolescence. *Journal of Early Adolescence, 9,* 247-268.

Simmons, R. G., & Blyth, D. A. (1987). *Moving into adolescence: The impact of pubertal change and school context.* Hawthorne, NY: Aldine.

Simmons, R. G., Blyth, D. A., & McKinney, K. L. (1983). The social and psychological effects of puberty on White females. In J. Brooks-Gunn & A. C. Petersen (Eds.), *Girls at puberty: Biological and psychosocial perspectives* (pp. 229-272). New York: Plenum.

Simmons, R. G., Blyth, D. A., Van Cleave, E. F., & Bush, D. M. (1979). Entry into early adolescence: The impact of school structure, puberty, and early dating on self-esteem. *American Sociological Review, 44,* 948-967.

Simmons, R. G., Burgeson, R., Carlton-Ford, S., & Blyth, D. A. (1987). The impact of cumulative change in early adolescence. *Child Development, 58,* 1220-1234.

Sonis, W., Comite, F., Blue, J., Pescovitz, O. H., Rahn, C. W., Hench, K. D., Cutler, G., Loriaux, D. L., & Klein, R. P. (1985). Behavior problems and social competence in girls with true precocious puberty. *Journal of Pediatrics, 106,* 156-160.

Spencer, M. A. & Dornbusch, S. M. (1990). Challenges in Studying Minority Youth. In S. S. Feldman & G. R. Elliott (Eds.). *At the Threshold. The Developing Adolescent.* (pp. 123-146). Cambridge, MA: Harvard University Press.

Spencer, M. B., & McLoyd, V. (1990). Special issue on minority children. *Child Development, 6.*

Sroufe, L. A., & Rutter, M. (1984). The domain of developmental psychopathology. *Child Development, 55,* 17-29.

Steinberg, L. D. (1981). Transformations in family relations at puberty. *Developmental Psychology, 17,* 833-840.

Steinberg, L. D. (1987a). Impact of puberty on family relations: Effects of pubertal status and pubertal timing. *Developmental Psychology, 23,* 451-460.

Steinberg, L. D. (1987b). Pubertal status, hormonal levels, and family relations. In E. J. Susman (Chair), *Hormone status at puberty: Consequences for adolescents and their families.* Symposium conducted at the biennial meeting of the Society for Research in Child Development, Baltimore, MD.

Steinberg, L. D. (1988). Reciprocal relation between parent-child distance and pubertal maturation. *Developmental Psychology, 24,* 122-128.

Steinberg, L. D. (1989). Pubertal maturation and parent-adolescent distance: An evolutionary perspective. In G. R. Adams, R. Montemayor, & T. P. Gullotta (Eds.), *Biology of adolescent behavior and development* (pp. 71-97). Newbury Park, CA: Sage.

Steinberg, L. D., & Hill, J. P. (1978). Patterns of family interaction as a function of age, the onset of puberty, and formal thinking. *Developmental Psychology, 14,* 683-684.

Stone, C. P., & Barker, R. G. (1939). The attitudes and interests of premenarcheal and postmenarcheal girls. *Journal of Genetic Psychology, 54,* 27-71.

Susman, E. J., Dorn, L. D., & Chrousos, G. P. (1991). Negative affect and hormone levels in young adolescents: Concurrent and predictive perspectives. *Journal of Youth and Adolescence, 20,* 167-190.

Susman, E. J., Inoff-Germain, G., Nottelmann, E. D., Loriaux, D. L., Cutler, G. B., Jr., & Chrousos, G. P. (1987). Hormones, emotional dispositions, and aggressive attributes in young adolescents. *Child Development, 58,* 1114-1134.

Susman, E. J., Nottelmann, E. D., & Blue, J. H. (1983). *Social competence, psychological states, and behavior problems in normal adolescents.* Paper presented at the biennial meetings of the Society for Research in Child Development, Detroit, MI.

Susman, E. J., Nottelmann, E. D., Inoff-Germain, G. E., Dorn, L. D., Cutler, G. B., Jr., Loriaux, D. L., & Chrousos, G. P. (1985). The relation of relative hormone levels and physical development and socio-emotional behavior in young adolescents. *Journal of Youth and Adolescence, 14,* 245-264.

Tanner, J. M. (1971). Sequence, tempo, and individual variation in growth and development of boys and girls aged twelve to sixteen. In J. Kagan & R. Coles (Eds.), *Twelve to sixteen: Early adolescence* (pp. 1-24). New York: Norton.

Tanner, J. M., Whitehausen, R. H., & Takaishi, M. *Standards From Birth to Maturity for Height, Weight Height Velosity and Weight Velosity, British Children, 1965.* Archives of the Diseases of Childhood, 41(1966), 455-471.

Thurber, S., & Hollingsworth, D. K. (1992). Validity of the Achenbach and Edelbrock youth self-report with hospitalized adolescents. *Journal of Clinical Child Psychology, 21,* 249-254.

Tobin-Richards, M. G., Boxer, A. M., & Petersen, A. C. (1983). The psychological significance of pubertal change: Sex differences in perceptions of self during early adolescence. In J. Brooks-Gunn & A. C. Petersen (Eds.), *Girls at puberty: Biological and psychosocial perspectives* (pp. 127-154). New York: Plenum.

Tobin-Richards, M. G., & Kavrell, S. M. (1984, April). *The effects of puberty on self-image: Sex differences.* Paper presented at the annual meeting of the American Educational Research Association, New Orleans, LA.

Udry, J. R. (1988). Biological predispositions and social control in adolescent sexual behavior. *American Sociological Review, 53,* 709-722.

Udry, J. R., & Billy, J. O. C. (1987). Initiation of coitus in early adolescence. *American Sociological Review, 52,* 841-855.

Udry, J. R., Billy, J. O. C., Morris, N. M., Groff, T. R., & Raj, M. H. (1985). Serum androgenic hormones motivate sexual behavior in adolescent boys. *Fertility and Sterlity, 43,* 90-94.

Udry, J. R., & Morris, N. M. (1985). Validation of a self-administered instrument to assess stage of adolescent development. *Journal of Youth and Adolescence, 9,* 271-280.

Udry, J. R., & Talbert, L. M. (1988). Sex hormone effects on personality at puberty. *Journal of Personality and Social Psychology, 54,* 291-295.

Udry, J. R., Talbert, L., & Morris, N. M. (1986). Biosocial foundations for adolescent female sexuality. *Demography, 23,* 217-228.

Warren, M. P., & Brooks-Gunn, J. (1989). Mood and behavior at adolescence: Evidence for hormonal factors. *Journal of Clinical Endocrinology and Metabolism, 69,* 77-83.

9. Reflections:
On the Past and the Future

Gerald R. Adams

The authors have provided a valuable form of description and analysis of theory and research on the variables under examination in this volume. Each of the chapters provides insight on the nature of individual differences, change or development, and contextual features of adolescent behavior, psychological functioning, and physical development. Several key points will be highlighted in this chapter and reflections advanced regarding the future use of a developmental contextualism perspective on the study of adolescence.

THE PAST AND PRESENT

Autonomy

Adolescence has been connected with issues of autonomy from the early beginnings of scholarship on this life stage (Hall, 1916). Silverberg and Gondoli (Chapter 1, this volume) have recognized that this interest is highly connected to cultural themes of self-reliance (in North America) and the importance autonomy has in the transition to adulthood. However, these authors recognize that subcultural distinctions and relational aspects of autonomy compel us to contextualize this psychosocial construct and recognize both the individuality and relatedness of the developmental features of autonomy.

This contextual theme is examined through the detachment debate. In their analysis, Silverberg and Gondoli conclude that early notions arguing that emotional distancing from parents was a necessary condition of healthy growth and development for adolescence can no longer be unqualifiably accepted, given the wealth of several decades of research with nonclinical samples. It should now be recognized widely that emotional autonomy does not require a radical detachment or distancing from parents. Rather, new appraisals

300

and relationship adjustments occur as part of the social features of increased striving for autonomy. Aspects of emotional autonomy and cognitive decision-making behavior are examined by Silverberg and Gondoli within the contexts of family, school, and workplace. Their analysis of much of the past research suggests, again, that dimensions of individuality and connectedness are central features within the environment that provide the basis for an enhancement or promotion of autonomous feelings and behaviors. The authors reviewed the central work of Hill and associates, Steinberg and colleagues, and the research team of Eccles. Placing an examination of these three differing, but associated, research programs into a single chapter readily demonstrated how autonomy needs to be examined from the perspective of how the environs of adolescents provide for unique and differentiated as well as connected or affiliated contexts.

Sexual Development

The very definition of adolescence includes connotations of sexual maturation and impending reproduction. Perhaps early interests in adolescent sexual behavior were peaked by implications of pregnancy. However, as Herold and Marshall (Chapter 3, this volume) recognize, the implications of the widespread introduction of AIDS for political and health concerns have expanded interest in adolescent sexuality. These authors review much of the evidence on changes in coitus experience, pregnancy rates, and contraception use. Much of this material is standard information obtained in current summaries of adolescent sexual behavior. The authors provide a more novel perspective, however, as they explore the role of developmental theory and the implications of recognizing individual differences, developmental change, and social and cultural context as interacting and associated dimensions of understanding sexual behavior. They include in their chapter an examination of both coital and noncoital behavior and the connection between sexuality, identity, and intimacy. Aspects of romantic attachment and affective expression are intertwined in their examination of selective components of available research literature. Likewise, varying forms of aberrant or unconventional sexual behaviors are examined. The authors conclude that in the past 20 years, the concern about sexually transmitted diseases and AIDS has widened the study of sexual behaviors beyond coitus to include condom use, negotiation and communication patterns, and other aspects of sexual identity and intimacy. One limitation of this review is the absence of a thorough consideration of the connection between childhood socialization and adolescent sexuality and adolescent sexuality as preparation for adulthood.

Intimacy

It might be argued that intimacy has been mostly treated as an adulthood issue. With unfolding sexuality, however, there is also a corresponding sense of intimacy. Fischer, Munsch, and Greene (Chapter 4, this volume) provide an expansive examination of issues of intimacy that has application to both adolescence and adulthood. They recognize the early influences of Sullivan's writings on interpersonal relations and Erikson's theory of psychosocial development for the study of intimacy. But more important is their identification of contemporary topics in the study of interpersonal relationships and the recognition of both the bright and dark side of each. Furthermore, the reader is likely to have found the examination of definitional issues most clarifying and pragmatic in nature.

The processes of intimacy, such as self-disclosure, openness, support, and nonverbal behaviors, are highlighted and useful in understanding what intimacy is in its manifested form. To guide a reader, Fischer et al. provided a useful conceptual model that provides a proposed association between individual, social, ethnic, and familial contexts that are either distal or proximal predictors of the process and content of intimacy and positive or negative personal or interpersonal outcomes.

This chapter is filled with an examination of experimental, cross-sectional, and longitudinal panel research findings. The findings reflect how cultural issues of individuality and connectedness are social processes that underlie much of what we know and how we study intimacy themes.

Identity

Like autonomy, identity is viewed as a central feature of adolescent individuation. This construct has been given increasing attention due to the influences from psychoanalytic authors such as Peter Blos and Erik Erikson. Scholars with backgrounds in developmental, clinical, and social psychology have expanded the examination of this construct and devised ways of assessing identity. Much of the available research on identity has taken a strong psychological perspective, however, with less attention given to the social component. In Côté's chapter (Chapter 5, this volume), this was addressed by a wider lens of attention.

After providing a general analysis of sociological and psychological theories of self or identity, Côté examined the corresponding empirical approaches to the study of identity from these two theoretical viewpoints. This was followed by an extensive analysis of developmental patterns in identity formation and an examination of the social contextual features of such development. Ethnicity was given a brief examination, whereas gender was more thoroughly examined and analyzed. The final section of this chapter included some important theorizing about identity and culture. In such theorizing, Côté used the previous work of sociologists such as Mead and Riesman and combined these macrolevel perspectives with the psychological views of such notables as Gergen, Marcia, and Kroger. The final product was a social-psychological blend of macroprocesses and microprocesses of identity formation.

In the conclusion of this chapter, the author addressed John Hill's earlier question of whether we could do without the concept of identity or not in the study of adolescence. Côté's response is placed within a cultural or evolutionary view of the so-called postmodern society. In a very concise way, he argued that if adults lose their identity, so do their offspring, and if a postmodern society provides no avenue for a firm sense of self, then surely it will be difficult for young people to form an identity when the world and its future is uncertain and transformative.

Achievement

Adolescence is filled with opportunities to identify and achieve goals. Most often, this achievement is examined in the context of school performance and opportunities. However, Dornbusch, Herman, and Morley (Chapter 6, this volume) have broadened their examination beyond school to several other important contexts.

In this novel review, the authors began with five fundamental questions. Using questions regarding adolescents' vision of role models, social contextual features of adolescent life, context specificity versus context generalization, and so forth, a wide examination of the social processes and structural features of achievement were examined in connection with such settings as school, extracurricular activities, work, peers, and neighborhood.

The various theoretical perspectives to achievement were reviewed and summarized. Psychological, sociological, and social psychological theories are briefly detailed. The lenses of each perspective were recognized as helping to shape the authors' descriptions and focal points in their analyses of the various domains of adolescent achievement. Of particular usefulness are the various definitions and functions of achievement in each domain. Among many other important contributions, this chapter provided a broad recognition of the power of context in understanding achievement. Such contextual features as ethnicity, social class, size or type of school, organization of the curriculum, tracking, and other features of the settings of adolescents' daily lives both mediated and moderated achievement behaviors.

Cognition

The study of cognitive development as proposed by Piaget and Inhelder, amplified by Elkind and Flavell, and generalized to social-cognitive perspectives such as Selman's or Kohlberg's has waned in recent years. Cognitive sciences have moved to mechanistic models of information processing, the study of mind, and to processes of critical thinking. As a strong reflection of this movement, Keating and Sasse (Chapter 7, this volume) selected a cognitive socialization theme in their chapter on adolescent critical habit of mind. In particular, they addressed the question of whether adolescence is a critical period for the development of critical thinking.

As Keating and Sasse began, they caught our attention by citing several sources that suggest schools are not promoting thinking that is serious, rational, and critical. To address this criticism of school, however, they began with an insightful discussion of what critical thinking involves. Keating and Sasse then focused on conceptual flexibility, reflective thinking, and cognitive self-regulation as related but distinct aspects of critical thinking as a purposeful action to use one's intellect. Within conceptual flexibility, they examined research on divergent and analogical thinking and applying algorithms. Under reflective thinking, they explored formal logic, informal thinking, and skepticism. Cognitive self-regulation included comprehension monitoring and curiosity. It became very clear that although these constructs hold a bridging association with prior work driven by Piaget and followers, it has moved far beyond toward cognitive operations that are less stage specific.

Keating and Sasse provided the reader with an examination of potential constraints on critical thinking and addressed evidence regarding adolescence as a critical period for the formation and development of critical thought processes. Should we accept their evidence for this assumption, as well as the arguments by many that not much critical thinking is found within the high school setting, then we found Keating and Sasse's analysis of educational practices that facilitate critical thought most practical and important. Unfortunately, Keating and Sasse fell short of a detailed analysis, in this otherwise excellent chapter, in their examination of teaching practices. Nonetheless, they vibrantly pointed the way to the next generational wave of research that will be investigating adolescent cognitive development.

Pubescence

Adolescence is readily recognized as a period of physical and sexual maturation. And the study of potential implications of pubescence for psychosocial development has gained considerable research attention over the past 20 years. In their analysis of the interplay between biological and psychosocial processes during puberty, Connolly, Paikoff, and Buchanan (Chapter 8, this volume) examined an amazing amount of research on this subject. Not many years ago, it would have been impossible to complete such an undertaking with the depth and breadth that these authors provided on this dimension of adolescence. Simply, the published research did not exist.

The reader was likely to have found, in the early pages of the chapter, the initial material to be an excellent and approachable review of the many biological processes and features of puberty. Furthermore, the authors provided a concise statement on John Hill's life span theory of development and the role of personal and situational variables. Using this framework, Connolly, Paikoff, and Buchanan explored the context and meaning of puberty. In this discussion, the authors drew heavily on Brooks-Gunn's considerable contributions to the study of puberty.

In a very noteworthy section of this chapter, Connolly et al. addressed the measurement and design issues involved in the study of pubescence. They pointed to the substantial difficulties in both measurement and method and noted the difficulty one has in integrating the research into some organized whole. The problematic features are amply recognized, but the authors were fortunately not daunted by this seeming disarray of indirectly comparable findings between many studies. With noted cautions, the authors examined the links between pubertal and psychosocial development during adolescence. They examined and explored puberty as an affective experience, the attentional behaviors accompanying puberty, the possible associations between puberty and noncompliant or nonconforming behaviors (e.g., aggression, delinquency). Less developed sections are provided on puberty within the context of sexuality and within family relationships. These authors concluded the chapter with important suggestions on what is yet to be examined, what must be considered to be more inclusive, and issues of funding.

THE FUTURE:
A BRIEF REFLECTION

Hill's (1973) original call for a form of developmental contextualism in the study of adolescence that includes a life span ecological framework has been partially fulfilled. There is increasing recognition of the role of the social address of adolescents in the research agenda of social scientists studying adolescent psychosocial development. Aspects of gender, ethnicity, peer group, school, neighborhood, and poverty (socioeconomic status) are being intertwined into the research, although the research efforts are far from being systematic and integrated. However, the contributions of childhood to adolescence and the role of adolescence for understanding adulthood remain less understood and investigated. The importance of understanding adolescence as a transitional state between earlier and later life cycles and the nature of continuity and discontinuities remains yet to be fully explored (see Montemayor, Adams, & Gullotta, 1990). Placing the adolescent into space and time through historical, cultural, or economic conditions is only partially developed (see Moen, Elder, & Luscher, 1995). Looking for the universal versus particular trends and patterns of adolescent development will require greater effort to include these features into our investigations as well as the use of cohort-sequential and time-lagged research methodologies. The potential use of a bio-psycho-social research perspective is gaining wider interest and recognition. However, such perspectives are mostly used by investigators interested in pubescence and sexuality during adolescence.

In many ways, we have created a perspective of developmental contextualism that is only used at a surface level. Much of the research on context is merely asking if there are setting or situation differences in how adolescents behave, develop, or grow. A stronger developmental contextualism has been suggested elsewhere (e.g., Ford & Lerner, 1992), and the variations of scientific contextualism (Hayes, Hayes, Reese, & Sarbin, 1993) have been detailed; but such scholarship is yet to have any wide effect on the study of adolescence. Perhaps, on reflection, the next essential step is to not just study adolescent behavior and development within context (using a person × situation design) but to delineate and investigate the social processes that create contextual influences, at the microlevel and macrolevel, on individual development. This will require some very critical theory construction on the behalf of researchers, the sharing and borrowing of social-psychological processes understood by psychologists, sociologists, anthropologists, economists, and other allied social and behavioral scientists, and the construction of methodologies that allow for the effective study of context, role, social processes, and individual development. Anything short of this will leave us with a promise unfulfilled and a shallow or empty form of developmental contextualism.

REFERENCES

Ford, D. H., & Lerner, R. M. (1992). *Developmental systems theory: An integrative approach.* Newbury Park, CA: Sage.

Hall, G. S. (1916). *Adolescence.* New York: Appleton-Century-Crofts.

Hayes, S. C., Hayes, L. J., Reese, H. W., & Sarbin, T. R. (Eds.). (1993). *Varieties of scientific contextualism.* Reno, NV: Context Press.

Hill, J. P. (1973). *Some perspectives on adolescence in American society.* A report prepared for the Office of Child Development, U. S. Department of Health, Education, and Welfare, Washington, DC.

Moen, P., Elder, G. H., & Luscher, K. (Eds.). (1995). *Examining lives in context: Perspectives on the ecology of human development.* Washington, DC: American Psychological Association.

Montemayor, R., Adams, G. R., & Gullotta, T. P. (Eds.). (1990). *From childhood to adolescence: A transitional period?* (Advances in Adolescent Development, Vol. 4). Newbury Park, CA: Sage.

Index

Private sphere, 155
Problem behavior, 23
Process of negotiation, 31
Profile of adjustment, 20
Prostitution, 66, 79, 80
Psychological separation and
    individuation, 24
Psychosocial identity, 136
Psychosocial maturity, 15
Pubarche, 263
Pubertal
    change, 112
    height spurt, 267
    status, 111, 261, 274
    timing, 2, 265
Puberty
    and affective experiences, 275
    and aggression, 283
    and attentional behaviors, 282
    and family relationships, 286
    and sexuality, 285
Puberty, 259, 260, 262, 263
Public sphere, 154

Racial discrimination, 218
Radioimmunoassay, 85
Rapprochement, 29
Rational choices, 48
Reflective thinking, 236
Reflective thinking, 240
Reflexive, 132
Relational context, 69
Religious institutions, 73
Resolution of the identity stage, 136
Risk taking behavior, 48, 49
Risk vulnerability, 49
Risky behavior, 45
Role of intimacy, 111
Romantic attachment, 97
Romantic partners, 120
Runaways on the street, 81

School pregnancy prevention
    programs, 85
School, 35
School achievement, 73

Schooling and occupational attainment,
    190
Second individuation, 14
Secondary schools, 35
Securely attached adolescent, 104
Self, 134
Self and identity, 133, 134
Self-assertion, 28
Self-consciousness, 279
Self-disclosure, 98, 99, 108, 114
Self-efficacy theory, 185
Self-esteem, 279
Self-governance, 44
Self-identity, 201
Self-reliance, 13, 14, 15, 41, 43
Separateness, 28, 115
Sex willingness, 80
Sex role identities, 110
Sex role orientation, 109
Sexual
    abuse, 78
    assaults, 79
    conduct, 82
    development, 67
    ideation, 75
    identity, 76
    identity formation, 62, 77
    intercourse, 63, 70
    offenses, 78, 81, 83
    risk acts, 65
    values, 74
    violence, 78
    socialization, 77
Sexuality, 1, 5
Sexuality and intimacy, 99
Sexuality education, 84
Sexually aberrant experiences, 78
Sexually transmitted diseases, 62
Situational or topical variations, 46
Skeletal and muscular growth, 263
Skepticism, 242
Smoking, 76
Social acceptability of intimacy, 114
Social achievement, 198, 200,
Social capital, 187
Social class of the parents, 194
Social commitment, 15
Social context and development, 147

About the Editors

Gerald R. Adams is Professor of Family Relations and Human Development at the University of Guelph. His research interests include the study of personality and social development, family-school contexts and individual development, and developmental patterns in identity formation during adolescence and young adulthood. He is a fellow of the American Psychological Association and American Psychological Society. He has editorial assignments with such publications as the *Journal of Adolescent Research*, *Journal of Adolescence*, *Journal of Early Adolescence*, and the *Journal of Primary Prevention*, among others. He teaches courses in adolescent development at both the undergraduate and graduate levels at the University of Guelph.

Raymond Montemayor is Associate Professor of Psychology at Ohio State University. His research interests include parent-adolescent relations, especially the study of conflict and stress between parents and adolescents. In addition, he is interested in the effect of peer relations on adolescent social development. He is Associate Editor for the *Journal of Early Adolescence* and is an editorial board member for the *Journal of Adolescent Research*.

Thomas P. Gullotta, MA, MSW, is CEO of Child and Family Agency of Southeastern Connecticut. He currently is the Editor of the *Journal of Primary Prevention*. For Sage Publications, he serves as a general series book editor for *Advances in Adolescent Development* and is the senior book series editor of *Issues in Children's and Families' Lives*. For Plenum, he serves as the series editor for *Prevention in Practice*. In addition, he holds editorial appointments on the *Journal of Early Adolescence, Adolescence*, and the *Journal of Educational and Psychological Consultation*. He serves on the board of the National Mental Health Association and is an adjunct faculty member in the Psychology Department of Eastern Connecticut State University.

About the Contributors

Christy M. Buchanan is Assistant Professor of Psychology at Wake Forest University. She received her PhD in developmental psychology from the University of Michigan in 1988 and worked as a research associate at Stanford University before moving to Wake Forest in 1992. Her research interests focus on children's adjustment to adolescence and how it is affected by biological changes as well as family circumstances. Her dissertation examined the role of hormonal change and observable pubertal changes on moods and feelings about self among very early adolescents. She has also studied adolescent adjustment to parental divorce and has recently finished a book titled *Adolescents After Divorce*. She continues to research issues involving the reactions and adaptation of both parents and children to the pubertal transition, including the effects of parents' and children's expectations for adolescence on that transition.

Sucheta D. Connolly is Assistant Professor of Psychiatry in the Department of Psychiatry at the Institute for Juvenile Research, University of Illinois, Chicago. She received her MD from Washington University Medical School, completed her residency in psychiatry at the University of Illinois and her fellowship in child and adolescent psychiatry at the University of Chicago. She teaches several courses to child psychiatry fellows and provides clinical supervision to a variety of trainees. Her clinical work emphasizes a multidisciplinary approach with children and adolescents. She collaborated with Roberta Paikoff on a research grant supported by the National Institute of Mental Health collecting data on adolescents and their families with the goal of creating more effective programs and services to reduce high-risk sexual behavior among youth. Her research interests include the influence of ethnic and cultural factors on psychiatric diagnosis and developing a curriculum for teaching clinical supervision.

James E. Côté is Associate Professor of Sociology at the University of Western Ontario, London, Ontario, Canada. He received his PhD from York University, Toronto. His research interests include the empirical investigation of Erikson's neopsychoanalytic perspective from a social structure and personality perspective; identity, culture, and history; cross-cultural and historical analyses of youth and adolescence; the changing life course in late modern society; and personal development associated with higher education. He has published two books and has authored and coauthored articles for many journals, and has recently completed a longitudinal study of university and high school students designed to determine the effect of higher education on these students' identity, moral, and cognitive development. Current theoretical work includes formulating a framework to clarify the identity-culture link and developing an account of the role played by "identity capital" in late-modern society.

Sanford M. Dornbusch is currently Reed-Hodgson Professor of Human Biology and Professor of Sociology and Education, emeritus, at Stanford University, where he also serves as Chairman of the Advisory Board of Stanford Center on Adolescence. He received his MA and PhD in Sociology from the University of Chicago. He has received the Walter J. Gores Award for Excellence in Teaching and is the first sociologist to chair three different sections of the American Sociological Association. He has been president of the Pacific Sociological Association and president of the Society for Research on Adolescence, the first nonpsychologist to receive that honor. He is the author of numerous articles and the author or editor of six books. His current research includes the study of family practices and educational achievement; the effect of divorce on adolescent children, community influences on school performance; the effect of perceived ethnic discrimination; tracking in schools; and homeless families, youth, and children.

Judith L. Fischer received her PhD in social-personality psychology from the University of Colorado in 1973. Her bachelor's and master's degrees in psychology are from the University of Denver. Her research interests include parent-adolescent relationships, intimacy, transitions to adulthood, addictions in families, and codependency. Currently, she is Department Chairperson for the

Department of Human Development and Family Studies at Texas Tech University. She has been on the faculty of Texas Tech since 1979, having taught previously at Penn State and Indiana-Purdue Fort Wayne. She is a member of the National Council on Family Relations, the American Association of Family and Consumer Studies, the Society for Research on Adolescence, the International Society for the Study of Personal Relations, and the Groves Conference on Marriage and the Family. She is on the editorial boards for the *Journal of Marriage and the Family, Family Relations, Journal of Adolescent Research,* and the *Journal of Social and Personal Relationships.*

Dawn M. Gondoli received her PhD in family studies from the University of Arizona in 1994. Currently, she is Assistant Professor of Psychology at the University of Notre Dame. Her research interests include psychological determinants of parenting, interpersonal vulnerabilities and adolescent depression, and close relationship influences on the development of self-concept in adolescence.

Shannon M. Greene received her PhD in marriage and family therapy in the Department of Human Development and Family Studies at Texas Tech University in 1995. She has master's degrees in counseling and in science with a concentration in marriage and family therapy, both from Arizona State University. While at Texas Tech, she was involved in research on family process using microanalytic methods of coding and analysis. Her dissertation research examined expressions of negativity in family interactions of mothers, fathers, and two same-sex adolescent siblings. She is a member of the American Association of Marriage and Family Therapy.

Melissa R. Herman is currently a doctoral candidate in sociology at Stanford University. She received her BA in sociology and psychology from Wesleyan University in 1990 and her MA in sociology from Stanford University in 1993. Her research interests include the sociology of education and the study of formal organizations, focusing particularly on tracking in high schools and the effects of school and student cultures on adolescent achievement. Her current studies examine status inconsistency in high school

Her current studies examine status inconsistency in high school tracking and the relative influence of regulation, emotional autonomy, and parental involvement on various adolescent outcomes.

Edward S. Herold, PhD, is Professor in the Department of Family Studies, University of Guelph in Canada. He has taught courses in human sexuality and conducted research on a diversity of sexuality topics for over 20 years. His major research focus has been on the sexuality of adolescents and young adults. He is the author of *The Sexual Behavior of Canadian Young People* and has published more than 60 articles and chapters in books. He has received several research grants from Health and Welfare Canada and the National Institute of Health. He produced and directed the film *It Couldn't Happen to Me,* the first film based on research documenting reasons for nonuse of contraception among many sexually active adolescents. He is the founder—and for 16 years, the chair—of the annual Guelph Conference and Training Institute on Sexuality, the largest annual conference on sexuality in North America. He has collaborated on studies in the Dominican Republic and presented papers at several international conferences. He has been a consultant to the World Health Organization and to the International Development Research Centre in Canada. He is a consulting editor for the *Journal of Sex Research* and is on the editorial board of the *Canadian Journal of Sex Research.* He is also an international representative on the board of directors of the Society for the Scientific Study of Sex. His current research interests are focused on casual sex and tourism and sexual behavior.

Daniel P. Keating is Professor in the Centre for Applied Cognitive Science, Department of Applied Psychology, at the Ontario Institute for Studies in Education, University of Toronto. At present, he is a Fellow of the Canadian Institute for Advanced Research and serves as director of the Canadian Institute for Advanced Research Human Development Program. He has published a number of empirical and theoretical articles in the area of adolescent development, with a particular focus on adolescent thinking. Among these publications are integrative reviews for Adelson's *Handbook of Adolescent Psychology* and Feldman and Elliott's *At the Threshold* (1990). He received his PhD from Johns Hopkins Univer-

Sheila K. Marshall is a doctoral candidate in the Department of Family Studies, University of Guelph in Canada. Her research interests focus on adolescent development in the family and peer context, with particular emphasis on social identity, romantic relationships, and friendships. Her most recent publication is titled "Attitudes on Interfaith Dating Among Jewish Adolescents: Contextual and Developmental Considerations" in the *Journal of Family Issues*. She holds a doctoral fellowship from the Social Science and Humanities Research Council of Canada.

Jeanne A. Morley is currently a doctoral candidate in sociology at Stanford University. She received her BA in sociology from Northwestern University in 1989 and her MA in sociology from Stanford University in 1991. Her research interests include social psychology, race and ethnicity, sociology of the family, children and youth studies, and the methodology of evaluation research. Her current research includes a review of research on alcoholism treatments, a meta-analysis of parenting education programs for infants and toddlers, and a decomposition of ethnic differences in adolescent school performance. Her dissertation research examines the contextual effects of schools on adolescent learning and psychological outcomes, with a particular concentration on the effects of the ethnic mix within each school.

Joyce Munsch received her PhD from Cornell University in human development and family studies in 1990. She also holds an MS from Cornell University and an MA from Yeshiva University. While a doctoral student at Cornell, she was a member of the Understanding and Building Teen Competence Project. She is currently Associate Professor in the Department of Human Development and Family Studies at Texas Tech University. Her research interests have included adolescent stress and coping, with a particular focus on coping by minority adolescents and adolescent social networks. Her most recent research has involved examining adolescents' relationships with nonparental adults, or what she calls "natural mentors." She is a member of the Society for Research on Adolescence, the Society for Research on Child Development, the American Psychological Association, and the National Council on Family Relations and serves on the editorial board of the *Journal of Early Adolescence*.

Development, the American Psychological Association, and the National Council on Family Relations and serves on the editorial board of the *Journal of Early Adolescence.*

Roberta L. Paikoff is Assistant Professor of Psychology in the Department of Psychiatry at the Institute for Juvenile Research, University of Illinois, Chicago. She completed her BS in human development and family studies at Cornell University and received her PhD in child psychology from the Institute of Child Development at the University of Minnesota. Her postdoctoral training was completed in psychology at Hebrew University of Jerusalem and in education policy research at the Educational Testing Service. Her current research interests focus on understanding the preadolescent and young adolescent years by emphasizing the interplay between biological, cognitive, and social relational factors in contributing to individual outcomes. In particular, she is interested in understanding the relationship of early sexuality to other normative developmental processes and in using information derived from research to create more effective programs and services to reduce high-risk sexual behavior among youth. Her work is supported by the National Institute of Mental Health office on AIDS and the William T. Grant Faculty Scholar Award.

Doris K. Sasse is a postdoctoral Fellow in the Department of Psychology at Brock University. She received her PhD in developmental psychology from Temple University in 1995. Her research interests include math and science achievement and disordered eating among adolescents.

Susan B. Silverberg is Assistant Professor at the University of Arizona in the Division of Family Studies. She received her BA in psychology and sociology from the State University of New York at Binghamton (1980) and her PhD in child and family studies from the University of Wisconsin-Madison (1986). She also completed postdoctoral work at the Max Planck Institute for Human Development and Education in Berlin, Germany. Her research interests include maternal mental health and adolescent adjustment, psychological and contextual determinants of parenting, single-mother to daughter relationships, and youth at risk.